In DeLor

The Drug Trial of the Century, by the Sole Surviving Defendant

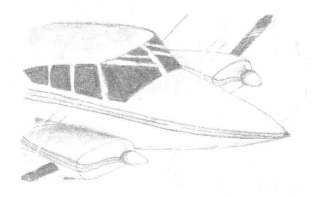

By

Stephen Lee Arrington

Pardoned by President Obama 2017

Drugs Bite Publishing
PO Box 3234
Paradise, CA 95967

Drugs Bite Publishing
PO Box 3234
Paradise, CA 95967

2nd Revision, January 2021

Although the author and publisher have made every effort to ensure the accuracy and completeness of information in this book, we assume no responsibility for errors, inaccuracies, omissions, or any inconsistency herein.

Library of Congress Control Number ISBN: 978-0-9799575-6-7

Cover Design and text by Stephen Lee Arrington
Cover Photography Matt Duhamal
Cover Photograph of DeLorean courtesy of Dr. Jay Shetlin
Cover Photoshop by Cheyenne Summer Arrington
Illustrations by Stetcyn Arrington, Andy Charles, Dominique Serafini, and Margery Spielman

Note: Previous versions of this work were published under the titles *Journey into Darkness* and *Extreme*.

Printed in the USA

Dedication

I dedicate this book to the inmate firefighters, who collectively are known as the Flame Brigade. They save lives, protect property, and guard our wilderness. Some have made the ultimate sacrifice for little pay—just for the chance to give something back to society.

This book is especially for my lifelong companion, Cynthia Elizabeth Arrington. I could not have written this book without her love, support, and adventurous spirit that teaches me about life, wonder, and the magnificence of a truly shared existence.

Also, for my childhood hero, Captain Jacques Yves Cousteau, and his son, Jean-Michel Cousteau, who put me in-charge of their expeditions and allowed me to lead their dive teams into extreme danger and on wonderous adventures.

Table of Contents

Cinema Productions Related to DeLorean Case

"Driven," by Embankment Films, directed by Nick Hamm, starring Jason Sudeikis and Lee Pace. The Story of John Z. DeLorean and James Hoffman. A black comedy with Hoffman as the hero. Now that is an interesting twist. The film was very entertaining, inspired by a true story.

"American Made," by Universal Pictures, starring Tom Cruise, Domhnall-Gleeson and Sarah Wright. The story of Barry Seal who was assassinated by a Medellin hit team coordinated by Max Mermelstein who also provided the guns. Max was arrested from evidence from the DeLorean Case and Hetrick's cooperation.

"Framing DeLorean," by XYZ Films, Producer Tamir Ardon, Docudrama starring Alex Baldwin.

"Out of the Night," Wyland Production Group, Starring Stephen Arrington, docudrama. Winner Gold Remi at WorldFest International Independent Film Festival & Winner Best Non-Broadcast Christian Video of the Year.

"Journey into Darkness," CDR Communications, Starring Stephen Arrington. Aired live internationally and across Holland on Dutch Public Broadcasting Network. Winner Bronze Telly Award

"The Man Who Made It Snow," Based on the Autobiography by Max Mermelstein, listed on IMDb as in development.

Note: Out of the Night and Journey into Darkness are available as DVD's at www.drugsbite.com.

Winner Amazon, Readers' Favorite 5 Star Book Review Award

"In DeLorean's Shadow is a story of hope and it is stunning in its message. If there is one book, one nonfiction book, one inspirational book you must read this year, let it be Stephen Arrington's story. It doesn't fail in any aspect! Great dialogues, awesome scene narratives, and an evocative, spellbinding style of writing…"

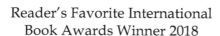

Beverly Hills International
Book Awards 2017
In DeLorean's Shadow
True Crime Finalist

Reader's Favorite International
Book Awards Winner 2018

Stephen Arrington is an award-winning author of seven books. His documentaries dealing with motivation bullying, drugs, and teen suicide prevention have won prestigious awards including a Gold Remi at WorldFest, the largest independent film festival in America.

Dangerous Reef, South Australia

I need a volunteer to jump inside an experimental plastic shark cage. We are amongst the Great White Shark. Chief diver Stephen Arrington is an instant volunteer, just as he was with munitions in Vietnam when deactivation was required.

As you read Steve's book, you will discover his sense of courage even as it gets confused with a blind acceptance of orders — perhaps submission due to an "overdose" of confidence. It is easy to abuse such people, and Stephen Arrington was taken advantage of and misguided.

I feel good to have contributed to the recovery and success of this kind human being. People should receive a second chance when they have been abused. — *Jean-Michel Cousteau*

Chief Diver & Expedition Leader Stephen Arrington inside world's first all plastic great white shark cage with a 17 ½ -foot-long shark, by Dominique Serafini

Preface

The true story of the "Drug Trial of the Century," needs to be told with all its secrets revealed. Be advised that though I write about John Z. DeLorean, this is my story. I have the court files and the FBI's transcripts of their secret tapes and investigative case reports, and the files from the investigative law firm that DeLorean hired at great expense. I know the things the jury never heard and what federal agents tried to cover up because I am the last surviving defendant. As such, I know the hidden criminal intrigues never revealed. Within these pages, you will discover why I never cooperated against anyone but myself.

I have applied for a presidential pardon. It required a lengthy interview with a senior FBI agent. He wanted answers to mysteries in the case that had eluded them. Four hours into the interrogation, the agent voiced his surprise that I was being open and completely honest. He became personable. "I've never seen a criminal file as big as yours," he said shaking his head. My FBI files filled a five-drawer filing cabinet. "For your pardon application," he continued, "a dozen FBI agents are conducting interviews on both coasts."

It was a big case, and it commanded the full attention of the highest levels of the FBI, DEA, CIA, IRS, DOJ, Interpol, Number 10 Downing Street, and Reagan's White House.

It also included Pablo Escobar, Rafael Salazar, "AKA Rafa," Escobar's #1 hitman, and Max Mermelstein, who was the #1 man in the United States for the Medellin Cartel.

My codefendants were John Z. DeLorean, ex-executive vice president of General Motors and founder of the DeLorean Motor Company, and whose car, the DeLorean became famous in the blockbuster movie, "*Back to The Future*." My other codefendant, Morgan Hetrick, was an aviation-engineering genius. Raised on a ranch in Texas he considered himself a maverick and not held to the restraints of federal law.

For the first time, I am free to tell my whole story how two ounces of marijuana led to my co-piloting a drug plane that according to the federal prosecutor of the DeLorean Case, Mr. James Walsh—had over a quarter of a billion dollars' worth of cocaine in its hold. Note: that was the estimated street value.

Warning: this is a true story written in the intensity of the moment. It contains real depictions of the criminal underworld and of life inside prison walls. This story may be disconcerting to some, yet it is necessary to convey the magnitude of where choices can lead those who would dance the criminal waltz. This work is also designed to help youth as such I have tried to present it in a way appropriate to teens.

Some names have been changed to protect the innocent. Instructor McNair is a real person (name changed) who is given credit for statements and actions of other bomb disposal instructors to move the story along more rapidly.

The events in this book are documented by the U.S. Navy, the DEA, the FBI, the DOJ, the Department of Corrections, and by numerous newspaper and television reports.

My underwater expeditions with the Cousteau Society are documented in films, books, and articles. Some of the still images from my 5½ years with the Cousteau's as a chief diver and expedition leader can be viewed at **www.drugsbite.com**.

Some events happened 35 years ago, yet I have tried to remain accurate to the intent of the conversations as I remember them. I used creative license to make the timeline more understandable and entertaining for readability.

Mine is a true story about hope in a very cruel criminal world. Prepare to take an extraordinary journey into darkness, and eventually come out the other side, as a commitment of faith to Jesus Christ leads to a childhood dream morphing into an ex-felon's reality.

Stephen Lee Arrington, Paradise, CA May 16, 2016

There are several timelines in this work, which is why on pages 349 and 350 you will find a Timeline Directory

Introduction

My job is the prosecution of serious federal crimes — for the most part, narcotics crime. So why am I writing introductory remarks for a book written by Stephen Arrington?

I first met Stephen in my professional capacity, as a narcotics prosecutor. He was there in court, in handcuffs, wearing a prison jumpsuit, looking somewhat dazed. Well, he might since he had been arrested by federal drug agents as part of one of the most celebrated narcotics undercover investigations — the DeLorean Case, as it came to be known to most of the civilized world.

His lawyer eventually negotiated a plea agreement for him. He was convicted on his guilty plea and received a five-year term of incarceration.

Four years later, Steve called, he had done his time in prison and been released. He invited me to an award ceremony by the Red Cross to recognize his successful effort to save a person from drowning in Long Beach. It was an unusual pleasure to see tangible proof that someone who has descended into the underworld of drugs and danger can resurface, with his character intact, and make his way to a successful and fulfilling career. It was even more of a pleasure to see such a person be willing to share his experience with others to ensure that they won't have to make that full journey themselves.

While I can claim no credit for the resurrection of Stephen Arrington, I am pleased and flattered to have been a part of the publication of this project. The raw material was sound, and so the job was perhaps deceptively easy. Nevertheless, his story is an important example to make the point that you can go home again if you want to. He did, and we are richer for it.

— *James Walsh Jr., Federal Prosecutor, DeLorean Drug Trial*

Chapter 1 - Los Angeles & Colombia, May 1982

I am driving Morgan's Cadillac down Century Boulevard. I glance at Morgan, who is counting money — a lot of money. He glares at me, "Know where all this cash comes from?"

"Your offshore investors?" I asked. Morgan has alluded there are people overseas who send him serious money. He owns an aviation business at Mojave Airport in the high desert. It is not a large operation, but everything in it is first class. Burt Rutan owns the hanger next door; he is building an aircraft called *Voyager* to fly nonstop around the world. Morgan said there are a lot of dreamers at the Mojave Airport implying that he is one of them.

"But do you know why they send me so much money?" he asked with a leer. "It's because I fly their cocaine."

"You what?" I ask stunned.

"I'm a smuggler. I fly coke from Colombia through the Gulf of Mexico a quarter ton or more at a time." Reaching into his satchel he greedily stirs bundles of money, like a toddler with both arms in a toy box. "So much money," he chuckled, "it's like being a king."

Morgan holds up thick bundles of hundred-dollar bills. "This is fifty thousand. Co-pilot my plane to Colombia and it's yours"

"No way," I snarled feeling betrayed.

I had recently gotten out of the Navy under a cloud of shame for selling marijuana to another sailor. I was attached to the elite Explosive Ordnance Disposal Command as the chief of Team 11. A number of us Vietnam Vets bought small amounts of pot. We sold or shared it with each other. The Navy had an attitude about marijuana. I was lucky to get out with an Honorable Discharge. I was trying to put my life back together, going to San Diego State University while working at a surf shop. My life was not going anywhere as dope was my constant companion. I was folding T-shirts at La Jolla Surf Systems when Morgan called.

Seven years earlier, I had taught Morgan how to scuba dive. He paid me for a while to run his yacht and to take young women diving.

On the phone, Morgan bragged about his wealth, which was in the tens of millions. Said he wanted to hire me as a pilot and as his right-hand man. Said he thought of me as one of his own sons.

When I left the ocean for the Mojave Desert, I tossed my dime bag of marijuana out the window. This was a chance for a new beginning. Now, I realize he had no interest in Steve, the supposed son. No, he wanted the Steve, who got in trouble for selling weed to his friends.'

"Fifty grand!" crowed Morgan waggling the bundles of cash.

I shook my head, "I will not be a part of this."

"But, Steve," Morgan said deviously, "you already are."

"What do you mean?" I blurted.

"Don't be stupid. You spend my money, drug money, which makes you a part of it whether you like it or not."

"I am not doing it," I snarled.

Morgan shoves the money back into his satchel. "Pull into the Marriott Hotel," he ordered abruptly.

A valet takes the silver Cadillac away while Morgan stands at the curb holding a black leather briefcase and his money satchel. He shoves the moneybag into my hands with a crafty smile. "Get used to carrying real money around," he said with a leer.

I take the satchel though I am feeling grumpy about it. The thought that I am carrying at least $150,000 in cash does not go unmissed by the greedier part of my character.

Morgan has a room on the fifth floor. He places his briefcase on a dresser and opens it. I toss the money satchel onto the bed as if it is nothing. Morgan glances at me, smirks and turns away. I step closer to see what he is up to—just as he turns around and slaps a Colt 1911 45 caliber pistol into my hand. "I want you to carry this."

The heavy handgun felt inordinately sinister, something from the dark underside of social order. By reflex, I drop out the magazine and work the slide, ejecting a round that flies in a shiny trajectory to land on the bed.

"What in the hell is going on?" I demanded.

Morgan shrugs, "We're here to pick up a lot of money. The gun is to make sure that no one tries to take it away."

"Forget it," I toss the gun onto the bed.

"Okay, leave the gun," Morgan griped, "I hope you don't have a problem helping me carry the money."

He steps to the door, opens it, and stands there waiting.

We walk deeper into the hotel. Morgan stops at a door and knocks once sharply, then twice more softly. The door swings inward. A large, muscular Latin man stands just inside. Heavy scarring mars his face as if someone once ran upon it with spiked track shoes. He is dressed all in black including the automatic pistol in his hand, a Mac 10. He uses the gun to wave us into the room. Against the wall are two more men with guns, but the most threatening of all is a man standing in the room's center—his empty hand extended in greeting.

Morgan strides to him and grasps his hand, "Max, this is Steve. He is my right-hand man; I trust him with my life."

The salutation impresses Max. I watch his hooded eyes as his hand takes mine. "Morgan has told me a lot about you," he said tightening his grip on my hand. I am very aware of the man in black behind me with the Mac 10. I glance at the other two men, one of which is leaning against a wall. He is wearing a white T-shirt with an automatic in a shoulder holster.

Max's grip pulls my eyes back to him. "Morgan said that you're an ex-frogman, an expert with weapons and explosives." Max still has not let go of my hand — it is as if he is tugging at my soul.

"Do any time in Vietnam?" he asked releasing of my hand.

"Four tours, mostly with the fleet rescuing downed pilots."

"Kill anyone?"

"No." Sweat gathers at my armpits.

He nods toward the Colombian casually leaning against the wall, "He has and so has Rodrigo Restrepo, standing behind you." Rodrigo, the man in black, holds up four fingers. Max's eyes cut back to me, "So you know how this works. All my boys are shooters, but they love their knives. You understand?"

My mind boggled at the death threat so casually flicked in my direction. One of the men picks up a heavy suitcase and drops it onto the bed. Max opens it. It is full of bundled bills.

"$700,000 just like last time," said Max.

Morgan grins at the stacks of bills. "Bring the suitcase, Steve," he said heading for the door. Max moves aside as I lift the heavy luggage. I glance at the two shooters against the wall. They smile like hunters sizing up game.

At the door, I turn and look at Max. It dawns on me as I return his ice-cold stare that he was waiting to see if I would look back at him — or just scurry out the door like a cowed dog.

Max slowly smiles and nods once.

I look at the shooters, burning their faces into my mind. Rodrigo Restrepo's glare hardens when I make eye contact with him.

Lugging the suitcase down the long corridor, I realize I have made an enemy. How foolish of me. In the primordial world of killers — one does not make eye-lock with a predator like Rodrigo. Stare into the eyes of an angry dog and it bites.

We stop at Morgan's room to collect the pistol and his satchel of money, which now seems oddly smaller.

I got on the freeway for the long drive back to the Mojave Desert while Morgan naps in the passenger seat. I spend the drive trying to think of a way out of this mess, but nothing comes to mind.

The sun is slipping below the horizon, silhouetting the tall cactus when Morgan stirs and wakes. He puts on his thick glasses and turns toward me, "Want to know who Max is?"

I shake my head.

"Max Mermelstein," Morgan deadpanned, "with that dark skin you wouldn't guess that he is a New York Jew. Max is the number one man in the United States for the Medellin Drug Cartel. His boss is Rafael Cardona Salazar, AKA Rafa, who is one bad hombre. Rafa is Pablo Escobar's main shooter," said Morgan.

Morgan's stare hardens, "You know you're going to have to make that airplane trip, don't you?"

"Morgan, I don't want to do it." Both of us noticed my choice of words, will not, had become, don't want.

"You don't have a choice, Stephen," Morgan glared. "You have to prove yourself to Max — and to the Medellin Cartel."

Morgan's side of the car is in shadow except for the strobe of headlights from passing cars. The bright lights flicker off his thick glasses magnifying them in an inhuman way. The ugliness of his true nature seeps out of him like a demon throwing off its human guise. An animal musk exudes from the man, a feral smell, like the muskiness of an old, furred predator.

"You leave first thing in the morning."

* * *

Stretch, the pilot, checks the gauges as we pause at the end of the Mojave runway in the twin-engine Aztec. The plane has many modifications for maximum performance and range. There are four wing tanks, two wing-tip tanks, and a 100-gallon fuel bladder lying on the back deck. We have a range of over 2,000 nautical miles.

The landing gear is beefy. The Aztec Twin F-Series can operate out of short field runways under a thousand feet long, making it a great cargo plane or the perfect long-haul drug plane.

The engines roar as the Aztec accelerates down the runway. I watch the ground falling away, knowing that my life will never be the same again.

At a cruising altitude of 9,500 feet, I switch to the outer wing tanks to reduce the chance of a Dutch Roll in bad weather. At altitude, the cockpit has grown cold.

Stretch asked me to turn on the heater.

I scan the gauges as I turn on the heater knob. It opens a fuel valve in the heating system and activates a gasoline-fired heater. I check the sky for traffic then check our location on the air chart. I glance at our flight plan. We will make a stop in Texas to refuel then onward to New Orleans where we will top off the wing tanks. The 100-gallon fuel bladder is for crossing the Gulf of Mexico.

I close my eyes then suddenly get a whiff of gasoline fumes just as a volatile cloud fills the cockpit.

"The heater," yelled Stretch, "shut it off!"

I turn off the heater then check the fuel bladder. The black rubberized skin is reassuringly taut.

Stretch alters course for an isolated desert strip. Abruptly, the port engine sputters and dies. The twin rapidly sheds speed and yawls to port. Stretch frantically cranks the engine as the plane vibrates from the excessive torque. The left wing falls away as the nose drops sickeningly. Massive thrust from the starboard engine is threatening to flip us upside down. Stretch pushes the yoke forward as the twin plunges into a spiraling dive throwing me against the instrument panel.

"Switch to the main tanks, hurry!" Stretch yelled urgently.

Outward centrifugal force is holding me against the door and instrument panel. It takes a huge effort to reach the fuel selector between the seats. I turn it to the main tanks.

The desert floor is rushing up at us at an astonishing rate. Stretch is applying right rudder decreasing the speed of the spiral, but he can only lightly engage the ailerons. He keeps the nose down as he fights to trim the crippled twin.

Abruptly, the port engine coughs then belches a cloud of black smoke. The propeller surges as Stretch slams the port throttle to the firestop. The turbo-charged engine races, yet we are still losing altitude. The spiral slows, yet the desert is still rushing up at us. Stretch pulls back harder on the yoke; the Aztec begins to respond as our airspeed increases. With the desert floor flashing beneath us in a blur, the twin finally levels out.

We are under a thousand feet of altitude as Stretch points the Aztec back toward the small desert runway. He glances at me,

"That was too close. If we had flipped upside down or gone into a full spin that fuel bladder would have smashed our heads through the windshield!"

Stretch spots the tiny desert strip in the distance. We do not dare declare an emergency. I monitor the radio for other traffic and hear none. Stretch ignores the traffic pattern and wind direction. We go straight in. His hands shake on final, and then the wheels hit the runway with a hard, but reassuring jolt.

We taxi to a clear part of the small airport before shutting down the engines. The hot desert air reeks of gasoline inside the cockpit. I jump out onto the runway and look beneath the plane. A solid quarter-inch stream of 100-octane aviation gasoline is pouring from the fuselage onto the hot asphalt.

Opening an access door, I stare at the bottom of the forward fuselage — it is awash with gasoline. Above the heater, a fuel line nut is loose. The volatile gasoline has been spilling onto the gasoline-fired heater and pouring over the hot exhaust pipe. I do not know why the plane did not explode.

"There's a good chance that nut didn't vibrate loose by itself. The flange and nut should have had a safety wire wrap locking it, but I don't see any loose wire in the compartment."

"Should we cancel the trip?" I asked hopefully.

Stretch shakes his head, "No, they are waiting for us down south and I don't need Max looking for me to tell him why we didn't make it. Besides, I need the money."

Stretch opens another access panel, "Let's thoroughly check out this aircraft — assume it wasn't an accident."

Thoughts of McNair's booby traps echo through my mind. I find the reflection downright depressing. Yet the training will help me now as we thoroughly check the aircraft. Whoever did this was good. There would be not debris evidence of a bomb, timing device or altimeter trigger.

Later, we taxi to the fueling station and fill the outer wing tanks. The port engine failed because the left 20-gallon wing-tip tank dumped the remainder of its gasoline into the forward compartment after I turned on the heater.

We refuel in Texas and then continue into the night.

* * *

At dark thirty the next morning, we taxi out onto a wet airstrip at an airport in New Orleans. The runway glistens darkly from a steady rain. I watch lightning bolts strike across a broad front. Rolling thunder intermittently overwhelms the roar of our engines as we race down the runway and lift off into a dark sky.

Stretch likes that the storm shrouds us from coastal radar, but then it gets far worse. Lightning bolts shatter the darkness outside the tiny cockpit. I see thunderheads advancing before gale-force winds. The Aztec tosses and bucks in the turbulence. Weaving between the towering dark walls is like flying through the Grand Canyon of the heavens.

The storm buffets us for hours, and then with the red glow of dawn, we pass from its embrace into an open sky filled with white clouds. Stretch slumps at the controls. He jerks upright then looks at me with red-rimmed eyes. "You better take the stick," he said, "I'm going to lie down in the back." He rests his head on the fuel bladder. "We are southwest of Cuba. Just stay on a compass heading of 140 degrees and keep an eye out for Cuban fighters. That storm has driven us towards their air defense perimeter."

I stare at the stained air chart. I can't believe that I am in a drug plane in the Gulf of Mexico watching out for Cuban fighters. I'm just a single-engine pilot. I have never flown a twin, nor a turbocharged aircraft. With only 72 hours of flying time, I'm an amateur. There is a reason why they call the single-engine pilot the most dangerous thing in the sky.

In the early afternoon, Stretch is back at the controls. He checks our heading by tuning in the Bogota airport's radio beacon. Soon the green coastline of Colombia appears low on the horizon.

Stretch keeps tapping the fuel gauges, but they stay in the red. Fighting the storm has cost us our small fuel reserve. The 100-gallon bladder behind us is flat.

From 3,000 feet, the Savannah and jungle terrain stretches into the distance. Its vastness broke only by winding muddy rivers and long ridges. We are lost and low on fuel when a weak whistle interrupts the static of the radio, two long warbling highs followed by a short descending note.

Stretch grabs the microphone and whistles back, two long, one short. They have seen us from the ground. "Del Norte, amigo, via Norte," urges a voice. Stretch turns north and lowers the nose of the aircraft. We lose altitude as the small plane bucks into a wind pushing over a ridge. We descend toward a dirt strip. Stretch pulls back on the yoke as the twin flares and cuts our throttle. The plane quickly settles to the ground with a heavy thump.

At the end of the runway stands a stout man with a black handlebar mustache. He is wearing a Yankees' ball cap, a sweat-stained khaki shirt, and greasy jeans. A bandolier of red shotgun cartridges drapes over his shoulder. He uses a double barrel shotgun to wave us under a Banyan tree. The engines rev as we taxi beneath the broad canopy. Stretch reduces the throttle to idle, letting the engines cool. The man with the shotgun waits tapping the big bore gun repeatedly against his hand.

Finally, the temperature gauges slip into the green. Stretch shuts down the engines. After many hours of listening to the continuous roar of the propellers, it is abruptly quiet inside the cockpit. I hear the engines creaking as they dissipate heat and the scrape of the door as I open it.

"You're late, Gringos," said the stout man with the shotgun.

Two pickup trucks barrel down a dirt road trailing clouds of dust. Men with guns jump down to stare curiously at us. No one smiles. The men are grim. Guarding this drug airstrip from police, soldiers, and other cartels is a grievous business.

I step out into the tropical heat. Rivulets of sweat run down my back. A flatbed truck skids to a stop in a cloud of dust as more armed men jump down.

Stretch steps out of the aircraft and yells, "Hola, hombres."

"Hola, Gringo," shouted a short man missing half his teeth. He and the others lower their guns, but a few stare warily at me. They are hardened criminals—robbers, smugglers, murderers, and rapists. They do not trust strangers. These coarse men from rural villages are leery of outsiders.

The short man offers a hand. I take it as he pulls me into a man hug. He smiles as he rubs my back in a friendly way. The man does not look bright, but it is a charade, he is expertly frisking me. He puts an arm around my waist as if we are compadres, while he checks my waist and lower back for a wire. He said something in Spanish and the tension amongst the men comes down a notch. His smile does not extend to his eyes.

The man with the shotgun shouts orders. The men organize into their various jobs. Even though the plane is under the tree's canopy, black removable numbers are taped to the tops of the wings should a government plane or helicopter flyover.

The truck carries five-gallon jerry cans of aviation gasoline. The men form a line to pass the cans. I join them as working with the men should make me more acceptable. Standing in the line taking and passing the cans, I glance at the outlaws about me.

Inside, I shudder. Just two months ago, I was sitting on a surfboard at Black's Beach surrounded by surfer friends. At this cartel hideout, I have never felt so lost or alone in my entire life. Abruptly, without doubt, I know that a prison cell or a moldy jungle grave lurks in my future. *My mind builds a mental image of dark earth, closing over body rumbles through my mind.*

Long shadows drape across the plane's hot metal skin as the last of the five-gallon jerry cans pass along the line of weary men. Mosquitoes descend upon us with the tropical twilight.

Standing on a wooden stepladder with the last full jerry can in my hands, I worry. If we are attacked, I would be nothing but a fleeing target — soon to be a pile of meat rotting in the jungle. I stare at the lengthening shadows until the man beside the ladder nudges me irritably to finish, "Oye, gringo."

I look at the bearded outlaw. It is sickening to realize that I am on the side of the bad guys. Wearily, I pour the last of the fuel into the wing tank. I feel the gasoline's icy bite as some of it spills down my bare arm in cold rivulets chasing mosquitoes from the sweat-covered skin.

As night descends, I follow a jungle path toward a crude cement house with a thatched roof. Through gaps in a weathered wood door, I see the flicker of an open flame. Spanish music weeps out into the night, along with the smell of roasting meat, eliciting hungry growls from the men as they shove past me.

The rusty door hinges squeak loudly as the man with the shotgun jerks it open and shouts a greeting to the cook inside. The cook glances over his shoulder and laughs. He is turning a charring animal carcass over a raised open fire pit. He is a big man with a huge belly that bulges against a greasy leather apron. A large butcher knife half hidden by a roll of fat protrudes from his thick belt. He says something in Spanish, which sends the men scurrying toward a rough-hewn table. I stare at the animal carcass, globs of fat drip wetly into the fire where they sizzle in a searing hiss amongst the red flames licking at the blackened meat.

The cook motions for me to join the men noisily taking seats at the table. The desperadoes lean their rifles and shotguns against the wall, but they lay their pistols and knives next to their plates.

I take a seat between Stretch and a man with a black-and-grey beard. He grins at me, exposing yellowed and broken teeth. "Muy sabroso," he said rubbing his hairy hands together in anticipation.

The cook makes repeated trips from the kitchen. He brings out blackened pots of beans, rice, chorizos sausages, fried chilies, onions, and cornbread. He returns, carrying in the animal carcass on a wooden platter and dumps it in the middle of the table. The men attack the charred carcass, ripping chunks of meat away with their knives and hands. Blood and grease leak from the wooden platter onto the table and then trickle across the rough surface to fall onto the dirt floor. A skinny dog licks the fat off the dirt.

I stare with reluctance at the carcass, its bones exposed, the crust of the meat blackened and leaking grease. It looks like a large goat.

"Aren't you going to eat?" asked Stretch.

"I'm a vegetarian," I whispered.

"They wouldn't understand," he said with a sober look.

The cook plunges his butcher knife shoulder-deep into the half-dismembered animal cutting away an entire limb. He drops a kilo of meat, bone, and charred gristle onto my plate. Leaning close, he rumbled, "Eat, Gringo." Then he piles on rice, beans, fried onions, and cornbread before lumbering away. Red flames from the fire pit silhouette his massive body as he passes from sight.

I attack the plate mimicking the coarse behavior of the men. The man next to me has a snub-nose revolver lying between us. He notices me staring at it then possessively slides the gun away. He snags a bottle of Ron Caldas rum from the table and urges me to drink with him. I never drink hard liquor yet grab the bottle and take a pull. The Colombian rum burns my throat. I feel its heat flaring upward numbing my brain. He grunts his approval then raises the bottle and swallows repeatedly. I watch his hairy Adam's apple sliding up and down.

The cook up-ends a paper sack onto the table. Marijuana spills across the wood planks. The men roll joints with yellowed paper. The room soon fills with the pungent smell of marijuana smoke. Other men touch lit matches to Camino Real cigars drawing them to bright red embers in the shadows across the table. The smoke rises thickly into the air, curling around the smut-stained rafters before drifting out into the night through the thatching. When the fat joint passes to me, I take a long pull. The joint burns fiercely, its harsh smoke irritating my throat and despite the burning in my chest, I hold in the smoke. I am hoping for a drugged drowsiness to help me sleep. I stare at the moving shadows the men cast on the wall from the flickering fire and feel my gut burning from the rum. I close my eyes when the room begins to spin then shuffle to a sleeping mat of hay covered with torn burlap in a side room.

Throughout the long night, paranoid and restless, I toss and turn upon the grass mattress. I listen to the guards conversing in soft Spanish outside the window. Finally, I fall into a troubled sleep only to be prey to bizarre and dark dreams.

* * *

In the morning, we are out early to load the plastic-wrapped kilo bricks of cocaine. They take the bricks from a concrete block house where there are thousands of them stacked in rows to the ceiling. The headman counts out 300 bricks. The men stuff the bricks into sea bags that we load into the grossly overweight airplane. The cargo compartments were designed to hold just 150 pounds. The men jam them to capacity — a full 325 pounds per compartment for a total of 650 pounds of cocaine. I look at the plane's bulging tires, the plane squats heavily upon the ground.

Stretch starts the engines and taxis out from under the tree. He crosses himself, which startles me.

'Why would he ask for God's blessing for a criminal enterprise?'

Stretch runs the engines up to max RPM. The twin vibrates and shudders as it strains against the brakes then with a lurch the plane rolls ponderously plowing through the gravel and dirt. Our speed laboriously climbs to 60 mph, as the end of short runway looms. At 85 mph, the waiting trees are beginning to fill the windshield when the wheels leave the ground. I retract the gear as a tree sweeps beneath us. At 500 feet, we begin a slow banking turn to the north.

Two hours later, Stretch is nodding. He jerks upright and says, "I need some shut-eye. Take the stick, keep us on a heading of 331 degrees." He tunes in a VOR (radio direction device) waypoint as an aid to help me navigate then lies down and is instantly asleep.

Soon, I am wondering if I am doing something wrong. We seem to be drifting off course. I tap the needle on the VOR then correct to a course of 332 degrees, but the needle still has that slight drift. I re-center the needle on the VOR. I repeat the process several times wondering if a wind is blowing us off course. I wake Stretch.

"What?" he demanded sitting wearily down in the pilot's seat. He adjusts the VOR, checks the frequencies — then glares at me. "You're 80 miles off course. Planning on overflying Cuba?"

I wince, "It's why I woke you."

"How many flight hours have you logged?"

"Not counting this trip, 72 hours." I am trying not to cringe.

"I don't mean twin time," he said carefully, "total stick time."

"That is my stick time," I said lamely. "I've never flown a twin. I'm not particularly good at radio navigation either."

Stretch stares at me. It is quiet in the cockpit for the next hour.

Late that afternoon, Stretch vectors in the radio beacon at the New Orleans International Airport. As soon as Stretch gets a radio signal confirming our heading, he drops the aircraft lower toward the ocean not that far below us. By flying under the radio signal, we are also hopefully below the shore-based radar. Soon the altimeter reads 300 feet. The VOR swings five degrees to port. Stretch pushes the twin's nose down and corrects our heading. We level off at 200 feet with ocean waves rushing beneath us.

Soon, we see oil platforms on the horizon. Stretch gains altitude as we close then turns to parallel the rigs. "If we stay low it may make the rig crews suspicious," Said Stretch. "They might call us in as a drug runner. By angling to fly over them on the shore side, they'll think we are managers checking the rigs."

"What if they still think we're a drug plane?" I asked.

"That's the beauty of my plan. The workers can't be sure and won't call it in for fear of angering oil bosses."

"What about the shore radar? They'll see us."

"Yeah, but we aren't flying straight in, we're going slow and paralleling the coastline. Most drug smugglers take the shortest line possible. We don't fit their drug profile. If we stay over the rigs and fly at reduced speed, they are liable to paint us as a helicopter servicing the oil platforms."

An hour later, we land at a small Mom and Pop runway in rural Louisiana to refuel.

Better is a poor man who walks in his integrity. — Proverbs 19:1

Chapter 2 – Mojave & Fort Lauderdale, Jun 1982

We arrive over the Mojave Desert late at night. Below us is a vast empty darkness with pools of light shining from isolated residences. Stretch keys the mic four times. Bright dual ribbons of white lights flick on successively revealing the runway.

Landing, we rapidly taxi to Morgan Aviation. Stretch shuts down the engines as men reach for the cargo hatches. I open the cockpit door to see Buzz, Morgan's oldest son waiting. He hands me an envelope. "Here's first class tickets to the Bahamas," he said. Go to the Paradise Island Yacht Harbor. You'll find Morgan aboard his yacht, *Highland Fling.* The Cadillac is outside. There's cash in the envelope for expenses."

* * *

I find the *Highland Fling* at a finger pier. Morgan is on the deck "We got problems," he lamented as I stepped aboard.

My heart surges, "What kind of problems?"

"We're under investigation by the FBI and DEA," confessed Morgan, "for money laundering and transporting cocaine."

"And when did you find this out?" I queried wearily.

"The day you and Stretch left for Colombia. Why do you think I am here in the Bahamas? I couldn't come back to the USA until I knew you made it back with Max's load of coke."

"I didn't need to make that flight."

"Yes, you did. You knew too much. With Colombians, either you are in the business, or you're dead. Wise up, I did you a favor."

"Favor?" I questioned.

"I vouched for you. That ties us together. For Colombians, whatever happens to one of us happens to the other. I said I trusted you with my life, that wasn't an idle statement. We made a promise to one of the scariest men on the planet. These Colombians are not like the mafia. The mafia won't hurt your family if they don't have to, it's an Italian honor thing. Families are sacred. Colombians are at the other end of the scale. First, they kill your family one at a time while they make you watch. Then it's all about torture time before they kill you. Yeah, I did you a big favor."

"I'm not making any more flights," I said with a snarl.

"Don't worry about it," he said shrugging off my words. "I'm out of the business forever. That was the last run."

I feel acutely stupid, "So what happens now?"

"We take the yacht back to Fort Lauderdale," said Morgan.

The next couple of months pass slowly. I am a nervous wreck and want to get out from under Morgan's thumb. When I went to work for him, I brought Revelstoke. It's a Chevy panel truck that I made to look like a captain's sea cabin. Redwood strips cover most of the exterior. Revelstoke commands a lot of attention, and I am quite proud of it.

Morgan's main squeeze, a woman he had been dating for years, asked to use it. Morgan was making some big promises about my future. Back then, I thought he was a legitimate businessman. I gave up Revelstoke on his request — big mistake. If I wanted to leave Morgan's employ, I had no ride. The $50,000 he promised had not materialized. He claimed that with the investigation, it would not be a good idea for me to be putting money in a bank.

When I was in the teams, Mickie Doke said, "Arrington, you're not as smart as you think you are."

I laughed because I knew I was smarter than he was, but now, I was not so sure. Morgan was playing me like a fiddle.

Morgan wanted enough money on hand to run if needed. Like pursuing FBI and DEA agents or a Colombian hit squad with murderous intent. He noted I wear 501 jeans. He had me stuff a $10,000 bundle of hundreds in the right front pocket and a $5,000 bundle of fifties in the left pocket. Plus, there would be another couple thousand in my wallet, which was his walking around money. He kept track of the cash and replenished it, as necessary.

I could take off with a fistful of money, yet it was not nearly enough to start life over, particularly if I had to keep looking over my shoulder for Max, hit men, the DEA, and the FBI.

Morgan kept me close to him. However, I had come up with an escape plan. I asked Morgan for half the cash he owed me so a friend and I could go surfing in Australia. I said that by being out of the country, I would not be under close government scrutiny.

Morgan liked the idea because he figured I would not abandon the other $25,000. My plan was simple, instead of Australia; I was heading for the 700-mile-long California coast to begin a new life. I figured I might skim off some extra money just before I left. *What does Steve have in his pockets?*

The main problem was that Morgan kept delaying the trip. I realized that he was never going to let me go, which brought me

film, "The Silent World," won the academy award for best picture in 1956. More than anything I wanted to be a Cousteau diver.

I lived a mostly solitary life, hiking in the foothills behind our house and making friends with wild and domestic animals. I was rather old to have imaginary friends, but I did. On my hikes, I was accompanied by imagined bears, raccoons, and eagles. At the high school pool, I swam underwater with whales, dolphins and great white sharks.

It was my secret fear that drove me to work out with weights. I grew stronger, yet my secret fear still lingered. My high school graduation was uneventful as no one came to help me celebrate it. I felt so alone, there was nothing left for me in my hometown, so I joined the Navy. I was going to follow my childhood dream and become a deep-sea diver.

I made four tours with the Seventh Fleet to Vietnam.

In Asia, I began to study the martial arts earning a brown belt in Gung Fu, and a black belt in Mudokwan Taekwondo. I participated in contact karate competitions in Japan and the Philippines. Often, I advanced to the quarter or semi-finals, but never the finals. I stood up for others taunted by bullies. It was a passion of mine — I hated bullies. Some people buy guns for self-defense, but I decided to become the gun. I studied advanced techniques, developing weaponless maiming, and killing skills. I learned stick and knife fighting.

In 1972, I was finally accepted into the Navy's Deepsea Diver School and assigned to an Explosive Ordnance Disposal Detachment (EOD). Four years later, I became a Bomb Disposal Frogman. I thought I had finally overcome my secret fear when I joined the Specialty Warfare Command. I had the comradery of my teammates. We stood together, 'No man left behind,' that was our motto and commitment. One can be brave and strong when doing what you believe in with comrades at your back. I was proud to serve my country as an underwater commando.

Now I realized that my secret fear had weakened my character. I did not get one of the most important lessons that a father teaches a son, strength of character. Morgan used my moral weakness to manipulate me, and I let it happen because he pretended to be the father I never had.

Staring at the various yachts tied to the dark piers, I wonder what happened to that boy who used to dream of being a hero? When had I let him slip away?

Stepping onto the deck of the Highland Fling I realize that I am adrift in a gathering of Colombian killers. I think how courage comes more easily when it serves a purpose, but without a worthy cause, bravery becomes elusive. I open the door and step inside the dark interior.

Not popular at school, I had many animal friends though
some were only imagined. Image by Margery Spielman.

*Man perfected by society is the best of all animals, he is the most
terrible of all when he lives without law, and without justice. — Aristotle
384 – 322 BC*

Chapter 3 - Fort Lauderdale & Los Angeles, Oct 1982

Weeks pass, while I work on Morgan's tub. I am suspicious of strangers. Scraping the bow, I discover rotting wood.

I call Morgan, "Your boat has a section of wood rot in the bow."

"How about if I have Sam come out to help?" he prodded.

"No, I can hire someone here." Sam is a surfer friend in California. He is 21 years old and lives for surfing. I introduced him to Sam before I knew about Morgan's criminal bent.

"I can have Sam on a flight out tomorrow," urged Morgan.

"No." I did not want Sam around Morgan's manipulations.

"Just get the job done as fast as you can." Morgan sounded angry and disappointed—I wondered why?

The next morning my phone rings, it's Sam. He just flew in and needs a ride. Sam is curbside when I arrive at the airport. He is wearing a T-shirt, shorts, sandals and holding a surfboard in a cocoon of bubble wrap—youthful innocence on vacation.

"What are you doing here?" I asked angrily.

"Morgan gave me an airline ticket to come out and help. He also gave me $500 in cash. Want to see it?"

I have known Sam since he was a 16-year-old surf rat in Hawaii. He arrived in the islands as a military dependent, where he soon discovered surfing and marijuana.

Two days later, I am on the bow of the Highland Fling when I see Morgan standing in the boatyard smiling up at me.

"Want to leave early for Australia?" He asked jauntily.

I am suspicious of Morgan bearing gifts, "What's the catch?"

"No catch," he said, "I need you to drive a car to California."

His offer did not seem odd. He has been looking at a Rolls Royce in Florida to avoid any California record of the sale.

He was quite cheerful as he said, "You leave tomorrow night."

The next day, I am with Morgan at the Pier 66 restaurant overlooking the yacht harbor. "You want to be very careful how you drive this car," he cautioned.

"Of course, we'll be careful. It's not like we're going to be racing about in your Rolls Royce."

"What Rolls Royce?" he asked startled.

"You're not buying a Rolls Royce?" I asked surprised.

"Just doing a favor for a friend. It's his car, not mine."

"Morgan," my heart sinks as I asked fearing the answer, "is there anything, we should know about this friend's car?"

"Don't ask, what you guys don't know can't hurt you."

"Can't hurt? Are you out of your mind?" I snapped.

"Do this, and I'll give you an extra $20,000 for Australia."

I had told Morgan, that I needed some time, that Sam and I were going surfing in Australia. In fact, I was going to run. I needed the money to do it. My silence was all the answer Morgan needed.

Walking out of the restaurant, I am mentally struggling with the fact that I am heading right back into the nightmare of the criminal machine, but then again, I never actually left it.

Morgan had me take his girlfriend to the airport. I brought Sam along for the ride. They chatted about suntans, bikinis, and other nonsense while I pondered Colombians and prison cells

After dropping her at the terminal, I turn to Sam, "You're getting out here too. I want you to take the next flight home and wait for me. I'll join you in four or five days."

"No way," Sam argued, "I'm going with you."

"Sam," I placed a hand on his shoulder, "Trust me on this."

"I know something is going to be in the car," proclaimed Sam. "Morgan called and offered me $5,000 just to ride shotgun with you — pretty neat, huh."

We argued, but Sam was adamant. So, I make him promise that if anything happened, he would deny knowing anything.

It's coke, isn't it?" Sam's face suddenly lite up, "Hey, does riding shotgun mean I get a gun?"

Sam and I are at the Pier 66 Hotel anxiously awaiting the car. The telephone rings. It is Scar Face calling to say he is outside.

Scar Face waits for me in the dark parking lot. I note other Colombians lurking in groups of two or three in the shadows. Scar Face is leaning against a light blue Chevy Caprice. He opens the door and points at a button hidden under the dash, then pats the rear seat. "Understand?" he asked. "The button is the trigger that releases the backseat. The stuff is in between the seat and the trunk. He opens the truck. "That's a false wall. The coke is behind it

I stare at the trunk, which is empty but for a spare tire, and web bag of pineapples. Scar Face picks up two of the pineapples and bashes them together repeatedly. He is amused by the clunking sound, like two heads forcefully colliding. Juice leaks from his fingers as he drops the cracked and bruised fruit. "Pineapples," he explained, "they mask the smell of the cocaine."

Chapter 4 – Los Angeles, Oct 18, 1982

Inside FBI Headquarters, I sit in a chair bolted to a cement floor in a white room with my hands cuffed behind my back. A bare wooden table is before me. I am facing a large pane of one-way glass. The door bangs open and Scotti storms into the room. He prowls about me. "Get used to the cuffs and chains, Arrington. You'll never be a free man again," he threatened. "Answer my questions without hesitation or grow old in prison."

"I want to talk to an attorney," I said with my head hanging.

"Do you have an attorney?" asked Scotti.

"No."

"Well there's the problem," he shouted leaning into my face. "To get you a public defender takes time and that is something you don't have right now. We got Hetrick," he said smugly, "he's on his way to a room just like this one." Scotti slammed his fist down on the wood table. "Right now, you're the lucky one. First one arrested gets first chance to cooperate."

I keep thinking about what I have seen in the movies and read in books. When cops get someone to talk without a lawyer, it always winds up bad for the guy sitting in the chair. I urgently want to cooperate, to get back on the right side of the law. How do I do that without giving up Sam? Prison would eat Sam alive. That thought leads to another. Sam is Morgan's insurance that I wouldn't cooperate against him. Morgan is still manipulating me even now. I am a lousy criminal; I don't think like one. I am drowning in a world I do not understand.

"Remember flying up to San Francisco to get a wad of cash?" he asked. "Morgan made you an accomplice to money laundering. That's three counts. See if you can do the math. That's 15 years each, so that's four-and-a-half a decades behind bars," he jeered.

He slams something down onto the table. "Want to tell me about this? It came out of your wallet."

'Oh no!' I lamented to myself. I stare at my 'Save the World Card.' I got it when I joined Team 11. On the front of the card are my picture and a physical description. A slashed red banner proclaims, 'Top Secret, CNWDI,' which means Critical Nuclear Weapon Design Information. It is an extremely high top-secret rating. On the back, it reads, 'The bearer of this card is qualified in the rendering safe and disposal of conventional, chemical, biological, and nuclear weapons. Due to the potentially catastrophic nature of a possible WMD (Weapon of Mass Destruction) event, all federal, state, and county agencies are directed by the President

of the United States to render whatever assistance is required. Authorization can be obtained by calling (telephone # deleted) however, assistance will be initiated before seeking authorization."

The 'Save the World Card,' was for a 'Broken Arrow Incident,' which is a terrorist or war event that involves WMDs or a nuclear incident. Foolishly, I had kept the card as a souvenir to show my kids one day.

"Having this card when you no longer have that clearance is another federal offense. Carrying it when you're involved in numerous felonies is good for another 10 or 15 years by itself," Scotti taunted. "That's 60 plus years, and we've just got started."

How could it get any worse – and then it does.

"Your 25 kilos of cocaine qualify you for the Rico Act. That is an ongoing criminal enterprise, which is an automatic 15 years to life. Then there are three more felonies: intention to distribute, conspiracy to sell, and possession of 55 pounds of cocaine worth tens of millions of dollars!"

'What did 300 kilos of cocaine from my trip south equal?' I wondered.

"We're going to find out everything," he crowed. "Someone is going to talk. Once Morgan starts flapping his jaws, you're going down. I figure you're looking at 150 years of hard time. The Rico Act means no chance of parole."

"I need a lawyer," it is all I could think to say.

"There's someone else tied into this case. He's big, and we're going to nail him. Morgan is going to get the chance of a lifetime to roll over on this guy. Your boss is going to cut himself one sweet deal, and he is going to throw you to the sharks."

I know he is talking about Max – who threatened to go through my family like a chainsaw. What had I done?

"I need an attorney," I said despondently.

"Man, you piss me off," raged Scotti. "I'm going to make it a personal vendetta to take you down hard. You are not going to like the hole I am going to bury you in. No attorney is going to be able to help you, certainly not a sad-assed public defender because that is all you're going to get. You think Morgan's going to pay for an attorney for you—no way!"

He stomped to the door and threw it open. "Get this piece of garbage out of my face!"

Two agents storm in and hustle me out the door.

A stupid thought comes to mind as they jostle me into a black sedan. In the movies, they always use the good cop/bad cop routine. Why did I only get the bad cop?

Morgan smiled, missing my point, as usual, "But you're going to get to drive me around in one of them. We'll keep one in the hanger for driving only on special occasions."

"How expensive are they?" I asked.

"I'm getting a good price, but one of them is rather expensive because it is gold-plated."

"A gold-plated DeLorean?"

"Twenty-four karat pure gold-plate," Morgan had a wistful look. "DeLorean only made three of them. Two were pre-ordered by American Express as an eye-catcher for their catalog. He is hoping he can get a high-ticket price for the last golden DeLorean."

"Wouldn't a gold DeLorean bring unwanted attention?"

Morgan smiled, "Yeah, I'll keep the gold DeLorean in the hanger."

"But why would he sell you his gold DeLorean?"

"Got a deal going down with John Z.," quipped Morgan.

"What kind of deal?" I asked hesitantly. 'Is Morgan up to something illegal again?' I wondered. Going straight was not working out so well for him. He likes fast money.

"It's not what you're thinking," said Morgan. "His car is hot because there is nothing else like it. I can help him incorporate aviation engineering into it. Make it lighter, tighter, and faster to augment the DeLorean's stainless-steel body and low-wind resistance concept. It has some steering performance issues that I can help to fix too. Remember, I designed the anti-skid system for Lear Jets. A sports car's steering would be far simpler. I flew him up to our hanger to show him some of my aircraft modifications. He was impressed."

This is great news. Morgan is an engineering genius. He has the talent and the imagination to think out of the box. He was doing great with his engineering ideas when I worked for him seven years ago at the Oxnard Airport. He could do it again if he put his mind to it. The DeLorean was intriguing enough to capture his full attention. I liked it, out of the cocaine trade forever and me in a DeLorean maybe even on occasion a golden DeLorean?

* * *

"Did you hear me?" asked Morgan interrupting my thoughts.

"Yeah," I whispered back, "what's he doing in the next cell?"

"He's our codefendant."

"What?"

Abruptly, I remember we should not be talking. I put a finger to my lips silencing Morgan. I jump down from the top bunk go over to the toilet and motion for him to join me.

He hustles over and leans into my ear as I flush the toilet, Morgan whispered, "The cocaine in your car was for him."

The next morning, I am sound asleep.

"Steve," whispered Morgan his halitosis washed in a lingering cloud over me. I wake up abruptly.

"What?" I grumbled. I do not like having Morgan in my face.

"I want to talk with John." Morgan leaned close, his perpetual body odor is overwhelming, and now he has toxic breath issues. It is our second day without a shower. Morgan grinned, "I want you to do that flushing thing while I talk with DeLorean."

Morgan's idea of having me flushing a toilet repeatedly so he can try to manipulate John Z. DeLorean, Cover of Time Magazine kind of guy, is a major wake-up call. Morgan has been manipulating me for seven months, and I need it to end — now he is about to help me in that effort.

"Sure," I jump down to begin the flushing thing while he scurries over to chat with our "Cover of Time Magazine," co-conspirator. The flushing thing is good for about 30 bowls of swirling water before they finish.

* * *

What neither of them realizes is that it is not working. The toilet is in the back of our cell. Morgan and DeLorean are talking at the front of the cells right up against two huge glass panels. The toilet sounds would not affect DeLorean's panel and ours only minimally. They might as well be talking straight into a microphone. It should have worked for us last night because we had our conversation over the toilet bowl and far from the glass panels with our backs to the hidden cameras. Morgan doesn't realize that the repeated whooshing of water down this toilet is washing away his control over me. I desperately needed cleansing — a toilet bowl seemed an odd place to do it. Yet, staring at the shiny stainless-steel bowl with the clean water swirling and gushing down it was purging my troubled soul. I have always loved to watch flowing water. It offers a spiritual cleansing in a deep way for those who take the time to notice it.

I did a lot of soul-searching last night and did not like who I had become. Before marijuana, I had been an honorable person proudly serving my country. As a bomb disposal frog, I often worked with law enforcement agencies, including the Secret Service, Alcohol, Tobacco and Firearms, police departments, military intelligence, and once with the CIA. I had been a good person. I taught CPR and first aid for the Red Cross for free and earned the Navy's Commendation Medal for multiple lifesaving efforts over the years. I had my flaws, but I was fundamentally a good person and liked helping others.

Marijuana changed me in subtle ways. The weed's corrupting high masked that my life was quickly going straight down a drain. Just like the gurgling sounds of this toilet bowl that I was standing over. It sucked away my challenging and adventurous career as a special operations frogman and sluiced it down a sewer pipe. How could I have been so stupid and foolishly corruptible? Yet, last night I realized that Morgan did not corrupt me – I did. He had seen what was wrong with me. It was a powerful lure for him, and he simply took advantage of what I offered him. He had been corrupting and stealing my soul. How foolish, Stephen.

I wanted to be on the right side of the law. Instead, I was in for a long dark journey. My foreseeable future was a prison cell and immersion in a stark inmate reality. However, I had one thing to cling to – the arrest had set me free, which was a strange way of thinking, but oddly true. With Morgan, I was headed for an early grave. Instead, I am on a journey into darkness that will require all my frog and martial arts training to survive. I am determined to one-day walk out of prison as a good person again.

* * *

I watch Morgan strutting back towards me. He steps close and takes over the flushing. "John was willing to talk because of the flushing noise," he whispered. "We have to stand together," he said punctuating the declaration with a toilet flush.

I stared at the water swirling down the bowl. "Twenty-five kilos," I said despondently, "that is a lot of cocaine."

"Try 225 kilos; your load was just the first installment. Just hang tough," Morgan said knuckling my chest in a fatherly way. "That $50,000 I owe you; it's going to buy you the best attorney I can find."

Morgan washes his hands in the steel sink. He paused and got a faraway look as he ponders something. "When the press gets wind of this," Morgan shakes water from his hands, "it is going to be a real media circus." Morgan smiles, he loves attention.

Neither of us had a clue that the presses of the nation and the international newspapers were already in DeLorean overdrive.

Breakfast arrives, and Morgan demands to call his attorney.

"Phones open at eight," said the guard relocking our door.

When they came for the empty trays, they took me with them.

We go down the elevator to the ground floor. The guards take me through a corridor and out a security door to a marshal's van. I realize that last night, the guards took me the long way to the glass cells, through the rowdy cellblocks, and down threatening-inmate filled corridors. They were trying to scare me into cooperating. I realize that lined up against me were all the resources of the federal and state agencies. How depressing.

Hours later, I am in a courthouse holding cell watching a bizarre argument. The news media has descended enforce on the courthouse. The curb out front is full of television vans. Filming crews are prowling about in the lobby. The courtroom upstairs was so packed with reporters that they are moving the proceedings to a larger courtroom. All the media attention is electrifying the marshals. They are arguing about who gets to escort me upstairs.

"I have been here over 20 years," stated a senior marshal, "I've never seen anything like this media circus."

Abruptly, a beefy female marshal comes up with a simple solution. "Why don't we all go?" she urged.

A general nodding of heads lends approval to the idea. The Sergeant volunteers two of the youngest marshals to stay and watch over the holding tank. Then he suggests, "Let's dress him up in lots of chains, make him look like a serious bad guy." He looks at me despondently realizing I do not look the part of the scary hardened criminal. He shrugs, "Just throw the chains on him, the more, the better; the press will love it, big time photo op, it might even get our picture on the front page."

They wrap a chain around my waist and then cuff my wrists and lock them to the waist chain. The woman marshal attaches leg irons to my ankles with a two-foot chain leash. Then they attach a chain from the cuffs to the leg irons, which the female marshal called a decorative touch. I have a metallic rattle when I walk.

They frog march me to the door that leads up to the main floor. Seven burly men and one macho woman pack tightly about me, whispering excitedly to each other—federal marshals at play and I am their new inmate-action figure.

The Sergeant leers, "Ready, Hot Shots?"

There is a high-pitched giggle of anticipation, which did not come from the female marshal.

The Sergeant slams open the security door. The heavy steel bangs against the wall commanding everyone's attention in the lobby. Abruptly, they see a phalanx of marshals charging up the stairs like a herd of stampeding welter beasts. They plow into the crowded lobby. My feet are only occasionally in contact with the floor. The marshals are carrying me like a trophy, a flying wedge of malignant glee shoving people out of the way.

Everyone stares excitedly at the chained super-criminal. They shout questions and offer up bogus answers. Most figure me to be a serial mass murderer or crazed sexual predator. We pass a nice-looking, little old lady — she glares at me with hate-filled eyes and mutters something foul.

I want to shout that I am not that bad of a person, but the chains and heavy marshal escort nullifies my unspoken words.

The marshals force their way into an elevator; the people inside are rousted out. A lawyer protests as the female marshal grabs his lapels and sends him spinning into the crowded lobby.

After the elevator doors close, the marshals chuckle amongst themselves; a gang of playground bullies happily comparing the individual damage they have done in the packed lobby. One marshal brags that he copped a feel off a foxy reporter.

The doors open to a corridor full of more reporters. Seeing the phalanx of determined marshals, the reporters quickly clear a path as we jostle our way into the courtroom.

Two marshals hustle me to a long table; the other six stand at the back wall — apparently ready to take me down if I tried anything. Morgan sits at the table rubbernecking at the sea of press. He has two attorneys with him.

A frazzled man in a cheap, ill-fitting suit introduces himself as my temporary public defender. He is looking worriedly at my stainless-steel hardware. "Is he a problem?" he asked nervously.

The female marshal is standing with one restraining hand on my shoulder. "No," she said, "just being careful. He's been a bit feisty."

I look at him and grin — he slides his chair further away.

The court proceedings are short as this is just a bail hearing. On the request of DeLorean's lead attorney, the judge reduces DeLorean's bail from $20,000,000 to $5,000,000. Morgan's bail is also dropped to $5,000,000, and mine is dropped to $250,000

The DeLorean case would be called The Drug Trial of the Century, and it became an international media blitz. The extensive coverage would last for years with feature articles and leading stories on every major network and newspaper in the modern world. Playboy Magazine would run a feature article on the case, which would please Morgan to no end. The most surprising aspect of the media coverage was when I read my name with DeLorean's and Hetrick's in a Doonesbury cartoon strip that ran for months. I was about to learn a new term, celebrity inmate, which was not good news.

With the courtroom drama over, my marshal horde descends upon me. As they hustle me past Hetrick and DeLorean I note that they only have two marshals each, but then again, they have all their attorneys as escorts.

Revelstoke, my home while living in Hawaii.
The living area, was 6'4" tall, 8' wide, and 12' long

It is curious that physical courage should be so common in the world and moral courage so rare. — Mark Twain

Chapter 5 - Terminal Island Prison, Oct 1982

I began my sojourn in prison early that evening in lockstep with eight other inmates. Our hands are cuffed in front of us, our ankles shackled with a two-foot long chain that drags. We are chained in groups of three. We walk in line with short steps known as the inmate shuffle. Getting out of step causes the ankle manacles to gouge the skin of the other two inmates, this equates to instant rage from stressed out criminals with serious attitude problems. I am carrying terrifying notions of what is waiting for me beyond the prison's dark walls. My secret fear is in full panic mode.

The stainless-steel chain drags across the dark parking lot making a merry tinkling sound that is at odds with my anxious state. We hobble through twin chain link fences topped with razor wire. A sea fog drifts in the harbor coating my skin with a wet, chilly mist.

Terminal Island Federal Correctional Facility (T.I.) squats on a man-made peninsula at the entrance to Los Angeles Harbor. The prison sprawls across 20 acres in a long, bleak rectangle. Before us looms a depressing concrete building three stories tall with dark barred windows on the top floor. On both ends of the foreboding wall are gun towers that drift in and out of a shifting fog. A guard stands outside a tower watching us — a riot shotgun rides casually on his shoulder. My upward gaze attracts a rap from a marshal's baton, "Move it, boy."

I shuffle forward, shoulders slumped, head down. The chain plays its merry tinkling cadence while I desperately try to deal with the reality of the looming prison. I am losing control of my life, yet all I can do is hobble forward as the prison sally port opens to swallow me. A dirty yellow light looms from the open steel door. All my senses argue against going through that ominous port. Reluctantly, I shuffle into the gloom of federal custody swathed in a musty feral smell.

We are in a dim entry at the base of a rusted steel staircase. The cement walls press in upon us. The walls are damp from moisture-laden air with patches of peeling pea green paint. My arm brushes against the damp metal scaffolding and comes away slimed with grime and wet rust. We climb the staircase in cadence, the solid thump of our shoes and tinkling of the chains echo off the walls. I accidentally break step earning a snarl from the hulking criminal behind me. At the top of the staircase, they herd us into a holding cell where they remove the leg irons and handcuffs. I rub my bruised ankle.

The inmate whose ankle I gouged glares at me as he walks over to a toilet with a half-busted off seat. The cell smells of tobacco, pungent body odor, and then strongly of urine as the man relieves himself. I step to a barred window with small glass panes painted brown. One of the upper panes has been broken out. I go up onto my tiptoes to peer out. The metal rim has sharp glass fragments embedded in it. They gleam like teeth. I peer out at the prison's North Yard. Through the swirling fog, I see walls stained in shades of black and gray from long exposure to smog and soot. The prison wall built during World War II. Formidable dormitories border the yard. They are two stories tall with twin rows of dirty windows leaking pale yellow light. The yard is black tarmac and cracked cement, with a few small lawns. A stunted tree squats alone in the middle of the yard.

"Get away from that window," bellowed a guard as he drags his truncheon across the bars. The large inmate I offended stands in a shadowed corner glaring at me.

After being fingerprinted, photographed, strip-searched, and issued prison jumpsuits, they lead us down corridors to a heavy steel door. The guard inserts a large brass key. Shoving the door open, he grins, "Welcome to The Hole, boys."

Jail Unit 1 (J-1) has three tiers of cells stacked inside a three-story building. I am dumbfounded seeing a huge steel cage squatting inside the confined concrete structure. We climb a steel staircase to the second tier then walk along a row of cells with their despairing human cargo. The cells are ten-feet long, six-feet wide, and less than eight-feet tall. From the cells, adult male eyes stare; some are fearful or hopeless, but most are predatory. I walk close to the railing, avoiding verbal threats exuding from the cells.

The guard stops at a cell midway down and opens the grill. "Arrington," he ordered, "inside."

I peer into the dim interior—abruptly the guard shoves me into the cell and slams the grill. It smells rank and stale like a damp cave. A steel toilet with a busted seat, its bowl soiled, crouches in the corner. I place a hand against the wall to steady myself. The concrete is grimy. My hand comes away slimed with a caking of tobacco residue that over the decades has turned a greasy nut brown. A dull glow from a dim yellow light recessed into the ceiling barely reaches the lower bunk, which is shrouded in shadows. A huge black man lies there. He is naked but for a pair of torn and stained boxer shorts. The man emits a heavy musk that fills the tiny cell. I look at his thick muscular arms, barrel chest, and hateful stare. I am instantly terrified but know not to show it. He glares with bloodshot, red-rimmed eyes.

"Hello," I said warily, "My name is Steve."

He shakes a meaty fist at me. "Don't gives a damn what's your name is whitey, stay out of my face, or I'll bust you up."

Under threat and feeling exposed, I climb onto the top bunk. The concrete ceiling looms above me. It is like lying down in a cement and iron coffin with a partially closed lid. I shut my eyes and listen to the sounds of the cellblock. An argument spiced with foul words, and vile threats reverberates from the cell above. I hear the flushing of a toilet, a cell door slamming, and the creaking of bedsprings from the bunk beneath me. As the huge man rustles about, the upper bunk magnifies his movements — it is a very weird and disturbing feeling.

I push my thoughts on an inward journey to happier times.

* * *

It was December 1979, and a big winter swell was pounding Oahu's northern reefs. I would remember it as the day I met Susan.

Standing on the beach, I am capturing spectacular wipeouts with a three-foot-long, 650 mm telephoto lens. The monstrous waves have closed out the North Shore. Only the big breaks, Waimea, Sunset, and Pipeline, are rideable. The trade winds are holding the four-story waves super-critical before they break with the crashing sound of rolling thunder. Only a few surfers are riding the huge waves. A half-dozen broken surfboards have washed up on the shore, when I see two exquisite blond women striding across the sand. I just did not expect them to stop right in front of me, but then I recognize Caroline whom I met several months ago at a beach party.

"What happened to your hair?" Caroline found my near baldness amusing. I avoid the subject of the naval brig where they shaved my head as I think about my recent release from there a week ago.

Caroline is on the University of Hawaii's swim team. Her figure is sleek as a seal's. She looks ravishing in her white nylon dolphin shorts and red bikini top. However, my attention rivets on her friend who is stunning. "This is Susan," volunteered Caroline, "meet Steve, he looks better with hair."

Susan is wearing jeans and a white cotton blouse. Her long blonde hair falls in a silken cascade halfway down her back. She is a few inches shorter than my six feet with the physique of a dedicated athlete. She is unaware that my heart is flopping in the hot sand at her feet.

"Mind if we join you?" asked Caroline, laying down a towel.

"Sure," I said grinning happily.

Hidden behind my sunglasses, I ogle Susan as she slides out of her jeans. I noticed that she has the kind of figure surfers daydream about while waxing up their surfboards. She checks that her burgundy bikini is in place. Then she lies down on a beach towel. She and Caroline share a bottle of coconut suntan oil. I take off my sunglasses to wipe away the sweat hindering my vision. I miss shooting some hot double overhead, tube rides. My surfer friends will be upset; however, I did not care.

The girls are basking in the tropical sun when a black Great Dane arrives at a run spraying sand everywhere. Caroline glares at the big dog as she brushes at the sand sticking to her oil-covered skin, but Susan does not mind. She pushes playfully at the Dane, "Who are you, mutt?"

"His name is not mutt, it's Puu," I ruffle his floppy ears. "His full name is Puu Kane. I thought it meant mountain man in Hawaiian, but it means lump man. So, I just call him Puu."

"Hi lump," said Susan as she scratched him under his muzzle.

Puu leans against my legs sopping up the attention, "He tends to be rather possessive of his dog dish and me."

Puu barks then pulls on my swim trunks with his teeth.

"What does he want?"

The Dane braces his paws in the sand and tugs harder. "He wants to be fed," I laugh, "Want to watch? It's amazing what he can do to a 40-pound bag of dog food."

"Sure," Susan's smile is radiant in the morning light.

I shoulder the camera and tripod as Caroline elects to work on her tan. I like the idea of being alone with Susan.

"How long have you had Puu?" Susan asked rubbing Puu's ears.

"Just five months."

"Really?" she asked. "You two are like soul mates."

"I hear that often. Puu and I have much in common. I stole him from a sailor who was abusing him something terrible."

"You stole him?"

"Yeah, the guy kept him tied to a tree in his backyard, often without food or water. The neighbors came out to encourage me to take him. He was howling and whimpering a lot." I rub Puu's ears while smiling at Susan. "When I took Puu he was covered in sores, skinny as a rail and beginning to turn mean."

Susan stares at Puu's black shiny coat and muscular body. "He seems to be recovering quickly."

"He's young and getting the best of care. We do a lot of hiking, and he loves running on the beach."

"Is that what you have in common with Puu? Have you been abused too?" asked Susan, her eyes full of innocence.

I stare a moment into her deep brown eyes, "Couple of months after I grabbed Puu, I was confined in the Navy brig in Pearl Harbor because of marijuana. So yeah, I guess I'm a little abused too."

Startled by my straightforward answer, Susan asked, "When did you get out of the brig?"

I glance at my watch, "Eight days and three hours ago."

Susan stares then picks up a stick and throws it for Puu. He is off in a burst of speed and flying sand, snatching up the stick. He charges back. Arriving in front of Susan, he chomps down crunching the stick in half. The crunched pieces fall at Susan's feet."

"Does he always do that?" Susan picks up and inspects the two-inch thick pieces of crumpled wood.

"It's why I usually throw much bigger sticks," I offered.

In the parking lot, Puu leads the way to a commercial van. Susan peers in as I open the backdoors. "Is this where you live?" she asked in wonder.

Puu jumps inside. "It's where we live; he considers it his mobile doghouse. I call it Revelstoke."

"You made this?"

"Yeah, it used to be a Chevy commercial van until I altered it a bit." From a heavy bag of dry dog food, I half-fill monster dog's dish, which is the lower third of a metal trashcan. Then I plop in a can of Mighty Dog. Susan watches in amazement as Puu inhales his mountain of food.

"Do you need feeding too?" I prodded.

Susan grins, "Yeah, but I wasn't going to tug on your shorts to ask."

I fill two wood bowls with plain organic yogurt and top it with fresh tropical fruit, granola, nuts, and seeds.

Susan looks at her bowl. "Certainly, looks healthy."

"I'm a bit of a health fanatic. I want to die healthy."

"Isn't that a contradiction in terms?" she asked.

"When I was a teenager, I read an old Arab saying, "Health is a crown, worn by the well, that only the sick can see." It opened my eyes. I try only to eat what's good and am addicted to self-propelled and gravity sports. I love to exercise."

"We have a lot in common," said Susan. Her brown eyes are captivating. I try not to stare. "I work at a health food restaurant" she continued, "and I ran with my school's cross-country team."

"I love running," I said eagerly. "I finished the Honolulu Marathon in three hours and forty-one minutes."

Susan grins, "That's a great time."

What Susan does not share is that she ran the Honolulu Marathon last year and beat my time by 18 minutes. Susan is a class act I, however, am an egotistical dope.

After we eat and Puu has gone out to play, I realize she probably wants to go back to the beach. If I am going to ask her out, now is the time, the thought makes me tongue-tied. Susan crosses her long legs, brushes a wisp of hair from her face, looks right, then left, and takes several deep breaths, while I struggle with embarrassment issues.

"Anything you'd like to ask me?" She smiled innocently.

"Ah, want to have dinner tonight?" I croaked.

"Hmm," she pondered my offer.

"Well?" I asked.

Susan, that 1st day at Pipeline, Hawaii. Photo Arrington

"I'm thinking about it," her eyes glint mischievously. *"Okay, can you pick me up at the restaurant where I work? I'm off at nine. If you arrive early, I'll make you dinner, and then we can go out."*

Susan stands. *"I'm glad we finally got that over with,"* she teased.

Later, we are standing in the parking lot beside Caroline's VW bug. Susan smiles and innocently asks, *"Do you want to know the name of the restaurant or maybe its address or my telephone number?"*

I feel like a clod as she writes on a piece of paper and stuffs it into my T-shirt pocket. *"Don't lose that,"* she quipped.

My heart and I stand there watching them drive out of sight. I do a happy little jig about the parking lot. In the middle of a one-legged spin, I notice two of my surfer friends watching me with their surfboards tucked under their arms. Water drips from their wet shorts. They are standing in a puddle of their own making, which means they have been standing there for a while — they do not look happy.

"Don't tell us that you haven't been shooting pictures."

"Ah..."

"This is the best surf we've had all year. I almost killed myself out there thinking you were getting it all on film," he complained.

"Ah..."

"Do you see his dog?" asked one of the surfers, *"I swear, I am going to kill him, but we better not try it in front of that crazy dog of his."*

My shrill whistle brings Puu bounding up. He laps water from the puddle at the surfers' feet and then jumps into the back of our truck.

"Well, got to go, guys," I said making a fast exit.

That night, I park on a tree-covered street by Susan's restaurant. I pull on a pair of old jeans and my favorite Hawaiian shirt. I give Puu orders to guard Revelstoke as I step out into the tropical evening.

A bell attached to the door tinkles as I walk into the quaint café.

Susan steps over to greet me. We grin at each other while the little bell jingles cheerfully above us.

Laulima is one of those Hawaiian hippie-type restaurants where customers sit on rugs and pillows while eating from low Japanese tables. Soft, environmental music drifts from hidden speakers and sandalwood incense wafts lightly in the air.

On Susan's recommendation, I order a bean tostada. I watch her serving other tables, while I try to look as though I am not watching her every move. She turns to smile at me then walks into the kitchen.

Unbeknown to me, she and the Chinese cook are building a monster bean tostada. When Susan exits the kitchen, she is carrying a large plater upon which squats a respectable bean mountain. I am wondering if it is for the family of four sitting at the next table when she plops it down in *front of me, some of the frijoles slop off the plate. I stare in awe at the size of the miniature bean volcano. "This is a tostada?" I blurted.*

"Anything wrong with it?" Susan asked smiling innocently.

"No, it's, fine." If my Hawaiian shirt had long sleeves, I would have rolled them up and traded the fork for a small shovel."

Susan returns as I am sopping up the last of the beans with a tortilla. "You ate the whole thing," said Susan as she gaped at the plate.

Leaving the restaurant, we walk on the beach in Waikiki under a crescent moon. Susan and I are discovering each other with words that go far beyond social chatter. I am baring my soul to her. My naval career of 14 years is ending in disgrace. I don't know why such a beautiful woman would have any interest in me. She gently probes encouraging me to reveal things that I have never shared with anyone. I bond with her on a level I have never known before.

Returning to Revelstoke, we romp with Puu and then go inside. I put soft Hawaiian music on the stereo and lit a few candles. The stained-glass skylight admits a color-softened glow from a streetlamp. A candle flame flickers between us; its radiance reflects in Susan's eyes. As we stare at each other, she raises a hand to her ponytail and removes a hair tie. I watch her soft blond hair fall across her shoulders in a golden cascade. Susan's eyes open very wide as I lean forward and kiss her.

* * *

A deep rumbling voice jerks me back into the prison cell.

"The name's Mose." The cavernous voice speaks slow, "Looks man, since we be bunky's, we gotta talks some, but it don't mean we be friends or nuthin. If sumthin goes down, Mose is gonna waste ya ass. Nothin personal whitey, just the way things is."

I say nothing.

"Hey, whitey, you listening to Mose?"

"Yeah, you said you might have to waste me."

"So, longs as ya understands. You gots any cigarettes?"

"Don't smoke."

"Knows you don't smoke; you don't carry da smell."

Mose is aware of my odor with his super funk clouding this small cell?

"What's the stupid white boy doing? Walking into my crib with no cigarettes," the deep voice grumbled.

Fear courses through my veins like ice. I say nothing, wondering what is coming next.

The night grows older as I listen to the guard's heavy boots on the steel catwalk with the tinkle of his keys preceding him.

The bunk shifts as Mose stands up. He is like a grizzly bear coming out of his cave. He stretches, pressing his huge hands to the ceiling then turns to stare, "Got anything to eat?"

Mose's huge head and shoulders tower over the edge of my mattress. He looks like a hopeful bear. "Didn't see ya carrying nuthin in, figured you might have sumthin in your pockets." He paws at my mattress.

I shake my head, "No, I don't have anything."

"So, what good are ya?" he growled then stomps a single partial pace to the opposite wall, "Why do I always gets da losers?" He rustles about in a beat-up locker. "Nuthin," he slams the metal door then drops his bulk onto the bunk grumbling despondently.

'Mose thinks I'm a loser?' What a startling thought.

The lights go out abruptly as the tier guard yells for the shutting down of radios, which few possess.

I listen to the pacing of the guard, the scuff of his boot, the grumbling of the inmates and then someone crying.

Mose growls from his man cave, "Good thing that ain't you sniveling, white boy. Can't stand men blubbering. Makes me wanna break sumpin to shut em up."

The bunk shifts as Mose snickers, "Now that would give em sumpin to cry about. You ever heard a grown man squeal?"

My heart races. *'Is he threatening me?'*

"I's heard em hit the high notes, just likes they's a little girl."

My blood surges and there is a rushing sound in my head.

Is Mose working himself up for something? I wonder fearfully.

My fists clench and unclench as something primal stirs deep down inside of me. My body readies to defend itself.

The deep baritone fills the cell with sudden deep mirth. "Youze one lucky white boy cause Mose ain't into none of that queer-boy stuff." He chuckled, "Bets you glad to hears that ain't ya?" He punches the metal springs beneath my mattress. For him it is a playful contact, but I feel the massive power behind that solid blow. "Youze glad Mose ain't gay ain't ya?"

"Absolutely," I replied, as a nervous laugh escapes my lips.

Mose snorts then chuckles deeply. "Bets you didn't think you'd be giggling on ya first night in da joint."

"No, Mose," I said smiling in the darkness, "I surely did not."

*   *   *

In the first waking moments, I hope beyond reason that it was all just a bad dream, that I am not confined in a prison cell. Then I hear the rumble of cellblock iron as steel security doors bang open then slam closed. There is the angry grumbling sound of inmates awakening as the reality of captivity rushes back and pounces upon me. There is a ratcheting of heavy circuit breakers being thrown in rapid succession as big bulb lights over the steel-grate catwalks sweep the darkness away. I close my eyes, not yet willing to let the chaos of a waking cellblock descend upon me.

Lying on my bunk, I refuse to acknowledge the morning. Mose leverages his huge bulk up and plops down on the toilet. Not wanting to witness the repulsive event, I roll over to face the wall.

What happens over the next few minutes includes thunderous sounds and beyond imagination smells that would scar a child for life. He finishes with a loud grunt and the whoosh of the toilet flushing just as breakfast arrives.

The guard pushes two plastic trays through a slot in the grill. Mose sets mine on the three-foot tall locker and then sits down on the lower bunk with his tray.

I climb down to look at my breakfast. I see an unrecognizable greasy liver-colored disk with curled crispy edges. *Liver pancake?* I wonder dejectedly. There is a mysterious lumpy white pile. *Some sort of clumpy cereal?* Beside it is a hard-boiled egg, two pieces of burnt white toast, a pad of butter, and a crushed carton of milk.

"You sits on the toilet." Mose seemed extraordinarily excited.

I look at the recommended seat dubiously "I do?"

My subconsciousness slips into shock.

"So, we can visit while we eats." Mose grins lopsidedly. Unfortunately, Mose has little practice at smiling in prison. It looks like he is grimacing as if his toiletries are not quite over.

Holding my tray, I notice there are still some chunky things clinging to the inside of the steel bowl. Hoping I am not making a major inmate etiquette faux pas, I push and hold down the handle giving the toilet a thorough washing out. It does not accomplish all that I hoped as I consider a second flushing.

"Would you sits down and stop screwing around," Mose is apparently impatient to visit.

"Do you know what that is?" I asked pointing at the thin slab of what appears to be abused processed meat.

"It's fried baloney, don't ya wants it?"

"Gross!" I recoil at the thought, "I am a vegetarian."

Mose snatches the fried baloney from my plastic tray. He jams it in his mouth and chews enthusiastically, then says, "Never met no vegetarian in da joint before. So, what douz you eats?"

Mose seems genuinely interested, "I only eat what's good for me, such as vegetables, fruits, nuts, and grains. I avoid most animal products like cheese…"

Mose strikes again, interrupting my discussion. The hard-boiled egg is no longer next to the unidentified white pile. He pops the egg into his mouth, "Animal product," he said.

Mose eats with his mouth open. It is like watching a garbage disposal that frequently spits out slimy chunks dripping saliva.

"I was going to eat that egg. I'm a Lacto-Ovo vegetarian."

Mose stares at me clueless. His mouth hangs open while he chews my egg. Regrettably, I see he is missing teeth while chunks of egg white and yellow yolk revolve about becoming wet and squishy. Drool leaks from his thick lips. I look away, but the mental image lingers. I fear I am mentally scarred for life.

"A LactoOvo vegetarian eats eggs, cheese, and drinks milk."

Mose just stares vacantly. I notice how massive and muscular he is with biceps the size of my thighs. He sits leaning forward, his wide shoulders are layered with corded muscle and a covering of black heads and pimples—some of which are big enough to warrant a name, like a puss volcano.

Mose shrugs off my explanation, "You want them grits?"

Ah, white pile identified.

I plunge my fork into the grits. Mose is not trying to be social at all. He wants me on the toilet so he can raid my tray.

"You wants to look real good at them grits," he said opening his eyes wide, the whites around his pupils flash in the shadow of his bunk. "Pries it apart and looks for lumps or anything stringy."

"Lumps?" I probed the grits, which are indeed a bit chunky.

"They snots in it.

"What!"

"Snot," Mose rubs his nose then realizes it needs picking, which he does with an index finger the size of a large sausage. He wipes his finger on a bit of sheet hanging from the upper bunk.

'That's my sheet!' My survival instinct cautions me to remain quiet about the slimy bugger hanging off my sheet

Mose snorts up loose snot in his nose, and swallows wetly, then says, "Inmates cooks da food. Sometimes they blows snot into it outta da nose—same for da meatloaf, and especially da puddin."

I stare at the pile of grits harboring who knows what and then offer Mose the tray. He wipes the grits off with his blunt fingers.

I can't help checking my tray for snot trails, and yes, there is a dubious sheen the width of a large index finger on my tray.

I look at the two pieces of burnt toast, the tab of butter and half-crushed milk carton and wonder how I have been conned out of most of my breakfast. I see Mose getting eye-lock on my milk. I snatch up the milk carton.

After breakfast, I clandestinely inspect my sheet. Once seen, some things cannot be unseen.

The guard opens the cell doors on our tier, "Yard time," he yells.

We file out from the dim interior into a cold late October morning. The sea fog is back; it drifts about the narrow J-1 yard, which is a constricted rectangle, 120-feet long by 55-feet wide. Tall walls topped with concertina wire hem in the concrete yard. A bent basketball hoop hangs from a pole, and in a corner, there is a rusted-out universal gym. Mose lumbers over to the machine, stepping to the front of the fast-assembling line. The inmate on the flat-back bench quickly finishes his set, stands up, and scurries off. Mose sits down with his ample buttocks overlapping the bench. He lifts the entire weight stack effortlessly.

"The guy's an animal," someone said from behind me.

A lanky white man stalks behind me. He has stringy brown hair, acne scars, and an Adam's apple that bobs when he talks. He has a shifty look that misses nothing in the yard as he shuffles, shoulders rounded, chest concave, a serious drug abuser. Normally I would avoid a character like this but glancing around I notice that odd characters are in the majority amongst the whites. Most of the inmates are South of the Border Latinos or BlackAmericans.

"Hey, new meat," he drawled, "I'm Clem."

I can tell this idiot mentally does not have both oars in the water.

"My name's Steve."

"Everyone knows what your name is, new meat," Clem said. He smiles showing gaps between crooked yellow teeth with visible cavities that resemble miniature coal mines with fractures.

"Because I'm the new guy?"

"Nah, you're DeLorean's codefendant, seen your picture in the paper." Clem nods toward the far wall of the J-1 yard. "That's Jail Unit 2. It's where they put DeLorean and Hetrick last night. It's a lot better than The Hole."

I wonder what other tidbits of information Clem might know, but then he drops a bombshell.

"Looks like they got you flagged to cooperate."

"What? What are you talking about?"

"Ratting off DeLorean," he shook his head. "Come on, aren't you curious why they stuck you in The Hole while your two buddies are cruising in J-2?"

"Hadn't thought much about it," I answered honestly.

Clem nods toward the universal where Mose has a 200-pound black inmate riding the weight stack. The half-inch-thick steel lifting bar is bending under the massive load.

"Yeah, well I bet you thought plenty about your cellie. Ain't an accident you being in Mose's cave and all."

"What are you talking about?"

"Man, you are dense." Clem looked at me like I'm a dimwit. "You better smarten up or you ain't gonna last long, homes."

Smarten up? I have the village idiot looking at me like I am stupid. Maybe the smartest thing I can do is gather information. Just seems strange soliciting it from the local doper.

"The hacks don't normally put new white meat in with the baddest and the meanest black dude in the whole joint," said Clem raising a shaggy eyebrow, "Understand now?"

"Meanest and baddest?" I questioned unhappily

With his eyes wide, he looks like a surprised scarecrow, "Mose is not allowed in general prison population because he doesn't play well with other inmates."

"They put me in his cell to scare me into cooperating?"

"Well, duh! Look, I don't want to be seen talking to you. When you rat out DeLorean, it's not going to look too good my hanging with you."

Walking within the rectangular edges of the small yard, I ponder Clem's words. I then think about Scotti saying he was making it his personal vendetta to take me down hard and, "You are not going to like the hole I'm going to bury you in."

'J-1 is The Hole.' Scotti arranged this to get me to cooperate.

Back in the cell, Mose has some advice for me. "You better hit the weight pile," he said sagely, "so you looks less like prey."

As an ex-Navy frogman, I'm in excellent physical condition. I do push-ups in sets of 50, and pull-ups in sets of 20 — and Mose thinks I look like a walking victim? Dang!

"Wants some advice? Wouldn't be chattering about your vegetarian thing, you sound like a bunny to be swallered up."

"Better if I look like a predator, huh?"

"You? A predator?" Mose belly laughs, "Ain't happening, veggie man. Got sum more advice. If you survive being in my cell, ya gonna get some respect out in da yard."

"We back to talking about cigarettes again?" I asked cynically.

"Na, I ain't into smoking, but if you shares your meat, I'll keep our secret about you being a rabbit and all."

"Not a problem for me," I said with a shrug.

Mose and I were bunkies for the first week of my incarceration at Terminal Island (T.I.). It was the most intense seven days of my life. He was a man boiling with anger and resentment. His rage lurked just beneath a fiery temperament that needed the barest excuse to come roaring forth. He lusted to break things. Though we were crammed in a cell for seven days, I did nothing to trigger Mose's wrath, or maybe he just tolerated me for my fried baloney and snot-laced grits.

When asked what it is like to be incarcerated, I say, "Go into your bathroom, invite two of the scariest people you can find inside, and then stay there for a couple of days."

The guard yells, "Yard time," as he walks the tier dragging his truncheon across the bars. Twenty cell doors open as 40 men step out and descend a metal staircase to file out into the yard. Mose heads for the universal gym scattering inmates along the way.

I watch teams gather for a game of basketball, no whites or Latinos allowed. The older Mexican inmates sit at a concrete table rolling cigarettes while enjoying a boisterous game of dominos where the tiles are slammed down with all the zeal and vengeance of a knife thrust into an opponent's back.

Tightening the laces on my running shoes, I launch off on a fast-paced counterclockwise run. I could not generate much sustained speed with so many of us in the narrow yard. So, I made fast sprints with rapid decelerations. As happens in a confined place with people moving randomly about, I had a minor collision with a black inmate trying to save a basketball from going out of bounds.

Avoiding physical contact with other inmates in prison is a serious matter, particularly between the races. He curses me though I do not think the fault is entirely mine. As our attention focuses on each other, the game pauses, inmates stare. The man is tall, muscular, sweating, and upset. He glances about noticing that the other players are watching.

"Sorry," I offer. He is still trying to decide what to do so I am giving him an easy out.

I watch him laboring to decide. One of my blessings and greatest faults is that I have a fast mind. I am not referring to a superior intellect. If I were that smart, I would not be here. I am referring to the speed that my brain processes information. The problem with a gift like this is that I often must wait for others to make their decision. Since I also have ADHD DE (Attention Deficit Hyperactivity Disorder, Deluxe Edition), it means I can get bored waiting. It can lead to antisocial, and sometimes borders on downright rude, behavior on my part.

"Sorry?" he asked, still trying to make up his mind where he wanted to go with this.

Well, actually, neither have I. They say everyone is tested in prison, maybe this is my moment. The guard is watching from behind the chain link fence. He should shut this down; instead, I guess this is just another aspect of a corrections officer at play. Unconsciously I roll my shoulders as I consider the value of proving myself in the light of day with even odds, and no visible weapons present. It has a certain merit – or so I foolishly thought. Remember fast mind, but not the best decisions, particularly not in this perilous inmate alley.

The man tosses the basketball to a friend and glares at me.

Okay, playtime, the words thunder through my mind. I drop into a defensive stance. Bending my knees lowers my center of gravity. My arms hang like a praying mantis. To block a strike, I raise my arm brushing the fist to the side, just enough to miss me, then slide my cupped hand over his wrist and pull down, accelerating my opponent's forward momentum downward. It brings his head in for a reverse back fist to the nose with the same hand. Over in less than two seconds.

The man I am facing is right-handed, which he reveals by dipping his right shoulder, he is telegraphing a right punch. My Praying Mantis back fist will light this turkey up.

"Hey, Lewis," Mose had not spoken loudly from his seated position at the bench press, but he instantly has the other black man's attention. Mose does a shoulder shrug; a let it go kind of motion. The black man looks back at me, sneers then snatches the ball from his companion and returns to the game.

Back in our cell, I watch the barred grill slide closed. I turn towards my bunk—just as Mose slams me against the bars. He is furious. Up close, he towers over me. His muscles, swollen with blood from his work out, stretch his sweat-stained T-shirt across his massive chest. He glares, then jabs two thick fingers into my chest. "Youze one stupid white boy!" he raged. "What you doing runnin all overs da yard likes you owns it and getting in everyone's business?"

"I was just running."

"Don't you knows about respect or nuttin? Everyone be needin their space and youze out theres running through it likes you got no respect for them. Be drug deals goin down, and gangs jiving bout their private stuff, while youze rabbiting about putting everyones on edge. Then you gets a run in with Lewis. Shoulda said sorry and moved on, but rabbit gots to stands there in his face egging em on."

"I wasn't egging him on," I argued.

"Wasn't that you getting ready to do some of that karate dancing? So, what was your big plan after you hits him?"

"Plan?"

"Don't plays stupid," said Mose poking harder with his two fingers. "Thinks if you hits him it's all over? You knuckles a gang member front of his brothers and you thinks he's gonna just forgets bout it? You be dead afore ya even knows it."

"I was going to pop him in the nose," I admitted reluctantly.

"I knows that," Mose turns away and sits down on his bunk, a bear with a problem cub. "So, did everyone in da yard. Dis place is a jungle; ya survives by being a smarter predator than the rests of da pack. Ain't no rules in here. It's bout survival. He who is standing wins. Da sucker laying in a puddle of blood dun lost for good. Just do da dude and disappears afore the hack sees ya."

Mose puts his face in his hands then looks at me with a great sadness. "You listens to me rabbit, dis place ain't what you thinks it is. You don't pays attention—ya winds up with a toe tag or workin as some man's boy toy."

Toe tag? That is dead. I see an image of me on a gurney. I do not like it—not hot on the boy toy idea either.

"Don't be thinking inwards in here, you gots to be thinking outwards all's da time. You be paying attention to them cuz theys be watchen you homes." Mose slaps his chest with a meaty hand, "Ya think Mose is so big and mean I got nuthin to be afraid of? Smallest inmate in da joint tapes a knife to a broomstick and nails ya throughs da bars while youze sleeping. Or maybe's they puts rats poison in yur oatmeal or throws something flammable on ya and sets your carcass on fire like pork on da barbeque."

Mose gets a faraway look in his eyes. I know he is thinking about that pork barbeque he just mentioned.

"Sorry, Mose," I said.

"Sorry? I'll tell you what ta be sorry bouts. Ya done made an enemy of Lewis. He being a gang member means you gots yourself a wholes passel of new dudes to contends with and theys be talking about you right now."

"Should I apologize?" *I don't like the thought.*

"Hell no, just stays outta his face. Act like nuthin a matter. But tells ya what. Next time you start rabbiting around da yard, I'll knocks your butt down afore someone else with attitude messes you up sum kinda permanent."

"Thanks, Mose, I appreciate your calling off Lewis."

"Did him a favor too, man didn't knows he's messing with a frisky bunny."

I crawl up onto my bunk wondering about my stupidity; I was the fool dancing in a minefield.

Mose shifts the whole bunk. He gets restless before meals. The cellblock reverberates in waves of conflicting sounds: inmates bickering, cellblock iron clanging, and playing beneath it all, a mixed tempo of warring music from radios tuned to rock, heavy metal, Latin, and country western music with blasts of static from the guard's radios. The cellblock is a ruckus of warring noise.

I grab my rag of a pillow and tuck it around my ears. I think about the cascading echo of small breakers on a beach and of flowing sand as the water rushes back to the ocean. I strip away all sound of the cellblock and will myself to remember.

* * *

Susan and I are sitting on a blanket watching the sun setting into the ocean. Puu arrives dripping wet and shakes, throwing water droplets everywhere. Tropical winter in Hawaii, the drops are refreshing. Susan unpacks a picnic basket full of vegetarian treats. Puu snuffs hopefully, then buries his black muzzle into the basket, but it holds little interest for him. He snorts, looking expectantly at Susan. She playfully offers him a leafy celery top, which he consents to sniff, and then with a disappointed exhalation, he puts his large blocky head between his big paws and groans. Rubbing the Dane's ears, Susan asked, "Didn't you bring anything for Puu?"

I dig to the bottom of the basket and hold up a large can of Mighty Dog. Susan opens the can and dumps the 16-ounce cylinder of meat onto a paper plate, which Puu inhales in large gulps. He licks his muzzle clean then contentedly lays his head in her lap. Puu gazes at Susan with adoring eyes and then loudly passes gas.

We are sitting in the lee of the Royal Hawaiian Hotel's lanai where a Polynesian show is just beginning. As the red sun slowly disappears into the calm water, Hawaiian hula dancers flood the stage, moving in rapid sync to the beat of drums.

Susan leans back into my arms. I stare at her while she listens to the music and watches the exotic dancers. The beat of the drums increases as fire dancers leap onto the stage, twirling batons tipped with swirling flames. The heavy rhythm of the drums matches the beating of my heart. I let my hand slip slowly from Susan's hair.

"Stop that," complained Susan. "This is just our second date. You can't just maul me whenever you want, and don't give me that hurt puppy dog look of yours."

I nodded not sure I could keep that promise. Susan smiles and leans against my shoulder. To keep from getting into any more trouble, I pick Susan up and run down to the water with Puu running alongside barking. "No!" yelled Susan as I cast us both into the cool tropical water.

* * *

"I smells lunch," blurted Mose. He pads to the bars to look.

Instead, a guard arrives, "Arrington, you're moving."

Stepping out of the cell, I softly say, "See ya, Mose."

Mose reaches up and snatches my pillow. He crawls with it back into his lair and rolling over faces the wall.

Mose, the meanest and baddest black man at T.I. The man who was supposed to terrorize me into cooperating, instead became a friend and my first inmate mentor.

If one advances confidently in the direction of his dreams, and endeavors to lead a life whichhe has imagined, he will meet with a success unexpected in common hours. — Henry David Thoreau

I arrive in J-3 with my possessions in my back pocket. It is a single-level cellblock beneath the prison hospital. Dual banks of nine each cells run the 90-foot length of a 12-foot-wide corridor. At one end is the television room where we eat. It is a serious improvement over the J-1 toilet seat with Mose eyeballing my tray. The guard stops at a steel cell door with a window and nods. I am surprised that the door is unlocked, so I open and close it twice.

"Hey idiot, open it or close it but get it over with," said a little middle-aged man sitting on the lower bunk reading a book.

"I just came over from J-1," I said cheerfully.

"And that explains exactly what?" he grumbled.

"I can open and close a door in this place."

"How long were you in J-1, a couple of decades?"

"No, I was there for a week, well actually eight days."

"Eight whole days and now you have this thing with doors?"

"I'm Stephen Arrington," I said offering my hand.

"Hey! You're the Fall Guy," He said standing up, "I'm Morris." He is in his sixties, five-feet tall with a slight frame and an old man's paunch. He is an Armenian doing time for the tax fraud.

"Why'd you call me Fall Guy?" I ask.

"Everyone at T.I. is calling you that. You're going to take the fall for DeLorean. "So," Morris grins, "is DeLorean guilty?"

Morris could not have been more obvious if he had written the word snitch on his forehead with a *Sharpe*. Large scary cellmate did not work, so the Feds are trying a friendly Armenian snitch.

"I don't have a clue," I answered warily.

"It's okay," Morris puts one hand up defensively, "and just in case you're thinking it, I'm not a snitch."

Not in a trusting mood, I place my few things on my bed.

"That's all you got?" laughed Morris. "That's nothing; you're like the poorest inmate I've ever seen."

I look at my compact tube of toothpaste, toothbrush, and plastic comb. "I didn't exactly have time to prepare."

"Well, I sure did," bragged Morris.

On the shelf in the locker, there are some socks, two T-shirts, soap, shampoo, letter writing materials, a paperback, and a few other personal items. "Yeah, so I see."

"Not there," he lifts his mattress, "here." It looks like a store. There are cartons of cigarettes, candy bars, beef jerky, a half dozen flattened *Cup of Noodles,* salted nuts, and more.

"Want one?" Morris offers a flattened *Cup of Noodles.*

I shake my head, "How do you protect all this stuff?"

"That's why I'm offering the noodles. One of us has to be in sight of this cell when the thieves are prowling about."

I glance at the upper bunk and do a double take; there is a window! The glazed glass prevents my seeing out, however, a pane of glass is missing. I have a four by six-inch view of the J-3 exercise yard. I spend five minutes watching a passing cloud.

Dinner arrives at 5:00 PM, and it is a great indulgence to eat in the television room. I sit at a table with three other inmates where in just a few minutes I learn how to steal a car.

That evening, I lie down in a non-threatening cell. I revel in a breath of wind blowing through the broken pane. It is a relief to be in a cell with a nonaggressive inmate. I fluff the pillow, and though it smells of old mildew, I close my eyes and happily fall asleep.

I wake to shadows of jail bars marching across the cell wall in sync with the rising sun. The metal bunk lightly shakes as Morris, who is snoring on the bunk below, farts. I strike a match to mask the foul odor seeping into the air. Morris gave me the matches thinking I might need them. It qualifies as inmate good manners.

Later, I am in the cell reading a paperback when the guard opens the door. "Arrington, attorney visit."

I follow the guard down the corridor. He opens a security door. Opposite his office is the attorney/client room. A slim man with dark curly hair in a black business suit is waiting for me. "Rick Barnett, I received a check for $50,000 to represent you.".

I am surprised that Morgan honored his promise. Taking Rick's hand, I realize I am now broke. It is a strange feeling, particularly after a $50,000 handshake. I sigh.

"Something wrong?" asked Rick.

"Just realized that I'm stone broke," I said shrugging.

"Just so you know, I don't represent snitches," said Rick. "I'm here to defend you to the best of my ability.

"I have a ground rule too," I said watching Rick's eyes. "That was my fifty grand, even though Morgan wrote the check. That means you represent me and only me, not Morgan's interest."

"Absolutely, not a problem."

"What happens if Morgan and I get adversarial?"

"Doesn't matter, I only represent you." Rick grinned at me, "By the way, I am glad you asked that question. With three defendants one always flips. So, just know this, I am your new best friend."

Back in the cellblock it is yard time. Stepping out the yard door, I look eagerly about the J-3 yard. It is a bit larger than the J-1 yard and has a better view of the North Yard through a 12-foot-tall chain-link fence. The yard is surrounded by three concrete walls. There is a frayed volleyball net, a rusted exercise machine, and a bent basketball hoop on a pole. The cracked concrete deck has a dirt section that is 6' wide and 30' long. I walk over to peer at the dirt while inmates walk or run the small perimeter.

I join the joggers. While running the small loop, I stare through the chain link fence at a couple of small lawns and a dwarf tree in the North Yard. Standing under the tree is a stooped old inmate feeding a flock of pigeons. Every so often, an inmate will walk by and give him a couple of slices of bread smuggled out of the chow hall. The old man shreds the bread as he shuffles amongst the crowding birds. When the crumbs are gone, the pigeons fly up to settle on a ledge. The old man stops his shuffle and just stands there, head down staring at the grass. Two more inmates arrive with bread; it is like putting coins into an antique toy machine as the old man shambles, shedding breadcrumbs. The birds arrive pecking and head bobbing about his feet as he shuffles, head down.

Repeatedly passing the dirt section, I notice there is a bit of dead brown grass under a layer of trash and cigarette butts. I see a dented bucket, and then I watch two inmates getting a drink from an old faucet. I stop running and look at the dirt section. An idea is forming. Fetching the bucket, I carry it to the strip of dirt. It is here in a small section that the dead grass lingers. I wonder about the roots deeper in the soil. I rake a patch of dirt clean with my fingers and take the debris away. I carry the pail to the faucet, which only produces a dribble of water. It takes two minutes to fill the bucket, which I carry to the cleaned patch of dirt. Kneeling, I pour the clear water onto the cleaned dirt. It is a privilege to do this.

My action prompts a memory of an old Asian saying from my martial arts dojo, *"The wonder, I carry water."* A simple concept yet its significance is impressive when one ponders the essence of it. This five-word maxim implies that the person has access to clean water. Because the bearer carries the water, it infers that it is being taken to a home and probably to a family, which equates to love, service, and responsibility. The author appreciates the wonder of such a simple act. After air, nothing is more important to life than water. I earned my living in water as a Navy frog and scuba instructor. Water is also where I played as a diver, surfer, sailboat sailor and snow skier. I am into water in a big way.

With these thoughts flowing through my mind like a mental waterfall, I do my bucket chore every day for two weeks. The other inmates think I am looking for an insanity defense, but I just keep carrying the sloshing bucket and pouring it over my patch of dirt. It is interesting how action can suggest possession. I consider the tiny patch of grass as mine by right of claim, and no one refutes it. I have bonded with something waiting beneath the soil's surface.

It happens on a Monday. I know because they served eggs over-easy, fried sausage, and baked beans for breakfast. I traded my sausage, which looks like something dug out of a cat's litter box, for another inmate's beans. He thought he got the best of the deal.

After the orderlies clean the television room, the guard lets us out into the yard. I look at my section of dirt, and stare in awe at dozens of tiny green sprouts of grass just breaking through the soil. I have made something beautiful happen in the bareness of prison. I happily fetch my bucket, and I slowly let the water dribble over the fresh sprouts of grass. "*The wonder, I carry water.*"

At the faucet again, I watch the water slowly dribbling into the dented bucket. I listen to the change in pitch of the falling water as it spills into the empty bucket with a hollow, tinny sound that becomes a brook-like gurgle as the pail fills. I inhale the crisp water vapor rising from the bucket and dunk my hand into it then let the water dribble from my fingertips onto my upraised face. The cool water wets my lips quenching a deep inner need for something good outside the ponderous negative sameness of prison. It is pleasing to be doing something so simple, yet so wondrously good.

I am on my third bucket of water when the guard calls my name, "Arrington, get over here."

I set down my bucket and walk warily over to the guard who looks me up and down, "What's with this bucket thing?"

"Just trying to grow some grass."

"Why?"

"Not much else to do here and it feels good," I said honestly.

"Think you're accomplishing something?"

"Yeah," I said, knowing that my bucket thing is about how I think and feel about myself. I am dirty inside and know it. It is as if I am pouring that bucket over my soul.

"Want a job? I am losing an orderly to general population today," he said. "You serve the meals and clean the cellblock."

"Okay," I nod, having noticed something special about the orderlies. Whenever they clean up the television room or the corridor, the rest of us have to stay locked in our cells. They are also the first ones out to prepare the morning meal. Being an orderly equates to less time confined in a prison cell.

"It pays seven cents an hour. If you're here long enough, it can really add up." He walks away chuckling.

"Hey Arrington," yelled an inmate, "get off the man's leg."

"What's that mean?" I asked in a friendly way. My positive response takes him off guard.

"Aren't you over there sucking up to the hack?"

"Nope," I put a smile on my face even though I would like to pop this worm's head like a zit. "Didn't you see him order me over to the fence? He wants me to be an orderly."

"You going to do it?" he asked suspiciously.

"Absolutely, pays a whole seven cents an hour."

Back inside J-3, I ask Morris, "What does it mean when an inmate says get off the man's leg?"

Morris laughs, "Think small dog humping a person's leg. It's an inmate slam, means stop sucking up to the guard."

"Everybody here sure wants to know a person's business."

"So, what did the guard want?"

"Wants me to be an orderly."

"That means they will move you into the orderly cell."

"I also get seven cents an hour."

I collect my toothpaste, toothbrush, and comb, drop them into the rusty bucket and walk out of the cell. Following the guard, I glance down at the bucket I am carrying. It is now my possession, though I do not own it. I get to carry it about, and no one bothers me about it. This rusty bucket, dented and oblong, is giving me purpose and meaning—and now a new job and I get paid, a whole seven cents an hour. As a child, an older woman next door offered to pay me cash to pull weeds. Three hours later, she paid me with three dimes. I felt I had been ripped off. Now as a 32-year-old adult, I am earning seven cents an hour—because of a rusty bucket.

In the orderly cell, an inmate is moving bedding from the top bunk to the lower bunk. "Hope you don't mind if I take the lower bunk, been here longer, earned it, name's Clayton."

"Don't mind at all. I'm Steve."

the night in a jail cell wearing a wrinkled suit. Now he is groomed, sits tall, and owns the courtroom. He is the center of attention, which is probably why Morgan looks grumpy.

Rick leans over and says, "This is just a procedural thing. The defense teams are making discovery motions."

"What about me?" I asked.

"You and I are just along for the ride."

"You mean we are just going to sit here and do nothing?"

"Yep, better than rotting in a jail cell isn't it?"

I glance about looking at real people, "You got that right."

The court proceedings take 15 minutes then the handcuffs go back on. The marshals lead Morgan and me separately from the courtroom. My escort and I join a young couple in an elevator. She has blond hair, a nice figure, innocent good looks, and radiates happiness. He is thrilled to be with her. They are discussing lunch plans. When the elevator doors open, I watch them walk towards the front exit. Sunlight halos her hair then my marshal escort pushes me toward the staircase that descends into the basement.

In the cell, I trade my baloney on white for a bruised apple. It is late afternoon before the marshals' van is ready to go back to T.I. Morgan has not returned to the holding cells, which means he is upstairs cutting a deal. I am alone now and have my own decisions to make, they will not be easy, but they will be mine.

Back in the cellblock, I have missed dinner so am treated to another sack lunch with baloney on white. I chuck the baloney but force down the bread. I do not like the taste of the white bread that harbors a salty residue seasoned with toxic nitrates, and the smell of the processed baloney, but it fills a hole.

The next morning, I receive a tiny bag from the commissary cart. Inside are four chocolate bars, paid for with my seven cents an hour orderly salary. That evening, I go into the shower stall. Hidden in my towel is half of a candy bar. If anyone sees me with it, they will ask for—or demand—a share. I am enjoying the inmate intrigue of the moment as I savor the rich chocolate with hot water washing over my face. In prison, imaginative inmates create special moments to what is otherwise a boring existence.

* * *

A month drags into the next month. It is 4:00 AM, I am awake with nothing to do and nowhere to go; it is an inmate thing. A rumbling sound drops out of the floor of the nut ward above us. It rushes through the adjacent cell then scuttles toward my bunk. The thick iron pipe above my head vibrates, emitting a gurgling sound that sloshes as the effluent flow hits an elbow then plunges down the pipe that runs past my head on its race to the sewer. A final swooshing noise trickles to a softer dripping tinkle that lingers for 10 or 12 seconds. A drop of condensation from the moist pipe drops onto my pillow.

I stare at a puddle of light on the cinderblock wall. A shaft of brightness from an exterior security light throws shadows of jail bars on the cinderblocks. A cockroach climbs into the pool of light then disappears back into the darker shadows.

Climbing down from the bunk, it is chilly just in my boxer shorts. I ignore the cold as I work to build discipline. I assume the posture of an alert praying mantis. In slow motion, I go through katas (martial arts routines). It is tricky to move about the limited space of the narrow cell. Next, to the bunk, I have less than four feet of width with five-plus feet of length; the locker takes up the other one foot. The cell's floor space then widens beyond the bunk by the door, which is where the toilet squats in J-3.

I use the tiny floor space to discipline my movements. Snap kicks go over the toilet and locker, back fists, snap punches, and thrust hits stop just short of the bunk or the cinderblock wall. I settle into a low horse stance with my spread legs all but touching the bunk and wall. I am preparing to practice an Iron Palm Strike. I block a kick from an imagined opponent to my front then turn to confront another. I step forward using momentum to accelerate the strike while concentrating on driving my palm through the locker door — my imagined opponent. I thought I would be short of contact — I am not. The resounding metallic clash just two feet from Clayton's head brings him instantly vertical in his bunk.

"What are you doing?" he blurted.

"Being an insect."

"Killing an insect?"

"No being one."

"A bug, you think you're a bug?" said Clayton, he has that look one reserves for demented, or drugged out, inmates.

"No, I am imitating the movements of a praying mantis," I said looking at a palm-sized dent in the locker's steel door.

"Sorry about the noise."

"What did you do, kick the locker?"

"No, just a palm strike."

Clayton stares at the deep dent in the metal. "You did that with the palm of your hand?" he asked surprised.

"Well, yeah, kind of."

"Karate, you're doing karate."

"It is Praying Mantis Gung Fu."

"So how good are you?" Clayton asked.

"Not good enough for hanging out in a prison." I shrugged.

I hear keys clacking followed by the door lock opening. "What are you guys doing in here?" demanded the guard.

"Nothing," Clayton and I answered in unison.

He does not notice the dented door, which is hard to miss except most of the locker doors have dents from frustrated inmates. "Get the room ready for breakfast, you two."

An hour later, I hear rolling wheels, faint clanking noises of trays bouncing, and then see an inmate pushing our food cart to the North Yard door.

The guard locks us behind the grill to wheel the cart inside. I can smell the oatmeal from behind the bars. Funny, I never noticed that oatmeal smells so good. As the guard unlocks the grill he whispers, "You guys did an excellent job cleaning yesterday, so I ordered an extra two rations."

Startlingly, I am excited about an extra bowl of cold oatmeal.

Unpacking the cart, I find the tray with my name then peruse the other trays for two bowls of relatively lump-free oatmeal. Only my vegetarian tray and a Jewish inmate's kosher meal have name labels. Having my name on a tray is an invitation for some snot enthusiast in the kitchen to put something nasty into my entrée. For a demented inmate, knowing the name of the victim getting his body wastes in a bowl is just too alluring. I am taking no chances on bugger seasoning and spit garnish.

"Gate!" yells the guard. The waiting inmates quickly move away from the grill so the guard can unlock it. The television room floods with boisterous, hungry inmates, and for the next half-hour, Clayton and I are busy serving in a riotous tip-free milieu.

After locking the rest of the inmates back in their cells, Clayton and I give the television room a serious cleaning. It is an every-meal event, as the men enjoy making messes, like frustrated children who resent mom-enforced table manners. What troubles me the most is the clusters of caked on hardened snot under the table—so I ignore them. Otherwise, Clayton and I do a good job; after all, there is an oatmeal incentive to consider.

Later the guard announces yard time, and we line up at the J-3 yard door for our coveted hour of sunshine. I am standing near the front of the line with an old black man glaring at me with bulbous eyes. He tries to edge a little closer to the front of the line, but an inmate pushes him back. The old man glares at me then sticks out his elbows to make sure I stay behind him.

I am highly amused.

When the guard opens the door, the men file out. When the old man is out the door, he dashes off in shuffling arthritic gait. I pretend to chase after him, but cackling with happiness, he beats me to the lawn by two-steps, unzips his fly, and begins peeing onto my grass. It goes on for a rather long time. I believe he saves up for this moment. He is in absolute bliss watching his pee stream. I am sure that he is reliving boyhood memories.

I walk over to the faucet with my dented bucket and stand there holding open the spigot's rusty spring-loaded knob. The small spout coughs up a weak water stream or leaks a downward dribble. I continuously adjust the bucket's height to catch the flow, so I turn it into a musical event. I listen carefully to the trickle of the water slowly filling the pail; I enjoy the gentle waterfall-like sound. The trickle of falling water creates a soft liquid melody. The sound of the spilling water delights me. Lately, I have been creating water music, which starts with a hollow drumming cadence when the bucket is empty, and then becomes a splash fest until the water level reaches two inches. By raising, lowering, and tilting the bucket, I change the pitch and depth of the aqua music. I watch the water level leisurely climb and hear the pitch deepen as the bucket gradually fills. Then I am off to the grass to watch what is so clean and pure pouring from the bucket onto the green living sprouts.

This is my main recreational moment of the day. I watch the spilling water turn the dry earth beneath the sparse grass a wet vibrant brown. What was once a litter-strewn patch of dead dirt is now life producing soil. I smell the damp earth scent of the dirt sucks up the water.

Six buckets later, I set the pail down then eagerly take off for my morning run. Now that I am familiar with all the inmates in my cellblock, I know who to avoid as I run at a faster pace than the confined area would normally allow.

Lately, a Latin smuggler named Cortez has been making unwanted advances. I am hostile in return, yet he continues to harass me. I think it is the publicity thing. The DeLorean Case is regularly on the front page of the Los Angeles newspapers and is a nightly feature on the news. Maybe the Colombian is jealous of the attention or wants to make a name for himself. Physically he is not especially threatening, six feet tall and weighs about 200 pounds with a gut. I may have to hurt him if he does not back off.

Lunch is a real inmate pleaser, hot dogs, cold beans, and stale potato chips with a soap opera blaring from the television. The Latin dude is bragging about an alleged reluctant inmate conquest. Apparently, the story is for my benefit as he keeps throwing looks in my direction. I am feeling downright hostile toward him as I drop his tray onto the table from a height of about a foot.

"Hey, homes," he glared, "careful with the groceries." He glances at his cronies, "Housewives can be so darn moody."

Yep, I will hurt him. Fighting can land both of us in The Hole, and I have no desire to go back to J-1. I need to confront him when no one else is around, which is not easy in a crowded cellblock.

"Clayton," shouted the guard, "attorney visit."

An hour later, I am mopping the television room when I see the guard open the security door at the end of the corridor. Clayton scurries rapidly down to the television room. I have never seen him move in such a hurry before.

"Steve," he said nervously, "my attorney wants to see you."

"Me," I ask, "why?"

"Says he can help you," Clayton glanced worriedly about, "but you got to tell the guard you want to see him. Otherwise, my guy said it's a violation of attorney-client privilege."

"Sure, I'll see him." I said handing the mop to Clayton, "Got to be better than slinging a mop about."

"Thanks," muttered Clayton as I walk down the corridor.

The guard sees me coming and opens the security door. I step through and go into the attorney/client room.

An overweight man with a food stain on his white shirt is waiting for me. Sometimes they call a crooked attorney a shyster. This character looks to fit the bill.

"Smart," he said shaking my hand, "would have been a big mistake not to have seen me."

"How's that?"

"Cause, I can get you out of here."

"Just like that?" I ask.

"Yeah," he snaps his fingers, "just like that." He leans back in his chair, "No problem at all."

'Who is this guy?'

"I run snitches, lots of snitches. I'm a regular Rat Wrangler."

"Really," I am intrigued, "so you work for the government."

"Not exactly, I'm more like a sub-contractor, gives them and me a couple of degrees of separation. I'm a troubleshooter."

"Is that what this is — rat recruitment?"

"Think of it more as serving your country," he shrugged, "you want to do the right thing don't you."

'Wow, this guy has read my file,' I thought. He looks sloppy, but now I know it is all a guise. He cut straight through to my biggest issue. 'Yeah, I want to serve my country, but not as a lowlife snitch.'

"Sounds like you've been psychoanalyzing me," I replied.

"Of course, you're being psychoanalyzed," he leered at me. "The FBI has a whole department dedicated to figuring out hotshots like you. What's the point of putting half a dozen snitches on you if we're not crunching the data?"

"Half a dozen snitches?" I am surprised.

"Yeah, it's a group effort. I got a whole snitch squad on you. Think of J-3 as snitch central." He said leaning forward, "We put a couple of them right in your face to distract you."

"Morris and Clayton," I offer.

"Maybe, in any case, I know everything you've said and done in this cellblock including your stupid bucket fetish."

"Look, I'm not the snitch type."

"Yeah, but you want to serve your country."

"Get that from Morris?"

The Rat Wrangler shrugs. Then he reaches into his pocket and drops a set of keys onto the table. "Listen closely; I'm your key out of here. But I need you to earn it," he coaxed.

"You've got that kind of horsepower?"

"Yeah, watch." He stepped to the door. "Hey, guard."

The guard stands up from his desk and walks to the door.

"Get lost," ordered the Rat-Wrangler.

The guard's anger surges, he is not used to controlling his emotions. Red-faced he turns abruptly, opens the security door, and goes into the cellblock. He slams the heavy steel door shut behind him — the sound reverberates loudly.

"Yeah, I got that kind of power," he said with a smirk. "I got more play than you can imagine. Remember your run-in with Louis? We had you moved out of J-3 before you got killed. The other option was to leave you there. Now no more stupid word games. You were Morgan's right-hand man. You know stuff. It means you are the key to busting this case wide-open."

"I'm not a snitch," I said standing up.

"You're going to wish you were! Get along with that guard?"

"He's okay," I shrugged again.

"Well, he's not going to be okay anymore. You saw me throw him out — I didn't belittle him on accident," the Rat-Wrangler leans forward, "He hates you now."

"Thanks," I said sarcastically.

"Lose the sarcastic act," he sneered. "You don't want to make me angry — you're in the wrong place. Some of my rats bite. Right now, this is me being nice." He smiled cruelly.

I turn and leave. If the Rat-Wrangler was trying to scare me — it worked. I did not doubt he could make my life inside a lot more terrifying. The Rat-Wrangler apparently has that kind of power — terror on a short leash with fangs prowling the corridor of J-3.

I knock on the security door and see the guard turn angrily to look at me. He stomps down the corridor and throws open the door and then slams it behind me.

"Move it, Arrington," ordered the guard.

I look him in the eyes, which is a huge guard/inmate mistake. "I'm sorry," I offered, "he did that to make you mad at me."

I see the guard's demeanor slowly change. "Nobody likes him, but he could care less. The guy's connected." The guard looks at me sympathetically, "Not someone you want on your wrong side."

"Yeah," I nodded, "that's what he said."

"Call your attorney and make a complaint," said the guard.

"Will it help?"

"Maybe, at least it will put that turd on notice." He looked at Clayton busily mopping the floor in our direction.

"Clayton," he yelled, "get in your cave."

Clayton stares then goes into the cell taking the mop with him.

"Make your call without anyone listening," he cautioned, "and remember to speak softly, particularly around your cellmate."

The next morning, I wake up early. The Rat Wrangler's threats are troublesome. Anything can go down in prison.

I spend the time concentrating on my Gung Fu moves. I am working on increasing my speed. To attain faster reflexes requires loose muscles and a calm focused mind — not easily achieved during the intensity of a fist or knife fight in prison.

My opportunity to discourage the Latin predator arrives abruptly. I had no time to think, only to act. We are standing in line at the yard door. I am last with my T-shirt off. It is sunny outside for a December morning, and I want to feel the warmth of the sun on my skin. The guard is holding the outer door open counting the men as they step out into the yard. There is a 12′ long corridor to the inner yard door. He cannot see inside the cellblock, which is an opportunity for inmate mischief.

Cortez stands ahead of me. I am about to lean down and pick up the bucket. We are the last two inmates in J-3 when he abruptly turns and leers at me. "Hey housewife, daddy's here," Cortez sneered as he aggressively places a hand on my pectoral muscle and squeezes hard.

My reaction is instinctive as I feel his disgusting hand on my bare skin. Cortez is about to say something raunchy. Instead, the only sound that comes out is a shriek of severe pain as I grab his hand and twist it violently inverting it toward his wrist. Applying pressure to the thumb joint and savagely rotating his palm inward means I own this dirt wad. With little effort, I could shatter his wrist joint. Instead, I slam my left forearm into the back of his elbow making an armbar for leverage and force Cortez to bend over at the waist. I drive his head down below the level of his butt. The man is in severe pain, which is very gratifying. From his touch to my achieving this takedown has taken less than two seconds.

I now have many options, from dislocating his shoulder to taking the joint apart with the bonus of an accelerated face smash into the tile floor. Instead, I hold him helpless. I whisper fiercely into his ear, "Touch me again, and I will break your wrist and tear your shoulder apart." I shoved him away, snatch up my bucket, and walk down the short corridor and out into the sunshine.

Three bucketsful later, my heart rate is still elevated. Cortez is playing dominos, pretending nothing happened. His defeat is not something he will talk about; it would destroy his reputation as a bad dude. However, I now have a lifelong enemy.

Instead of the usual six bucketsful of water for the lawn, I stop at three. I have too much energy bubbling in my veins to wait for the dribbling fountain to fill the bucket. I run the small perimeter, but the pace is too slow for all my energy with a dozen pacing men always in the way. So instead, I jog to the wire fence and do pushups, burpees, or sit-ups. When my arms or stomach tires, I leap up and sprint for the opposite wall where I drop for more pushups, sit-ups, and burpees, then sprint again, repeatedly.

I know why I am doing this. It is an animal thing, showing an adversary your strength and endurance, letting him know that it would be a huge mistake to challenge this feisty animal. How primal, how very appropriate it is in this inmate alley. I am enjoying myself immensely. I want to pound my chest and howl. I have passed my first real physical confrontation.

Back inside, I choose not to shower. I want to stink — I am in predator mode. At lunch, I eye the rows of blackened burgers in the cart wanting to eat them all. I am in a mood. Munching a carrot returns me to vegetarian sanity. War Bunny placated.

I gobble everything on my veggie tray where the main event is two scoops of white rice with a small pile of peas and two pieces of white bread. Still hungry, I go to my secret hideout during meal prep. With a broom handle, I raise a ceiling tile where I hid two cereal boxes. Clayton sees me, but it is no big deal, I know where his secret stash is too, only he is into hiding desserts.

Clayton and I are heating burgers in the microwave when the guard opens the cell doors. It becomes boisterous as the men fill the tables. I spy Cortez at a corner table and drop his tray the usual twelve inches, but he ignores me, pretending great interest in what the ignorant jerk next to him is saying. I resist the urge to paw the floor with my sneaker and growl; I am on a primal high.

The rest of the week passes uneventfully, which in prison is darn good. The other inmate bullies notice that Cortez is now ignoring me, even though I foolishly bait him. Fewer inmates listen to his stories; he struts less. In our primal society, where almost nothing goes unnoticed, a predator has been defanged. It interests me to watch the pecking order reshuffle itself.

After 4:00 PM count, the guards shift changes. The guard, who let me make the semi-private telephone call, opens our cell door. "Clayton, Arrington, get the television room ready."

Clayton is first out the door. As I pass the guard, he presses something into my hand. "Thought you would enjoy seeing this," he smiled and walked away. It is a newspaper clipping from the San Diego Union-Tribune. The headline reads, "DeLorean Defendant Complains of Unlawful Attorney Visit."

On Friday, they transfer Cortez out to the general population. Clayton and I are cleaning the television room after lunch. The rest of the cellblock is on lockdown. The guard locks us behind the grill, and then the North Yard guard opens the outer door and takes Cortez out into general population.

"That guy hates you," said Clayton. "He used to like trying to bully you. So, what did you do to him?"

"It's not what I did," I answered, "it's what I didn't do."

I watch Clayton knowing he is not my friend. He is a snitch who tried to set me up with the Rat Wrangler.

Wednesday morning is commissary day, the highlight of the week. Waiting for the commissary cart, I glance over my shoulder at the kindly old black man, who so likes watering my lawn with his pee. A homeless man from the streets of Los Angeles, he has no family or friends to send him money. He is too proud to beg or borrow from the other inmates. When the commissary cart makes its weekly appearance, he shuffles down to his cell and sulks.

As I see his cell door close, I think about the surprise I have for him. He is a chronic cigar smoker. In the yard, he handrolls cigars from the cheap bulk tobacco issued to the inmates by the prison staff. He begins by wadding up a handful of the loose tobacco into a fat cylinder, which he carefully lays into a paper towel. Rolling the paper towel, he tamps it into a zombie cigar that he lightly dampens with water from the drinking fountain. The process caught the attention of Shorty.

Shorty is shy of five-foot, with a passion for robbing banks, only he is not particularly good at it. Tellers have a problem taking him seriously. As a frequent offender, he has spent most of his adult life in prison. He always wants to know everyone else's business.

Shorty leans over the old man's shoulder at the concrete table in the yard to investigate. "What ya doing?" he asked.

"Dampening my cigar," the old man replied patiently.

"Why don't you just lick it?"

"Can't, I ain't got that much spit," grumbled the old man.

"Well, how come you got to wet it anyhow?"

The old man regards Shorty, "If I don't wet the paper towel, the fire will run right up the sides of the cigar and fry my lips."

"Oh," shrugged Shorty, who walked away, interest satisfied.

At the commissary line, I receive a brown paper sack with my name printed on it. The sack is from my attorney Rick depositing a hundred dollars into my prison account as a Christmas present. He indeed has become my new best friend, which means I truly have someone I can trust on my side.

I take the sack to my cell. It is not wise to let other inmates see your purchases. I set the sack on my bunk and remove two small packets of five cigars each. I carry them to the old man's cell and tap on his door. I never enter a prison cell without knocking. I am liable to see totally disgusting things that can be haunting.

"Come in already," grumbled a raspy voice.

I step inside. The close air in the cell carries the old man's funk — death lurks here. "What do you want, youngster?"

I hold up the cigars, "The commissary man made a mistake and put these cigars in my sack. I thought you might want them."

"Don't want no charity, boy."

"I got them by mistake," I murmured, "this isn't charity."

"Saves your money for yourself," he grumbled.

I lay the cigars on his bed and walk out.

In the corridor, I take several deep breaths purging my lungs of the death smell that lingers in that cell. The commissary cigars will not do his lungs any good, but they will be better than inhaling burning paper towels and wads of loose tobacco. I return to my cell and tear open the commissary sack. Inside is a little box radio. I set it on the dented locker. It is just a little mono unit with a two-inch speaker. I tune the radio to a sixty's station and hear one of my favorite songs from high school. I turn the volume up as the fifty-cent speaker fills the cell with a surfer riff that reverberates off the walls driving away the noise of the jail unit.

Later, In the corridor, I see the old black man shuffling along with a big toothless grin wrapped around a store-bought cigar. His eyes look more bulbous than normal as his jaw works that cigar. As he passes, he quietly said, "Thanks, youngster."

In prison, no one would dare complain about someone smoking. It could well be your last conscious act.

Four days later, he died in his sleep. As they take the thin body away on a gurney, I will always remember seeing his lanky frame poised over my lawn with the stub of a cigar sticking out of his mouth while he happily peed on my grass.

I go into his cell on a whim. Lying on the locker is one of the empty cigar packets. Wrapped in a paper towel next to it are ten cigar stubs. I pick it all up and go back to my cell.

At yard time, I use the bucket to scrape out a chunk of grass and dirt. I stuff the cigar butts with a wad of grass into the cigar box then place it into the hole. I offer up a silent prayer for the old man's soul. Then I flood the lawn with buckets of water.

That night in my cell, I dwell upon the vitality of life — I am missing within these prison walls. Instead of morbid thoughts, I build a mental picture. Susan is on the beach throwing a stick for Puu to fetch. I see her long blond hair blowing in the trade wind, and just beyond her the wave faces are running twenty-foot plus.

* * *

I am in the lineup at Laniakea and see Susan on the beach waving at me. I am in perfect position to catch a set wave. I paddle furiously as I drop into an elevator plunge screaming my lungs out. I make a long curving bottom turn and accelerate rapidly across the wave face. Despite my speed, I suddenly know I am not going fast enough. The whole wave face pitches as it washes over a shallow inner reef. Then the thick lip comes crashing down like a liquid door closing; trapping me inside a spinning fluid barrel that is rapidly collapsing. Angling the board hard into the wave face, I desperately try to arrow the board through the thick wall of rushing water — I almost make it.

Caught in the vortex of turbulent water, I can see I am within a foot of the surface as I try to punch out the back side of the massive wave. Then watch the rapidly receding sky as I am pulled backwards knowing I am in for a severe thrashing. The lip slams its small human cargo into the sandy bottom. I am lucky not to have hit the jagged reef. All about me, bubbles swirl distortedly in a wildly spinning turmoil of rolling water. My surfboard leash snaps. I curl into a protective ball. I fear I am about to do the reef-shredding, human-hamburger, drowning thing with Susan watching from the beach.

Desperately, I make it back to the surface just in time to be hit by another wave. My surfboard has long since departed for the beach as I begin my second underwater excursion. I finally arrive back at the beach, pick up my surfboard floating in the froth and totter wearily across the sand with my broken leash dragging behind me.

I see Susan throwing a stick, which Puu fetches back to her. Staggering up to her, I ask, "Did you see that magnificent wave I caught?"

Susan gives me the look — I know it well. She has a low opinion of girls who sit on the beach watching their boyfriends surf.

"No," she answered, "I was throwing a stick for Puu. Why?"

Standing there with wet sand stuffing my swim trunks, I realize that the throwing motion Susan was making with the stick looks exactly like the waving motion I saw from out in the line-up. She was playing with the dog, not waving at me.

"Oh, no reason," I replied, dragging my thrashed body toward the truck and a bottle of aspirin.

Susan catches up. "Stephen," she said taking my hand in hers, "you don't have to impress me with your surfing, I already love you."

I could feel the surfboard wax melting in the pocket of my trunks.

Stepping close Susan raises her face and smiles in a way that needs immediate attention. As I lower my face to hers, I see Susan close her big brown eyes. Abruptly, my sinuses drain a cargo of salt water that the big wave had packed into them. In shock, Susan's eyes fly open as snot and sinus water flushes across her face.

* * *

Revelstoke at sunset, La Jolla Shores, San Diego, CA.
Photo Arrington

The next morning, I am in the television room mopping the floor. When it dries, the guard opens the grill, and the inmates rush to place chairs in front of the television. Again, the guard locks the grill, only now I am on the other side as I mop the corridor. From the television room, I hear the men shouting at each other as they argue about what to watch. Shorty wins the argument with support from four Latinos who could have cared less—they just liked going against the black inmates while they played dominos.

The guard switches the channel to Shorty's soap opera. Two men who wanted to watch cartoons sit angrily at a back table.

After finishing the floor, the guard unlocks the grill, and I retire to my cell to read. I am two pages into a paperback when Shorty opened the cell door and asked me to change the channel.

I am reaching for the television when I hear a growl of outrage. I spin about to see a large, muscular black man hurling a chair from his path as he comes at me shrieking, "I'm going to rip your face off, white trash!"

The paperback falls unnoticed from my hand. I cannot show fear as the enraged man stomps up to me. Fury distorts his face as he growls, "What gives you the right, white boy?"

A mist of spittle sprays my face. The black man's eyes are fierce, lips curled, shoulders hunched, muscles bulging as an icicle of fear knives through my groin.

"I'm going to kill you!" he raged.

Other inmates move quickly away from us.

'Why me,' shrieked my mind, but I know as an orderly, I have taken a position of authority and privilege. He probably thinks that I am pretending to be a trustee-wannabe. The stupidity of it all makes me angry. Like a furnace door slamming open, my anger blazes to instant fury. I have contained myself for so long. My sanity flees before the fierce winds of a burning rage. Focusing on my adversary, I have become a primal male animal ready to fight for its survival.

There is crazed wrath in the man's eyes. I glare back. Hot blood pounds at my temples. Just when I think he will attack—he hesitates, breaking eye contact to glance at those about us.

Instantly, I know he does not want to fight either. He did not expect me to stand up for myself. Now he is probably thinking, 'Why give up cruising in J-3 for The Hole?'

I look at him in a sober way as calmness settles upon me. "Man does what a man has to do," I said without thinking.

'Where did that come from,' I wondered. Yet, my words recognize him as a man, but so am I. It is assertive, yet non-confrontational. It is as if the words were given to me. Instantly, I know it is over. From this point, it is all about bluster, a bully working on his image. It is not that I have won, but rather that I stood my ground. As we continue to glare at each other, I realize he is re-evaluating me. I was a surprise for him.

I have no more problems with the black man though I often catch him watching me through hooded eyes. His presence keeps me on my toes. I find that when I am around him, which is often in our confined cellblock, I am more alert, more keenly aware of what I am doing. I pay greater attention to what I say and keep my body orientated to repel any sudden hostility. I am in the constant company of a powerful adversary.

There was a concept taught to young American Indian warriors who were encouraged to seek a worthy adversary. The tribal elders knew that it was good to have a strong and cunning opponent upon which to sharpen your wits and abilities — a forced awareness with serious survival incentives.

* * *

I am in the television room scrubbing a table when an inmate says, "Hey Arrington, you made the funny page. Doonesbury, the cartoon strip," he points at his newspaper. "Trudeau is doing a strip on the DeLorean Case becoming a movie. Duke, one of the cartoon characters is telling a bag lady that you and Hetrick had a boat berthed next to his in-Fort Lauderdale."

I walked closer to peer over his shoulder.

The man snaps the paper and continues to read, "Duke boasts that he loaned Hetrick and Arrington his deck gun for one of their clandestine operations."

"I'm in prison with a cartoon character," he cackled. "Hey, how about autographing this for me?"

* * *

The next day a toilet clogs in a cell. The guard admits two inmate plumbers from the general population to fix it. It is a rare event. The staff segregates jail unit inmates from general population inmates to prevent murders during court cases.

The guard retires to his office, which is at the other end of the cellblock behind a thick security door. From there he cannot monitor the cellblock. Abruptly, the two inmate plumbers walk boldly into my cell.

I am on my upper bunk idly reading *Lord of the Rings*. I am engrossed in the fantasy story of trolls, dwarfs, wizards, elves, and hobbits. I casually look up from the page to see who is coming through the door—my alarm is instantaneous. The two burly inmates crowding into the cell are bikers. The headbands they wear identify them as members of the Aryan Brotherhood, a white gang known for its violence against other inmates. I realize that a hit is going down, and I am it!

The first one through the door has deep-set, wild eyes that glare from a bearded face. At the lower corner of his eye, there are three tattooed teardrops, one for each murder he has committed. "Are you Arrington?" he demanded.

My eyes fall to his right hand, which grasps a screwdriver. Rust covers most of the shank, except for the nicked tip that is shiny from a recent sharpening. One biker is at the foot of my bed and the other approaches from the side. I have no escape as death crowds against my bunk. The brute with the screwdriver leans heavily on the edge of my mattress, "Hey," he growled, "I asked you a question."

The other inmate glances out the door, "Hurry, man."

I want to scream, instead, in a weak whisper I hear myself insanely say, "Yeah, I'm Arrington."

Stupid, stupid, yelled my inner voice, *'Why did you tell them your name.'*

The inmate transfers the screwdriver to his left hand while his right-hand he reaches into his pocket and extracts the Doonesbury comic strip. "Mind signing this for me?" he asked hopefully.

Forgiveness is the fragrance the violet sheds on the heel that crushed it.
— Mark Twain

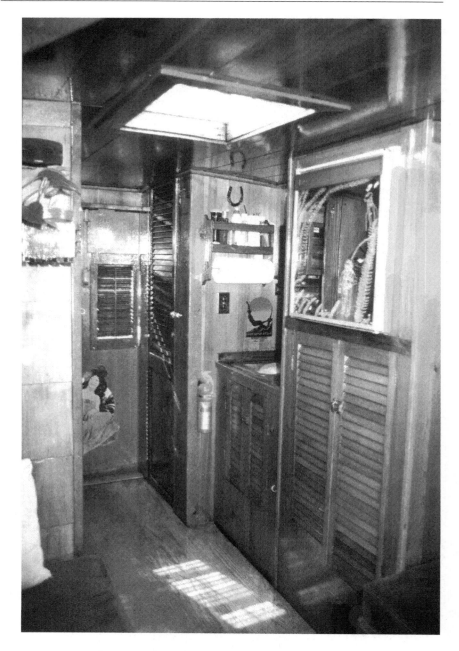

Interior Revelstoke looking front to back.
Photo Arrington

Chapter 8 - J-3, Dec 1982

From my bunk, I hear inmates shouting and the crash of chairs hitting the walls. The guard runs down the corridor yelling, "Lockdown! Lockdown!" as he keys his radio for assistance.

Clayton is in court. I am alone in the cell wondering who just got beat up in the television room. Inmates run for their cells as a posse of guards charge down the corridor. One of them takes his ring of keys and locks all the cell doors with two inmates in them.

Looking through the small security window, I see one of the older men, his white shirt splattered with blood, hands cuffed behind his back, being dragged down the corridor by two guards. The man is in his late sixties. He is a white-collar criminal. What would he be fighting about and with whom? The senior citizen inmates can get cranky if caught cheating at dominoes or cards. With three or four convicts in a card game, cheating is rampant.

I see a bloody, unconscious body being wheeled out on a gurney. The shocker is that the victim is a young man. He is new in the cellblock. Blood-soaked bandages cover most of the young man's head. Whatever happened, he lost big time — to an old man?

"Arrington, out!" snarled the guard. He stomps into the television room. A fan of blood splatters one wall, and before it, more blood pools on the floor. There are multiple boot prints from guards having walked through the puddle of crimson.

"What happened?" I asked.

"Soap opera fight," he answered gruffly. "Clean it up."

He marches angrily away to begin a long report.

Alone in the shadow of violence, I stare in horror at a bloodbath. A banged-up mop bucket with its attached wringer lies tipped over by the blood-splattered wall. The wringer's metal handle lies on the floor in the pool of blood. I right the bucket then pick up the metal handle, careful of the dripping blood, and drop it into the bucket. I roll the mop wringer down to the deep sink room where I rinse off the handle, fill the bucket with warm water, and return to the television room. I mop up the blood on the floor and sponge the blood from the wall.

I think that the old man's prison profile just got dropkicked to the top of the violent behavior charts. From a low-risk, white-collar prisoner with modest privileges to violent, high-risk inmate headed for The Hole where there are no privileges. Whatever charges he was facing before are modest compared to assault with a weapon in prison with murderous intent. At his age, he has probably just sentenced himself to the rest of his life in prison, and it will not be at a low or medium security facility. He will do hard time with the most vicious of inmates. Since he is old, he will be a perpetual victim. All because in a rage he picked up a metal handle from the mop bucket and walloped a younger man in the head with it over a stupid soap opera.

I wheel the mop bucket down the dim corridor of repeating steel doors to the deep sink room. The dented steel bucket wobbles, rippling its cargo of crimson liquid as I stare into its depths. Though it is mostly water, it looks like gallons of blood. I flick on the deep-sink ceiling light. The recessed low-watt bulb lies behind a thick yellowed piece of a rusty wire screen covered in dust. From it, a dim cone of yellow light bathes the deep sink leaving the rest of the tiny room shadowed.

Picking up the bucket, I slowly pour the crimson liquid down the drain. I am unable to look away. The sink is old, cracked, stained, and mildewed with a rusty drain half-clogged with human hair and other filth. I watch the blood swirling down that black drain hole like a giant leech sucking life's blood and suddenly feel physically ill—it is as if I am seeing my life swirling down the gaping maul of a giant leach.

'I am never going to get out of here alive.' The thought smothers me in the dark, cramped room, 'I am going to die in this prison.'

The bucket falls from my hands and clatters into the sink. It leaks rivulets of blood that crawl slowly toward the red-stained drain. I back out into the corridor just as the guard arrives.

"Get back into your cell; we are on full lockdown."

In a daze, I stagger into my cell with hands covered with blood. The door slams and locks behind me. I wash at the sink where there is only cold water. I strip off my blood splattered T-shirt and soak it. After several rinses, I wring it out and hang it on the bunk corner to dry. It is mid-December. I am cold as I climb onto the bunk and pull the threadbare blanket around my shoulders. In a deep depression, I stare at the ceiling pipes and shiver.

The guard lets me out to serve dinner. My T-shirt is damp and cold as I push the food cart down the corridor. He unlocks each door, so I can hand in two trays, and then he slams the door.

The main course is meatloaf with a dollop of oven-blackened ketchup on top. There is a scoop of mashed potatoes with brown gravy, canned green peas, two pieces of white bread, and a carton of milk. Dessert is a square of yellow *Jell-O* with some suspicious white streaks embedded in it. Only a fool would eat that *Jell-O*.

I am a robot as we go from cell to cell. Closing the door to the last cell, we return to where we started to collect the empty trays. The contaminated *Jell-O*. is missing from most of the trays. Back in my cell, I realize I forgot to take a tray for myself. Not that I am in the mood to eat, yet I know the hunger will come.

Two in the morning and I am awake, depressed, dead tired and chilled to the bone. I am pondering how I, just like that old man, have foolishly thrown away my freedom and my life.

There has got to be more than just trying to survive in prison.

My thought is a plea cast out into a dark void while I struggle with images of blood gurgling down black drains.

Notions of salvation pull at me. I know almost nothing about it. However, a vague memory echoes across my thoughts, a Bible verse, "The blood will set you free."

I know about blood. It stains my T-shirt. The verse is a promise, not that the blood may set you free, but that it will set you free. I feel so lost and alone.

'Can Jesus Christ's blood free me inside this prison cell?' I wonder.

A thought like a fast-rising bubble rushes upward to a turbulent surface where it bursts. I realize that I am alone only because I have chosen to live my life that way.

I have always lived alone. My family moved often. I built no lasting friendships. I convinced myself that being a loner was my choice when it was not. I had few friends. My friendships were shallow — that is what I got, and that is what I gave. I spent years actively designing a self-image without considering what or who I was becoming. All my choices were a continuous quest for self-fulfillment on my terms. I was totally self-absorbed.

I climb down from the bunk in my shorts and get down on my knees on the cold concrete floor. The last thing I see before closing my eyes are the shadows of the jail bars silhouetted on the lower corner of the cell's wall. It is an aptly visual reminder of how far I have fallen. I have no idea how long jail bars will shadow my life, I just sink down into myself and ponder the misery that promises to lurk far into my future. I am not sure that I will pray until it just happens.

"Holy Father, I am so terribly sorry. I have thrown my life away. My friends have turned their backs on me, and society has locked me away, but what about You? Are You there for a sinner like me, a felon in a prison cell?"

The answer is immediate, not a spoken word heard, but a powerful feeling of acceptance that fills my soul. I take a deep soul-cleansing breath. I am a new person as I lay my sins at the foot of the cross. The tragedy of the moment dissipates as hope floods through me and in its wake walks a simple joy. The fatigue of moments ago washes away in a deluge of emotions. I simply know that God has taken compassion on me. I am not a wasted person. I have value, the coin of which is that God loves all His creations, even a felon in a prison cell.

Climbing onto my bunk, I want to lie awake all night to treasure this moment. Instead, I fall into a deep, restful sleep.

The next morning when the guard opens the door, I go to the bookshelf in the television room. There are a dozen paperbacks, all rejected by the other inmates, and four Bibles. I look for an intact one. Some are missing pages. The men sometimes use the extra thin pages from Bibles to roll joints.

I return to my cell and open the Bible. I have just taken the first step of a never-ending journey towards a better understanding of whom I am and who I would like to become.

The days pass quietly. A temporary peace settles upon the cellblock as Christmas approaches.

The guard raps my cell door, "Get out here, Arrington."

I step out, but he has gone into the television room, so I follow. I find him standing over a beat-up cardboard box.

"What is it?" I asked.

"A Christmas tree," he said gruffly, "Put it together."

The dust-covered, plastic tree is a wreck, like a logging truck ran over it. There is a string of petrified popcorn covered with green mold and black rot. There are also scratched ornaments and many colorful shards of what used to be ornaments.

My mind plays with the concept of Christmas at Terminal Island Prison. It is just what I needed, a holiday distraction. I carry all the parts into the shower and give them a good dousing with warm water and soap. Then dry the plastic tree off with used towels.

In the television room, I assemble the battered tree with a lot of twisting and bending to wind up with something that looks like an evergreen roadkill. I hang the few intact ornaments with cracks, chips and scrapes then ponder the heap of ornament scraps.

Imagination can take you to some fascinating places. I went from cell to cell gathering empty toilet paper rolls. With toothpaste for cement, I attach the colorful scraps of plastic to the outside of the toilet paper rolls. Not only does this add color, but also the toothpaste looks like globs of snow. I discovered that if I tear the toilet paper rolls open and fan one end, they look like angel wings. That goes on top of the tree. I wrap one of Clayton's spare sheets around the base to add to the snow effect. A few prominent stains increase the realism of the great outdoors.

The guard swings by with a string of colorful lights and half a roll of tin foil. I make homemade tinsel and wrap each light and the angel on top with a reflective aluminum shield. I run another idea by him and soon he has me locked in my cell with a bowl of popcorn from the nut ward upstairs, a spool of thread and a needle. If the other inmates got ahold of the needle, they would use it to make gang tattoos.

Turning off the ceiling lights on the Christmas tree side of the room sets the mood, and the guard releases the men to a mixed review. Most are happy to see the tree; some are not.

The next day the guard agreed to leave me locked alone in the cellblock while everyone else goes out to the yard. From my cell, I watch the last of the inmates walk out through the yard door, then the guard looks back, "Have a good time." He said stepping through the yard door and locking it.

I step out into the corridor. It is weird and strangely odd to be alone in the cellblock, the silence is enticing. I am like a child whose parents have finally decided that he can stay at home alone without a sitter. The house takes on a strangeness that is ever so alluring. I only have one hour, so I step back into the cell and quickly strip down to my shorts and pull the bedding off the bunks. I go into the deep sink room and get the roller bucket, fill it with hot water and wheel it into the cell. Armed with two cans of scouring powder, I scrub the cell top to bottom. The overhead pipes are the worst with layers of rust, hardened grime, and decades of dust falling on old but still growing, mildew. I throw around water, lots of water; it drips from the pipes, murky brown at first, and then shades of tan. I am a cleaning slob; the floor is awash with wet muck.

It feels good watching the dirty water chasing down the sink drain. This is an outer and inner cleansing of the deepest kind. I refill the bucket, rinse out the mop, and attack the cell. I discover that our cell is not dull yellow, but rather a flat white. I have accumulated a half dozen of the least soiled towels from the laundry cart and wiped down the ceiling pipes and walls. I scrub the window, smiling as it gets progressively brighter in the cell. With the time winding down, I grab more towels to dry the floor. I place fresh sheets on the bunks and am behind the supposedly locked cell door when the inmates file back in.

The guard pretends to unlock my cell door then looks inside at the freshness of the cell. He smiles and walks away. Clayton opens the door and stares, "Whoa, what happened in here?"

"I have been cleaning."

"Tell me I am not living with a nutcase."

"I just didn't like living in a dirty cell and decided to do something about it." Yet, it is much deeper than that. Washing the cell was like scrubbing my soul. I enjoy the sunlight pouring through the window that brightens the cell. Life is good for being a jail unit inmate.

After lunch, the guard arrives with a few Christmas boxes. One is for me. A friend sent the box. One of only three in the cellblock. Inside were pictures of Puu and Susan and a pound of assorted teas.

That night, just before lock-down, I heat a cup of water in the microwave and drop in a bag of herbal tea. Smelling the fragrant scent of the tea, I climb onto my bunk to look at the pictures. When the lights go out, I slip off to sleep wrapped in dreams of happier times.

Around midnight a winter storm descends on the prison waking me. Thunder reverberates through the cellblock and echoes off the prison walls. I stand at the window wrapped in a blanket watching raindrops pound against the warped glass. I stick my arm out through a broken pane to feel the cold rain washing over my hand. Bold flashes of lightning intermittently shatter the black shroud of the night. The strobing brilliance flashes against the scalloped glass, casting running shadows of rain rivulets into the cell. Shadows of the scuttling rivulets make it look like the cell walls are crying in shades of black and white.

I open the locker and remove a picture of Revelstoke parked in a tropical forest above Waimea Falls. Striking a match, I see Puu at the open back door with his floppy ears down. Susan was inside baking cookies, and I could almost hear her ordering Puu, The Nose, out of her way. I wish with all my might that I was in that picture right now. Instead memories will have to do.

* * *

I am standing beneath a towering tropical tree. A trade wind is blowing. I listen to the rustling leaves while looking at the soft yellow light coming out Revelstoke's open backdoors. Puu is standing there with his tail wagging; he woofs at me. I see Susan taking cookies from the oven. She turns and smiles. The wind has the feel of rain. The interior of Revelstoke looks warm and inviting with the enticing aroma of cookies fresh from the oven. I step inside.

Susan sweeps her long blond hair to one side as she closes the oven door. She is wearing a blue silk crop top and black nylon Dolphin shorts. It is a runner's outfit, and she wears it well. I collect a hug, two cookies, and a kiss. Outside I hear the wind blowing amongst the elephant bamboo. The wind is bending the tall bamboo's leafy tops, causing the trunks to clack and rattle against each other like a giant wind chime. I take my cookies to the back door and look out as Susan steps up behind me and places her arms around my waist.

"When do you expect to leave Hawaii?" she asked.

Susan and I are living on borrowed time. The Navy machine is awaiting my transfer papers from the personnel department. For some odd reason, they are slow in coming, which pleases me greatly. After my release from the brig, I reported as ordered back to the command. The Executive Officer had been reluctant to have me back around the rest of the men, so he ordered me to go back out the base gate and to pretend I was on leave.

How startling was that order, pretend I am on leave? I am in big trouble, soon to leave the Navy in shame, and he orders me to go play? My only responsibility was to check in once a week and to pick up a paycheck. I thought the transfer process would take two weeks, but three months had passed. Three glorious months of surfing, hiking with Susan and Puu and being totally in love in an island paradise.

Watching Puu running and barking among the swaying bamboo with Susan's arms around me, I am so incredibly happy and so afraid that I will lose her when my orders come. "I don't know why they haven't arrived already," I answered.

Susan rubs her head against my shoulder as a strong gust of wind blows through the elephant bamboo forest, the answering sound is magnificent. The trees thunk and clack loudly. She burrows her face into my neck. I feel her warm breath caressing my skin as she says in a soft voice that has lodged in my heart ever since, "Steve, I love you so much, please don't ever let me go."

A tropical rain comes down abruptly in heavy sheets.

* * *

Standing at the cell's window, I feel the bite of the icy wind blowing through the broken panes as a shudder runs through my body. The rain is splashing against the window like an ocean of tears. Thick drops run in rivulets down the panes to puddle on the sill, and abruptly I am crying—not crying in self-pity, but rather for the happiness I have known and so treasure. The images are a bandage that caresses my battered soul. Turning away from the window, I see the lightning strobe against the cell wall. It paints abrupt shadows of the jail bars with a splash of tears. The rain thunders down harder, dampening the dim glow from the security lights as the cell fades to darkness.

Interior of Revelstoke looking front to back. Note surfboard hanging over the bed, which folds out into a queen-sized bed.
Photo Arrington

Everything has its wonders, even darkness, and silence, and I learn whatever state I am in, therein to be content. — Helen Keller

Winter in the cellblock plods by, but finally, the weather warms. Both Morris and Clayton pled guilty months ago; were sentenced and transferred out to the general population. Standing at the fence in the J-3 yard, I stare at the men in the North Yard, envious of their freedom. It sounds strange yearning for the rights of a sentenced inmate, but such is the fortune of a long-term jail-unit inmate.

I see inmates walking down an outside corridor between two dormitories that lead through a breezeway to the South Yard. To walk where there is consistently a breeze. We rarely feel the wind in this confined yard. The breezeway parallels the breakwater. Beyond the breezeway is the South Yard, where they house the honor inmates.

The South Yard has no walls on two sides. One can see outside the prison through a double row of 20-foot tall chain-link fences topped with razor wire. On one side is the Pacific Ocean, on the other is the channel that leads to the Port of Los Angeles Harbor.

The looming DeLorean trial commands the nightly news, and I am in DeLorean's shadow. It will not bode well for me as my trial goes first. The prosecutors are coming after me with a vengeance as per the Rat-Wrangler and Agent Scotti.

With my depression hovering closely, I carry my rusted bucket to the lawn. It has grown substantially. The 30' by 6' section is now a lawn with thriving grass. There are no bare spots. Parts of it are a foot tall. I decide to do something odd. I set my bucket down beside the grass, walk to where it is tallest, and lie face down upon it. I turn my head to one side; all I can see is lush green grass. I inhale its fragrance and stare at the densely growing green grass.

"What are you doing, Arrington?" demanded the guard.

Not wanting to break the magic of the moment I continue to stare at the blades of grass, "Just lying here," I replied softly.

"You're not losing it, are you?"

"No sir, just wanted to look at the grass up close."

"Well stand up," he ordered. "You are being just too weird."

Rather than take any more chances with me, the guard goes for the easy solution, which is always their default solution to any problems--he terminates our yard time early. There is a saying amongst prison guards that is regularly enforced with bias and pleasure, "Inmates have nothing coming." It is a barrier between the staff and us convicts. In prison there are walls within walls

As we shuffle back inside an inmate glares at me, "Thanks, Arrington." He is one of the new snitches, so I just blow him off.

That afternoon an inmate gardener arrives with a power lawn mower. He does the pull-start thing, and three passes later, my little patch of grass is mowed, butchered more like it.

The next day, I clean up the grass and collect a cigar box full of the cuttings and take them back to my cell. On my bunk, I lift the lid and inhale, the fragrant bouquet. It carries me back to Hawaii.

* * *

Susan and I are walking on the grass at the Waikiki Memorial Park. We each have one arm around the other's waist. I enjoy the feel of Susan's silk dress as it slides with each step. I love this woman so much it hurts. I fear losing her after four wonderful months together. I lean close to nuzzle my face in her thick mane of blond hair. I smell the fragrance of coconuts and think what it would be like to spend the rest of my life with her — then fear fills my stomach with a sinking feeling.

"Susan," I said tenderly, "my orders arrived today."

"I know, I could tell by how withdrawn you are acting. When do you leave?" A sad look in her eyes is ripping my heart apart.

"Next week," I said unhappily.

Susan stares, it is a penetrating look right into my soul. Everything depends on her answer what I am about to ask. "Susan," I said softly, "would you like to come to California with me?"

Susan's smiles and he eyes shine as she says with her voice full of excitement, "Yes Stephen, I would."

The fear of losing her evaporates in the furnace of our love.

We sit on the grass lawn and stare out at the ocean while happily planning our future. Puu is sleeping with his head on my lap. He snores with one paw occasionally moving in pursuit of dog-dream adventures. Susan's head lies against my shoulder as she lightly strokes Puu.

"Steve," she asked timidly, "what about Puu?"

"What about Puu?" I rub his ears.

"Well," said Susan, her words coming out slowly, "if two of us are going to be living in Revelstoke, it will be cramped, but with Monster Dog it will be crowded. You have friends who would love to have Puu."

Susan is worried about what she is voicing. I want to comfort her because I, too, am anxious about Puu. I look at the two individuals I love most in the world. I am heading into the unknown. Eventually, I will wind up at college, but until then — all is in doubt. The two most vital

parts of my life are with me now, and one wants me to leave the other behind – what should I do?

Susan takes a deep breath, "That couple that watched Puu when you were in the brig, he liked it there. They have such a big backyard. They asked me to tell you that they would love to have Puu."

The sky is cloudy when I pull into my friend's driveway. I take Puu to him and hand over his leash. I kneel and ruffle Puu's ears, so he knows that I love him, and then with my heart breaking, I leave quickly. Puu barks once to let me know that I have forgotten him. I hurry out to Revelstoke and drive away, refusing to look back. I hear him barking anxiously. Tears stream down my face. As I round a corner, the barking gives way to a long-drawn-out howl that slowly fades with distance but keeps echoing inside my heart.

Susan must work that evening, so I spend a rainy night alone on the North Shore. I miss Puu terribly and feel empty inside.

The next morning, I miss Puu's wagging tail and his big sad eyes begging for attention. I go to a pay telephone and call Susan. As soon as I hear her voice, I know something is wrong. Stuttering and crying, with her words broken with sobs, she said, "Steve, I'm so sorry."

"Susan, what's wrong?" My heart thumps wildly.

"Puu jumped the fence," she gasped. "A car hit him. He's dead."

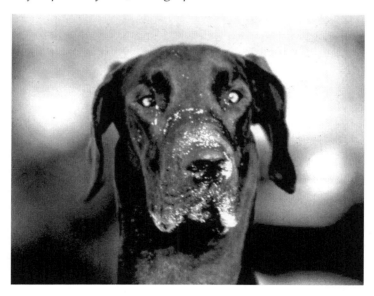

Puu Kane after romping in the sand. Photo Arrington

Although the world is full of suffering, it is full also of the overcoming of it. – Helen Keller

* * *

The months pass, new inmates arrive, go to court a couple of times, plead guilty, get sentenced and then go to the North Yard. Not one case went to trial.

At 5:30 AM, I hear the swish and click of the guard's keys. I get ready to begin the morning breakfast routine, but when the guard opens the door, a set of cuffs dangles from his hand.

On the ride up to the courthouse, I thrive watching the civilian world. Too soon, the case will end when I plead guilty. Then I will be years behind gray walls living a shadow life.

After the anticipated long wait in the holding cells, they take me up to Judge Takasugi's courtroom. Rick is waiting at his regular spot. One of my marshal escorts removes my handcuffs. DeLorean is with his battery of attorneys and legal aids at the other table. Morgan is in conversation with his lead attorney at the other end of our table.

I glance around the room as always full of press. I am mostly looking at beautiful women, something that will not be happening in prison. It is a stark reality of the dismal future awaiting me.

One of DeLorean's attorneys stands and walks over to Rick and whispers in his ear. "Rick nods then turns to me and smiles, "Want to meet John Z. DeLorean?"

"What?"

"He wants to talk to you."

"Me?"

Rick points towards DeLorean's table with his chin.

DeLorean is smiling at me, even his attorneys are beaming.

The marshals to my back are startled as I stand and walk with the attorney. DeLorean stands and meets me halfway. He offers his hand and a big grin. "I hear they're calling you Upright Steve."

One of the newspapers printed that, and it rather caught on.

"Yeah, I guess it is an odd nickname for a felon."

"My attorneys had you checked out. Everyone says you're going to do the right thing."

"It's just who I am, wish I would have done things differently."

"Who doesn't?" DeLorean said, his smile infectious.

"I just wanted to say I appreciate it," he said shaking my hand again, "Nice to know there's at least one person I can count on my side." He looks towards Morgan's table and frowns.

DeLorean leans in, "Are you going to trial?" he whispered.

Judge Takasugi will not allow any cameras in the courtroom, and there is no mic close to us. I feel safe to answer softly, "I'll listen to Rick, but I will not testify against anyone."

"Nice to know," I feel DeLorean's warm breath on my cheek, "Rick is a good man, so are you."

I wanted to say something, but his words were so startling I just stood there. DeLorean walks back to his table.

Walking back across the court, I glance about the packed room. Everyone is staring. I notice several attractive women reporters smiling at me. I know they are hoping to get a comment. It lifts my spirits, particularly considering that I am wearing prison coveralls with an inmate cutting my hair with old prison clippers.

As I sit down, Rick asks, "That was interesting. Anything I need to know regarding his whispering to you?"

I leaned toward him and said softly, "Only that I won't snitch."

I glance at DeLorean, who leans back in his chair, and shoots his cuffs as Judge Takasugi walks out of his chambers.

The court proceedings are for discovery of evidence, which the government is reluctant to release. I do not know it, but things are happening behind closed doors that are about to be revealed.

The marshals cuff my hands behind my back. This is a surprise as they have been cuffing my hands in front of me for the walk to and from the court. *Am I in trouble?*

They walk me at a brisk pace out of the court. While waiting for the elevator, they are in a whispered conversation. "We shouldn't have let the idiot walk away from us."

"No kidding, every time he just sits there. I didn't expect that attorney to walk over and escort him over to DeLorean."

The elevator door opens, and we step inside. When the door closes, one of the marshals asked gruffly, "Was that planned?"

"No, I had no idea it was going to happen, why?"

"Because you're in our custody," he growled, "you're not to be out of arm's reach. If the Sargent finds out, we're in big trouble."

"If? Are you kidding?" complained the other Marshall, "They did it right in front of the prosecutor. Don't you think he's dying to know what they said and mad as hell that they got away with it?"

"What did he say to you?" the other marshal queried.

I just give them a weak smile and shrug.

The elevator door opens, silencing the marshals.

Every time I have been in court, I said and did nothing. That makes the whispering intoxicating for the lawyers.

Going down the stairs, the lead marshal growls, "You try that again, I'll bounce your face off the floor a couple of times."

I sit idly in the holding cell, so I let my mind drift.

* * *

I arrived at Treasure Island Naval Base in California, on March 15, 1980. I was going on appellate leave while awaiting final disposition of my Bad Conduct Discharge. My hopes were not high for a favorable ruling from the military court. I spent two lonely weeks processing through the Navy's paper machine. As a chief petty officer, they did not assign me to a work detail. My time was my own. I spent most of it just walking around San Francisco or sitting on a beach watching the sunset. It was a time of raw emotions. I felt empty from Puu's death. The Navy had been my home for almost 14 years. I had been so proud to be a frogman and war vet, and now it was all ending in disgrace. The future was uncertain. At the end of each day, I stood alone on a beach facing Hawaii, which lay beyond the sunset, and thought of a woman with golden hair – and a sad-eyed Great Dane that was no more.

At the naval base, the personnel department was not aware of my full situation. My orders had simply read "Process for discharge," but in the service jacket, there was a thick manila envelope, stamped on its cover and back in bold red letters was a warning, "TOP SECRET, FOR COMMANDING OFFICER'S EYES ONLY." I assumed it contained the results of my court-martial with orders to initiate my appellate leave.

On March 31, my papers were ready.

A scrawny clerk wearing oversized wire-rimmed glasses smiles as he pushes papers at me to sign. Astonished, I stare at the ornate document. The words "Honorable Discharge," sear themselves into my brain.

"You okay, Chief?" asked the skinny clerk.

"Yes, I'm fine," I said as I realized, this was a colossal mistake.

"Just sign right here," said the clerk. With his thick glasses, he looks like a helpful little mouse with his narrow face and big eyes. He slips the discharge papers into a manila envelope then leafs through the remains of my service jacket. He pauses seeing the manila envelope stamped in bold red ink. He flips it over, glances at the still-secure seal, then shrugs. He places the Honorable Discharge into an envelope and gives it to me.

I snatch it up and get halfway to the door when the clerk yells, "Hey, Chief, hold on, your check is still coming over from disbursing."

"Check?" It arrives ten minutes later.

"Just sign here," smiles the helpful clerk. The check was for $524.00. "What's this for?" I asked.

The clerk is surprised, "You have 22 days of leave not taken. You get a portion of your base pay back. Is there a problem with the sum?"

I could only stare at the helpful young man. After all the Navy's effort to punish me, a couple of clerical errors had wiped most of it away.

* * *

A few weeks later, two new inmates arrive in J-3. I thought little about them—until one of them steps boldly into my cell.

I am reading my Bible when he comes aggressively through the door. He steps right up to my bunk, which is way outside inmate protocols. He stares at me then whispers, "Don't say anything. Just listen. We don't have much time."

"Who are you?" I blurted.

"I'm a federal agent," he whispered, "I'm here undercover. You need to listen to me."

He has an athletic build, short sandy hair, and he looks like a grave person. He has a military attitude and bearing.

"What do you want?"

"Morgan is flipping sides, so are his sons and Stretch. There's no point in your protecting them."

"I could care less about protecting them!" I growled. "Don't you guys get it? I am not a snitch. I just want to serve my time and pick up what's left of my life again."

"You're not going to have a life. You are the one who is not getting it. This case is much bigger than you think. It involves the highest levels of the FBI, the DEA, the IRS, the Department of State, and the Department of Justice. The Attorney General of the United States, Edwin Meese, is watching this case closely because Reagan is breathing down his neck. It also has action on the other side of the pond. Interpol is all over this. They are determined to take DeLorean down. The Irish Republican Army and #10 Downing Street are competing to see who is going to take out DeLorean."

"You mean the Prime Minister of England?"

"Yeah, she wants DeLorean's head on her wall, and Ronnie Reagan is hot to give it to her."

"Why?"

"The government of England invested £138,000,000 in the DeLorean Motor Company. That is more than a quarter billion of our dollars, and it seems that John DeLorean misappropriated a big chunk of it. As I said, she wants his head."

"What's the Irish Republican Army got to do with it?"

"That's DeLorean's fault. We videotaped DeLorean boasting that he had a very tight relationship with the IRA. They wanted to keep DMC open in Northern Ireland. The IRA is not happy about DeLorean involving them. They said, 'We do not take Mr. DeLorean's lies lightly, nor will we forget them should he ever bump into us.' They aren't happy with you either."

"Me?"

"Guilt by association, another reason to get your butt into the Witness Protection Program—while you still can."

"Look, Morgan, his sons, and your pilot buddy have already told us all about you. We know everything you did, and I promise, you don't want us to play hardball with you."

"Why me, if everyone else is cooperating?" I asked.

"We know there isn't anything new you can tell us. We need you out of the case. DeLorean's attorneys are delaying his trial with a sheaf of discovery motions. You go on trial first, and that means your lawyer will depose all our witnesses. That's like letting the other players at a poker table look at your cards before the betting even starts."

He leans in closer, "If you cooperate it puts DeLorean on notice, who knows he might even cop a plea, which is why we are taking the chance of my talking with you. We will play you and Hetrick against Max and Rafa, and all their boys. Some will flip, and they will help us to take down Pablo Escobar, and the Ochoa Brothers too. They could all fall like dominos."

Max, Rafa, Pablo Escobar and the Ochoa Brothers are the Who's Who of the top drug cartel on the planet. They are vicious, cold-blooded killers with the war chest of a small country. In the prisons, they have an army of assassins. The only way I would leave the prison as a snitch is with a toe-tag and wrapped up in a black body bag.

"My cooperating is not happening. I have a family, and you can't protect them."

"If we say we will protect them then we will. We are people of our word," he said forcefully.

"If you're so honorable why were the FBI and DEA agents following my friends and breaking into their cars and houses?"

"You're talking about Scotti, the DEA guy who busted you."

"Yeah, he's one of yours. Isn't he?"

Buzz, Morgan's oldest son, came home to find a burglar in his house. When he confronted the man, the burglar produced a badge and his ID, agent Gerald Scotti. The newspaper headline read, "Federal agent uses Burglary as an Investigative Tool."

"Was one of us," corrected Scotti, "the guy is on his way out. He got caught with his hand in the cookie jar."

That thrilled me to no end. *Gerald Scotti, the pretend bad guy, really was a bad guy. How cool is that?*

"Cookie jar?" I asked leading him to say more.

"You know about the Grandma Mafia Case?" he asked

I shake my head, surprised he is sharing all of this.

"It's a group of old lady housewives who were laundering millions for cocaine traffickers. Someone tipped their defense attorney that they were under investigation by the DEA."

"Gerald Scotti?" I asked hopefully.

"Bingo."

"Someone got paid $160,000 for that news, but we can't prove anything except he was the only agent that accessed that file on the DEA's top-secret supercomputer. We got his computer code after we ran a trace. It almost sank our case."

"If that wasn't bad enough two of the Grandma Mafia women drove into an underground parking at of our bank. It was an FBI sting. The women were delivering $630,000 in cash, plus $90,000 in Canadian dollars. They no sooner stepped out of the car with the money than a car skids to a stop next to them. Two masked men with guns throw down on our girls. They nab their cardboard box with the cash and escape."

"You think Scotti was one of the gunmen?" I asked eagerly.

"Na, Scotti had nothing to do with that. It looks to be an IRS insider job. The IRS agent that uncovered the evidence in the Grandma Mafia Case," grumbled the agent. "He suddenly up and resigned from the IRS two months before the robbery. That was suspicious as he got the case going. We think he was mad because he didn't get the lead role."

"Was?"

"He's dead, his chute cartwheeled when it deployed while base jumping off Half Dome in Yosemite last August. He hit the cliff face repeatedly then dropped 600 feet like a rock. Two men who were with him fled the scene. In his motorhome, park rangers found receipts for large cashier checks. There were also math equations divvying up $630,000 and converting $90,000 Canadian to US dollars. The guy spent $200,000 in two months."

The agent throws up his hands, "Yeah, we're having some difficulties with two back-to-back major drug cases, and we need not just a win, but a homerun. Scotti is a loaded canon. He's messing up our case."

"What's that got to do with me?" I asked.

"We want him out and you in. You would be a credible witness against DeLorean and Max," the agent said. "The main gal in the Grandma Mafia Case had a condo at Miami Lakes — sound familiar?"

I am speechless.

"Yeah, Max lives in Miami Lakes. Follow the strands of the web and there will be a spider lurking in it somewhere. Anyway, one of the Grandma Mafia gals filed for dismissal of charges claiming one of our agents blackmailed her. It was all bogus, but during the dismissal trial Agent Scotti was called to the stand — he took the Fifth because he didn't want to incriminate himself."

The agent paces, "I have told you far more than I should, but I read your file. I believe deep down you are a standup guy. Tell me that you will cooperate, and I can take you out of here right now. We have a nice facility in San Diego for keeping high-profile inmate's safe. In fact, we've already protected you once. Remember your run-in with Louis in J-3? We pulled you out of there just in time. Next yard period you were going down!"

I am stunned into silence.

"If you're wondering what to do with everything, I'm telling you," quipped the agent, "you're too late. One of the lawyers defending the Grandma Mafia's head broad is Howard Wiesman."

The agent smiles at the startled look in my eyes. "Yeah, he's DeLorean's lead defense attorney. He knows about all this stuff, so I haven't told you anything he doesn't already know. You can bet they'll try to turn this to their advantage."

I shake my head, "I am serious about not cooperating. I don't want to live the rest of my life fearing retaliation from the Medellin Cartel against me or my family."

"Are you that crazy?"

'The cartel leaving me alone is all I got,' I think wildly to myself. The only honorable act left to me is to protect the ones I care about, my family and Sam.

I look at the agent and say the word that terrifies me deep down inside — am I making the right choice? The word came out more reluctantly than I intended, "No."

"It ends right now. I gave you all I got. Cut a deal and flip or all the weight of the United States Government is coming down on you like a load of bricks." The agent stares at me, "Don't pull another newspaper stunt about unauthorized visits. It won't play out well for you." He steps to the door, "I'm going to summon the guard. He is going to walk me out through that security door. We could have walked down that corridor together." He steps out and hails the guard standing at the ready by the television room grill.

The guard looks at me sitting on my bunk. "What are you," he asked shaking his head, "a fool?"

The agent finger shoots me then says, "Watch your back, Louis hasn't forgotten about you."

I climb down from my bunk and watch the two men walking down the corridor. The agent has shed all pretense of being an inmate. He strides proudly, the heavy guard hurrying to keep up. They arrive at the security door and step through it.

That evening I retired to my cell. My dilemma is that I deserve this. I have a debt to pay and a time to serve, which is the only way I can ever be totally free again. Something is nipping at the edge of my consciousness. They are going to extraordinary measures to get me to flip, but they do not really need me, except regarding their witnesses being disposed of by Rick. That means they are sweating something so big it could destroy their case.

As the days pass, I withdraw more into myself. I think about happier times and often look at my handful of pictures because it was the time of my greatest freedom. The pictures carry me away to a place not 30 minutes from the prison.

* * *

For two weeks after my release from the Navy, I have been in a perpetual state of worry wondering if Susan will really join me.

It is a sunny day when I park Revelstoke at the industrial side of Los Angeles International Airport and walk eagerly into a terminal. I find the arrival gate and stand there with my heart beating wildly. Soon people are walking down the ramp as I peer impatiently. Then I spot her blonde hair in the crowd. Seeing me, she runs down the ramp and throws her arms around me. My world brightens like morning sunlight spreading across a high mountain meadow. Holding her tight, feeling her heart beating wildly against mine, I feel wonderfully happy.

For three months, we are nomads traveling little-used roads and lonely highways. We begin by driving north to Sequoia National Park in the

Sierra Nevada Mountains. At sunset, we camp at Wolverton, a mountain valley where winter snow still lingers. Wisps of fog drift through the tall redwood trees as I light candles inside Revelstoke.

June finds us camped in Tuolumne Meadows in the upper Yosemite Valley. Patches of snow cover the ground where shadows dwell most of the day. The campground has just cold running water, and chemical toilets. The campers are shivering in their tents or trying to huddle close to campfires wreathed in smoke. In Revelstoke, Susan and I are in the lap of nomadic luxury. We are warm and snug; Hawaiian slack key guitar plays on the stereo as I lounge in my hot tub. It is a deep sink where wetsuits and clothes hang to dry. The tub is just big enough to hold me in a tight sitting position. I watch Susan in the kitchen; I am incredibly happy as she carries in a steaming pot of water and pours it into my tub.

The next day, we bathe in a mountain stream. The water is melting snow runoff. We find a secluded spot, strip down to our swimsuits, and then run together screaming into the chilly water. Susan stops midstream to wash her long legs. I watch her with my heart pounding wildly for the words I am about to say. "Susan will you marry me?"

All is still but for the quiet gurgle of water flowing over rocks and a bird chirping. Susan smiles, "Oh yes, Stephen, "I will."

Susan just before I asked her to marry me. Photo Arrington

Reluctantly, I take Susan back to Los Angeles. She must use her return ticket back to Hawaii before it expires. Susan is all for getting married at a courthouse, but I want her parents' permission first. I walk with her to the gate. I wait with her until she must walk down the ramp. She walks backward waving and then she steps around a corner and disappears from my life forever.

Standing alone, I suddenly know I will never see Susan again.

Her parents argue against our marriage. Friends counsel that she should give it more thought. Not being together, we drift apart. I enroll at San Diego State University. During Christmas break, I am working at La Jolla Surf Systems when a letter from Susan arrives. I open it eagerly then read that she is seeing a surfer friend of mine in Hawaii.

Months pass, my longing for Susan intensifies. I often think of Puu. Marijuana is now my constant companion as I sink into depression. Facing finals, I realize I must get it together. I stuff my marijuana in a little-used drawer. I should have flushed it down the toilet — but did not have that kind of moral courage.

In May, I get another letter. I fear to open it; May is the wedding month. I place it on the teak dresser. Each time I walk by, I pick it up but cannot bring myself to open it.

Days later, a storm rips through La Jolla. The surf is too turbulent to ride. Pulling on my running shoes, I go out an hour before sunset onto an empty beach. I run along the seashore in the blustery wind and heavy rain. It is half a mile from La Jolla Shores to the UCSD Pier. I run in the deep sand and through shallow water. I sprint under the pier racing between barnacle-encrusted pilings. I splash through a stream racing into the ocean from the steep coastal cliffs. I run until the sun sets and only slow my pace when I cannot see what is beneath my feet.

Back inside Revelstoke, the wind buffets the truck. In the darkness, I see the deep sink where I remember my profound happiness in Yosemite while watching Susan making banana nut bread. In the dark kitchen I touch the cold oven. I step to the dresser where the envelope waits. My hands are chilled, but that is not why they are shaking. I strike a match and lite a red candle. I pick up the envelope in the soft flickering light with a feeling of extreme dread and gently open it.

I read the words slowly as they rip like a spray of bullets into my heart. Susan was married two weeks ago on the North Shore. She wants to share her happiness, as she describes the ceremony at the beach on the North Shore. It is a joyful ceremony attended by all my surfer friends. Susan and her new husband are honeymooning in New Zealand.

I hold the letter to the candle flame and watch it catch fire. I drop it into an abalone shell where it blackens as flickering flames consume the *words that are tearing at my soul. At first, the tears come softly, but then a broken hollowness spills out from deep down inside of me and I sink into despairing grief.*

I have no idea how long I stood there in the dark shivering before I opened the drawer where I placed my stash of marijuana.

Revelstoke while in the woods with Susan. Note how high the side windows are for privacy. Photo Arrington

Character cannot be developed in ease and quiet. Only through experience of trial and suffering can the soul be strengthened, ambition inspired, and success achieved. — Helen Keller

Chapter 10 - J-3, July 1983

The North Yard guard arrives at the door with two inmates. One of them is Morgan Hetrick. He is carrying a large cardboard box as he follows the guard to a cell. Morgan and I make eye contact but say nothing. This whole time he has been in J-2 and using the other exercise yard. I am wondering why they have moved him to J-3. It must be a government ploy of some sort. I do not want him in my life, and now there will be no escaping him.

I go into his cell without knocking. He is unpacking his box into the locker. There are cartons of cigarettes, candy bars, beef jerky — *inmate having-things* on a grand scale kind of stuff.

"Why the cigarettes?" I asked, "You don't smoke."

Morgan smiled, "Influence, and protection. How are you?"

"I'm doing time. How do you think I am doing?"

"So, cooperate, that's what my boys and I are doing."

It is interesting that he does not feel threatened standing alone with me. He knows I can kill someone in seconds. I imagine a right-hand praying mantis back fist to his nose, breaking the cartilage. The follow through is a left-hand iron palm strike driving the broken cartilage into the brain. The left hand then accelerates the head into a right elbow strike to the temple where the skull is thinnest. Last, a right arm headlock with a sharp twist using the falling body as leverage to snap the neck — over in three seconds.

As these thoughts play out in my brain, I realize that it says a lot about me that he stands there with complete trust. My nature is that I want to be a good human being. I learned these skills to protect others and myself. Morgan knows that about me. I have issues with harming someone without grave justification.

I calmly ask, "So, what's the deal?"

"Cooperate against DeLorean, Max, Rafa, and their people." He paused and stared at me, "Oh, and you too, sorry. I also have to give up the drug routes and surrender my offshore money, the *Highland Fling,* my 53-foot Hatteras yacht, houses, and planes." Morgan said. "In return, they won't prosecute my boys."

"What are you doing in J-3?" I asked.

"The Feds sent me hoping I could talk you into cooperating. You might get off with only five years. With good time, out in three. You don't think you can beat this do you?"

"No, I'm just waiting to see how it plays out," I said shrugging

"I had to tell them a lot," Morgan grimaced.

I glare at Morgan. Why did he have to promise me a new life in aviation, when his real intent was crime and my corruption.

"I wish you would have just left me alone," I said bitterly.

"Stephen, I rescued you from that loser job at the surf shop."

"You thought pulling me into a cocaine smuggling operation was a better option?" I asked incredulously.

"Better than selling dime bags of marijuana out of your truck."

"I wasn't selling; I was using."

"It was only a matter of time." Morgan said smugly.

"Not a chance. Yeah, I was addicted to marijuana, to the instant high, but I was working that out. Just not fast enough. You pulled the father figure stunt on me. You used that, manipulating me into a direction I wouldn't have chosen on my own."

"Look at what I was offering, you could have lived like a king."

"What did it get you?" I countered. "You and your family are ruined. What about the damage from the drugs? How many families have suffered because of you and now because of me? I have to live with that for the rest of my life. "

"Would it help if I told you that I am truly sorry?" he asked.

I look at Morgan for several long seconds as my Christian walk pushes to make its presence known. "Yeah Morgan, it helps," I surrendered almost reluctantly.

We are both silent then Morgan says, "I keep thinking about when we first met in Oxnard. We had some good times. You were like the son I wish I had."

Morgan pauses and glances towards the cell door. "Remember what I said when I introduced you to James Hoffman?"

"Yeah, you said to be quiet around him, not to trust him."

"That's because he's a pathological liar and a master conman. I've known him a long time. He is so fat and ugly he needs an edge, so he lies. Hoffman is the Feds' key witness, and he sucks. He boasted a month before the investigation got started that he was going to deliver John Z. DeLorean. That's entrapment." Morgan grins at me. I know he is trading information for forgiveness.

I dredge up a half smile, "Thanks, Morgan."

Morgan chuckles, "You know why they want you out of the case? You have credibility. They're worried you'll pull sympathy from the jury, which could help DeLorean. That's why John Z. wanted to meet you in the courtroom. He knew I was going to flip.

He wanted to affirm that you two are both victims and that you are standing together. That would play well before the jury.

"The jury isn't going to buy me as a victim," I said soberly.

"The Feds are worried they will. I told the FBI, that Max threatened to kill you several times. Once while Rafa stood at your back with a gun to your head. That concerns the Feds."

"But I wasn't exactly innocent."

"True, but it was coercion on a Medellin Cartel scale, and that's something a person can understand. You need only one juror to be sympathetic, and it becomes a mistrial. A high-powered defense team could raise serious doubt amongst the jurors. Think about this from DeLorean's perspective. His attorneys are going to throw themselves at the prosecution's case against you with everything they got. You're going to have a battery of attorneys standing behind Rick to find out what the Feds know and how to defeat it. That's why the Feds are worried."

"What about my trip south of the border?"

"I had to tell them," Morgan sighed, "but, I also told them how you adamantly didn't want to do it. Steve, you fought me every step of the way. The Feds don't want the jury to hear that."

Morgan smiles slyly, "You know you dodged a bullet big time. I was in a real bind because I bragged to Max that you were going to be a great asset with all your skills from leading combat frog teams on dangerous missions. Max talked with Pablo Escobar about you. They were figuring you as the answer to their biggest problem. The Feds were throwing high-tech assets at his low-tech smuggling operation. Pablo wanted a team of Navy frogs with you in a command role. Max would provide all the sophisticated assets.

"Command role?" I asked startled at the implication.

"The kid's gun in your face was a test and you passed."

"You knew about that?"

Morgan nods, "Yeah, the Colombians are big into high-stress tests. Pablo Escobar and Max had such big plans for you. Pablo wanted to size you up in person. We were going to fly down to Medellin for a meet and greet but the investigation got personal."

"I was going back to Colombia to meet Pablo Escobar?"

"And the Ochoa Brothers, along with Max, and Rafa. They were going to drop a bundle of money into your pockets. Millions to buy planes, boats, and military gear. You could have recruited from the teams. Men like you who were driven out for a stupid marijuana mistake or who wanted to make a pile of money. For some of them, the rogue adventure would have been enough of a lure."

"This is crazy talk," I stared at Morgan.

"Pablo Escobar didn't think it crazy at all. He was willing to front tens of millions to make it happen. That's why I couldn't tell Max that you were balking at flying that one stupid load. Look at it from my perspective. You're an adventure guy, and this was crazy dangerous. I had to present you to Max to save your life. I told you too much," Morgan looked away. "Max couldn't have you walking around knowing about his and Pablo's business and not being fully committed to it. When I promised to turn my business over to you in San Diego I wasn't kidding."

"It was the cocaine business that you were talking about?"

"Duh! What other business was I in?" quipped Morgan. "What a recruitment pool, all those hot special operators. With a skilled team of commandos, we would have been untouchable."

Morgan leers, "Know what else Max smuggles? Weapons, he could get anything: M-16 assault rifles, hand grenades, C-4 plastic explosives, detonating cord, even anti-tank weapons."

Morgan began to pace, "Max's planes take weapons and money down and bring back cocaine. Sometimes the Feds would bust a plane bringing in the coke, but they never got one of the planes going south. That was stupid on the Feds part; their problem was that the various agencies didn't play well together."

Morgan is getting excited talking about his big plans. "These cartel dudes are crude and unsophisticated; it's all about being macho and instant primal gratification. Most of them are high or drunk most of the time and few graduated from middle school. Put a ragtag bag of those idiots up against our special warfare operators, throw in high-tech weaponry, night vision goggles, sophisticated coms and military planning—and bam," boasted Morgan. "We would have been rich beyond our dreams."

"You really thought this out, didn't you?" I asked.

"Max and I had a great plan. He is the one who realized that cocaine floats. We could do night drops, shove bales of cocaine out at low altitude into the ocean with low watt beacons and marker lights. We do this in the radar shadow on the backside of Anacapa Island. It's part of Channel Islands National Park. That means there is no one there at night, except for the caretaker at Lander's Bay on the northern tip of the island. We have a couple of rubber Zodiacs grab the bails. From Anacapa, it is only an 11-mile run to the marina or we could buy a house with a dock in Mandalay Bay where you first met me."

I ponder what my life might be like and I not met Morgan.

"It wouldn't have worked," I said flatly, "your plan was stupid. I was stationed at Point Mugu Naval Air Station, which is the headquarters for the Navy's Frontier Control Command Center. Anacapa Island is inside the Navy's Pacific Ocean Missile Testing Range. Frontier Control is wired into the powerful radar station at San Nicolas Island, which has a clear line of sight of the backside of Anacapa Island. Just up the coast is Vandenberg Air Force Base with its Minuteman Inter-Continental Ballistic Missile Silos. There are more underwater listening devices and radar units covering that part of the California seaboard than anywhere else on the west coast of the United States. That is an incredibly sensitive area with highly restricted access. Fighter jets and helicopter gunships would have intercepted your drug plane with guns hot. To get to your house with a dock in Mandalay Bay, you need to transit Channel Islands Harbor, which has a Coast Guard Base at the entrance. Imagine them stopping your boat for a routine safety inspection. You know there's no place to hide kilos of coke in a rubber boat."

"See why we needed you in a command role." Morgan said.

"You and Max were crazy to think I would recruit men from my command. I would never have done that, Morgan," I said angerly.

"Don't be so sure," snapped Morgan, "Pablo can be quite persuasive. You were lucky you got out when you did."

"Lucky? Do I look lucky?" I challenged.

"Do you know how Rafa pulled Max into the Cartel?" asked Morgan smugly. "He killed a guy right in front of him and then made Max help get rid of the body. Max was scared to death. It's how the Colombians work. If Rafa did Stretch like they were planning—he would hand you the shovel. You dig Stretch's grave, so you're culpable. Refuse, and you're digging your own grave."

Morgan slips past me and steps to the door again. He peers out the security window checking the corridor.

"I have daily attorney visits. We're getting a lot of information, some of it uncovered by reporters, freelance investigators, and conspiracy nuts," confides, Morgan. "I'll share what I can before they pull me out of here."

* * *

Over the next couple of days, Morgan shared that Agent Gerald Scotti was the lead suspect for disclosing secret government information that benefited the defense attorney in the Grandma Mafia Case. It made him a poor witness for the government in the upcoming DeLorean trial. Scotti was looking better as a defense witness. He said that the White House is trying to manipulate the trial and that the prosecutor, James Walsh was hoping to make the cover of Time Magazine. Scotti also alleged that Hoffman got paid rewards for his work. He far out earned Scotti. Think $160,000 in one year. That gave him a financial incentive to coerce DeLorean into the conspiracy. Together these add up to a case buster.

* * *

Laying on my bunk, I wondered what made me so susceptible to Morgan's manipulations. To understand, I let my mind drift back to when Morgan re-entered my life.

* * *

I am a photojournalism major at San Diego State University. I take the bus to keep down wear and tear on Revelstoke. Getting off the bus in La Jolla, I drop my books off in Revelstoke, which I park outside of La Jolla Surf Systems where I work. I go into the surf shop and say hello to my boss Jeff. He is a terribly busy addict. I smoke marijuana. Earning not much more than minimum wage, I am on a tight budget.

I go over to a shelf full of T-shirts and begin refolding the ones dropped by customers. I often try to convince myself that I am happy, but lately, it has been getting harder to make that mental leap. The only high point in my life is that I am living a surfer lifestyle. I surf a couple of times a day, but when the surf is down, the beach gets boring. I am into jogging in a big way, but like most of my activities, I tend to do a couple of bong hits before beginning the run. I was dissatisfied. My masquerade as a radical character immersed in the local surf culture stood revealed as a fool's blunder. I thought I was living for the moment when I was living for the next high. That is when Morgan Hetrick called.

I am still folding T-shirts when Jeff yells, "Phone call for you." He covers the mouthpiece, "Don't be long. I'm trying to score some dope."

"Steve Arrington," I said into the mouthpiece.

"Steve, it's Morgan Hetrick," his commanding voice recalls memories of airplanes, yachts, and fancy cars. I had not seen Morgan since I left Point Mugu Naval Air Station seven years ago in 1975.

"Steve, I had been wondering where you'd gotten to after leaving the Navy," he said kindly. "It took quite an effort to run you down."

"I'm just getting in some college time and a bit of surfing," I try to sound upbeat. It is exciting to have a multimillionaire call when I am barely on the upside of down and out.

"What are you doing for money?" he said, getting right to the point.

"Oh, a bit of GI Bill for college and I work part-time at the surf shop for the fun of it," I answered flippantly.

"How much do you get paid?"

I told him, implying that it was more for recreation than survival.

"Are you kidding? I pay my janitor three times that," he snickered.

Well, that put my lack of success under a bright mental spotlight.

"How about coming to work for me?" he asked jauntily.

"Work for you?" My heart leaps.

"You're still a licensed pilot, aren't you?"

"Yeah, but I haven't flown for a couple of years."

I have not flown since starting my marijuana habit. It is a surprising realization. I enjoyed flying, spent a couple of paychecks to learn how. It is a rude awakening to realize marijuana had stolen something else once important to me and I did not notice it was missing.

"Doesn't make any difference, I can get you up to speed. Why don't I fly down there so we can talk tête-à-tête?"

"Fly down?"

"Let's do lunch tomorrow," he named an airport not far away.

The next morning, I am up early. It takes a strong effort not to light up a joint — my usual morning routine. I needed to see Morgan with a sober mind. He does not drink alcohol or do drugs and has a negative attitude about those that do. Instead of recognizing my problem, I self-congratulate myself for my force of will. This is Steve being oblivious.

Arriving at the small county airport, I join a couple of airplane enthusiasts at a waist-high chain-link fence. We watch small planes landing and taking off when one of them comments, "Here comes a Mooney 231, now that is one hot airplane."

I watch Morgan's plane land and taxi to a row of tie-downs. I block the main gear as Morgan steps out and says, "Let's eat her," Morgan throws an arm over my shoulder as we head for the Flight Line Restaurant. "So why are you going to college? I never figured you for the diploma type."

"Just looking to broaden my education." It is a truthful answer. My interest revolves around English and writing classes. I am still trying to work out an occupation while taking advantage of the GI Bill.

The restaurant features aviation memorabilia with model airplanes hanging from the ceiling. I like the place, then realize I have not been in a restaurant in over a year. I eat in Revelstoke or pack lunches, most of my money went to feed my marijuana habit.

Morgan opts for a steak and fries. He is 30 lbs. overweight. I consider the chef's salad hold the ham, but figure as a vegetarian I should order something manlier, "Grilled cheese on whole wheat, please."

Morgan watches the young waitress walking away until the kitchen door closes. "Oh, my!" he said longingly with one hand over his heart.

He has not changed from the man I knew seven years ago. Morgan was always chasing a skirt — come to think of it, so was I.

"Remember how successful Morgan Aviation used to be?" he asked.

"Sure, you had quite an operation."

"Well," he opens his arms and leans back expansively. "I've got seven domestic corporations and two international companies. I have a hanger in Mojave next to Burt Rutan's facility. He's the guy looking to fly around the world nonstop without refueling."

Morgan continues to brag, his voice getting louder as the young woman arrives with our order. "Last year we brought in over three million dollars," he said leering as she sets his plate down. She is not impressed, but I am — no doubt with tips the waitress out earns me.

"I want you to be my right-hand man," Morgan announced.

I choke on a French fry, "Right-hand man?"

"I'm rich and want to enjoy it. I'm retiring in three or four years, you learn the ropes, and I'll make you Executive Vice President."

"Vice President of Morgan Aviation?" I asked in astonishment.

"No," he laughs, "Executive Vice President of all my companies.

I stare at him speechless.

"We'll start you off right away at $50,000 a year till you get up to speed, then we'll double it," Morgan smiled, "repeatedly."

A French fry hangs halfway to my mouth.

"Course we have to get you a commercial, multi-engine instrument license, and your own airplane."

"My own plane?" Did I just gasp?

"Of course, your own plane," he slugs me happily. "You're in the aviation business now, son."

Having a multimillionaire affectionately calling me son means a lot. I was drowning in failure in San Diego, and Morgan just tossed me a huge life-ring. In a celebratory mood, I squirt a glob of ketchup onto my plate then dunk the grilled cheese sandwich into it.

Driving Revelstoke back to La Jolla Shores, my mind is in a whirl. Suddenly, all my problems had an answer compliments of an old friend.

I dropped out of college, quit my job, and said goodbye to my few friends. All of them are smokers and dealing with their own various levels of un-admitted addiction."

I arrive at Morgan Aviation at sunset with half a tank of gas, $20 in my pocket and a highly motivated attitude.

Over the next eight weeks, I discover that my job is about hanging out with Morgan. He spends little time in the Mojave Desert. All of Morgan's recreation revolves around the pursuit of women. He has a couple of yachts in Florida used for trolling for new girlfriends and for scuba diving in the Bahamas. I mind the dive gear, teach diving when required and run the boat. Many of the young women that Morgan takes out on the yacht have tried to set me up with their girlfriends, but I have no interest. These are party girls, young women looking for a fling and trailing a social disease in their wake. Morgan scoffs at my notion of love.

The other thing missing is a paycheck. Morgan gives me spending money, but it's not for depositing in a bank. Now that was very odd. I also did not know Morgan was arranging my first big test and looking forward to introducing me to Max Mermelstein.

Morgan with a friend. *Highland Fling* in the background. Morgan did not like to be photographed. He had issues that the image might wind-up on the FBI's Most Wanted poster.
This is my only photograph of him. Photo Arrington

* * *

I am watering the grass in the J-3 yard when Morgan strolls over. "So, this is the famous Arrington lawn. It and you are a point of interest at T.I.," said Morgan as we walk to the water fountain. "Is that dribble all you get?" he asked.

"I don't mind; it's not that I have anywhere to go. If you listen carefully, the water makes a sort of aquatic music."

"Going for an insanity defense?" teased Morgan.

"Do you know that Reagan declared the war on drugs while I was driving the drug car? It was like he was talking to me."

"Actually, Regan was talking about you. It was no coincidence that he announced his war on drugs just before your arrest in what would become, 'The Drug Trial of the Century.'"

I gaped at Morgan. "It wasn't a coincidence?"

"President Reagan and Prime Minister Thatcher met in London a month before the DeLorean investigation began. Thatcher wanted to take DeLorean down. He took $18,000,000 of her money. He was in the States outside of British jurisdiction and she needed Reagan's help to get him. Reagan owed her big time after failing to help her during the Falkland War. She lost a couple of ships and 255 service personnel. Britain could have lost that war. This was payback."

"Both governments conspired to get DeLorean?" I asked.

"Absolutely," said Morgan with great assurance.

"That means DeLorean has a real chance of getting off," I said.

"Yep, but that defense doesn't work for us," grumbled Morgan.

"Which means testifying against me." I stated bluntly.

Morgan is stunned. "Sure, I had to tell them about it, But I will not take the stand against you or DeLorean."

"What?"

"Come on," Morgan prodded, "I'm a Hetrick not a Hoffman. I won't testify against friends or family. It's why the negotiations have taken so long. You're family."

"And DeLorean?" I asked.

"He's a friend of sorts."

"How could he be your friend?" I asked.

Morgan laughs, "I've known John DeLorean for over a decade. I was the pilot for Fletcher Jones a mega-millionaire. He owned a computer company worth hundreds of millions of dollars. Fletcher was just 40-years old and retired. He had a swingers thing going on at his 3,900-acre ranch, the Westerly Stud Farm, in San Ynez. Fletcher had me flying Hollywood starlets in for wild weekends."

"With DeLorean," I am stunned.

"Yeah, but then Fletcher met and fell in love with a real star," Morgan said. "It put an end to his swinging days. He wanted to marry her. I flew her in frequently and we became good friends. It's because of her that I won't testify against John DeLorean."

Morgan is blowing my mind. "Who was this woman?"

Morgan smiles, "Cristina Ferrare, DeLorean's wife. She gave me a note that said, 'I didn't know that men like you existed.' So yeah, we were close. We had deep conversations during those flights to and from San Ynez. A year later, she ups and marries DeLorean. I couldn't take the stand against him with her staring at me. You don't have a proper picture of who I really am. I may be a smuggler, but I have my own code of Texas cowboy ethics. I grew up on a ranch in Texas. When I was 14, I started flying airplanes, and was hooked. Years later, I bought two war surplus B-25 bombers. One for spare parts, the other I flew to South America to acquire exotic cargos."

"What kind of exotic cargos?" I asked.

"Mostly monkeys, they're small. You can jam a lot of them in a cage. They did quite well and could go longer without water. I sold them to zoos and research labs who bought my monkeys by the crate. These were legitimate businesses, but all they cared about was their bottom line which makes sense to me. I'm a cowboy and a maverick. I don't hold to all the laws of the United States," Morgan said, then he changed the subject. "We locked our deal with the government yesterday. I am pleading guilty on June 13."

That evening, Morgan waves me into his cell. "I'm leaving in the morning. Our discovery motions paid off. We got all the transcripts of the FBI's secret tapes and investigative reports, as well as other stuff that they don't want anyone to know about."

"Rick, my attorney, has copies of this?"

"When you and DeLorean merged your defenses, Rick also got copies of all the investigative reports from that expensive firm John DeLorean hired. The press filed dozens of motions trying to get their hands on this stuff, but it's locked under court seal. The FBI files and tape transcripts are going to blow big holes in their case."

"Really?" I said, quite entertained.

"Absolutely, because it's all tied to James T. Hoffman. Their whole case is totally dependent on the testimony of a man who has repeatedly perjured himself in court. Remember, I've worked with Hoffman for a couple of decades. He's a conman. It's embedded in his black soul. He lies because he needs to turn everything to his advantage. He's like a spider weaving a multifaceted web, only a master con artist can hold something this complex together."

"So, he's addicted to the con?"

"It's why he is one of the best and why I worked with him for so long. Look, I knew the man and was on my guard. Yet still, he hit me up for a hundred thousand bucks. I am a hard person to take advantage of the Feds would never have got me, but for him."

"They took you down in just a few months," I countered.

Morgan laughed, "Not a chance, Stephen, I've been under government scrutiny for over 25 years."

"What?" I asked stunned, "you said you only found out about the investigation when I made that stupid flight to Colombia."

Morgan smiled slyly, "Stephen, I'm afraid that James Hoffman is not the only con artist in this case."

"I got conned!" I paused to think about what I just said.

"Stephen, I always had your best interests at heart. With me as your teacher, you could have been a magnificent smuggler."

"Thanks," I said dryly still pondering Morgan conning me.

"The FBI and DEA agents didn't know what they were up against. Hoffman always goes for the throat. He takes his victims down hard leaving them with no options to defend themselves. The FBI agent Tisa and Scotti thought he was just a loser snitch, which gave Hoffman the opportunity to con them. They didn't respect his sly intelligence and long experience of conning federal agents, police detectives, prosecutors and even judges."

"Hoffman wants to get paid for his efforts, but more than that is the satisfaction of conning someone who thinks they're your intellectual better. Hoffman thrives on proving himself superior, and he will take the most outlandish risks to accomplish it. The crazier the ride, the more it becomes believable to the mark. Right now, he is working the con of a lifetime."

"How is that possible when he's working in custody for the government as a snitch?" I asked.

Morgan peers out the cell door's security window. "Have to give him credit. He gets busted for smuggling, turns evidence, and converts snitching into a profit. Instead of sleeping in a lockup or safe house he is staying in expensive hotels. He plays it off as part of his cover while he skims cash from every case he works. You can bet the Feds going after me was his idea. The FBI, DEA and DOJ are just along for the ride. Hoffman is driving the whole case."

"How did he achieve that?" I asked.

Morgan smiled, "It was Hoffman setting up the agents so he could weasel his way into my case. He saw a report on his old buddy Morgan Hetrick from the Venture County police chief about money laundering. The cop was requesting Federal assistance."

Morgan squints his eyes, rolls his shoulders, and clinches a fist. I know that combination. Morgan does it when he is so mad, he is ready to clobber someone. He may be overweight, but Morgan is a scrapper. He takes a deep breath then continues, "When Hoffman saw my name associated with money laundering, it was like being dealt double aces in Black Jack, and then spitting the aces and drawing face cards and hitting an unbeatable 21 with both hands. With my file Hoffman is looking at a pot of gold!"

"Your gold?" I probed.

"Damn right," he snarled, "my gold!"

Morgan sweeps a fist under his nose. He takes a deep breath to settle himself. He glares at me, "When you went to work for me in 74, Hoffman was also working for me. He was in the shady side of my business, I made sure your paths didn't cross."

"Morgan Aviation had a shady side?" I asked astounded. I had never saw a hint of anything nefarious.

Morgan looks out the window then his eyes slide back to me. "You saw the legitimate side of my businesses at Oxnard Airport. Let's just say there was a creative side too. That's where Hoffman worked, until he stole a hundred grand of my money and split."

Morgan is angrier than I have ever seen him. "Hoffman knows me better than anyone else. He knew I flew a hundred kilo load of cocaine into Alabama in 1980 and smuggled multiple massive loads of marijuana throughout the 1970's. He shared all of that with the FBI. Thing is he knows I'll kill him for it. So, the *piece de resistance* of his master con is that he had to get the Feds to take everything I had and send me to prison for a long time. And don't forget he would be angling for his cut of the spoils."

"Abruptly, something even bigger than me falls into his lap. Remember, he's in the federal offices. Hoffman is hearing things and seeing paper on the cases they're working. Then he sees a file on John Z. DeLorean or hears the agents talking about him. Hoffman claims that he was DeLorean's neighbor in Pauma Valley in San Diego County. He only met DeLorean once, yet he plays it like they're old buddies."

Suddenly, I figured it out. "The Feds sic Hoffman on DeLorean, and he ties it to your investigation because they need a real drug smuggler with actual product to build their case around."

Morgan nodded, "Hoffman realized that this was a historical con. In the criminal world it would make him famous. When he threw me to Scotti, I was the perfect fit. James Hoffman handed the Feds a homerun case. But because he was laying it all out and pulling the strings the Feds knew without Hoffman there was no case against me or DeLorean."

"But how is this the con of a lifetime?" I asked.

"It's all about the players. Imagine them sitting at a poker table in a dark room playing, "Texas Holdem.""

"Texas Holdem?" I asked. I knew nothing about the game.

The dealer gives everyone two cards face down and the betting begins. Then he lays out three cards face up in the middle of the table. Each player uses them to build their hand. After another round of betting, the dealer flips up another card and then after the betting settles, he flips up the final card. Best out of five cards wins. The game can get intense, people have been shot. I saw a guy get his throat cut in a rough border town in Colombia after bluffing a hard man to throw-in a winning hand. His mistake was laughing at the looser. South of the border they take their machoism to a knife in the gut level."

"Anyway, across the table from Hoffman is John DeLorean, a head of industry and maverick automaker with an urgent need for cash. Next to John is me. I set up Pablo Escobar's whole West Coast smuggling operation for Max Mermelstein. I was now the top West Coast cocaine smuggler with tens of millions of dollars in drug money that needed to be laundered. Sitting on each side of Hoffman are FBI agent Benedict Tisa and DEA agent Gerald Scotti. Everyone must put something in the pot except for Hoffman. Behind Hoffman is James Walsh. The players have no idea that he is a senior federal prosecutor. He is acting as the pit boss. Secretly he is overseeing the action for the Department of Justice to make sure no one blows the case."

"For Hoffman to con this group of savvy men it's going to take boldness, a web of outrageous lies, and serious talent."

I ask, "Why doesn't Hoffman have any money on the table?"

"Because Stephen," Morgan said with a laugh, "Hoffman is the dealer. He's running the game, and he's pulling cards from the bottom of the deck."

"So, here's how the con begins. Hoffman has convinced DeLorean that he can get him a $60,000,000 loan to save his company. In return, Hoffman wants 1.8 million dollars as a commission, but he wants it up front. Then he lies to Tisa and Scotti telling them that DeLorean said that he wanted to put up two million bucks to buy cocaine or heroin to save his company. This is a total lie, but it is the best news the Feds could have heard. They had nothing and suddenly Hoffman is offering them DeLorean on a platter with me as a side dish. Hoffman is orchestrating both sides, everyone is dancing to his tune. It's a classic con, the agents think their running Hoffman—but he's the one doing the driving and they're cluelessly sitting in the backseat celebrating their good fortune. Actually, they're just along for the ride for when Hoffman needs them and their guns with arrest warrants."

"What made Hoffman think he could pull it off." I asked.

Morgan laughs, "Because James Timothy Hoffman's real name is Timothy William DeJong. He worked for the New York FBI for ten years as a snitch after getting caught smuggling. He cut his teeth on setting up cases, ripping the criminals off for their assets, and then bringing in the FBI to arrest the marks before they could do anything about it."

"He never got caught?"

"Not exactly, he was masterful. He would look out a window or down a street and yell that FBI agents were descending on them."

"DeJong would have already marked out what he wanted to steal, cash, drugs or both. He would order the mark to run while he hid the evidence. Figure the mark is in full panic mode and Hoffman is offering him an out. He's even willing to take the fall. For the mark, worse case scenario, it is better to be arrested for a half-pound of cocaine with $500 in cash than a kilo with $10,000. Think shorter sentences. But his real hope is that he might escape." Unfortunately for him,

Hoffman warned the FBI that the guy was a runner. The mark is going to prison with nothing. That means he's not a threat to Hoffman for a long time.

"The FBI had suspicions about what Hoffman was up to but didn't want to blow their case with unnecessary complications."

"What did you mean by, 'Not exactly.'" I asked.

Morgan grins, "DeJong has spent more time in courts than most prosecutors, getting sued and dodging convictions. He is an expert at shedding evidence against him. The prosecutor would have DeJong locked up in an airtight case, then DeJong would start digging cracks in it. Say that he was working a FBI case and had to show credibility to whomever he was conning so the Feds could arrest him. The District Attorney is told by the FBI to drop the case against DeJong because he is giving evidence in another much more important case. It makes sense to the local prosecutor to give up a small fish for a much bigger fish. It is completely in line with the Feds, 'Let's make a deal way of winning cases.' Sometimes the prosecutor balks so the FBI gets the court to draw up a letter for Hoffman where he promises that he won't steal, smuggle, or deal drugs again. The prosecutor is pleased to draw up a binding document that will land Hoffman back in jail if he violates it."

"You're kidding?" I asked. "He actually got away with it?"

"Repeatedly," grinned Morgan. "In fact, the last time he signed one of those FBI engineered documents, 'I promise not to steal evidence and smuggle anymore,' was just eight months before the DeLorean trial."

I look at Morgan stunned. My perception of the DOJ and FBI being mostly honest is taking a severe beating.

Morgan continues, "Rick, your attorney, has a copy of the latest letter signed by Hoffman and an Assistant District Attorney for the Los Angeles Federal Courthouse. An agreement not to prosecute Hoffman for alleged smuggling and other criminal activity for the last five years. In return Hoffman would provide evidence against the criminals and smugglers he was stealing from. Just another day at the office for James Timothy Hoffman."

Morgan cracks his knuckles, "Things got too hot in New York for DeJong. People were gunning for him on the streets after they got out of prison. He convinced the Feds to move him to the West Coast with a new name. The FBI created James T. Hoffman, but they never got a leash on him."

I shake my head, "This is crazy, but couldn't DeLorean figure out that he was being conned?"

"Not at first, but when he got suspicious, Hoffman says that his investors are Colombian drug lords. DeLorean wants out. Hoffman threatens that the Colombians will kill his daughter and give him her head in a paper bag. DeLorean panics. He figures he needs some serious backup, so he lays down a bluff to protect his family. He brings the Irish Republican Army (IRA) to the table. DeLorean tells Hoffman that the 1.8 million is coming from the IRA because they want to keep his factory open in Ireland."

"Picture the IRA now standing behind DeLorean at the card table. But they are not on DeLorean's side. They'd rather put a bullet in the back of his head for lying about them. But Hoffman doesn't bluff that easily and counters with a threat from the Cali Cartel. Envision the Cali Cartel standing behind Hoffman sharpening their knives while the IRA wants to bomb DeLorean's car."

"John is desperate. He said he had to pay the 1.8 million to his receivers. Thus, DeLorean claims it kills the deal."

"Therefore, it should have ended there," I said.

Morgan shook his head, "Nope, FBI agent Tisa acting as the dirty banker just needs a new angle. He and Hoffman want DeLorean to put something else in the pot. He has John provide the VIN numbers of 40 DeLorean cars as collateral for the 1.8 million to purchase the cocaine. John puts the VINs for the DeLoreans on the table because he thought he was pulling off a fast one as 40 DeLoreans are only worth a half mil, not the 1.8 million dollars needed to buy the cocaine."

"Did John actually come up with the DeLoreans?" I asked.

"He moved 40 DeLoreans to his residence in Plumas Valley. However, now the agents want DeLorean to sweeten the pot, so he throws in half of the shares to DeLorean Motor Cars. It all goes into the pot."

"Well that's worth millions," I surmised.

"Nope, they're bogus. The DeLorean Motor Car is a shell; the stocks are worthless. Get this, DeLorean is now trying to con the bankers and Hoffman with an empty shell game."

"Are you telling me that DeLorean is a con artist too?"

Morgan chuckles, "It wasn't an accident that DeLorean had his hands knuckle deep in $18,000,000 of Margret Thatcher's money. I see DeLorean as a likeable rogue. But the man is a genuine con artist from a business perspective. It means he is not exactly a crook. Yet, stealing $18,000,000 from the British Government is not the work of an amateur. That kind of con takes serious experience."

Morgan offers a wry smile, "His real corporation, the DeLorean Motor Company, was not yet a part of the deal."

"Not yet?" I asked.

"Wait for it," said Morgan.

"But why would the FBI and DOJ fall for a scam like that?"

"Simple, DeLorean will never get the money.

The agents arrested me with the $1.8 mil in cash, which is what the Feds put on the table along with my 55 pounds of cocaine. Hoffman totally conned me, again! But, as I said, for it to be a master con Hoffman must strip me of all my assets, which also go into the pot. You see the FBI is planning on taking everything on the table. Being greedy they're looking at ways to make the pot grow — really grow!"

"This is when the case almost took a very scary twist. Hoffman and Agent Tisa, acting as the corrupt banker were trying to get me to put $15,000,000 into the real DeLorean Motor Company in Ireland for a partnership stake."

"You had that much offshore?" I asked surprised.

"Yeah, more than twice that," Morgan shrugged. "My $15,000,000 is still out of their reach in a Bahama bank. Hoffman is trying hard to get it into the pot. Yet, it is not nearly enough. To buy a 50% share in DMC was going to require $100,000,000 in cash. Remember, the original $60,000,000 is just to save DMC. Continued operations and development needed continued investment in the hundreds of millions. So, I flew down to the Cayman Islands for a secret meet with the Medellin Cartel."

Morgan wipes his brow as he remembers the meeting. "Pablo Escobar and the Ochoa Brothers had a serious money problem. They were buried in cash, storing it in closets, mattresses, and in bedrooms filled with 100-dollar bills. They were losing millions annually to rats that were eating packets of hundred-dollar bills as snacks. So, I urged Pablo and the Ochoa Brothers to put up $60,000,000 as a stake in DMC. They agree, but the money isn't in the pot yet."

"But it is time to put Pablo Escobar and the Ochoa Brothers at the poker table behind me with their army of hit men from the largest drug cartel on the planet. Yet, it's still not a hundred million. So, Pablo Escobar offers a piece of the action to Max Mermelstein and Rafa. For a piece of DMC, they agree to put up the 25 million. That's now $100,000,000 in drug money being boxed up for delivery to the poker table."

"This is a secret inside look at how Pablo Escobar likes to operate. He is the one driving to get the $100,000,000 onto the table. He gets his top people financially invested in this operation which means they're totally committed to working for him. No one is secretly looking to take down the, "King of the Cocaine Drug Trade because they would be cutting their own throats. The other option is getting their throats cut by an enterprising Colombian looking to move up in the cartel."

My mind is boggled, it's all too much for me to take in — then Morgan grabs my attention back with a startling statement. "Slide Max and Rafa in behind you because you're my sidekick — whatever happens to me happens to you."

A sudden memory of Rafa standing behind me with the gun and twitchy trigger finger boggles my mind. It also means that Scar Face would be there with his knife.

Morgan continues, "Rafa has a car dealership in Medellin. He's into cars big time and is suddenly eager to open the first DeLorean dealership in South America. Imagine the macho prestige it would bring him. Rafa is overly excited, he is seeing legitimate cash flowing into his coffers accompanied by gorgeous women and hot cars."

"But if those murderous men lost that kind of cash, you could guess what would have happen to you and me."

"Pablo Escobar, the Ochoa Brothers, Max, Rafa, Scar Face, the IRA, the FBI, the DEA, the DOJ, and the Cali Cartel — that is one scary poker table," I am mentally visualizing them in my mind and it is all too real.

"Don't forget about Pablo Escobar. He's spinning his own web inside Hoffman's and Tisa's scam. Pablo doesn't think small. He is possibly the richest man in the world. For him, his investment of $60,000,000 is just seed money. He is figuring on using DMC to launder billions of dollars. DMC is the ultimate big-time façade. All he needs is a front man."

"Which is who?" I asked.

Morgan offers a huge grin, "Me," He bragged. Morgan adds almost regretfully, "I'm afraid you had a part in Pablo's Ireland plan. Hoffman wanted me to fly over to Belfast and get myself established as DeLorean's new executive engineer and as an agent for a massive investor conglomerate."

"Why did I need to be there?" I am almost afraid to ask.

"Pablo smuggles cocaine mostly to the United States. The DeLorean deal is a perfect opportunity for him to expand to the European Continent. He saw the IRA as a perfect partner. They were fighting the United Kingdom and had an extensive underground network. With my help he wanted you to set up and lead a smuggling operation out of Ireland."

"I would have had no idea how to do that!" I stated the obvious.

"No problem, I set up the West Coast Operation for Pablo and Max," Morgan boasted. "I would have mentored you."

"A mentor!" I growled. "You and Pablo were totally missing the fact that I am not that kind of a character. I never could have pulled this off. I don't have a criminal bent."

Morgan nods, "That is so true, Stephen. I had such high hopes for you," he said sadly. "You would have been untrainable. Probably would have gotten yourself killed."

"Anyway," Morgan pickups his original conversation. "DeLorean wanted me to provide plausible deniability for him. DeLorean needed billions of dollars to build DMC into a true auto industry giant with a whole line of various models."

How do they hide that from DMC corporate?" I asked.

"They had no idea this was going down. That was DeLorean's problem. But getting the corporate board to accept a massive infusion of cash would have been easy."

"To seal the deal, I flew DeLorean up to Morgan Aviation to show him some of my aviation designs." Morgan gave me a satisfied look, "He was impressed enough that we started talking serous business." Note: *I have the secret file where Morgan confesses all of this to the FBI, including Hoffman's involvement.*

"Anyway," Morgan continued, "Hoffman and Agent Tisa lost control of the con, when the FBI and DOJ arrested the three of us prematurely."

"Why didn't they wait?" I asked.

"Because DeLorean's whole goal was to save DMC. It was going into receivership the very next day. If DeLorean lost DMC, then all bets were off. It would have killed the deal. Bright lights of scrutiny would be shining on the poker table so all the bad people standing in the background fade away with their money as fast as possible."

"So, it's over," I breath a sign of relief.

Morgan says, "Not quite."

"Tisa, the FBI Agent, slides a single card and a piece of paper facedown across the table to you. He is making a side bet. The prosecutor, James Walsh, acting as the pit boss picks up the paper and reads it. He says, "Yeah, I'll allow this and flips it up.

"What is it?" I asked nervously.

"It's your Grand Jury Indictment with a dozen counts — think life in prison, no possibility of parole." Morgan looked at me like he is taking my measure. "You're not cooperating is you taking that side bet—so, your butt goes into the pot."

"What's with the single card in front of me?"

"It's the joker, of course. You're the wild card, Stephen. No one knows what you are going to do. The FBI's chances of losing gets very real because of you. Since you go to trial first it exposes everything, they got for DeLorean's attorneys to see. The Feds are sweating that big time because one more person is still standing in the back of the room." Morgan pauses for drama, "The President of the United States. Ronald Reagan is heavily invested in this case. Remember, he formed an oversight committee to ensure that all of his agencies cooperated, and Margret Thatcher has Ronnie's phone number on speed dial."

"So, what do you do, Stephen? Do you go to trial? Are you willing to risk the wrath of the United States Government? Maybe spend the rest of your life behind bars?"

"I don't know," I said truthfully.

"That's the problem," said Morgan. "Everyone at the table saw you as the wild card. Consider them all card sharks and you're the minnow who stumbled into their piece of the ocean. You can see that it would give some of them something to speculate about regarding your ongoing existence!"

I am so troubled by all of this. My mind is beginning to panic. Flight or fight hormones are kicking in but glancing about the J-3 prison yard I can't run. I am literally trapped prey waiting for them to decide what to do with me.

"So," asked Morgan, "what are you going to do?

"I don't know," I said. "I'm still waiting to see how it all goes down. What about you? Aren't you worried about snitching?"

Morgan stares blankly out the window, "I don't sleep well, not with a three-million-dollar price tag on my head. I understand that Escobar will pay an extra million if I suffer."

"What about me?" I asked nervously. "You said whatever happened to one of us also happens to the other."

"I said I trusted you with my life; you didn't say that about me. Think of it as a Colombian loophole for smaller guys like you. Means you're open for recruitment. Besides, you got credibility with Pablo. who has a lot of faith in American Newspapers. If they print it, it must be true. It is the ultimate test for him. The papers are printing that not only are you not cooperating but that you and DeLorean are merging your defenses. If DeLorean trusts you with his defense, well that's good enough for Pablo Escobar."

Morgan looked me up and down, "Steve, I am deeply sorry for bringing you into this. I am guilty of betraying your trust more than you will ever know. It's why I put up that $50,000 for you to buy your own lawyer. Steve, I want you to take down Hoffman!"

My mouth fell open. I could not have been more shocked. "You want me to what?" I gasped.

Morgan steps to the cell door, and checks the corridor, "It's not what you're thinking. I don't want you to kill him," he said with a disarming laugh. Morgan pauses to reconsider. "Well actually, I would very much like to do that myself." Morgan is doing his fist thing again.

"But I can't," he grumbled, "I want you to take him down in court. You could destroy the whole case, you're a con buster. Steve, down deep you're basically an honest guy and the jury will see that. If DeLorean walks, all deals are off with the Feds and Hoffman. His snitch career is over. He'll windup in the witness protection program selling insurance in some backwater in some place like a Nebraska farm town. He'll hate it and will know that I did it!" crowed Hetrick.

"What happens if I lose?"

"Stephen, you can beat this. You'll have all of DeLorean's lawyers defending you. You're his big hope. Even if you don't walk, he gets all the FBI's evidence. He can't lose."

"Your trial will be an international event. The masses will be judging you and that's a good thing. The press wants a hero in this case, it sure isn't Hoffman, and the Feds are dirty. They can paint you as the unexpected hero option standing his ground," Morgan took a dramatic pause. "It adds a new dimension that would sell mega millions of newspapers."

'There he goes again,' I thought. 'The master manipulator trying to work his black magic.' The secret of a con man is that they think everyone wants to cash in on a deal — money, fame, and power. Yes, I wanted my day in court, but I was looking for a way to do it honestly. I had a debt to pay, a time to serve, before I would be okay with myself or with God. And there is found the answer to my dilemma. I did not have just two choices, there was a third option. It would require a lot of hope on my part, but for me it was the only answer. I would plead guilty but refuse to cooperate. Which means I would be throwing myself on the mercy of the court. The prosecutor was going to want his pound of flesh. My hope was in God. I had surrendered my life to Him and had to believe that what every happened He would have my back if I did the right thing.'

Morgan sighs, "If you're lucky, you might come out of this okay. But there's nothing else I can do for you."

The next day, they transferred Morgan to a high-security facility in San Diego where they hid high-profile informants.

That morning while watering my lawn, I pondered what could have happened to me had Pablo Escobar gone ahead with his crazy plan. I did not doubt that when he focused his fanatically criminal mind on someone he would blow straight through their deceptions. He would instantly see that I am not a hardened criminal lusting for money and power. I would be an embarrassment to him. Better to just erase me out of existence. His go to solution was to kill what bothered him and to be safe, wipe out their family too. Problem solved.

Here is a key insight into who I am. I did not apply for training as a SEAL. It did not match up with my kinder softer character. As a bomb disposal frog, my job was to save lives. Worst case scenario, in a combat situation, I might have to kill with a bomb, bullet or even with my bare hands. Which I was perfectly willing to do and had trained for extensive with the martial arts. I would only kill to save others — period.

Faith is the strength by which a shattered world shall emerge into the light. — Helen Keller

In July, the government offers a deal. I have been waiting for this knowing how badly they wanted me out of the case. I hope that it will be acceptable. As anticipated, they want me out of the case before DeLorean's trial begins. Hanging over their offer is the threat of the full weight of the DOJ and a promise to bury me behind bars. If I plead guilty to two counts, one for conspiracy and the other for smuggling, they will drop possession, which was rather obvious — it was never my cocaine. There was no offer of minimum sentencing. I could get 15 years for each.

'This is a deal?' I asked myself. However, they agreed not to file additional charges, such as a certain airplane trip to Colombia.

On the 25th of July, marshals take me to the courthouse. After the usual long wait in the holding cells, they take me up to Judge Takasugi's courtroom. Rick is waiting at the defendant's table.

"We're not going to get a better deal than this," confided Rick. "If they charge you with your little jaunt down to Colombia then they also must bring charges against Stretch and Morgan's boys too. It complicates the deal they struck with them. Bottom line is they want you out of the case because you won't snitch, and they need their snitches out because they got protection and are liable to say something they shouldn't. It's all about getting DeLorean."

Just then, Judge Takasugi steps out of his chambers and into the court. The proceedings I have waited for so long, take all of five minutes. The judge accepts my guilty plea then orders me to return to court in two months for sentencing.

* * *

I am walking in the cellblock doing the corridor promenade. It helps to burn off my nervous energy. I follow inmate etiquette of looking at the tiled floor to avoid eye contact with the three other walkers. It is a modest effort at privacy that can get you beat up or stabbed for not observing this simple courtesy.

Abruptly, I notice the three other walkers eagerly gathering at the door that leads to the guard's office and the attorney visiting room. Other inmates' sense something is up as I walk up to the thick window and peer over the shoulders of a rapidly growing crowd. The guard is talking with a stunningly attractive woman. She glances at the window, which is full of lust-filled eyes and is about to look away, but then she turns back, meets my eyes, and smiles. She said something to the guard.

Unreal, I am avoiding looking people in the eyes, and suddenly I have a striking woman making direct eye contact with me in the J-3 corridor. It is overwhelmingly exciting and a bit weird.

The guard unlocks the door. "Back, perverts," he snarled

The men in front barely move as they shuffle to keep the men behind them from crowding forward.

"Arrington," barked the guard, "in here, now."

The inmates part reluctantly to let me through. One of them quipped, "Lucky dog." The guard closes the door behind me.

"Hello," said the woman offering her hand, "my name is Ginger Hartman. I am the federal probation officer assigned to prepare your pre-sentencing report."

I unsuccessfully try not to stare as I take her hand. Her skin is soft and smooth, her grip firm—it has been almost a year since a woman has touched me. I revel in the touch, trying not to show it. Ginger is a tall, athletic, sophisticated woman in her thirties. For her visit to our cellblock, she is wearing a white silk blouse with the top buttons undone and a tight black skirt that complements her long, shapely legs. She is wearing black stiletto high heels. Ginger has my, the guard's, and the drooling pack of fools' in the J-3 corridor complete attention.

"Want me to hang around?" The guard asked hopefully.

"Not necessary," Ginger favored him with a smile, "our conversation is confidential."

The thought of being alone with Ginger is so very appealing that I smile at the guard. He frowns. I will pay for that smile.

"Come with me," said Ginger as she steps into the attorney visiting room. I notice how the stiletto heels complement her long legs and try not to stare at her tight skirt. She turns and catches me, but then offers a friendly smile as she closes the door.

'Now that was rather provocative,' I thought happily.

Inside, there is a table with two chairs. Ginger tells me to sit then walks around to the other side of the table. She picks up a chair and carries it back to my side. She sits down facing me and crosses one leg over the other. I hear the whisper of her nylons as one-leg brushes over the other. Her perfume wafts lightly in the close room. I try not to stare at her glossy red lipstick and slightly pouting mouth. I have not been this close to a woman in so long, I could easily spend hours just looking at her, as could the rest of the cellblock. The inmates are still crowded four-deep at the security door with high hopes, though they cannot see her. They will wait however long it takes for another look at Ginger.

On a professional level, Ginger should be sitting across the table from me. As a representative of the court, her attire should be demure and conservative. I do not doubt the woman is using her sexuality to lure me into talking. I don't stand a chance.

Ginger takes a legal pad and places it on the table, then leans towards me. She takes a deep breath, which puts a serious strain on the third from the top button. The woman just doesn't play fair.

"I'm here to take a statement for the court in your own words as to how you became involved with Morgan Hetrick and John Z. DeLorean," she said in a slightly husky voice.

"How do I rate such a good-looking parole officer?" I quipped trying not to look at her blouse. Ginger is a real pro at dealing with lonely inmates who are starved for attention.

"It's a government plot," she said smiling with those rouged lips. "You're supposed to tell me everything you know."

Her words are like a thrown bucket of ice water. What she writes, and what I say to her is going to have a huge impact on my prison sentence. I lean back trying to escape from the mood she is creating; only the truth will serve me well here.

"I'll tell what I did, but I won't snitch on anyone," I said firmly.

Ginger looks up from her notepad, "Actually, with Morgan, his sons, and the pilot you flew with all cooperating, I doubt that you have anything new to tell us."

"I will be completely honest with you," I offered sincerely. "I stupidly got caught up with some very sophisticated criminals. I didn't know how to get out of it without being killed."

Ginger leans forward and looks deeply into my eyes, she places a hand on my knee, and blinks, "So tell me about it."

In prison, you are so very alone. I have been holding so much inside of me, and suddenly it becomes critical that Ginger understand why I am not snitching. I know what she is up to with her hand on my leg. Yet, I sense she is sincerely after the truth.

"I want to tell you the reason why I am not cooperating," I said decisively. "I deserve to do the time. Snitching would make my incarceration more difficult. Putting my time off on someone else and their families, just doesn't fit well with me."

Ginger stares, "You're not going to ask for time served?"

I manage a weak smile. "I can't blame Morgan for what I did. When he told me, he was a drug smuggler, I should have run, but I didn't. I am guilty despite the manipulations."

Ginger sweeps a lock of red hair from her green eyes. "So, what kind of a sentence should we ask for?" she asked staring so deeply into my eyes that surely, she must be glimpsing my soul.

My answer leaps out on its own, unexpectedly, "Five years."

Ginger looks startled. My quick response even surprised me. But it feels good and right with my soul. My deepest hope for a workable release date is putting out its first questing root.

I looked away from Ginger and stared at the wall. "A five-year sentence means I could be out in three years on good behavior. It's enough time to learn my lesson, but not so much that prison might change me from who I am."

Ginger regards me carefully, "Morgan admitted that he twisted your arm, but you're right that you still have to be punished."

Ginger stands and offers her hand. As I take it, I feel her fingers wrap around mine, "Steve, let your positive attitude continue to lead you. So many inmates come back after such high hopes, but I somehow know I won't see you in prison again."

She called for the guard, then said, "I hope you get five years."

She picks up her briefcase and walks through the security door to the outside corridor without looking back. Her delicate perfume lingers in her wake.

The guard snickered "How about that; she's hoping you get a five-year sentence. What did you do to upset her?"

"Upset?" I queried. "I'm hoping for the same thing."

* * *

On August 25, riding to court in the marshals' van, I am as nervous as a long-tailed cat in a room full of grandmothers in rocking chairs.

Two hours later, I sit anxiously in the courtroom watching the prosecutor's assistant, Mr. Phillips, presenting their case. He points an accusing finger at me and says, "The United States of America charges Stephen Arrington..." his words hammered at me like physical blows. He argued that by not cooperating, I am hindering the war on drugs. He talked about my prior trouble in the Navy (two ounces of marijuana) and references the $55,000,000 supposed value of cocaine that I delivered. He then told the judge about my airplane trip to Colombia to pick up 650 pounds of cocaine. Then added that because of my plea-bargain agreement, I, unfortunately, could not be charged for that offense. However, the judge should certainly consider it for my sentencing.

Mr. Phillips is again pointing his finger at me. "Though Count 2 Possession was dropped as part of his plea bargain, he did plead guilty to Count 3 Conspiracy to deliver 220 lbs. of cocaine to Mr. John Z. DeLorean. A substantial sentence is warranted here. This is a major, major case and the punishment should far exceed any possibility of reward.".

I was sitting there astounded. I had foolishly assumed that because of my plea bargain the airplane trip wouldn't be introduced into the sentencing trial, let alone without accompanying evidence, nor mitigating circumstances. I also had nothing to do with the 225 lb. DeLorean conspiracy. I had driven a car with 25 lbs. of cocaine with little or no forewarning. I felt betrayed, yet again Mickey Doke's words echo through my mind, 'You're not as smart as you think you are.'

Note: This and all following statements are public record.

Judge Takasugi asked a few questions of his own. "Sir, do you have any evidence that Mr. Arrington knew anything about this drug scheme before he took possession of the car or that he was part of the supposed conspiracy with Hetrick and DeLorean?

The prosecutor bobs and weaves as he takes over a minute to essentially say, "No."

The Judge continued, "Do you believe that Mr. Arrington has made any money off of this or any other crime and is there any possibility that he may have hidden any money away?"

The prosecutor looked unhappy as he concocted a long answer that ends with, "No, with Hetrick cooperating, we have complete access to all the appropriate bank records and accounts."

"You may sit down," said the judge.

My defense attorney, Richard Barnett, then stands up. He references my long list of community service. He notes I have been a volunteer CPR and First Aid instructor for the Red Cross for over a dozen years. He talks about my 14-year military career during which I made four tours to Vietnam and earned the Naval Commendation Medal, the Navy's highest non-combat award for lifesaving. He tells how I had risked my life as a bomb disposal frogman while engaged in dangerous missions for the Navy, the Secret Service, and one for the CIA. He references my preventing the launch of a Tom Cat fighter possibly saving two pilot's lives which can be authenticated in Naval Records. He points out that I resisted involvement in Morgan's criminal enterprise and that Morgan used threats and manipulation to force my cooperation.

Rick concluded his arguments, "We admit that Mr. Arrington is indeed guilty, but we are talking about two multimillionaires allegedly involved in a conspiracy and a young man who only had twenty dollars in his pocket when he arrived on the scene. A severe sentence is neither appropriate nor fair when you consider the level of his involvement and his significant resistance to participating in the first place."

Next, it is my turn. The reporters have packed the court. I must begin twice because my voice cracks with emotion as I try to speak. "The greatest words I have ever heard were, 'Federal agents, you are under arrest.' Those words freed me from a nightmare. I had been living a life of deceit. I did things I was afraid not to do. When Agent Scotti arrested me, he later said, 'Well, I guess this isn't the best day of your life.' I replied, 'Actually, I think it is.' My arrest was a new beginning. Those officers rescued me from a life that was wildly out of control."

"From my jail cell, I asked my attorney, not to request a bail reduction because, in prison, I was coming to terms with what I had done. I knew that the earlier I began serving my sentence, the sooner I could be a productive member of society again.

"As a Christian, I now know that good must come of all things. I want to share what I have learned from this situation. As soon as I am able, I would like to speak to high-school students about drug abuse and the realities of prison life. I want to prevent youths from falling into the same traps as me. Sir, I know that my crime calls for punishment, and I am prepared to pay my debt to society. Your Honor, I am sorry for what I have done and am ready for sentencing." Shaken, I sat down.

The clerk's voice is abruptly loud and impersonal as he orders, "The defendant will stand for sentencing."

I jump to my feet, fold my hands before me.

Judge Takasugi looks at Mr. Phillips, "Mr. Arrington's trip to Colombia cannot be ignored, nor should it be."

He shifts his gaze to Ginger Hartman, who is sitting in the front row in a stunning red skirt and jacket with a white silk blouse. "On the other hand," he continued, "there is a swell of supporting letters on behalf of Mr. Arrington, and a very, very positive Pre-Sentencing Report, and certain favorable aspects that were cited by Mr. Barrnet in his argument."

"Based on these factors," the judge peered solemnly at me over his glasses then calmly reads the sentence from his notes. "Mr. Arrington, for count one, I sentence you to five years. For count two, I sentence you to an additional five years." After a pregnant pause, he continued, "Both sentences will run concurrently. I also sentence you to three years special parole." The judge smacked his gavel down, "Court dismissed." *Author's note: A concurrent sentence means I will serve both sentences as one.*

Far away, there in the sunshine are my highest aspirations. I may not reach them, but I can look up and see their beauty, believe in them, and try to follow where they lead. — Louisa May Alcott

My J-3 Bucket. Illustration by Stetcyn Leigh Arrington

* * *

A week later, the North Yard guard comes for me. After over ten months in J-3, it takes just seconds to empty my locker into a small box. I left the bucket by the lawn in the hope that some kind soul would continue to water the lawn.

As I stand at the North Yard door looking out, there is a deep sense of dread lurking as I prepare to face real dangers. My hope outweighs my fears. I am ready to go forward in life, and that path leads into a concrete-and-steel jungle where depraved logic rules and human predators prowl looking for prey.

I am carrying a quote in my mind by M. H. McKee, a cerebral blueprint on how to model the rest of my life, "*Integrity is one of several paths, it distinguishes itself from the others because it is the right path and the only one upon which you will never get lost.*"

Finally, the North Yard guard opens the door, yet I stand there unable to move. Despite the beckoning sunshine, I am paralyzed. Every time I passed through this portal; I have worn handcuffs. Conditioned to orders, I look dubiously at the guard, who says, "So take off, Arrington, you know the drill."

With the box under one arm and integrity riding along like a hopeful passenger, I walk across the immensity of the North Yard. I felt naked and exposed to the harsh glare of general population inmates who stop what they are doing to watch new meat entering their domain. I glance backward at J-3, noting how small the building looks from the outside.

I wonder at a feeling of extreme joy as I move from jail inmate to sentenced felon. How do I explain the desire to belong somewhere, even if it is just a bunk inside *Chez Clink*?

I open the door to A Unit (Animal House) and step into the dim interior. A guard at the front desk gives me a bunk assignment. I count bunks in search of mine. At number 34, I stop and stare in acute disappointment. The lower bunk is covered with a disgusting array of stains, much of the bed's stuffing is missing, it resembles a filthy rag more than a mattress.

Unfortunately, the bed is the good news when compared with my new bunkmates. Four men are present in the eight-man cubicle. They are a mixed bag of druggies who at midday are high. One of them lays on my bunk drooling onto the pillow. Another squat in a corner with his head nodding back and forth as he tries to keep loose contact with reality. The other two are a couple of idiots staring at me with open hostility. I know that they will be up most of the night shooting up with heroin or cocaine. Since all their money goes for drugs, they cannot buy stuff from the prison store so they will be thieves. It means that there will be a lot of fighting and arguing, particularly at night.

I step past the two men staring at me. They are a scruffy lot with bandanas tied low on their foreheads. One is tall and lanky, the other short and dumpy. They both glare as they watch me store my few items in the rusted metal locker. "Hey, you got any cigarettes? The dumpy one inquired gruffly.

I stare at the misfits, "Don't smoke."

Dumpy looks like a puffed-up toad. "What about candy?" he asked glaring menacingly from under his stained bandana.

"Why don't you just watch what I put in my locker, then you won't have to ask me any more questions."

Mr. Toad and Mr. Stork slink down the corridor leaving me alone with the drooling slob and the stoned black youth, who I now notice has vomited recently onto his shirt. I flee the gray cubicle and head for the beckoning sunlight outside.

I eagerly turn toward the breezeway and walk toward the South Yard. I notice men turning in my direction—new meat alert. The corridor is 20-feet wide with high gray walls open to the sky, and then there is the breezeway stretching into the distance. The ocean is suddenly a living presence that extends outward to infinity. I walk slowly next to the chain-link fence, staring at the water, listening to the liquid sound of it lapping at the rocks and the occasional squawk of seagulls.

I arrive at the South Yard and see a baseball field of lush grass and wonder who waters it. There is a small dormitory, the Honor Dorm with coveted single-occupancy rooms. A debilitated building for the weight room. Most of its windows are broken out, a door hangs by one hinge and white paint is peeling from its walls.

I walk the yard's perimeter until the loudspeakers announce noon count time. I must hurry back to Animal House for count standing beside or lying upon my bunk. I do not look forward to meeting the rest of the midnight crew in the cubicle. I hear them arguing. To get to my bunk, which is now vacant, I must walk past two husky black men. They scowled and moved to block my way.

"What do you want?" demanded the larger of the two.

"You're standing in front of my bunk," I answered.

"Ain't your bunk," retorted the black man. "You've been moved white boy, Sanchez cleared out your stuff."

Wondering what is going on and where my few possessions have gone, I wander the dormitory and run into Sanchez.

"Hey, Steve, so they finally let you out of J-3." Sanchez had been one of the more normal men in J-3. "Check out this bunk," he said with a wink. "Think it's an improvement over number 34 and the sleaze patrol that slums there?"

Sanchez's hand is resting on a top bunk with a thick three-inch mattress, clean sheets, and an un-holed blanket. The bunk stands against a window with—an ocean view!

"For me," I gasped.

Sanchez beams, "You are standing in the older-inmates-having-things wing of Animal House."

The other men in the cubicle are mature businessmen, all are in for white-collar crimes. By the wealth of expensive clothes, they are men of influence. They voted me in for entertainment reasons. Celebrity inmate status paying dividends.

Lying on my new bunk I stare out the window. The panes are regular glass. There is no warping to spoil the view, just the ever-present jail bars. There is a flat 12-foot wide cement slab, and then a chain link fence. Seven yards from the window, the Ocean laps on moss-laced and seaweed-covered rocks. Some panes are broken out, I gratefully inhale the ocean smell.

After the count, I head for the chow hall, where I hear my name called. I turn to see Clayton.

"Hi, Jailbait," he laughed. "Welcome to the belly of the beast. Come on," he said putting a hand on my back, "let's do lunch."

We step through double doors into a vast chow hall that is a ruckus of noise. Two long rows of inmates stretch along the walls in twin food lines. Looking at the violent men, I think that this is the last line someone would try cutting then I watch it happen.

Heads turn as an enormous black man arrives merrily calling out greetings in a softened baritone. He is almost seven feet tall, weighs over 300 pounds, has massive shoulders, and a big gut. His shiny pink T-shirt only covers half of his gut as he prances between tables. He is wearing white nylon shorts that are busting at the seams leaving his drooping pimpled cheeks exposed. He has large, pink plastic curlers in his curly hair and a blue silk scarf tied around his beefy neck. His caked-on makeup under a black light would send a clown into therapy. He sashays to the front of the line and takes a tray as two gang members hurriedly step out of his way.

"What is that?" I whispered a little too loudly.

"Shush," cautioned Clayton, "that is Tiffany, AKA, the Tiff."

"Does he belong to the gay gang?"

"Nope, the Tiff is a gang. Everyone is afraid of him."

"He looks kind of, well, oddly friendly."

Tiffany is flirting with everyone around him, and every inmate is being extremely polite in return.

"That's the problem. When Tiffany falls in love, it makes no difference to him if it's just a one-sided affair."

At the serving line, most of the food is picked over. It is slim pickings for a vegetarian. Peanut butter and jelly sandwiches loom large in my future.

After 4:00 PM count, I head back down to the South Yard to watch my first sunset of 1983. I walk the yard's inner perimeter stopping under a row of eucalyptus trees to smell the pods, then sit down on the grass and lean my back against a tree trunk. It feels good to rest against something other than concrete. Imagine not touching a tree for almost a year — only concrete or steel.

To the west, I gaze at the sun, while it slowly descends behind the rolling hills of San Pedro. As the day fades to dusk, lights flicker to life on the darkening hillside. The seaport's streets come alive with moving ribbons of vehicular light, flashing yellows, glowing reds, and glistening whites. Traffic lights blink or flicker to their own rhythm, while the setting sun silhouettes the sloping hillside in a bright red halo. I spend the early evening wandering the South Yard watching the lights glistening in the darkness.

Abruptly I hear live music. It is coming from the channel of Los Angeles Harbor. I step up to the fence as the music swells, then I hear laughter and the tinkle of happy voices raised in celebration. Suddenly, appearing from behind a large, darkened warehouse, I see brilliant lights floating upon the dark water, sparkling whites, merry reds, warm blues, and emerald greens as a cruise ship heads out to sea. I hear a woman laughing. The sound touches my very core. I have not heard a woman laugh since my incarceration. I can see just a small section of the cruise liner at a time. I watch the great white ship slip from view, and then the laughter and the music fade as the moment is broken by a sharp, magnified voice, "Count time, count time."

I turn reluctantly away from the multicolored lights and walk back up the breezeway with the gentle sound of small waves breaking on the rocks, and I know deep in my heart that I am truly a very blessed and fortunate inmate.

That evening I sit upon my bunk staring out the window. In the distance is the Long Beach Naval Station, where I sailed for four tours to Vietnam and saw much of Asia. I have decided to re-exam my life beginning where it went wrong. When I met Morgan Hetrick is a good starting point.

* * *

I arrived at Point Mugu Naval Station in 1972 as a support diver assigned to the EOD (Explosive Ordnance Disposal) Team. As a brand-new diver, I was inexperienced and clueless. My first dive with Red Charlie, my Commanding Officer, was a disaster. But, diving became my passion. I took a basic scuba class, followed by a rescue diver course, then a dive master class, and within six months an instructor course. Charlie could hardly believe that his klutz support diver was abruptly the base scuba instructor.

That is how I met Morgan Hetrick. I had taught his secretary to scuba dive. She asked if I could certify her multimillionaire boss.

Morgan was a gifted flier and an engineering genius. He was Bill Lear's personal pilot for the Lear Jet Corporation. While there, he tinkered with ways to improve the plane's performance. He developed the first anti-skid system for Lear Jets, which led to him starting Morgan Aviation. He leased a large hanger at the Oxnard Airport. Lear jets flew in from across the nation to get his brake system upgrade.

Morgan saw another unique opportunity to make money with a 1956 version of a French military training jet, the Morane-Saulnier MS 760 Paris Jet. He claimed to have bought it from a man way ahead of his time. John E. Morgan, AKA Johnny Skyrocket, was also known as the father of private jet flying for the public market. However, his company in Las Vegas went bankrupt and Morgan Hetrick, with a co-investor, bought up his remaining inventory. He planned to convert the military trainers into the Morgan Paris Jet II and sell them for $300,000 each. It was the only four-passenger private jet available for under a million bucks.

Morgan's house had a dock in wealthy Mandalay Bay. He had a 32-foot Hatteras yacht for cruising at high speed to the Channel Islands. That was why he took up scuba diving, but he did not have a dive card. He had taken a scuba class but had not done the open water part. We went out to the Channel Islands where we made several dives. I found him to be competent, so I issued him a dive card. We became friends though he was 20 years older. He would hire me to go out on his yacht to teach his friends to scuba dive. Then Morgan discovered that I knew many young ladies. Being a scuba instructor was a terrific way to meet women. For some, Morgan's age and looks mattered little because of his expensive toys and eager willingness to shower the women with lavish gifts.

Morgan was a master at how to impress a money-susceptible woman, and I was along for the ride. He had me drive his Fleetwood motorhome up to Reno Airport in Nevada. He would fly up with our dates in the Morgan Paris II jet for the weekend. I would drive them up to Mount Rose Ski Resort where Morgan and his date would stay in one of the deluxe suites. My girl and I stayed in the Fleetwood. We flew back to Oxnard leaving the Fleetwood at the Reno Airport for the ski season.

I was having the most fun of my life and earning money for it. I would invite women to go diving on Morgan's yacht. Diving off a commercial dive boat is an expensive and crowded experience. Lunch is usually peanut butter and jelly sandwiches, and someone always gets seasick. Vomit smells have a way of damping appetites. On Morgan's yacht, *everything was first class. Usually there would be three to four women to the two of us. For a 24-year-old Navy diver, who had never had much of anything, Morgan was a dream come true. From middle school on, I had part-time jobs to help support mom and me. Now, I was living the high life. Just out of a bad marriage, I was on a wild streak.*

Growing up without a father at home, I followed my values, which was not a very high bar. I had no moral compass. My scuba class at Point Mugu was always full. I had free access to a 50-meter pool, a classroom, and the use of an 85' Navy drone recovery vessel for a high-speed dive boat. I only had to pay the crew $85 a trip. The base commander, an admiral, loved scuba diving and was pleased to offer it to naval personnel and their families and the civilian employees. The Admiral also had a stunningly attractive 20-year-old daughter, but that is another story.

That was about the time that my Commanding Officer, Red Charlie, transferred out to Hawaii. I missed Charlie a lot. He had become my first mentor and father figure. I respected his judgment. However, he had a rather low opinion of Morgan Hetrick and did not think he was a good influence on me. In hindsight, I wish I paid more attention to his advice.

* * *

While attached to the Point Mugu EOD Team, I was living in a single's complex in Oxnard. I was in my apartment on a Saturday when the telephone rang. A nurse lived across the hall from me, and she was calling because they had an unconscious diver in the emergency room.

At the EOD building, we had a recompression chamber, and I was an inside medical tender and a hyperbaric chamber supervisor. The nurse told the emergency room doctor about me and he was asking for my help.

I showed up at the emergency room in shorts and a T-shirt. I was a rather laid-back kind of guy. My nurse friend thought it would be a better idea to put me in hospital scrubs before I went into the emergency room. The patient was an overweight, middle-aged man who had surfaced unconscious from a 100-foot dive. That meant the prognosis was cerebral air embolism, which was almost always fatal. The diver needed to get into a recompression chamber fast, or he would die. Our chamber was down for maintenance, so I got on the phone and arranged for another chamber 50 air miles away. The ER doc called for helicopter transport. We needed to meet the chopper at the Oxnard Airport.

We rushed the patient down a corridor on a gurney where the physician stopped a passing nurse. "Roxanne, you're coming with us. I need you to prepare injections for me," he ordered.

Outside an ambulance was waiting with the back door open. The attendant helped to slide the patient in, then both he and the physician climbed inside the back. The nurse started to follow, but the doctor said, "It's too tight back here, you two ride up front."

Opening the passenger door, I paused as I saw a single bucket seat.

"Get in," ordered Roxanne, "I'll sit on your lap."

She settled onto my lap and the driver floored it.

I looked at her and grinned. Roxanne was athletic and very attractive.

While preparing injections, Roxanne tilted towards me for stability. She passed a syringe to the physician, then leaned close and whispered into my ear, "This is so exciting!"

"Oh, yeah," I agreed.

"Do you think they'll let me go up in the helicopter?" she asked hopefully.

"I certainly hope so," I answered while wondering if she and I might need to share another seat together.

Halfway to the airport, the patient went into full arrest. We dashed back to the hospital, but it was too late.

The physician shook my hand and said, "Thanks for coming in on such short notice."

"Call me anytime," I smiled at him. I turned towards Roxanne, just as the head nurse took her away. I walked disappointedly out of the emergency room. I returned to my apartment somewhat despondent that I did not ask Roxanne for her telephone number.

The next morning the nurse across the hall knocked on my door. She smiled as she handed me a scrap of paper, "Roxanne said that since she already had the privilege of sitting on your lap, you might as well have her telephone number."

Roxanne and I became quite the number. I even stopped chasing other women, which bothered Morgan Hetrick to no end. Within a month, Roxanne was making sutle marrage hints. That is until she realized that I was not a Navy doctor.

"You're not a doctor?" she asked with a look of horror.

"What made you think I was a doctor?" I asked startled.

"You were in the emergency room wearing scrubs. The ER Doc was asking you questions. You were consulting with him, and he was taking your advice. He doesn't take advice from anyone except another physician. Why wouldn't I think you were a doctor?"

"I'm a Navy diver who operates a hyperbaric chamber," I said looking at her in a questioning way. "I know how to treat diving maladies, which the doctor found helpful, but I was mostly there to help arrange for a recompression chamber."

Roxanne looked at me and blinked.

That was the sudden end of our relationship. However, Roxanne would have an unfortunate lasting impact on me. She liked to smoke marijuana and encouraged me to join her. I had rarely tried marijuana, usually at a party when I was under the influence of a couple of beers. I wasn't into it. As a diver, I did not want to compromise my lungs in any way. Roxanne pushed me to smoke marijuana with her on every date.

Many argue that marijuana is not habit forming. However, its mind-altering effect can certainly become habit forming. Later, in Hawaii, it became a problem for me as in the islands it was socially acceptable, very available and packed a significant higher amount of THC (the active mind-altering ingredient in marijuana).

* * *

As a Christian, I have a certain perspective about life. I believe our lives are like a spiritual garden. Through our actions and choices, we determine what is growing in our garden. Roxanne planted a weed in my garden that I would through my actions encourage to grow. There was a swampy area in my garden, it wasn't pleasant to walk through. Giving my life to Jesus Christ meant repenting a lifetime of sins. Now, there is no swamp, nor weeds in my garden. It is beautiful and a pleasure to walk through. I have an obligation to share the gifts God has given me. This book is an important part of my work as a Christian.

As social creatures, we like to do things with others. I have learned that when someone is doing something good, they want family and friends to join them. Unfortunately, when someone is doing something wrong, they usually target certain friends and sometimes family members encouraging them to share in that wrongness.

Roxanne opened a door into a world that only promised trouble. I chose to step into that shadow world because she was exotic and alluring. Our relationship was founded on a lie. She was only attracted to me because she thought I was a doctor. I was attracted to her not because of her good nature, nor her values or even a sense of happiness at being together. My physical desire for her overrode any sensibility that might have saved me from a bad path. In 1974, marijuana was an illegal substance. That is key to the argument I am presenting. To obtain a prohibited drug meant that I would seek out and associate with people who were prone to choose poorly. Corrupting influences are the gift of association with people of compromised character. So, my problems, did not begin with Morgan Hetrick, nor did they begin with Roxanne – they began with me.

* * *

The EOD Team at Point Mugu also supported marine operations at Vandenberg Air Force Base, which was up the coast. Jerry Fountaine and

I were sent there to participate in a top-secret operation purposely leaked to the Russians. The Secretary of State, Dr. Henry Kissinger, was in negotiations with the Russian General Secretary, Leonid Brezhnev, to limit strategic arms, and President Reagan wanted an edge. The Air Force came up with a radical idea--drop an 87,000-pound, 56-foot long Minuteman Intercontinental Ballistic Missile (ICBM) out of the back of a C-5 Galaxy Airlifter from an altitude of 20,000 feet. Twin parachutes would extract the missile on a specially designed carriage.

Minuteman ICBM being extracted from a C-5 Galaxy.
Photo United States Air Force

When the missile stabilized vertically, it separated from the carriage. Next, three parachutes deployed from the nose of the ICBM to keep it vertical. At an altitude of 9,000 feet, the parachutes fell away, and a timer fired the missile's engine. It was a spectacular success never to be repeated, and it brought the Russians to the negotiation table. They had no answer to this new strategic advantage.

During the launch at the Air Force's Pacific Missile Test Range, a Russian spy trawler was just outside the ten-mile international water's boundary monitoring the test.

The Russian strategy in the event of total war with the USA had been to do a preemptive thermonuclear strike on our ICBM farms (multiple silos laid out on a large grid). That strategy just got tossed into the trash can. We proved we could launch an ICBM with three independently targeted nuclear warheads in Russia from anywhere in the world. We had 105 C-5 Galaxy Transports, which means lots of incoming nuclear warheads from anywhere on the planet. It was a game changer!

This was a daring operation with a high risk of catastrophic failure. During the drop, the crew of the C-5 Galaxy was in danger if anything dramatic went wrong, such as the missile getting stuck partially outside the cargo bay with two large parachutes deployed in the C-5's jet stream.

That could drag the whole aircraft down. This almost happened during a previous test of an inert package. Fortunately, the crew managed to free it. Also, there was the threat of the Galaxy going into a nose-up vertical stall from an instantaneous change in the center of gravity with the dropping of an 87,000-pound package.

There was one more person under serious threat, that being me in a 12-foot-long IBS (inflatable boat small), with Jerry Fountaine running the outboard. We were alongside a USN minesweeper waiting for the package to fall into the ocean. The minesweeper was tracking the test with its radar to direct us to the point of impact for the ICBM carriage.

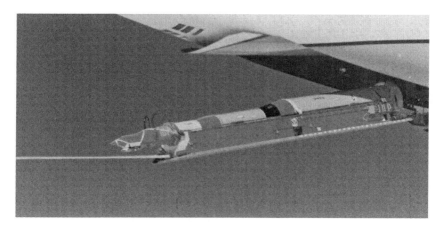

The ICBM rests on a contoured Styrofoam cushion.

The radio I held squawked, "Package splashdown in 90 seconds, 400 yards to port at ten 0-clock off our bow."

Fountaine opens the throttle wide. He needs to get us close. It comes down fast splashing into the ocean not 30 feet from us. I jump into the water to sink it. The carriage is floating vertically. The top of it extends five feet out the water. I swim through floating parachutes and shroud lines to pry away the ICBM's Styrofoam bed to sink the carriage. I fear that it could take me down with it if I am snagged by shroud lines or get wrapped into a sinking parachute like a sailor of old; sewn into a canvas sack with weights, and dumped overboard — as in burial at sea.

The carriage and its parachutes are a hazard to navigation, but if the Russians got the sled, it would be a significant intelligence haul. So, the whole package must go to the bottom of the ocean. I do my cutting and prying bit until there is just a foot of carriage floating out of the water. Then I cut a hole in a large section of Styrofoam and do a little careful prying. The whole time there is a swell running, the sled is bobbing and dipping. It scares me that a dip might become a sudden plunge, and off I would go on a 3000-foot plummet to the dark seabed far below.

Using my K-Bar knife, I cut a hole in a big chunk of Styrofoam and tie a rope to it. It is scary having to swim back to the IBS while avoiding dozens of floating shroud lines and two parachutes. I pull myself up onto the IBS and give the rope a gentle tug to pull out slack. The result is spectacular. The Styrofoam chunk spits out and the carriage goes down fast. The shroud lines and parachutes race across the surface creating a turbulent wake that disappears into the depths. The rope abruptly jerks from my hand as a taunt shroud line rips the floating Styrofoam section in half. One piece of the foam remains bobbing on the surface – the other half with my rope is on a race to the seabed thousands of feet below.

"Wow," exclaimed Fountaine staring at the severed block of foam, "that could have been you."

* * *

Statement by Red Charlie Morgan CW4:

Stephen Arrington reported to the Navy EOD Detachment at Point Mugu, California in 1972 as a Petty Officer 1st Class. I was his commanding officer and realized he was very intelligent to have earned that rank with only six years in the Navy. He had just graduated from the Naval Deep-Sea Diving School in Washington DC and reported in as a support diver.

Steve's first dive with the command was with me so I could assess his diving ability. As we sat in our IBS (Inflatable Boat Small), I asked Steve, "Ready to enter the water?"

He replied, "How do I do that?"

I was shocked; it should have been a big hint. I said, "Just hold to your facemask and roll in backward."

We swam down to a depth of 80 feet to search for a dummy ASROC (anti-submarine rocket attached to a Mk 46 torpedo) launched from a ship. We had a 100-foot circling line for laying a search grid. I was teaching Steve how to use a handheld sonar. We each had a set of earphones attached to the sonar.

As I slowly scanned the sandy seabed with the sonar looking for the torpedo, we heard a pinging of an object rapidly closing on us. Suddenly a dark object shot out of the gloom – it was only three feet away when we saw it. A huge sea lion was homing in on the sonar beam, and when it spotted us, it veered up and passed right over Steve's shoulder.

Abruptly, the sonar was tugged from my hand. I turned and saw that Steve was trying to swim for the surface, so I grabbed his ankle. He looked at me, and all I could see in his facemask were two huge eyes. He moved his fingers to gesture "bite" for "shark," and I gestured back, "no."

He had become entangled in the circling line and somehow had lost his knife, at which point I terminated the dive.

Back aboard the rubber boat, I asked Steve, "How many open water dives have you made?"

He replied, "Just this one."

"How could this be your first ocean dive?" I asked.

"Our school was on the Patuxent River in Washington DC. We never went out into the actual ocean."

Steve was a quick learner because six months later he had earned his NAUI certification to teach diving and was working on his off hours as a dive instructor at the Navy base.

That was where he met Morgan Hetrick, who wanted Steve to teach him to dive. Morgan had a 32-foot long yacht and plenty of money and enjoyed hosting beautiful women from Steve's diving classes aboard his party boat on weekends.

When Steve would return to the detachment on Monday, he would entertain us with stories of his fabulous weekend. Hetrick owned an airplane manufacturing business and Steve was overly impressed by his wealth.

I was concerned about Steve's relationship with Mr. Hetrick. Steve was only 24 years old and very naïve. I cautioned him that if the situation seemed too good to be true, it probably was. That turned out to be good advice. Steve's relationship with Hetrick was a cause of his future problems.

One Sunday, I went to the detachment and found Steve there with an attractive young woman. The EOD building is in a restricted area of the base. I called Steve aside and explained this was unsatisfactory, and he needed to take her out of the area immediately. He explained that she was attending his SCUBA diving class and wanted to see the recompression chamber. When he introduced her, I realized that she was the Base Commander's daughter. I about lost it. I could picture myself in front of the admiral explaining why his daughter was in my restricted building all alone with this rascal.

In 1974, I was transferred to Hawaii. In 1976, Steve was also transferred to Hawaii. He had graduated from EOD School and promoted to the rank of Chief Petty Officer.

After transferring to the EOD detachment at Bangor Submarine Base in Washington State in 1976, I learned about Steve's arrest for selling marijuana and his court-martial.

When asked to write a letter on Steve's behalf for the court-martial I did. I wrote that Steve had been an asset to my team at Point Mugu and had shown that he was of good character. I was disappointed that he had used and sold marijuana, which appropriately ended his naval career.

In 1982, I got a phone call from an EOD friend who said, "Your man Arrington was arrested last night by the DEA in possession of millions of dollars' worth of cocaine."

One evening in 1988, while watching a Jacques Cousteau documentary on television, I heard Jean-Michel Cousteau say, "Chief Diver Steve Arrington." I was shocked. My Navy EOD friend called to ask, "Was that the Steve Arrington we know?"

I met with Steve while on a trip to San Diego. He had called to let me know that he was working for Cousteau, and we met for dinner. My wife and I are honored to be the godparents for one of Steve's daughters. I am glad to have Steve back in my life and to know his wonderful family. His story gives hope to others who have made life-changing mistakes.

Life is a traveling to the edge of knowledge, then a leap taken. — D.H. Lawrence

Chapter 12 - Animal Unit, Sept 1983

The next morning I met with the Recreation Officer to request assignment to his department. "Why recreation?" he asked. "We pay the least. In the kitchen, you earn more, and you can lift food."

"I want to be in a department that makes people happy. I can run the theater's movie projector. I worked in a movie theater when I was 14-years old. They had a 1950's movie projector that I loved to watch it working. I spent my free time in the dark projection booth helping to thread the shiny 35 mm film through its pathways. It's an art to splice the film and load it onto the huge spinning drive platters with the right amount of tension. Then to thread the film through guide pullies up to the projector's synchronized gate, where toothed sprockets grab the film and thread it past the big projection lamp at 24 frames a second on its way to the recovery plater. Threading and splicing film is an art and I'm good at it. I can also help with the stage and I would really be into watering that baseball field in the South Yard."

"Yeah, the whole prison knows about your watering thing," he quipped. "Okay, so let's go water the baseball field."

I set out three large whirly bird sprinklers at one end of the field and slowly work my way to the other end. I only abandon the field for lunch and return with smuggled pieces of bread. It is for the birds that bathe in the shallow puddles of water on the grass.

Dragging the heavy hoses, watching the whirlybirds shooting their long wandering streams, dodging traveling spurts of falling water, and getting wet, I am completely in my element. I love water. It is why I became a diver. I have plenty of time for thinking. I pick up the memory thread after I left Point Mugu.

* * *

It is August 1975; I am at the Naval Explosive Ordnance Disposal School, which is south of Washington DC on the Potomac River. It is the first day of pool training, and I am swimming frantically. Taking a desperate breath of air, I peer underwater and see that Hank is two body-lengths ahead of me. Hank, a Navy SEAL, converting to EOD diver, is in superb physical condition. I lunge upward for a gulp of air, but then the 20-pound weight belt around my waist drags me back underwater. It is a buoyancy issue. My head weighs about ten pounds, but below the surface of the water, it is neutral.

The enclosed pool is 150 feet long, 70 feet wide, and 24 feet deep. It is an above ground, huge steel box inside a four-story building. The pool's wood plank deck is on the fourth floor. Floodlights hang from wooden ceiling rafters. At the pool's far wall, I see Hank do a flip turn despite his lead baggage. Then he shoots past me going the other way. I hit the wall and shove off. Surfacing for another breath, I hear my team cheering me on, but then I am back underwater — all too aware of the wild thumping of my heart. Hank touches the pool edge as a teammate dives over him into the water. Finally, I touch the edge and see a classmate diving over me. On the pool's deck the other students are screaming encouragement.

The instructors divided our class into two relay teams. The losers get to do 50 pushups before we go on a three-mile run in a forest.

I watch Hank propel himself up and out of the pool with a single push of his brawny arms. I struggle to get out of the water and then pass off my weight belt to the next frog candidate in line. As I watch the lead-weighted swimmers laboring across the pool, I have a disturbing thought. We are standing at one end of a long pool, and the swimmers are lumbering toward the other end with their lead handicap. I get out of line and walk cautiously over to our instructor, "Excuse me, Instructor McNair."

Master Chief Gunner's Mate McNair glares, then looks up my name on his clipboard, "What do you want, Candidate Arrington?"

"Don't you think I should maybe stand at the other end of the pool; in case someone gets in trouble?" I asked hopefully. Perhaps he will notice that I am thinking ahead — potential problem prevention. The best rescue is the one that is prevented, basic lifeguard training

Instructor McNair is from the South and strongly opinionated. He has a lanky build with deceptively strong ropey muscles and quick reflexes.

"Are you planning on being the class troublemaker?" asked McNair.

McNair is wearing mirrored sunglasses and a blue ball cap, even though we are in an indoor training facility. He looks less than friendly, like a rattlesnake eyeing a fat rodent blundering down a path.

"Just trying to help..." My words fade under the reptilian glare.

"This exercise is to see if you half-wits can swim with a load of lead and if not, have the good sense to drop the weight belt before drowning yourself. Go to the back of the line and give me 50 push-ups, clown."

Hank sees me drop for my penalty pushups. "Hooyah," he growled, which is a frogman shout of aggression for participating in physical training or combat. He drops alongside me, rapidly firing off four-dozen pushups followed by two one-arm ones.

I peer over my teammates and see that the fourth set of swimmers are now laboring across the water. Abruptly, at mid-pool, a swimmer begins to frantically dog paddle. He squeaks, gurgles, and chokes just before disappearing beneath the surface in a froth of wildly waving arms.

Running past the other men, I dive into the pool. Through the blur of being underwater, I see the student clawing upwards as he sinks rapidly toward the bottom. I swim to mid-pool and do a jackknife dive plunging downward. I am halfway down when Hank catches up with me. It is also when I run out of air. Oxygen deprived from the 50 pushups; I am on the verge of aborting. Abruptly, the student comes clawing upward minus his lead weight belt. Hank and I each grab an arm and head up with him.

On the surface, we assist the coughing man to the side of the pool where Instructor McNair is angrily pacing. "Hey, numbskull," he demanded. "What's with the drowning routine? Why didn't you drop that stupid weight belt sooner, idiot?"

"I guess I wasn't thinking," lamented the young man. I stare at a free-swinging three-inch-long strand of snot hanging from his nose.

McNair glares at him. "Bomb disposal frogmen always have to think clearly and decisively or people die. Obviously, you aren't cut from that fabric," said McNair consulting his clipboard. "You're Hopkins, right?"

"Yes sir," he nodded. The snot strand commands my attention, as it swings in sync with the motion of his head.

"Do not refer to me as sir. I am Instructor McNair or Gunner McNair. In any case, go clean out your locker, boy."

"Don't I get a second chance?" he pleaded, wiping the snot strand from his nose, and flinging it out toward the center of the pool.

"Not possible," McNair stated flatly, "this is not an elementary school recess situation boy. Explosive devices never give second chances. It is an initial success or spectacular failure."

In his gravelly voice, McNair says, "Go on, this job isn't for you."

Getting into EOD School is a long, arduous path. Thousands apply, yet few make it to training. We already lost two and now Hopkins has washed out. McNair growls, "What are you waiting for, Hopkins?"

Hopkins is a shattered man. He climbs out of the pool and with his feet slapping wetly on the wood plank floor walks dejectedly through the locker room doors. I watch the twin doors swinging back and forth. It is silent on the pool deck except for the slap of the water against the side of the pool.

Abruptly I see Instructor McNair glaring at me, "Arrington, who told you and your water rodent buddy that you could get into my pool?"

The locker room doors loom behind McNair as he orders, "Hank, fetch that weight belt. Arrington get rid of that wad of snot in my pool."

After a full load of punishment push-ups, sit-ups, and pull-ups, McNair takes us out for a three-mile run through a forest. Jogging three abreast on a dirt road, I ponder my rescue fiasco. Few of us frog candidates can expect to graduate. The dropout/failure rate usually takes 80% of the class. The few remaining graduates will join the Navy's elite Explosive Ordnance Disposal (EOD) Teams and participate in extraordinarily challenging adventures. When not involved as part of America's frontline of defense, bomb disposal frogs work with NASA's space program recovering reentry vehicles, deploy with Secret Service teams to protect domestic and foreign heads of state, participate in super-secret CIA operations, and top-secret military operations. A frog's job can include skydiving, helicopter water insertions, submarine lockouts, scuba diving to survey sunken wrecks, blowing up things in creative ways and touring the world on high-tech military operations. All these mission profiles can be life-threatening, which is why the command structure makes sure no one graduates who cannot be depended on in an emergency.

Listening to the cadence of our boots pounding along the dusty road, I think about where Hopkins' boots are now. He is probably in the administration building waiting for orders back to the fleet. Hopkins' blunder involved overlooking the obvious — not an optimistic statement regarding someone attempting to defuse high explosives. My blunder was more subtle; halfway down in the pool, I was ready to abort the rescue. In the clear water of the swimming pool, I would have had a second chance to save my classmate. In the open ocean, I might not get a second chance, which means my teammate dies.

In my rescue attempt, I failed because I had gotten mindlock. Running along the pool's side deck would have been faster than my frantic swim. From the deck, I could have seen Hopkins beneath the water, and dove in for a faster and more effective rescue.

'What was I thinking just before I hit the water?' I wondered. The answer hits me with the psychological impact of a speeding freight train. I thought this was my chance to look good. I even recall that I wanted to make sure my racing dive was impressive for McNair. It is such a startling thought. Am I that shallow? I mentally cringe as I realize that McNair no doubt saw right through my little drama.

We are nearing the end of the run as I cautiously glance over at McNair, noting he is not even breaking a sweat or breathing hard.

"You eyeballing me, Arrington?" he snarled edging closer to me.

No point in denying the obvious, "Yes, Instructor."

"What's going on in that little squid brain of yours?"

"That I screwed up, Instructor McNair."

"Really?" Did McNair almost smile?

"Running kind of airs out the old brain pan, doesn't it?"

"Yes, Instructor McNair," I grinned in a friendly way.

"Think I dropped Hopkins because he tried to drown on me? I dropped Hopkins because that boy is an accident looking for a place to happen. He is the kind of dope who always gets someone else hurt or killed. The drowning bit saved him the anguish of suffering through any more of my training. The idiot feared the water. Amazing, squeamish around water and thinks he can be a frogman."

McNair taps my shoulder, "Want to know a secret? I am going to be darn surprised if you make it through my class, Arrington."

"Not make it?" I echoed, my grin hanging in shambles.

"Yeah, that's what I said. We are team players. I think your favorite team is you and your stupid ego. Arrington, when the class falls out for chow, why don't you take that ego of yours around the forest loop again and try to wear it down some."

"Yes, Instructor McNair." The punishment felt almost welcome as I run away from that icy glare. I do not miss the sound of boots pursuing me. There is no way that I am going to turn around and let Instructor McNair catch me eyeballing him again. The running boots are gaining, I glance over to see the radiance of Hank's beacon-like grin.

"Mind if I tag along?" he asked, sunlight flashing off his teeth.

* * *

In the South Yard, the sunlight is painting wandering rainbows in the cascading water in the air above the wet green grass. I am like a kid in a water park. I give the whole baseball field a good soaking. I shut off the taps, coil the hoses, and carry them to the recreation locker. I enjoy the sound of squishing water under my sneakers. I am thinking, 'The wonder, inmate carries water-hoses.'

The Recreation Officer walks up. "You soaked the lawn," he noted, "but on Fridays, we only give it a light watering. It may not dry out by Saturday when everyone wants to run and lay on the grass. It is not going to make you very popular amongst the rest of the inmates," he said sagely.

* * *

I am in the chow line when someone grabs my arm. I turn to see an Arian Brotherhood gang member. He is a couple of inches taller than my six feet, has bulging muscles, face and neck tattoos, and wild roving eyes. He looks like a man with attitude problems.

"You're the dude who wants to write a book for kids?" he asked. "Warning them about drugs?"

"Yeah, that's me," I answered.

"Come with me," he said, pulling me toward a corner. "Got something to share and don't want anyone else listening in."

"It's personal, but you want me to write about it?"

"Yeah, soon it won't matter no how," he said bitterly. His eyes drift randomly. There is a lost connection or a detour to another planet in that drug-abused brain. One moment he is staring right at me, then his eyes are off on an adventure of their own, shooting about the room before settling on the ceiling. Then with a jolt, like a circuit connecting, his eyes rediscover me. He also has a lazy eye, which never quite focuses on where he is looking. It gives the impression that he is talking to someone standing beside me.

"They call me Loco. I'm also kind of gay."

I have no idea how to response a kind of gay pronouncement.

"That's why I'm talking with ya."

"What?" I said stepping back.

"Didn't mean that. Everyone knows you're straight." Wild Eyes grabs my arm again, "I want you to write about me."

"Why?"

"Cuss I'm dying. I got the Big A," he lamented.

"Big A?"

"AIDS man," the eyes take another tour of the room. "Don't talk about it or I won't have any kind of love life any more."

Love life? What a corruption of words. He has a disease that kills and is okay passing it around — murder by slow killing disease served up by a twisted aficionado with love. This place is just too twisted.

"I need you to write about my addiction." One eye is staring fiercely at me; the other is interested in a salt shaker on a table.

"I don't think I care to write about that kind of behavior."

"I'm talking about the drugs man. I'm a heroin addict. It's how I got AIDS, and it's what's killing me," he moaned.

I look at this man and see fear — deep hope-busting fear.

"I want you to write about what happened just before I got arrested. My road dog (inmate term for best friend) and I were shooting up. He was doing the first load when suddenly he starts shaking, vomits on his self, goes rigid, then quivers, and bam, the dude dies. I was wondering what to do?" he lamented.

"If you should call 911?"

"Na, he was stone dead. Weren't nobody gonna help Bobby Boy." The wild eye is examining the debris on the floor. "I was wondering if I should do a full hit."

"You're kidding," I asked stunned.

"Figured he OD'd, so I did only half a load. Shot up and passed out. Woke up in the night lying next to a dead guy. Man, he had one bad funk— starting to stink you know."

"You used the same needle?" I asked incredulously.

"Yeah, after I wiped the vomit off it."

"Your friend dies, and you shoot up with the same stuff?"

His good eye blinks, "It's what addiction is, dude."

The wild eyes look up at the ceiling, then vacantly across the room. "What do you think happened to the junkie when word got out that Bobby Boy died shooting up his stuff?"

"Someone turned him in?" I hazarded.

"Dude sold out his stash after doubling his price. Word was out that his dope was so good it killed Bobby Boy, and he was some kind of hard-core doper. It was a boss recommendation."

"That's nuts!"

"No, that's addiction," the biker nodded sagely.

"You want me to write about this?"

"You have to; it's all I got." Tears are streaming from those fierce eyes. They wet a tattoo on his neck of a biker on his machine going away down a desert road towards a setting sun. "I'm dying of the Big A. I got nothing to leave except for that story."

That afternoon I am still trying to shake Loco's story out of my mind while watering the baseball field. I have three hoses going with whirlybirds spraying long arches of shooting water. I dodge the water jets, not always successfully, which is cool because I am enjoying getting wet. It is a hot day, and I am a relatively happy guy considering the crazy residents I am meeting on a regular basis. I have just shifted all the hoses, so have a half-hour to pick up my memory thread.

* * *

At EOD School, we are in the hardhat diving locker for deep-sea diving rig training. McNair yells, "Grab the heavy gear and get out on the pool deck. You got five minutes."

Poolside, the instructors split us into four teams. It is race time.

A two-inch thick rope runs the width of the pool. At the rope's center hangs a 50-pound lead weight, which puts a deep V in the taunt line. The object of this race is to familiarize us with the Mark V Deep-Sea Diving Dress. After donning the heavy gear, which weighs 184 pounds, we have to climb down a ladder into the pool, submerge, and tug our way hand-over-hand down the rope to the lead weight at a depth of 18 feet. Next, we must pull ourselves up to the pool's opposite edge, where another rope plunges straight down from the surface. We grab the rope and descend to the pool's bottom where we walk across to an ascent line tied to the ladder where we started.

The team's combined race time determines the winners who only have do a three-mile run before dinner. The losers get to do pulls-ups, pushups, and sit-ups; the number of which is determined by the instructor's mood. Losing took on a new perspective at EOD School as McNair liked to remind us, "Sportsmanship is not a factor in your grade, nor is it a desirable quality for a combat frog. In Spec War, you get medals for terminating the other team."

"The idea is to teach you how to control the buoyancy of the hard hat rig," Said McNair. "Inflating the deep-sea diving dress with air makes it buoyant. Dumping out the air turns it into 60 pounds of negative buoyancy, which means an express trip to the bottom of my pool."

The race begins as I expected. The men are awkward and unsure in their movements as they muscle themselves down the rope to the 50-pound lead clump, and then pull themselves up the other end of the rope. Keeping a proper balance of air in the dress is challenging. It requires the constant use of both hands to open and close the air inlet and exhaust valves. The air exhaust valve is on the left side of the helmet, while the inlet valve is on a clip at the lower right side of the chest harness.

Ninety minutes later the teams are in a draw. While suiting up, I go over my plan and see no obvious flaws. I do not even notice that I am again letting my ego out of its cage. I have a secret advantage over my classmates. I spent three months at the Navy's Deep-Sea Diving School. I am very experienced with this old rig.

I tug on the heavy rubber and canvas diving suit. A teammate buckles on my lead boots. The boots have stout rope lacings under leather straps to ensure they do not come off. Losing a weighed boot underwater could flip a diver upside down. Any water in the suit (all canvas diving suits leak) would flood down into the helmet, drowning the inverted diver. Next, I don the breastplate then they sling a 70-pound weight belt from my shoulders and buckle it snugly at my waist. They pass a crotch strap between my legs and aggressively snug it tight, which pulls the breastplate down firmly onto my shoulders while causing serious discomfort in the groin. It prevents the helmet and breastplate from rising when the suit inflates. Last, they lower a helmet onto my head.

Inside the rig, I jack my shoulders to settle the breastplate and weight belt. I feel like a mule in a wagon harness. Hank thumps the top of my helmet twice, the signal to stand; I practically leap to my feet. I am anxious to get into the water, yet the ponderous weight of the deep-sea rig *limits me to short shambling steps. Shuffling quickly to the ladder, I descend into the cool water. The rig's massive weight begins to fall away. I hear the helmet mounted exhaust valve begin to gurgle as water covers the port. I watch exhaust bubbles breaking on the surface as I do another shoulder shrug to settle the rig and loop my arm over the downward slanting rope. Looping an arm over the rope allows that hand to operate the air inlet valve, which clips to a ring on my chest harness. It frees my left hand to work the exhaust valve on the side of the helmet.*

Stepping off the ladder, I take a deep breath, say "Diver leaving surface," and then shut off the air supply and spin the exhaust valve open. Immediately, the hard-hat rig loses its buoyancy as air from the suit compresses upward into the helmet before bubbling freely out of the exhaust valve. The top face port is awash with a cloud of ascending bubbles as I slide down the slanting rope toward the lead clump. The increasing water pressure presses the canvas suit tightly against my skin, so I slowly open the air inlet to keep from getting classic suit squeeze, which is what a boa constrictor does to a swallowed goat.

Rapidly, I slip down the rope to the 50-pound clump. At the lead weight, I spin the exhaust valve shut and twirl the air inlet valve open. I pass my hands over the clump as the increasing buoyancy helps to shove me up the rope on the other side. I arrive abruptly at the other end of the pool and quickly reach out to grab the descent line. Semi-shutting down the air supply, I slide down the descent rope like a 30-pound anchor. I hit the pool bottom so hard my legs nearly buckle. The crash of my impact echoes across the bottom of the pool in a small tsunami of sound.

I check for spinal damage as I attempt to stand upright at the base of the pool. Deciding that I am okay, I stride rapidly across the bottom to the ascent line under the ladder where I started. My tenders begin pulling me upward, and I help by climbing the rope. I know that the school record for the hard-hat race is toast. At the surface, I grab and climb the ladder, and then shuffle quickly toward the dressing chair. I am tempted to do a little dance step like a football receiver after a dramatic touchdown.

Not doing a shuffling boogie to the dressing stool turns out to be my only good decision. Had I attempted a victory rumba in the old dive suit, McNair would have tackled me. I hear him yelling, "Get his helmet off, I'm going to strangle him!" As Hank lifts my helmet off, McNair shoulders his way in, "This is not about racing, squid brain," he growled, "it's about learning to control the rig. You want people to notice you? How about clearing out your locker. The whole class will notice that!"

I hunker down inside the old diving dress as McNair's rage washes over me. "That was stupendously dangerous! Nah, it was imbecilic. What would have happened if your balloon stunt ruptured the canvas suit? Any idea how fast 70 pounds of lead ballast sinks?"

I slid down deeper into the clammy suit.

"Sit up straight, fool," he punches me in the chest, "you're making my suit look bad! Get those shoulders back, look like a man when I'm chewing on you. Now tell me what you were doing in my pool?"

"I wanted to be the best student you've ever had," I replied meekly.

McNair grabs the two ropes on my chest plate and hauls me to my feet. "Arrington, the best students always help their classmates. As a Navy hard-hat diver, you might have shared a few things to aid your classmates. But no, you had to grandstand. From now on your focus here is to support your classmates in every way possible. And if you're luckier than I think you are you might get to stand with the class on graduation day."

After storing the heavy gear, McNair decides that we need another mood adjustment. He takes us out for a little five-mile run through the woods. Running with my classmates is turning into my main opportunity for seriously pondering of my faults. I want people to like me. Yet, I am just beginning to realize that trying to look good in front of my classmates is not the way to win them over as friends.

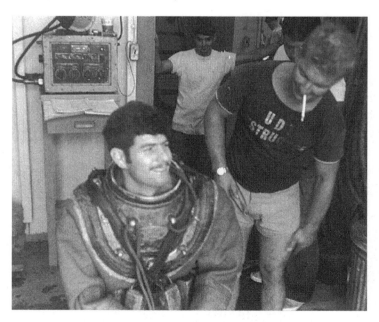

The Author at Naval School Deep Sea Diving,
Naval Shipyard, Washington DC 1972.

The unexamined life is not worth living. — Socrates 469–399 BC

Chapter 13 - A-Unit, Sept-Oct 1983

Each morning, I am up early. Running in the pre-morning darkness is the closest I can come to feeling free. I enjoy racing the sunrise, counting laps before first light, while most of the prison slumbers.

On the morning of September 27, I wait eagerly at the door for the guard. It is my 34th birthday. I hear the guard's shoes plodding on the concrete walkway that leads to the door. I hear the lock click open and wait until his footsteps fade. I step out and bolt for the South Yard.

A sea fog drifts on the ground and covers the smooth surface of the ocean. With each lap around the South Yard, I push the pace faster, racing against the dim red glow that is growing on the fog-bound horizon. I sprint the last lap, then pause breathing deeply to watch the rising sun, its light misted brilliant red by a curtain of white fog. Inhaling the fresh ocean air, I am riding on a natural high as I jog toward the open door of the weight room. There is no warning that I am going into a chamber of horrors.

A light mist floats in cold air inside the weight room. The few windows that are not broken out of the clapboard building are wet with dew. Iron weights and rusty steel bars lie scattered about the wooden floor. I stoop to pick up a long steel bar. It is cold. The dew that covers the metal wets my hands. Racking the heavy bar, I abruptly smell the pungent musk of marijuana smoke. That is when I see the two men. They are just outside the backdoor in the deeper shadows getting high. Their dark silhouettes, shrouded by the fog, have a disconcerting, sinister air. Suddenly the two men begin to walk toward me. The fog drifts from their bodies in long wispy tendrils that cling to their silhouettes in a smoky embrace. The barren room waxes colder at their stealthy approach. I have an intimidating feeling that they are stalking me.

They are only a few feet away when one of them, a Samoan with a massively thick body, raises a blunt finger to his nose. Pinching off one nostril, he leans forward and snorts forcefully. A thick wad of mucus lands inches from my foot. The other inmate looks like a Polish mercenary with a hulking muscular build. His blunt head is shaved and tattooed, the skin glistens with sweat. He grins evilly, revealing missing front teeth, then leers maliciously, "Ready for a little pony ride, boy?" he threatened in a gravelly voice.

I desperately try to remain calm, while sudden fear flushes through me. There is nowhere to flee. "It's a good thing there's no one down here but us men," I answered gruffly.

The bald man guffaws as he punchs me solidly in the chest with a beefy hand. I almost lose my balance from the unexpected blow. The man is fast. I feel a surge of adrenaline flowing through me. I am stunned that he landed a blow while I just stood there.

Deep inside of me, the primal Steve steps out of his cave and glares at the two dangerous adversaries.

"Acting tough ain't gonna help," sneered the hulking man. He was aggressively chewing something. I thought it was a piece of gum, but then I realized it was a clove of garlic. The odor wafted about him as he eyed me up and down.

Primal Steve wasn't going to wait for his attack. I am going to kick him in the knee. It is a tough decision, choosing to attack someone so big, particularly when he has a giant Samoan along for the ride. These monsters are seeking sadistic pleasure in the most demented way possible. They will laugh at the torment they render as they destroy another human being's life and spirit. Fierce anger sends hot blood coursing through my arteries. These are the ultimate subhuman bullies — so forget the knee or groin kick, which can go terribly wrong. It is an expected strike; a street fighter will try to capture your foot — then pound on your body as they ride you to the ground. I must fight smart — it is live or die.

I cannot overcome their brute strength, nor go toe-to-toe with these ogres. The man's missing teeth and face scars tell me he can take a lot of abuse and keep coming. I must take the fight to them and the bald man is in my face, so it must be him. I fear they might have weapons, so I am going after his left eye with a finger whip. It is a straight-in, lightning quick Gung Fu praying mantis strike.

For me, it is a flicking of the right hand while extending the middle finger supported underneath by the index finger to scratch or nick his eye. The middle fingernail slices across the eye from left to right. Think rattlesnake strike to his eyeball.

A fist must punch through its target for effect, meaning it must go further into his defenses and momentarily linger, which begs a counterattack. The flick extends and retracts in a microsecond. It is a whipping motion with an unlocked elbow. It leaves nothing for the opponent to seize. Instead, one or both of his hands will automatically move to protect the damaged eye.

I plan to dodge past the bald man to escape the Samoan. But, if that huge man gets his hands on me, I will probably get only one hit in and it must stop him completely. If I must, I will spear hand him in his larynx. It is a windpipe crusher, a possible killing blow — slow death by strangulation. The victim suffers. It is a straight in jab. The advantage of the spear hand is a four-inch reach over a fist; it is there and gone. Though the Samoan has a huge neck, his larynx is completely exposed. If he turns, I will change to a hammer blow, with the base of the fist hitting the main nerve bundle on the side of his neck. It is a stunning blow that causes temporary paralyses and can instantly drop a person despite their size. Unfortunately, the paralyses can be permanent.

My life and quality of existence are about to be determined in just seconds as I prepare to shuffle step into the beast before me. I drop into the Shuriken, which looks harmless, my center of gravity lowered, hands draped in front. It is a predatory Praying Mantis stance for throwing a fighting star, a shuriken. A martial artist can throw, jab, or flick a shuriken. Instead, I will flick my finger like a thrown shuriken. Yet, I hesitate, LORD help me, I cannot blind this man. Though the threat is still there nothing has happened to warrant my maiming him. I hesitate, which can be a fatal mistake.

Sudden voices pull our attention to the door. A couple of biker types are just walking in through the open doorway. "Hey, Bad Bill," yelled the beast in front of me, "lookie what I got me here."

With the bald man's face turned toward the bikers, there is a moment of inattention. I am going to use it to run. The Samoan is ponderous, I am fast and agile, I can dodge him—I hope.

"Hey, it's the Fall Guy," the bearded biker says cheerfully.

I freeze because the biker's voice directed at me--was friendly

Bad Bill holds out his hand. It is a welcoming posture. "Remember me?" he asked hopefully? He looks like a sad-eyed hound dog eager for attention. He grins, "You signed the Doonesbury comic strip for me." The memory floods back. He is one of the inmate plumbers who slipped into my cell in J-3.

"Hey, Gonzo, this is one right-on dude," he said while shaking my hand enthusiastically. "Gonzo calls me Bad Bill, but you can call me Sweet William." He turned to Gonzo, "Fall Guy refused to rat out DeLorean. He's an upright dude."

He asks me, "Wanna be my road dog? (biker speak for friend).

My status in the weight room shot up as Sweet William's brand-new road dog. Gonzo shifts roles in a heartbeat, from attacker to

want-to-be-best-of-friends. He insists on helping with my workout.
I load the bar on the bench press with 165 pounds and have a very
enthusiastic Gonzo spotting me. I do ten repetitions.

"Ah, you can do more than that," he lisped adding two ten-
pound plates. For the next hour, I lift *creampuff weight,* then get to
help spot heavy iron with Gonzo, Bad Bill, and the Samoan, known
for some strange reason as *Chick.*

Toward the end of the workout, Gonzo knuckles me good
naturedly in the chest and leers, "Ya gotta drive the heavy iron,
sugar." He smiled, a garlic cloud proceeding his words, "If you
wanna stay a virgin, you're gonna need bigger muscles, cutie."

*One's dignity may be assaulted, vandalized, and cruelly mocked, but
cannot be taken away unless it is surrendered.* — Morton Kondrake

Leaving the weight room, I go sit on the bleachers. In the future,
I will avoid Gonzo and Chick. However, I like Sweet William a lot.

I consider the horror of what almost happened to me. *'Did a
comic strip just help to save me from that?'* I wondered. I knew I owed
sincere appreciation to the three high school bullies who so shamed
me. That water hose incident drove me to study the martial arts
with a passion, particularly when I was in Asia.

I wondered how life's lessons, the good and the bad, morph us
into the person we will become. I look back toward the weight
room. In prison, the University of Life is one tough teacher. I
foolishly did not pay attention to my instincts. I sensed that the two
men were stalking me. I should have left immediately or even run
away. It is a fundamental strategy of martial arts.

'You're not as smart as you think you are,' echoed in my mind.

However, for my protection, I have been carrying around a
double handful of weapons openly. They have been in plain sight
for over a year, and no one has noticed them. My middle fingers
and thumb nails are a bit longer than most men allow. The finger
flick has a viciously maiming follow-up move. After the shuriken
strike by the right middle finger, the left hand strikes with the
thumb and fingers cupped. The fingers slide alongside the
opponent's head guiding and re-enforcing the thumb as it drives
straight into the attacker's right eye. It can gouge out or jelly the
eyeball. It is a blinding move, and it flickered through my mind
that I might have to do it. I am so lucky it did not come to that.

At that instant, a thought abruptly explodes in my mind that is so powerful it shifts the foundation of my inner perception. Just before the bikers walked into the weight room, I sent out a mental plea, "LORD help me, but I cannot risk blinding this man's eye."

My solutions to the confrontation were all violent. I would have wound up in 'The Hole' with new charges. Instead, an answer to a terrifying situation walked unexpectedly through the door — not a corrections officer as one would hope, but in the unanticipated form of a friendly biker gang member. I reject that it could have been simple happenstance because this was not a singular event.

In J-1, Mose was known for his fits of rage and violence against others. Rumor had it that he has broken men's limbs. However, in his way, Mose was polite, tolerant of my ignorance and stupidity — and he saved me from a bad confrontation with Lewis.

There was that moment with the angry black man in J-3 when the words, "A man does what a man has to do," leaped into my mind without thought and soothed his fury as well as mine. It allowed both of us to stand-down with honor.

In J-3, a new inmate arrived from J-1. While I was serving lunch, he loudly stated, "Hey, I hear Arrington is in here. He's going to rat out DeLorean for sure."

What an idiotic thing for him to have said. He had called me a snitch, which according to inmate rules meant I had to confront and probably hurt him. I had no desire to challenge the idiot, but then Shorty rode to my rescue. He challenged the man, "Arrington is an upright dude and my friend." Shorty pointed at me, "He is standing right there. You apologize, right now."

The idiot looked at me and said he was sorry. Just like that, an unwinnable situation defused. Why did Shorty stand up for me? Was it because I, unlike the others, treated him with respect?

It was my Christian commitment that gave me the courage to plead guilty instead of taking the easy way out by snitching. The judge all but rewarded me with a reduced sentence.

I think of all the times in my recent past where circumstance seemed to favor me, and I decided to believe that none of it was happenstance or luck. I consciously choose instead to believe that God was blessing me. If I followed that line of spiritual logic, then what must follow was that God had a plan — a path for me to walk. In that instant, I made a lifelong commitment to follow Jesus Christ, to surrender to his will and to live my life with Christian purpose. In the last hour, I had gone from stark terror to incredible hope. An encouraging thought slowly emerged into my awareness, that from this day forward I would live my life with a hope that never surrenders.

* * *

I am sitting on my bunk in Animal House for count. Inmates do a lot of waiting. This will be a 30 to 45-minute event unless the numbers don't add up — then it could take hours. To pass the time, I entertain a memory picture that bubbles up from a prouder past.

* * *

I shove my arms through the webbing of a scuba pack at the EOD School pool. I stand and lift the twin 90-cubic-foot scuba cylinders over my head and let them slide down onto my back. Picking up my dive mask, I spit into it and glance about while rubbing the saliva onto the faceplate to keep it from fogging up. There are only 18 of us standing at the side of the pool, and we are all nervous, except apparently for Hank.

"Look at Hank," bellyached Charlie. "You'd think he was a kid in line for the submarine ride at Disneyland."

Hank acknowledges the comment with his ubiquitous smile, "Oh, this is going to be way more fun than any old Disney ride."

"Fun," exclaims Charlie strapping on a weight belt, "McNair and his cronies are going to spend the next hour endeavoring to drown us, and you think it is going to be fun?"

"Pool harassment is a big confidence builder." Said Hank, "After this, there is not much of anything underwater we can't handle."

"Yeah? Well I could take a pass on this," lamented Charlie.

"No, you couldn't." Hank was not smiling. "You want to be a Navy combat diver, an attack swimmer? You must get through pool harassment first. It is not just a test — it is a rite of passage. All combat frogs know that every member of their team has been through this. It means when your dive buddy's life is at stake, you'll be there for him no matter what is coming at you."

Watching Hank laying it out for Charlie, I see his true character. Hank is a seriously dedicated warrior. It would be an honor to serve on his team. I look at Charlie and realize I could not say the same about him and then wonder what my classmates would think of serving with me?

Maybe that question will find an answer in the next 60 minutes.

Dipping my mask into the pool, I slosh the water around to wash out the saliva. Everyone knows that I will be McNair's prime target. Looking at the water lapping at the side of the pool I see floodlights shimmering on the rippling surface then a reflection of a diver stepping up beside me. Hank nudges my shoulder, "Hey, Arrington, want to be my dive buddy?"

"You bet." Hank was my first choice for a dive buddy.
"Mind if we're the last ones off the bottom? It's important to me."
"Wouldn't expect anything else."

"How much air you got in your tanks, Arrington?" McNair's gravelly voice surprises me. How long had he been standing behind us?

"Three thousand pounds, Instructor McNair," I shouted with all the enthusiasm I could muster.

"Don't waste any of it," warned McNair. He is carrying a mask, fins, and a snorkel. He has a large sheath knife (K-Bar) strapped to his narrow waist. I am wondering what he is planning on doing with that knife.

"Okay, girls," taunted McNair, "here are the pool harassment rules: go to the bottom of the pool, stay close to your swim buddy, and anyone who breaks the surface before their cylinders are empty gets to be a fleet sailor again. Pass this test, and there is a chance you will discover more underwater adventure waiting in your future than any of you clowns can imagine. "All you have to do is get past me. Any questions?"

"What's the knife for?" wondered Charlie nervously.

"In case I get inspired," cackled McNair. He glanced at his watch, "You girls got five seconds to get out of my sight."

Eighteen bodies hitting the water creates a pressure wave that sloshes over the deck. Hank gives me the thumbs up as we swim down. I want to be a Navy frogman more than anything. I just must hold my breath — while being abused by motivated instructors who will not share their aqua fraternity with anyone of lesser caliber than themselves. If an instructor has any issues with a student, this is his opportunity to do something about it.

McNair arrives in a flash of fins. He tears away my mask, rips the mouthpiece from my clenched teeth, snatches my fins and pops me in the jaw with his elbow. He is not being sadistic, rather mimicking getting banged about in surf and waves with loose equipment.

First, the air supply I tell myself, reaching over one shoulder to grab the thick corrugated rubber air hoses. I stretch them out and jam the mouthpiece between my clenched teeth. Exhaling into the mouthpiece to clear out the water I try to take a breath, but my air is off. I hit the quick releases, pull the bulky double tanks to my front and open the air valve. Grabbing a short breath, I peer through the water's blur to see that Hank is giving me the hand signal to buddy breath.

I quickly push the mouthpiece toward his beaver teeth. He takes two quick breaths to purge his lungs and shoves it back to me. I grab two short breaths, pass the mouthpiece back, then find my mask, put it on, and clear it. Looking across the bottom of the massive three-stories deep pool — it is an underwater war zone. Students are scattered across the pool bottom with their dive gear drifting about them like debris from detonations or strewn in heaps like underwater roadkill. A set of twin tanks thuds into the white painted, steel bottom in an explosion of bubbles from a free-flowing double-hose regulator.

McNair and his assailants are hitting each buddy team like a coordinated shark attack on a panicked school of minnows. Looking at Hank, I see why he must buddy-breathe with me. His twin tanks are missing their regulator. McNair has it attached to his knife belt. He and his band of pirates are free diving, which makes them quick and agile. Gunner McNair is elegant as he free dives down to attack a dive team from behind. He strips them of their gear, then uses the tank straps to tie the regulator hoses, fins, and dive masks into a large bulky knot. He then hovers like a shark eager to cause more mischief before heading up for air.

Hank and I are swimming three feet off the bottom, which somewhat limits the direction of McNair's next attack. Since we are still buddy breathing, Hank is riding on my tanks, which is the most efficient arrangement for swimming horizontally while sharing air off a double-hose regulator. I take two breaths, and then pass the mouthpiece up to Hank. Abruptly, I see the regulator drifting down in front of my faceplate. How did McNair detach it from my tanks without my feeling it?

As McNair rips away my mask and fins, I realize that this attack occurred when Hank was supposed to be getting his two breaths. McNair finishes his assault by ripping the tank straps off my chest and waist. He shoves the tanks away. Since they are negative, they sink to the bottom ten feet away. Finless, I frog kick over to get them back. I turn with the tanks and hold them out to Hank, who arrives with the regulator. He reattaches the double-hose regulator and offers the mouthpiece to me. I shake my head and nod towards him. He grins and takes two quick breaths. We go through several breathing cycles to purge off excess CO_2 then I settle the tanks onto my back while Hank retrieves our masks and fins. We gear up and begin swimming again.

Ascending bubbles from two vacant rigs draw my eyes upward where I see a buddy team hugging the side of the pool. I have no idea who they are because Hank and I are abruptly without masks again and under attack. This time, McNair has added a twist. He stretches the corrugated double-hoses the length of the tanks, wedging the mouthpiece between the bottoms of the twin 90 cylinders. He shoves the tanks away with the mouthpiece releasing a cascade of bubbles. With the hoses wedged between the tank bottoms, it is impossible to breathe off the mouthpiece. Hank stretches the hoses, pulling the mouthpiece out and snatches a breath. He passes it to me, and I am surprised to see he is laughing! A gurgle of bubbles ascends from his lips in a buoyant cascade. I take a breath, tilt my head back then *blow out an air ring. I watch it expanding as it ascends in a shimmering wheel of air. An instructor free dives through it causing the wheel to collapse into a shower of tiny bubbles that rushes upwards in a sparkling cloud to the pool's surface. My fear of pool harassment abruptly dissipates like the disintegrating bubble ring.*

Beyond Hank, I see McNair and his brigands stripping a team of their gear, and then one of the students loses it. It is Charlie. Don is on the bottom looking upward as his dive partner sprints for the surface. Charlie drops his weight belt on his way up. I watch the belt sinking rapidly. A great sadness washes over me as I watch Charlie treading water on the surface. I am a silent observer, incapable of sharing any encouragement, and deep down inside me something shudders. It is a compelling feeling of real loss. I have never had friends like these men. Our friendship has been tempered in the kiln of many hardships shared. It is not just the tragedy of losing a friend. It is that these men have helped to define my self-worth. Facing challenges as a team has established a warrior's camaraderie amongst us. Hank and I swim rapidly towards Don, but instead, he joins another diver who has just lost his buddy.

McNair and his cutthroats, flush with the success of culling our class of two more candidates, attack us enforce. Hank and I wait patiently while the instructors render violence upon us. True to my promise to Hank, we are going to stay down and be the last buddy team off the bottom.

* * *

Walking down the breezeway in early October, I glance at a large wart growing on my finger. I had tried to get some wart remover from the prison clinic, but they refused. Probably afraid I would try to feed it to another inmate, which in prison is a justifiable concern. I look at the abrasive concrete wall to my right and then resisting a powerful urge not to do this, place the wart firmly against the wall. For the first six feet or so it doesn't hurt much, and then it does—I continue to walk. After a couple of dozen feet of serious wart abrading, I look down at my bleeding finger. Yep, the wart is mostly gone. I put the finger in my mouth and chew out a bit of remain wart root.

It was not my first attempt at prison cosmetic surgery. In J-3, I had a nerve ganglion growing on my wrist. It was a gelatinous sac the size of a large marble. In the old days, people would strike the sac with a Bible to rupture it. My cellmate used a heavy law book from the prison library. It worked, but it took two firm whacks applied by an overly enthusiastic felon.

I stroll over to the lawn and sit down. It is an hour before sunset. I say a quiet prayer, open my Bible to a random page, and read a sentence. Abruptly, the stability of my world shifts.

When I sat down, my thoughts were speculative about my life in prison. I wondered how serving any more time in such a callous institution was going to make me a better person.

I stared in amazement at the words in Romans 5 3-5, "But we also exult in our tribulations, knowing that tribulation brings about perseverance, and perseverance, proven character and proven character, hope, and hope does not disappoint."

Prison is my tribulation! If my incarceration is an ordeal in which to temper my moral fiber, then the tribulation that is my daily companion is leading me to growth—growth in spirit and character. As I reach for greater comprehension, adversity aids me in that quest.

That evening, I climb onto my bunk and fluff the thin pillow. Folding it into a wedge, I lie on my stomach and peer out the barred window. I am waiting to watch the moonrise.

While living in Revelstoke, I patterned my nightly activities on the rising of the full moon. It is a terrific time for night surfing or an early evening hike. Tonight, I will be a passive observer of the moonrise. In prison, deviant behavior takes an uptick during the full moon. My bunk will be an early refuge from lunar inmate intrigues. I listen to the soft breathing of two men sleeping in the cubicle. They are resting up for late-night activities. I have no idea what they are planning, nor do I want to know.

Looking out the window, I mentally prepare for the celestial theater that is unfolding. A sliver of light slowly becomes visible in the approaching darkness with the arrival of the harvest moon. I stare at moonlight dancing on the ocean as a memory unfolds.

* * *

I mentally shuffle backward in time, sorting through a caravan of distinctive memories revolving around my many adventures in Revelstoke. I am heading back to the very beginning of my nomadic lifestyle; it is when my life shifted dramatically from the norms of daily existence to the unique challenges of becoming a road wanderer.

It begins on a fall day in Maryland where my mind captures an image of dense woods with tall trees swaying in a blustery wind. The leaves on the trees are changing colors as winter approaches. Nature has been busy with broad strokes of her brush painting the lush forest in a swarm of brilliant fall colors. Each tree is a biological masterpiece of tint and shading with flaming reds, vibrant oranges, and soft canary yellows. The gusting wind is stripping leaves in clusters from swaying branches, gathering them like flocks of colorful birds, before sending them swirling in an aerial dance of changing hues and shifting patterns. A ground-hugging breeze scoops up a thick blanket of colorful leaves hurling them across a black tarmac road where the passage of a large brown van scatters them. The leaves swirl in the wake of the vehicle and then the wind carries them swiftly away as the van slows to drive through a gate at the EOD School's blasting range.

Parking, I wait for my class to break. I have missed the chance to blow up several pounds of TNT while picking up my new van at the Chevy dealership. There is a final rolling explosion from the range. I see my classmates spilling out of a concrete bunker. They open the double backdoors of the truck as a dozen men clamber inside, jousting each other for a place to sit on the empty floor. Hank plops down in the passenger seat and cheerfully knuckles my arm. "You're going mobile on us?" he quipped. "That is such a cool idea."

"You can share in the experience if you want," I offered.

"Sure, what do I get to do?"

"You could cut a few holes in the metal siding."

"What?" he laughed. "This is a new truck, and you want me to cut holes into it?" he asked innocuously.

We drive to the dormitory where I have stockpiled motorhome parts and tools in my room. I am eager to get to work. Winter is coming, and I want to be into my mobile residence before the ice and snow hits.

Using a paper template, I trace out a side window. Revving a drill motor, I look at the truck's shiny fresh paint, and then push the spinning drill bit through the unblemished metal. I am about to cut a two-foot-square hole. Grabbing a power jigsaw, I insert the blade into the still-warm hole and cut out a large chunk of metal.

"Now that is what I call instant depreciation," quips Mickey Doke. Soon another chunk of metal hits the ground from the other side. "Hey, this is fun," said Hank revving the saber saw.

At the open back door, Mickey Doke steps in, "Hey if you need any more holes cut can I do it?"

"Sure, I need some holes cut in the roof." With templates for the roof vents, I mark out their pre-chosen location and turn him loose with the jigsaw. Soon there are half a dozen men involved in a diversity of projects. We install side-windows that are too high on the outside for people to see inside. We mount roof vents, and, over my yet-to-be-built bed, I fit a stained-glass skylight made by an artist friend. It is my third van conversion, so I am working from experience. I had been thinking about

building Revelstoke for months and fine-tuning the plans. My classmates are intelligent and capable men. They take care to do a good job.

The weeks pass quickly as I busily put all my spare time into creating Revelstoke. We framed the interior and covered it with fragrant cedars, redwoods, and mahogany. Some of my classmates brought personal treasures that they wanted to contribute or had found at a yard sale.

I moved into Revelstoke during Christmas break. With a week's leave before me, I found myself considering where to spend the night? I drove out the base gate and headed for the Atlantic Coast.

Sunset found me walking on an empty windswept beach. Day vacationers had fled the cold day as I shuffled across the sand watching the waves. A new sense of inner freedom was spreading its wings. Being mobile was expanding my prospects for adventure, challenge, and mystery. My nightly home was wherever I parked for the evening. I had grabbed more leisure out of each day as the constraints of time relaxed. I had a new independence that would enhance the quality of my life far beyond my expectations.

EOD class 76B in the practical problem forest. From left, Larry Cargill, Hank, Author, Lt. Phil Adkins, David Gill, Don Futrell (another SEAL) and Mickey Doke.

Unlike the mediocre, intrepid spirits seek victory over those things that seem impossible. – Ferdinand Magellan, Explorer 1520

Chapter 14 - A-Unit, Dec - Jan 1983

For my second Christmas inside, I track down the Recreation Officer to get access to the basement storerooms. It is creepy in the dark bowels of the old prison. Of the three overhead lights, only the one farthest away works. I see dust particles floating languidly in the still air. Boxes cast dark shadows on the walls. In a dank and moldy corner, I dig out a six-foot-tall plastic Christmas tree and four dusty cardboard boxes full of chipped Christmas lights and dusty ornaments — Christmas cheer stuffed in moldy boxes, cloaked in dust, and wrapped in darkness.

Placing the Christmas boxes in the recreation cart for hauling hoses, I tow my squeaky-wheeled sleigh to the visiting room. A guard locks me inside the large room as I go about my task. I string chipped ornaments and faded ribbon from the walls, then erect the plastic tree in a corner. I spend an hour weaving lights around the tree and hanging all the handmade ornaments in its branches.

I am wrapping empty boxes to put under the tree when I hear a tiny thump against a windowpane. Looking out into the night, I see a small movement on a concrete pad. Lying by a spool of razor wire lays a sparrow. I watch it slowly die — and with its little life went the last vestige of my wanting to celebrate Christmas at T.I. Staring at the artificial tree with its litter of vacant gifts, I wonder about the gay deception of celebrating Christmas in prison.

The next day, Sam comes for his first visit. Sitting next to the Christmas tree, we enjoy an amusing conversation. Sam is sharing what happened to him after my arrest.

"I went back to the Valley Hilton and caught a sci-fi movie," he said. "I spent the next day wondering where you were and then I saw you on the news wearing handcuffs. It blew me away."

"It was quite a shock for me, too." I added truthfully.

"Yeah, well my life got frantic after seeing that," Sam said seriously. "I snuck down to San Diego driving on side streets and spent the next few days sleeping in my car and hiding out."

"Hiding where?" I asked.

"Out in the water in the lineup at La Jolla Shores. I was watching the parking lot; nondescript cars caused me to panic."

"You were hiding at your favorite surf spot?" I asked.

"La Jolla isn't my favorite spot," said Sam, "Windansea Beach is much better, particularly with a south swell running. I missed some great waves hanging out at La Jolla, which is why I figured they wouldn't be looking for me there. I finally went home for a hot shower. I was washing my hair when mom knocked on the door and said that I had visitors--that they had badges."

Sam rolls his eyes, "Thought they were going to take me away, but all they wanted to do was talk."

"What did you tell them?"

"I told them that I didn't know there was cocaine in the car just like you told me to say. They didn't buy it, but then the agent said that they were not planning on arresting me."

I am stunned! "Sam, the DEA told you that they weren't interested in you?" I asked, trying to keep my voice dead calm.

"Nope, they said I would just complicate the case."

"Did they interview you again afterward?"

"No," said Sam, clueless.

"Sam, the reason I didn't cooperate was to protect you," I growled. If the judge knew that Sam was a victim of Morgan's manipulations, not mine, it might have shortened my sentence.

Sam replied, "You know, I can't stand pineapple anymore." To change the subject, he noticed that an inmate was staring at him. "Is that guy over there hitting on me?" he asked.

I glance over, "Yeah, that's Felix."

"But he has a hot babe with him, why's he looking at me?"

"Because he's gay and the hot babe is his sister."

"She's cute but chunky," Sam said thoughtfully.

"She has a stunning figure," I smiled knowing I am about to blow Sam's mind. "She looks chunky because she is wearing at least seven layers of lingerie under her clothes."

"What?" Sam asked confused, "Why?"

"Her brother, Felix, runs a lingerie shop in the Drugs and Drag Unit. In a few minutes, his sister is going to go into the ladies' room and remove all her lingerie. Then at the appointed moment, she will walk out and give it all to Felix, including the size triple extra-large that she has in her big purse." I said shrewdly.

"How do you know that?"

"Because Felix is wearing his jumpsuit."

Sam looks at Felix, who is indeed wearing a pink jumpsuit with a silk lavender sash belt.

"Felix will go into the men's room and put on all of that stuff. He needs the jumpsuit to hide the added layer of a triple extra-large lingerie, which is for Tiff."

"Who?"

"You don't want to know."

Sam is exasperated, "What are you talking about?"

"Felix runs, 'The Cat Lingerie Boutique,' out of his eight-man cubical. All the inmates in there are gay. When Felix goes back through security, he will slip a hundred bucks to the guard. At the Drug and Drag Unit, he will lay out all the new stuff. After dinner, the gay crew will gather there for dress up night."

"Dress up night?"

"Again, you don't want to know."

"And the triple extra-large?" urged Sam.

I smiled at Sam; apparently, he does want to know. "The Tiff weighs over 300 pounds; he loves to dress up — and he dances."

"Scary," said Sam with a shudder.

"That's right, it is scary, which is why you should be extremely glad that you are not here."

"Yeah, so I'm glad."

"Good, then I want your sandals."

"You what?"

"I want to trade sandals."

"Trade sandals?" he popped his head under the table to eye the decrepit flip-flops I am wearing. "Duct tape, they're duck taped?" Sam asked then peering closer, "Is that green stuff mold?"

Sam walks away awkwardly in my old flip-flops as he leaves the visiting room. It is difficult watching him walk through the door to freedom and unhindered surf adventures while I head for the metal security door with the bad-attitude correctional officers and psycho inmates waiting for me. However, Sam's sandals were quite comfy.

* * *

The prison has become my *dojo* (place of enlightenment). My intent is the simple perfection of action, no matter how trivial the task and total awareness of every act. "The wonder, I carry water," the realistic appreciation of simplicity in life. I ponder the Eastern teachings I have learned in dojos and from trips to Asia with the Pacific Fleet and think how often the goal of Eastern philosophy is to achieve perfected awareness and simplicity of life.

However, I find these goals better answered in the Bible. Enhanced awareness is part of following the teachings of Jesus Christ. Every morning when I wake, I pray asking for a closer walk with He who guides me. Being a practicing Christian is a self-correcting lifestyle that leads to heightened awareness as I strive to be a better human being.

Just before Christmas, I appeared before the Parole Board. Because of my excellent record, they decided on a minimum sentence. Which caused me to ponder something intensely. Scotti threatened me with 145 years, i.e. a life sentence with no possibility of parole. The prosecutor wanted 45 years, then settled for a max of 30 with my plea bargain. Judge Takasugi gave me five years. Now, the parole board just cut that to three years. What was causing all this good fortune? The biggest difference in my life is my Christian walk. I find that I want to grow closer to God. I want to do good things and to have the LORD's blessing. Here, in my adversity of prison, all my problems are coming wrapped in a blessing.

On Christmas Eve, I go down to the South Yard to watch the Christmas Parade of Boats. Up and down the channel, brightly lit yachts, all aglow with decorations, pass in a line. Staring at the marine pageantry, I realize there is something almost magical about serving my time at Terminal Island. I sit down with my back against a pine tree. Looking up at the branches covered with pine needles, I inhale deeply. It rained recently releasing an amazing forest smell that carried me to another forest, where dangerous problems lurked.

* * *

I stand on the edge of a forest. A bomb disposal tool pouch drapes over my shoulder. A light breeze drifting through the forest carries the fresh scent of pine needles. Nervously I wonder what awaits me inside the dense, almost haunting woods hiding an assortment of practical ordnance problems. Our class of nine remaining EOD candidates is working in teams of three. For the day's exercises, each of the team members must solve a practical hands-on problem. This is my turn.

Instructor McNair looks at me and grins, "Hey, meat, bet you're soon going to look like burnt hamburger oozing ketchup."

I thread carefully following the narrow trail with all my senses keenly alert for trip wires and other booby traps. In my back pocket, I carry a 3"x 5" situation card. It reads, "Vietnam, 1968 Tet Offensive. Your team is responding to a call for assistance from an oil storage yard where three Viet Cong sappers have penetrated the base defenses. You have one hour to clear the site and render safe any explosives encountered."

Creeping cautiously down the path, I hear the crunch of McNair's boots in my wake. Splitting my attention between the ordnance problems that lie ahead and the man with the explosive personality stalking me from behind is daunting. Somewhere ahead lurks a block of TNT attached to a trigger. If I blow the booby trap, a device will set off an explosion just far enough away to be a total shock.

Around a bend in the trail, I see the dull sheen of an oil tank. With each step, I pause and peer about, looking for twisted branches, damaged leaves or freshly turned soil. The dirt trail seems undisturbed – or is it?

Crouching down, I see the dirt line on a rock is a bit higher than the ground surrounding it. I look suspiciously at the dirt trail. There are a few crumbs of disturbed dirt half hidden by a leafy branch and some dead leaves. The pieces of dirt are slightly damp. Someone has been digging. The placement of the rock and leafy branch ensures that anyone coming down the trail will place a foot right here. Earlier, Instructor McNair confided that each situation could have up to three explosive hazards. I sink onto my knees suppressing a surge of excitement. McNair looks away pretending not to notice I am onto his booby trap. Unsheathing my K-Bar knife, I probe the ground. The blade tip sinks easily into the loosely packed soil, and then it grates against something solid. Carefully digging away the crumbly dirt reveals a homemade Vietnamese antipersonnel mine. I pull a pin from my pocket and slip it into the plunger rendering it safe.

I am about to lift it out when I hear McNair take a single step closer to look over my shoulder. What was he trying to see? He knows what is here since he probably did the digging. Warily, I wonder if a surprise lurks beneath the first device. Gently scooping the dirt out from under the mine my fingers find a taut wire attached to the mine's bottom. He booby-trapped the boob-trap. I unearth a second mine. It is a Bouncing Betty, an American device. If triggered, an explosive charge bounces the mine six feet into the air before going off, ensuring maximum personnel damage. The top mine had a plunger for a trigger; this one has a pull mechanism. Any disturbance of the top mine triggers the second booby-trap. Using another pin, I render safe the Bouncing Betty and then grin at Instructor McNair. He grins back, which is troubling. Setting the two mines to one side for later disposal, I feel the flush of success.

Obviously, the sappers wanted to blow the oil tank. Problem number three is attached somewhere to that tank. I head at a faster pace directly for it. I do not intend just to beat the practical problem. I want a good time and for McNair to notice my deductive reasoning leading me to the obvious location of the last device. I move forward at a rather reckless pace for someone playing hide-and-seek with lethal explosive devices.

Soon, I discovered an IED (Improvised Explosive Device) attached to the metal cylinder near one of the tank's welds. There are six sticks of dynamite taped to the steel plate with a simple chemical pencil fuse. After a short inspection, I confidently render the device safe by jerking out the chemical fuse and jamming its explosive tip into some loose dirt. I did the jerking out and jamming into the dirt with more flourish than necessary, but I wanted to make a statement. "Done," I announced proudly.

Instructor McNair smiles at me, which I should have recognized as not being a good sign, but I am flush with an overwhelming feeling of accomplishment. He glances at his watch, "Only 44 minutes. That is a good time. Some students use the whole hour to be sure they didn't miss anything." He said rubbing his hands together, "Sure, you're done?"

"Three problems," I answered confidently, "three solutions."

"Then call in your team," said McNair with a wry smile.

There was that warning smile again. I was feeling less confident. "No more than three devices per problem. That is what you said, right?"

"Yep," McNair grinned like a lion leering at a dimwitted cow.

"You guys can come in," I yelled while thinking maybe they shouldn't.

McNair has me take my team members to the landmines and the IED to show them how I found each device and explain what I did to render them safe. My self-assurance has returned. I can tell the other guys are envious of my 100% grade and with 16 minutes to spare. McNair glances at his digital stopwatch and then leads us to a gnarled old tree.

He looked at his watch again. "I want you all to stand here." He placed us just beyond the old tree trunk, then steps back behind the tree.

"I have a bad feeling," Hank said. He sniffs the air. "Smells like burnt gunpowder — this is a blasting site!" Just 25 yards away, a half-pound block of TNT explodes in a pool sheathed with ice. A 30-foot tall eruption of mud, ice-cold dirty water, and shredded leaves rains down on us.

"Four! There were four!" I yelled over the ringing in my ears."

"Idiot," McNair shook his head. "There were only three. The first two mines were connected, so they only count as one device."

"But that's not fair," I argued.

"Idiot, fair is not a factor. You just blew a war problem. Anyone smell American roasted hamburger blown into the mud, muck, and leaves of an Asian jungle? Come on," said McNair, "want to see what killed you?"

Walking doggedly in McNair's footsteps, I am not in the mood to see what killed me. Ten feet from the oil tank McNair points to a simulated explosive charge with a timer hidden in a bush beneath a transfer valve. "It's okay, Arrington," McNair offered, with a crocodile grin, "a lot of overconfident candidates fail this exercise."

"Fail," I echoed, "but I found and safed the first two problems."

"Get over it, Arrington," scolded McNair. "If this were real, you'd be shredded human meat pierced with hot metal shards and served up in a black zip-lock body bag for shipment home to your mother."

"Oh yeah, I forgot about that," I replied sarcastically.

"You've got nine more practical problems to pull your grade up. However, you need to be more focused on your real commitment here."

"I am committed." Did that just sound like I was whining?

McNair snarls, "You are attempting to become a bomb disposal frogman in my world. When someone plants a bomb, it is about turning people into corpses," McNair sounds like he is lecturing a child. "That could be you, me, or your entire team as you just so fatally accomplished. When it comes to bombs and booby-traps, anticipate the unexpected, take nothing for granted — be alert to everything, and commit to staying alive."

"But I was alert and..." I started to argue.

"Nah, Arrington," McNair knuckled my chest, "you are dense, self-focused, and inattentive. Thinking you could second-guess sappers, you hurried down a trail that was known to be booby-trapped."

"But I was right," I interrupted, "no more mines on the trail."

"So, how many mistakes can a bomb disposal technician make?"

"None," I hazarded meekly.

"Simple logic indicated that there was another device."

"I missed something?"

"Yeah, the answer is found in what was not there," said McNair. He points at the smoking hole, "This was the only device with a wire to trigger the TNT. The other devices weren't wired. "So, Rocks-for-Brains, what did hurrying gain you? You overlooked the obvious, made suicidal assumptions, wiped out your whole team — for a better grade?"

"I did fail." This was difficult to admit in front of my classmates.

"Yeah, you failed," McNair hoisted up on his fatigue pants. "I'm going to tell you a secret. It is better to show your ignorance than your stupidity. Prideful people are reluctant to ask questions. They blunder about when a simple question could point them in the right direction."

"I see," I replied warily.

"No, you don't," McNair sighed, "you don't ask questions because you're pretending you have all of the answers." He kneels on one knee and motions for us to join him. "My job is to weed out all the hot shots that are too stupid," McNair said glancing at me, "or too vain to realize why they are here. As a bomb disposal frogman, you get only one chance in a real situation. Make a mistake and people are going to exit this world. Arrington, if you survive the practical problems phase of your training; the next course will be the nuclear weapons phase. You make a mistake with a real thermonuclear weapon and a couple of million people die because you were stupid."

McNair stares at me. The extended silence is deafening.

"This is real," I said cautiously.

violence. Such as D-Unit, AKA Drug and Drag Unit, a reference to the vast availability of drugs tied to the gay crowd's prison livelihood. I sincerely hope not to be going to D-Unit.

The unit manager blurts two words, "G-Unit."

"G-Unit! I'm going to G-unit!" It is astounding news.

Five minutes later, I exit Animal House, happily carrying three stacked cardboard boxes. They are moving me incredibly early to the honor dormitory. Usually, it takes years just to be considered. The honor dorm houses 20 inmates. With over a thousand inmates at T.I., only a tiny fraction become honor inmates. I am buoyant as I stride along the breezeway with my three small boxes. I have become a man of substance—*I be having things.*

In G Unit, an inmate clerk says, "You're in four. Here's the key."

"I get my own key?" I asked startled. *I had no idea that any inmate got a key to anything. My projection booth I locked with a latch.*

Walking down the dorm's hallway, I notice how clean it is; the main bathroom is tidy. I arrive at my room, unlock the door and then with a surge of anticipation push it open. It looks like a college dorm room. Against a wall there are a hang-up closet, two drawers, and a built-in writing desk. On the other wall, there is a twin bed with an oak frame. The mattress is six inches thick. Light floods through an open bar-less window. A palm tree stands next to the window frame. The tip of one of its broad green leaves hangs just inside the sill. Setting the boxes on the desk, I lift a houseplant and place it on the windowsill. It is a fern that I dug up in the yard and planted in a colorful ceramic pot I made in the hobby shop.

I made friends with the clerk whose room was across the hall. Ralph was doing time right out of high school for bank robbery. He had a drug habit he couldn't break. A 15-year prison sentence cured him of that. He became a Christian. We got along well.

Living in the Honor Dorm for the next three months was as close to contentment in a federal prison as one could find. I enjoyed my job and knew whom to avoid in the yard. I liked to watch the big festive cruise ships go up and down the harbor. I had talked the recreation officer into purchasing *Frisbees,* and during free time, Ralph and I would sail them carefully over the baseball field. One must be very aware when throwing things in a prison yard. Imagine accidentally hitting someone in the back of the head such as Tiffany and having it stick in his pink hair curlers. I was a regular in the weight room, but only early in the morning before the weirdoes hit the weight pile with their Neanderthal mindset. I would run the South Yard perimeter for hours at a time on weekends.

Ralph (face blurred) and me outside the T.I. Theater

At count time, the South Yard would empty as the general population inmates headed for their bunks in the North Yard. With only 20 honor inmates, mostly older men, the South Yard became almost like a town park. For an inmate, life was so good, I just had to wonder what would happen next.

* * *

At 5:30 AM, a guard opens my door and flips on the light. "Arrington, get up," he barked. He tosses a small cardboard box at me, "You're leaving. The box is for your stuff."

"Leaving, for where?" I asked.

"Camp Boron, you're going to the high desert, boy."

I look at the box, "All my stuff won't fit in this little box."

"Tough, leave the rest behind, now you got nine minutes."

Dressed in two minutes, I pick up the little box. In goes the radio, my Bible, journals, pictures, and Sam's sandals. I leave my plants. Except for two ceramic pots I made in the pottery shop, I am back to what I carried out of J-3. Such is an inmate's life.

"Move it, Arrington," grumbled the guard.

We walk out into the morning darkness. The guard is quiet but for the sound of his boots and the metallic swish of his ring of keys. I am packing away memories of T.I. We walk across the baseball field; the grass is wet with dew beneath my sneakers. Walking along the breezeway, I stare out over the ocean, which I will not see again for a long time. I am trading ocean breezes for dry desert wind. Entering the North Yard, we pass Animal House. Ahead is J-3. The lights are on in the television room, and I see two orderlies setting up the room for breakfast. The little J-3 yard is dark. I know the little patch of lawn is again an empty stretch of dry dirt with a covering of inmate debris. There is no evidence that I have spent almost a year of my life there.

We pass J-1 squatting sinisterly in the dark. Mose is still there.

The guard opens the door that leads up a flight of stairs past the door to the projection booth. I place a hand against the metal door as it slides into the realm of memories. Entering Control, the guard opens the steel grill and shoves me into the holding cell. It is just a guard thing, an expression of authority over a perceived inferior.

I go over to the window where the broken pane remains and look out. The view is the same, but now everything has meaning where good and bad memories reside deep down inside of me.

I look at J-3 from this rare higher perspective, where I lived out ten months of my life. It looks so small and dreary.

The holding cell fills with four other inmates. I hear federal marshals stomping up the steel stairs. One of them glances in the cell, "I only see five. I have paperwork for six."

"Yeah, we had to find a last-minute replacement. The guy got caught smoking dope last night so no camp for him," said the guard. "They're bringing over a replacement right now."

The door opens as a guard shoves Ralph into control.

It is startling to see him, a warmness washes over me. What are the chances my best friend would abruptly join me? I am pleased to mentally chalk it up to the LORD's handiwork.

For me, the long ride is a miraculous journey of sights and sounds. The marshals are bored, except for Ralph and I, the other inmates sleep. We pick up Interstate 10 and go east. I came this way 18 months ago going west with the cocaine—how strange.

Hours later, we arrive at Boron Federal Prison Camp. It is at the foot of a modest hill in the middle of a vast desert valley with mountains in the hazy distance. Most of the camp's buildings are on the lower part of the hillside. Toward the top of the hill, which rises 300 feet above the desert floor, are the classrooms, wood and metal shops, and a radar dome. During World War II, this was an Army radar station. The buildings are weathered clapboard.

They assign me to a four-man cubical with three strangers. None has been inside a real prison. It fascinates me that these white-collar inmates carry none of the hardened wariness that a prison breeds into its charges. They thought the camp was hard time. I unpack my cardboard box, which takes about 30 seconds.

Ralph and I meet outside. Control and the visiting room are near the gate, six dormitories staggered up the lower part of the hillside. Across from us are the admin building, firehouse, honor dorm, and cafeteria. Opposite the cafeteria, I see something that brings me to an abrupt standstill. "Look," I blurted, "I see sunlight sparkling on water." A sign proclaims swimming on Saturdays and Sundays. It's a swimming pool, I haven't been immersed in water since Florida."

Ralph outdoes me, "Yeah, well I haven't been swimming since high school." He pauses and frowns as he realizes the significance of his words. He stands there acutely depressed.

We continue up the hill. From the top, we can see at least 20 miles in every direction. The flat desert flourishes with sage, tumbleweeds, and cactus. It is fascinating to see so far. I watch a giant B-52 bomber from Edwards Air Force Base fly low over the camp vectoring in on the radar dome above us.

We walk into the cafeteria for lunch. There is a total absence of gang bangers and drugged out weirdoes. I get stuck at the salad bar. There are carrots, tomatoes, cucumbers, broccoli, cauliflower, kidney beans, and croutons. I am in rodent heaven.

Boron Prison Camp viewed from the east. Radar dome on top of the hill. Photo Courtesy of Tim Tyler

After orientation, I see the Unit Manager for job assignment. The man does not like prison inmates. He is bald and has thick leathery skin, "Plumber or a dishwasher?" He asked gruffly.

"Actually, sir, I would like to be an inmate firefighter."

He glares, "Did I say firefighter? Plumber or dishwasher?"

"I said, firefighter because I have a lot of qualifications from the Navy and…" He cuts me off with a wave of his hand.

"Forget firefighter," he shouted. "That position is for honor inmates only. "You're a wise guy, get out of my office."

Outside his door, Ralph waits his turn, "What's he like?"

"A redneck Tiffany doing menopause without meds."

I did not know the Unit Manager had walked to the door.

"That supposed to be funny?" he snarled. He points at Ralph with his chin, "Get inside."

Three minutes later he walks out. "So, how'd it go?" I asked.

"Wanted to know who Tiffany was," Ralph said, "the guy's got issues so I told him."

While waiting for our job assignments, we stacked lava rocks, lots of rocks. During a break, I went into the firehouse to meet with the Safety Officer about a fireman job.

"Why do you want to be a firefighter?" he asked.

"I spent 14 years in the Navy. In damage control parties I was the #1 hose man. I led the attack on a fire in the ship's kitchen. I was a Machinist Mate Chief. I can maintain the equipment and fire trucks. Firefighters help people; maybe even saves lives. It would give my time here meaning and value. I was also a bomb disposal frogman and have extensive training at making right choices in emergencies. I take instruction well and follow orders."

"Really?" he asked, "an inmate who will do what he is told?"

"Sir, I would be the best firefighter you've ever had, I'll work long hours, will do my job efficiently and to the best of my ability."

"I know that firefighters go into life-threatening situations as a team. You must think with a cool head, make right decisions the first time and be willing to lay your life on the line for a victim or even another firefighter. I am focused and have no bad habits."

"You're informed, I will give you that," he said glancing at my file, which he brought to our meeting. "Your record from T.I. looks good, but you're asking me to go against my colleague." He closes my file and drums his fingers on it. A man in thought.

The next morning, Ralph and I are standing outside the Unit Manager's door, who steps out and posts the work assignment sheet. He glares at us as he slams the door closed.

Ralph stares at the list, "I get one word," he grumbled, "Plumbing shop. You get a sentence, Arrington, firehouse, assigned to the honor dorm."

Outside, Ralph asked, "So, what did you say to the Safety Officer? Maybe I should I write this down."

I carry my box to the honor dorm, which is the old military officers' quarters. The one-man rooms are in sets of two with a common bathroom. A firefighter named Henry shares the bathroom. He is an ex-CIA agent, turned politician — turned bribe taker. Henry is an easygoing, casual kind of man. "You are one lucky fellow," he said, "I've never seen the Safety Officer so fired up to get someone on the crew. He and the Unit Manager had one major fight, so he went to the Warden, who approved the deal."

"Hope I haven't caused any bad blood between them."

"No problem, the Safety Officer hates the Unit Manager. Everyone hates the Unit Manager — even the Warden."

"You think the other inmates will be mad that I am in the honor dorm so suddenly?" I asked.

"Na, you're a prison inmate, they won't risk setting you off, besides everyone's stoked that you put it to the Unit Manager."

"I did?"

"Yeah, that guy hates you now."

After dinner, I wash my jeans. They are worn thin from almost two years of constant use. I hang the pants to dry on the open window. Abruptly, the fire siren wails. I grab the damp pants and jam a foot through the crotch. I have torn the pants from the crotch to the knee. I drop them, pull on my sneakers and run down to the firehouse in my T-shirt and boxers. I wasn't going to miss this ride.

Each firefighters' turnouts are ready to don. Their jackets hang from hooks with their helmets. On the floor, the trousers are tucked over the boots. The men simply step into the boots, pull up the trousers, slip on the suspenders, grab their jacket and helmet off the hook, and step to the fire truck. I grab a pair of used trousers from a pile, pull them on, and jam my feet into a pair of too-large rubber boots. A suspender strap is broken on the trousers, but I worry that the truck might leave without me, so one strap and no jacket will have to do.

The chief engineer turns on the flashing red lights. I rush to the workbench where I spy a helmet and run for the truck. I jump aboard with the helmet in one hand and grab hold of a polished chrome handrail with the other. Henry hits a buzzer signaling all are aboard. The chief engineer kicks it into gear and pulls out onto the street. The big truck stops at the gate to pick up a guard escort, and then the fire truck accelerates down the access road.

As the truck gains speed, I am ecstatic. I have only ridden in marshal vans with their semi-darkened windows. I am standing the back of a speeding fire truck trying to snap my helmet strap only to discover it is broken. At Highway 395 we turn southbound. The road is straight as the truck accelerates to 60 mph. I feel the wind getting into my baggy trousers which begin to flap about wildly. I am holding the helmet on with one hand and hanging on to the truck with the other. I consider wedging the helmet into the hose bed when a sizeable bug splats into the faceplate. I keep the helmet on and hope that Henry does not notice my distress.

That is when my trousers begin to slip. The suspender strap is getting longer as it slides through the broken buckle. With my trousers bagging around my thighs, the wind has found ample purchase and is pantsing me. My boxers are waving about like a flag. I am careful not to make eye contact with Henry, whom I can plainly hear laughing.

We hit a long uphill grade, which slows the truck, reducing the wind, but it is too late for my trousers, which are now down around my ankles. Henry is highly amused. I see him push the buzzer on the intercom and speak loudly into it. I might die of humiliation and figure it could not get much worse, when I hear a horn and what sounds like two women hooting. I risk a glance over my shoulder and see the lights of a pickup about 30 feet behind us. They flick on their high beams. I do not doubt Ralph will hear all about it.

Finally, we arrive at the scene where a Volkswagen bug is completely enveloped with fire shooting out of the windows. The car's woman driver stands beside a highway patrol car. The patrolman yells that the gas tank ruptured ten minutes ago. With no threat of the fire spreading, the chief engineer decides that this would be a good time to test the coatless new guy with the droopy drawers.

There is no time to mess with the strap as Henry hands me the nozzle of a black rubber attack hose and points towards the back of

Chapter 16 – Boron Prison Camp, April – May 1984

At 6:00 AM, I stand at the door of the honor dorm waiting for the guard. I hear the crunch of boots on gravel. A flashlight plays over the door's glass panes. I wait until he walks away to step out. I take a few running steps, leap over a tumbleweed, and sprint for the road that leads uphill. I love running in desert solitude. In the predawn twilight, I anticipate surprising jackrabbits, desert mice, and birds. I inhale the crisp air. I am halfway up the hillside when the first Jack startles from a sagebush. It zigzags ahead of me as I put on a burst of speed, trying, but failing, to keep up. It is how I do my wind sprints, chasing bunnies. I love running in the early morning as the vast open vista comes alive with creatures.

I let my mind slip off to memories of deployment as part of a flying team to the Central Pacific.

* * *

In March 1979, my team deployed with Team 7 on an extended mission to check the sunken Japanese ships in Truk Atoll in the Marshall Islands for hazardous ordnance. These shoal-sheltered waters were a stronghold for Japan during World War II. American airplanes pounded the atoll into Japan's version of Pearl Harbor with the Japanese on the receiving end of a massive American fist. Almost a hundred ships lie on the bottom. We will check the ones that lay in depths accessible to divers. However, there was one wreck I was eager to dive. The vessel is lying at a depth of 144 feet. It is a Japanese submarine, the I-169.

As we descend the submarine slowly comes into view. She is resting upright. Sea-faded sunlight dapples the ocean floor. The rippled sand bottom is featureless, like an underwater desert. Passing below 100 feet, the depth compresses my thin rubber wetsuit, decreasing its buoyancy and accelerating my free fall toward the submarine. I pass slowly over the remains of the conning tower. I kick along just a few feet above the hull passing the deck gun. I follow the dark hull back toward the stern. I am almost out of time as I consider the fate of the Japanese sailors. A dive bomber forced the sub to crash dive; she went down with the engine room hatch open. All her sailors drowned or suffocated from lack of oxygen in a submarine tomb with no chance of rescue. Japanese divers heard the men inside pounding on the hull for 24 hours – then the sub went silent.

That evening I walk out to a deserted beach and stare out at the moonlit ocean. Glancing about to make sure that no one is about I reach into my pocket and take out a joint. Before Hawaii, I seldom smoked weed. In Hawaii, there was a casual attitude about it.

Later, one of the divers from Team 7 asked, "Loan me a joint, man."

"What!" How does he know I have pot?

"You know, dude, what you've got hidden in that regulator."

I rolled them while high with Bill, a support diver. He must have told this character, and now I am in a panic. "I threw them away," I lied."

"Yeah, right," he said frowning, not believing me.

I go to my room, remove the hidden joints, and flush them down the toilet. I promise myself that I am done smoking dope.

The heavy German battlecruiser, *Prinz Eugen*. Image shot
of the battlecruiser at Kwajalein Atoll for the nuclear tests.

Two months later we moved our operations to Kwajalein Atoll.

I walk barefoot on a white sand beach to a small catamaran drawn up on the shore. Shoving the light sailing craft into the water, I tow it over to a pier where I have stacked my dive gear and an underwater scooter. It is also where two members of my team, Mike Mullins, and Tommy Dye, are standing. Mike is a large Hawaiian with a deceptively sensitive nature. Tommy is a dedicated weightlifter.

"Sure, you guys don't want to come?" I asked. "This is going to be an exceptional dive, a once in a lifetime opportunity." I could hardly imagine that any diver worth their flippers would pass up a chance to dive on one of the most famous World War II shipwrecks.

"Come on, Chief," Mike said laughing, *"We have been diving on sunken ships practically every day for the past two months. It is our first Sunday off, and you want us to go dive on another wreck for fun?"*

"But it is the Prinz Eugen," I urged, *"How many chances does a guy get to dive on a heavy German battlecruiser?"*

"When does a guy get to get drunk on a Sunday afternoon," said Tommy, *"and there's no one to give him grief about it?"*

"But Eugen fought in one of the most famous sea battles of all time," I countered. *"She was with the Pocket Battleship Bismarck in the English Channel. When the British fleet pounced on her. Bismarck sent the massive Battleship HMS Hood straight to the bottom with one round."*

"Well, I'm about doing some serious drinking," deadpanned Tommy.

Giving up, I raise the catamaran's sail, its colorful canvas fills with wind as the little sailboat scuttles away from the pier. I steer toward the other side of the broad lagoon. The catamaran rapidly picks up speed, skimming across the water. A flock of seabirds flies squawking in my wake but soon abandons the catamaran for a school of fish jumping in the near distance. I imagine the finned predators below, tuna or barracuda, herding the smaller fish to the surface where there is nowhere for them to flee. Altering course slightly, I sail through the melee. The air abounds with shrill squawking as frantic seabirds, their wings beating loudly, dive bomb the surface on either side of the swift-sailing catamaran.

The sailboat is speeding at about 14 knots with flying fish leaping out of the water before the swift catamaran. I think how my teammates are wasting an incredible diving opportunity to get drunk. I am thankful that I threw my dope away two months ago. I think clearer with greater focus and my mental discipline has improved. I make a silent promise not to smoke marijuana again. I would remember that promise made impulsively and think how much different my life would have been had I honored that pledge. I have since realized that a commitment not honored is a lie fulfilled. The result can be devastating far beyond life's expectations.

I hear the twin hulls cutting the water, the ruffle of wind in the sail and the fading sounds of the seabirds. I gaze at cumulus clouds drifting across the horizon against a royal blue sky. Then there is a lush green barrier island. I head for its shore where there is a white coral beach with tall coconut trees leaning over pale blue shallows. The water becomes a dark blue as the white bottom abruptly falls away. I see sunlight glistening on a huge brass propeller protruding out of the water. I peer at the massive ship lying mostly upside down on the bottom.

Damaged during the Bikini Island nuclear tests, a storm drove her against the island where she rolled and sank. Her stern just protrudes from the surf with the bow lying at a depth of 120 feet.

Donning my dive gear, I plunge into the warm, inviting water and then pull in the underwater scooter. I stare through my dive mask at the capsized wreck that awaits me. The clear water is alive with schools of tropical fish. Below, I see the massive war ship with its living canopy of colorful corals and swaying sea fans waving back and forth in a light surge. Just a fraction of the enormous ship is visible. This is a world-class dive site. It's remoteness and security restrictions mean few will dive it.

Triggering the scooter, I begin a spiraling descent through the tropical water. Riding behind an underwater scooter is like flying in slow motion. Imagining I am a World War II pilot, I do a wing over as I pass over a twelve-inch gun turret that has fallen to the side of the wreck. As I pass over the armored side of the battlecruiser there is a sheathing of colorful corals that cover the superstructure. Various schools of fish, their scales glistening in the soft light, swarm the wreck, swimming into and out of deck compartments. They flow through doors and gush from round portholes like holiday streamers riding a gusting summer wind.

I must contain my urge to explore, wanting to conduct the deepest part of the dive first to build a safety factor for decompressing later. I skim just inches from the wood planks above me watching small tropical fish flee in sudden alarm as the headlamp paints them in their brilliant colors. To the little fish, my scooter with its dazzling headlight must look like an aquatic locomotive hurtling out of the depths. I am thoroughly enjoying this until I see a small fish, blinded by my light, flee right in front of a larger drab camouflaged fish hiding beneath a cleat. The bigger fish sucks the little yellow, blue, and black fellow into its jaws. The small fish wiggles frantically as the bigger fish's jaws flex, and then the little fish disappears down its throat. The image burns into my mind. I feel horrible about the little death in my wake as some of the magic of the dive drains away.

Approaching the bridge, I see a small, black-tipped reef shark cruising out of an open port. It is not a very big shark, but where there is one, there is probably more. Diving alone can be unsettling, particularly in deep water. Warily, I glance over my shoulder, not expecting to see anything. A giant 300-pound grouper swims just off my flank. Hoping he is simply curious; I turn the scooter right at him. With rapid beats of its tail, the monster fish swiftly disappears down into the darkness below.

I am abruptly having bothersome thoughts that in the deep darkness lurking below nature may be preparing to swallow me whole and spit my life right out of existence

My depth gauge reads 104 feet. The gloomy water gets darker. I finally see the shadowed form of the bow. Knowing that big predatory fish is lurking in the darkness, I promptly retreat to clearer and warmer water. I keep imagining that big fish skulking just over my shoulder. Big-mouthed groupers inhale their prey. I am having troublesome images of just my flippers sticking out from its massive lips. I am now regretting seeing that little fish swallowed. Knowing it was my fault gets me to worrying about things like karma.

Ascending to the 50-foot level without seeing the big fish, I am eager to explore the interior of the capsized ship. Tying the scooter off to a handrail, I cautiously swim into an open door aft of the bridge. The glow of my dive light plays off pale soft sponges and causes a spider crab to run for cover leaving little clouds of silt that traces his tiny steps across the ceiling of the upside-down cabin like the impact of tracers. Along the inside bulkhead is a rack of explosive-filled torpedoes. I know they are live weapons because the Navy wanted to see if their nuclear tests got any secondary explosions. Another reason why few will get to dive this wreck.

Swimming down a narrow corridor, I slip deeper inside the ship, a coating of silt covers all the exposed surfaces untouched by cleansing ocean currents. A spreading darkness precedes me the deeper I go. I am careful to keep my fin kicks minimal so as not to stir up the silt and ruin the visibility. Glancing at my air gauge and checking my watch, I know it is time to return to the scooter and ascend.

Twenty feet from the surface I pause for a short safety stop to out gas nitrogen, then take another two-minute decompression stop at ten feet. After attaching the scooter to a line hanging from the catamaran, I amuse myself by trying to make friends with a small fish, which flees in sudden alarm. I turn and see the big grouper. I scream at it in surprise, which comes out as a blast of bubbles. The big fish bolts for the bottom as I rocket out of the water and scramble up onto the boat.

Sailing back into a light tropical rain, I heel the catamaran tighter into the gusting trade wind. Entering the little harbor, I tie up the small boat and hurry off to find my friends. I cannot wait to tell them about the giant grouper and the magnificent wreck.

Entering the darkened bar, I smell the stench of cigarette smoke hanging in a lingering cloud. Loud music blasts from a jukebox, and I see the frogs from our twin teams at the bar. One of them snores loudly, his head resting near a puddle of spilled beer. The others are drunk and arguing some foolish point. Fortunately, they do not see me as I quickly step back outside into the late afternoon sunlight.

Following a jungle path back toward the harbor, I am pleased I threw away my marijuana. I had foolishly risked my naval career, but there is something more that I have stupidly put at risk, something so important that I have been working diligently toward its realization for two years.

The Navy offers its enlisted men the opportunity to join its officer's ranks through the LDO (Limited Duty Officer) Program. Enlistees who

*reach the rank of E-6 or above (I am an E-7) can apply for the program. I
have every reason to be hopeful. Unlike the rest of the Navy, EOD Teams
require a high ratio of officers to enlisted men. The command has billets to
advance four enlisted men this year from EODMUONE, and I am
determined to be one of them. Lieutenant (junior grade) Stephen
Arrington has such a nice ring to it.*

* * *

Weeks pass at the prison camp. I am in my room, while a late-spring sandstorm rages outside the window. Sand is seeping in through the weathered frame of the windowsill and falls in a steady stream to the floor. The falling grains remind me of the slow, relentless passage of prison time.

I figure nothing could lure me out of the room on a day like this — then over the mournful howl of the wind, I hear the wail of the fire siren and bolt from the room. Sprinting into the fury of the sandstorm, I see the Chief Engineer driving the red Mack fire truck out of the large, double doors. The older truck's headlamps, dimmed yellow by the blowing sand, resemble two huge eyes. For an instant, the red fire truck with the side aluminum ladders resembling wings looks like a raging dragon exiting its lair.

I don turnouts and leap onto the back carriage of the 48 Mack. We accelerate with the rear of the truck fishtailing into a high-speed turn. Our mechanical beast flies into the storm, the roar of its siren a primal scream that clears lesser vehicles from its path.

Clinging to the back of the truck, I revel in the excitement of the moment as the sand-laden wind whips past my face shield. Life inside prison walls has been slow and much too dreary, the prison sentence seems to drag. My spirit yearns for new vistas, outside adventure, passion, and excitement.

We climb the grade to the south, leaving the blowing sand behind, then top the hill, and arrive at the scene of a terrible accident, where a head-on collision occurred between a small pickup truck and a delivery van. The driver of the van is hurt, but his injuries are minor. In the wreckage of the pickup truck — the young driver is dying. I stand at the front of the crumpled vehicle with a charged fire hose in case of fire. Most of the shattered windshield has broken away. I have an unhindered view of the young man's last moments. After prying off the jammed driver's door, the other firefighters are trying desperately to keep him alive. The steering wheel pins him to the seat. There are cuts to his face, which hardly bleed—a sure sign we are losing him. I watch his eyes go out of focus as his head falls to one side, and then his body slumps as the life drains out of him.

We gently lay the body on the desert ground. I watch tentacles of blood weep from the body slowly soaking into the cracked dirt and porous desert sand. While waiting for the coroner to come I think about this young man's life so abruptly cut off. Nothing is fair or unfair about life—it simply is. Each human existence is a mystery waiting to be played out. Our best chance for a quality, meaningful life is to do good things, to be aware, to strive for excellence, to hold truth dear, to love, and to commit to a loving God who cares about us without reservation despite our faults and weaknesses. He knows that as our relationship with Him grows and matures our Christian walk will encourage hope and eagerness to change. Instead of being a slave of the sins of the world, we become enslaved by His righteousness.

When the coroner arrives, we help him bag the body and place it in his vehicle. Then I use the fire hose to wash the blood deep into the dirt and sand. "From dust to dust," has never had more meaning for me than at that moment.

That night, after the winds have subsided, the stars stand out clearly in the dark sky. Gazing into the black void of the desert sky, I listen to two Mexican inmates outside on the dormitory steps, playing guitars and singing a sad Spanish song. Their melancholy melodies lead me to think about the vibrancy of life and how suddenly it can end.

In my hand, I hold a ripe peach. It is my first peach in prison. I bought it at the camp store. A prison clerk purchased several lugs of the fruit as a treat for us. Turning the peach in my hand, I inhale its fragrance and look at the soft, subtle colors of the fuzz-covered skin. I have never so carefully looked at a peach. I realize how perfect of a creation a peach is as I sink my teeth into its succulent flesh. As this sad day ends, it feels good to be alive, and the peach tastes delicious.

Spring is sliding towards early summer. My day begins with an eight-mile run. On the final leg of my last loop, I slow to a walk and look down toward the firehouse a quarter mile away. It is such a profound blessing to be an inmate firefighter with such crucial responsibilities. The LORD has given me an extraordinary gift. The general inmate condition is a constant feeling of despair and lack of self-worth. To be a convicted felon is to be a flawed human being. It is like wearing your corruption on the outside for all to see.

I walk into the firehouse. All the men in the engine bay are looking sober as I remember this is the Chief Engineer's last day. He is getting out early and not sure how it feels about it. The biggest problem facing a soon to be released inmate is the lurking question of an uncertain future in a world that may not want him back. He shakes hands with each of us before walking away.

Henry, now the senior firefighter, asked, "Are we agreed?" There is a general nodding of heads. Then they look in unison at me. Henry walks to the chief engineer's hook and removes the red helmet. He walks to my firefighting gear, removes my yellow helmet, and hangs the chief engineer's red helmet.

I stand there stupefied. The senior firefighter should become chief engineer—not the junior man. As I watch, a smile creases Henry's face, and then the team files quietly into the office. I touch the helmet. My heart thuds in my chest with emotion. I have not felt like this since my graduation from bomb disposal school eight years ago. I am again part of something special. We may be incarcerated men, but we belong to a fraternity of heroes.

I spend the next 15 minutes walking around the Ford truck, touching its equipment and running my hands over the paint. I open the cab of the old Mack and climb inside. I say a prayer of thanks and ask that I might be worthy and that none of these men get hurt or die under my leadership. Then I start the engine and drive out of the firehouse.

Every morning the job of the chief engineer is to drive the fire trucks around the loop of the hill to make sure all is working. The last vehicle I drove was on the wrong side of the law. Now, because of the vote of inmates, I can honestly consider myself one of the good guys again. There is no doubt in my mind that God loves surprising us with the depth of his love.

I motor out onto the road and turn uphill. Two men are walking the tarmac. They are defiant, unwilling to step aside. I drive slowly, not minding that the walkers linger on the road. I realize that they are expressing their independence. To them, I am just another inmate. To honk my horn would be beyond foolish. Therefore, I drive up the hill in first gear at walking speed. Finally, they step grudgingly out of the way. They stare at me as I pass. I smile and wish them a good morning continuing up the hill at a slow speed. In prison, it is all about respect.

Later, at lunch, I see the two men who were walking the hill staring at me. They both smile and nod. On the hill, I could have encouraged the men to view me in a positive or a negative way. The right choice took a little extra effort on my part. Consideration of others is a key to finding simple happiness in life.

After lunch, I walk back to the firehouse and see the men waxing the big Ford. They will not let me share in the work, so I go into the safety officer's office.

"Morning, Sir," I said politely. He has his boots up on the desk as he reads the local newspaper.

"Hey Chief," he replied.

Those two words stop me in my tracks.

"Is it something I said?" he asked.

"After I left the Navy, I never thought I would be called chief again," I said in wonder.

He smiles, "I didn't have anything to do with that decision although I think they made a good choice. I figure it is better to let the crew pick their leader." He leans forward, "They can also ask you to step down. It's all about trust."

"I will not let them down."

"Figured that," he said flipping the page on his newspaper.

* * *

A week later, Ralph and I are sitting on a bench outside the honor dorm watching the fading sunset and talking.

"You know, Steve," pondered Ralph, "it's eerie how lucky you are for an inmate. The judge could have nailed you, yet he let you off with five years. Considering the magnitude of your case, that is a darn small punishment. At T.I. lots of good things happened to you including getting into the honor dorm amazingly early. You were in general population for what, just four months?"

"Yeah, but there were a few tough moments where I could have gotten hurt or killed."

"Yeah, but fortune smiled on you even then," said Ralph. "Here you not only score the best job in the whole Federal Department of Corrections, but you also move into the honor dorm in just a week. That kind of stuff just does not happen accidentally. Now a few months go by, and suddenly you are in charge of the fire department. Why are you so darn lucky?"

I smile, "I am not so much lucky, as I am blessed."

"What's the difference?"

"The difference is the source. Luck is happenstance, though you can aid your pursuit of being lucky by doing good with your life. However, blessed is purposeful—it comes from God."

"You are being blessed on purpose?" he asked, "By God?"

"I don't doubt it," I said with assurance.

"You believe God thinks you're special?" There was a ring of sarcasm in Ralph's tone.

"No more than anyone else," I answered honestly. "I simply believe He is laying the foundation for me to do something good with my life. He loves all of us and knows that doing good for others changes us. It allows us a closer relationship with God. Surrendering to the LORD and having Jesus Christ and the Holy Spirit abide in us changes a person in the best ways possible."

"But why are you being so blessed?" Ralph asked seriously.

"Ralph, I have always tried to be a good person, but I was harboring a lot of bad habits and was completely self-motivated. When things went wrong, I didn't have the character traits to make the right choices. Instead, I slipped over to the wrong side. God wanted me back. That's why reading the Bible is so important. It teaches us that only God can take evil and turn it to good."

. "You were guilty," exclaimed Ralph, "but there were mitigating circumstances. Do you believe you were evil?"

I nod, "The Bible is showing me the path back to the good side. That's where happiness resides and that is where I want to be."

"Yeah, but doing what?" Ralph said with a frown. "Good jobs are few and hard to find for ex-felons."

"It's not exactly a job, but rather a mission. I would like to talk with youth about hope."

"Then you're going to talk about choices, right?"

"No, youths have adults talking at them about choices all the time. I want to share a kind of hope that never surrenders. A foundational concept that youth can build their dreams on. I'm talking about the hope that someone can honestly believe in—the kind of hope that changes lives."

"That's it? Just hope."

"Hope that never surrenders, is a powerful way of thinking and being yet hope doesn't exist in a vacuum. I would tie it in with life skills and character traits that lead to happiness and success in life: discipline, a desire to succeed, commitment, team building, fitness, leadership, and the pursuit of adventure." I am thinking of a kinder Gunner McNair approach. Then again, many youths would love a McNair type of teaching without the softer side.

The sudden wail of the fire siren shatters the still of the desert night. I erupt from the bench and hit the ground running. *A blessing happening in real time, thank you, LORD! I send up a prayer of thanks as I run joyously.*

In the firehouse, I don my trousers and boots, climb into the driver's seat, and hit the ignition. My jacket and helmet are already lying on the seat where I placed them earlier. The helmet's visor is defogged by cleaning it with toothpaste. I am so ready for this moment, like a 16-year-old with a brand-new driver's license, his car freshly polished and poised for that first driving adventure. I pull the big truck out onto the threshold, and key the mic, "San Bernardino Command, Engine Company 52, standing by."

The reply is instant, "Roger, 52, respond Code 3 (red light and siren), single-car accident involving injuries, Route 395, two miles south of four corners."

"Roger, 52 responding Code 3," I have a sudden urge to pee, but with two deep breaths, it passes. Henry slides into the passenger seat followed by an escort officer. A buzzer announces that the last firefighter is aboard. I floor the pedal. The fire engine charges out of the bay. The camp gate swings up as we hurl down the road, lights strobing the desert landscape red, the siren like a primal scream challenging the night.

I glance over at Henry and the guard. They are both grinning at me, fully caught up in the excitement of the moment. I send a loud surfer hoot sailing out the window and go for fourth gear. I am ecstatic. In my excitement, my right foot trembles from jamming down the gas pedal. Even the guard is fully into it. I have seen guards angry, disgusted, bored, and occasionally smiling, but never excited in a happy way. We are sharing a human moment. It is not a guard and his charges—it is three guys inside a fire engine on a red-light-and-siren adventure.

Eight miles down the highway we come upon a station wagon with its front end embedded in a sandbank. A broken path of torn desert brush and deep tire marks in the brown sand tell of a car out of control. It had blown a tire and the elderly man driving it had almost rolled the vehicle. His wife sits beside the car with an injured leg. The rest of the crew quickly renders first aid while I confirm that the ambulance is only a short distance away.

This is a tame emergency response. We provide basic first aid for their minor cuts and lend comfort to the elderly couple.

After the ambulance departs with the couple, we turn the scene over to a highway patrol officer and drive back toward the camp. I have the window down to enjoy the warm desert air blowing into the cab. There is just something special about driving a fire engine, particularly during the magic of a dark night with all the lit gauges glowing softly against the chrome dashboard.

At Four Corners, we stop to fill the fire truck's gas tank. The guard treats us to a cup of gas station coffee, which is about five times better than what they serve us at the prison chow hall. It is the best cup of coffee I have ever had.

Later, lying in bed, I turn my thoughts to what I told Ralph about being blessed. I believe with all my heart that God wants to bless each of us in a good way. The good things that come of it will prompt us to share it with others.

"For I know the plans I have for you," declares the LORD, "plans to prosper you and not to harm you, plans to give you hope and a future." — Jeremiah 29:11 (NIV).

Therefore, I ask myself, *'What would be the most amazing gift God could have given me in prison?'*

In the Navy, my specialty training was leading a team of bomb disposal frogmen into dangerous and trying situations. It was the most meaningful and purposeful part of my life. Then the corruption of drugs perverted my values and destroyed my drive and motivation. I fell a long way downwards into oblivion.

What boggles my mind now was my willingness to stay in the hole I dug—smoking that stupid weed. Yeah, I was making motions towards a better life by going to college, but it was all a façade, I was hiding behind a smoke screen so to speak. I had no real-life plan, just rolling with the moment.

At Terminal Island, I found Christ and my life immediately began to change. Now suddenly, I am leading a group of inmate firefighters. We have little training and old firefighting equipment, yet we are on a mission to save lives. I mean who ever heard of an inmate driving anything? I am driving a fire engine out of prison in emergency response to save lives.

Now, that is an incredible gift, tailored for an inmate, by a very loving God. My chief engineer job is a complex blessing that gives my life meaning and purpose while in prison. Yes, I do not doubt that He is preparing me for something, and I will not fail Him.

Engine Company 52 at a San Bernardino training event
Henry is the tall man to my right.

The camp boils under the summer sun with no relief. Unable to sleep, I let my mind drift back to the end of my military career.

* * *

I am working in the Operations Department at Lualualei Naval Weapons Station when the Executive Officer posts a list on the bulletin board. "This is the promotion list from the LDO selection board." I rush over, my name is not on it. Two men deserve advancement, but two do not. I feel entitled to my judgment because I typed their applications.

There are guidelines on how to format the LDO application. Part of the selection process is to ensure that the candidate could originate official correspondence that meets the literary standards of the Navy. One of the applicants complained that I had an unfair advantage. In the Operations Department, I had the use of a magnetic card typewriter. In 1979, the personal computer did not exist. My IBM typewriter had a credit-card-sized slot into which I could insert a memory card. On it, I could type a three-page letter without error. In the late seventies, it was a big deal.

To eliminate my unfair advantage, the Executive Officer decided that the other candidates would print their letters with pencil and paper then give them to me to type. The document included evaluations, awards, recommendations, as well as correspondence and college courses completed. Having read the other applications, I was confident of my selection. I had spent over two years preparing and had far outperformed the other men. Two did nothing, just submit a weak application. None had attended college, while I was close to a two-year degree.

Reading the names of the officers on the selection board, I see that they only selected candidates from their own teams.

Enraged, I go to the commanding officer's office and knuckle the door. I step inside as the CO looks up at me and frowns. "I know why you're here, Chief. "You weren't selected because you have less than three years with the command. The other men were more experienced."

"Excuse me, but time in command is not part of the selection criteria."

"The experience requirement is the prerogative of the board. But the defining reason you were not selected is that you are too immature."

"What?"

"You live in a truck. A surf mobile I think they call it."

"That's ridiculous," I said insulted.

"What's ridiculous is to have one of our officers living in a truck like a surf bum. Wait until next year; I can guarantee you'll be accepted, particularly if you get rid of that stupid surf wagon."

I am speechless. Incredibly, the CO takes my silence as acceptance. He shifts gears, "We need to send a team out to the USS Enterprise. The officer-in-charge will be one of the new LDO's. He has never served on an aircraft carrier, so I want him to have a chief who has plenty of flight deck experience. You leave in a couple of weeks."

He just admitted I have plenty of flight deck experience having served on three carriers. So, I am supposed to babysit the E-6. On the verge of fury, I growled, "Not a good idea. You'll have to bring me back before the deployment is over. My enlistment is up in three months. I have given over 13 years of service believing that I would always be treated fairly by the Navy. I no longer hold that illusion."

Stomping out of his office, I think, 'Did I really just do that?'

Surprisingly, my emotional decision to leave the Navy resulted in my selling Revelstoke to Bill, a support diver who had long coveted it. I needed the money to return to California and finish my BA degree with financial assistance from the G.I. Bill. I moved in with Bill and his new wife in the enlisted housing to save money. It was astounding how quickly my life was changing.

USS Arizona BB-39, New York City on Dec 24, 1916.

A week later, I am on a 16-foot-long Boston Whaler tied up to the Arizona Memorial. The King of Tonga is going to lay a flower wreath at the memorial, and we are part of his security party, making sure that no terrorist has placed any bombs along his intended path. Bill is on my team as a support diver for this mission. We check under the Memorial's platform then descend toward the sunken wreck below. The water is murky. I switch on a dive light. The beam barely pierces the deep gloom. Tidal clouds of sediment drift in the murky water. Then in the wavering funnel of yellow light, I see a ship's hatch. This is America's largest steel coffin for the regiment of tortured souls entombed within.

Swimming the main deck of the ghostly ship, I ponder the last acts of the doomed men inside. On an early Sunday morning, the bombs rained down unexpectedly. Many men were still in their bunks when the massive explosions tore through the mighty warship. Plunged into darkness and surrounded by thunderous explosions over a thousand men died.

Placing my hand against a porthole's armored hatch, I mentally build a distinctive image of what it must have been like, the huge explosions within confined compartments, the roar of fire and the rushing sound of flooding water — and of men screaming their lives out. Then as the dreadnaught settled toward the bottom, they would have heard the groaning of steel bulkheads buckling — without even knowing that Japan had just thrown down the gauntlet of war.

Swimming along the deck of the stricken gray dreadnought, I stick my hand through a thick layer of clinging mud and sediment to touch the wooden deck. The timber is grimy and rotten. Each kick of my fins lifts a veil of black silt that rises slowly in a mushrooming cloud. It is soul-chilling cold down here. The water seeping into my wetsuit feels like an icicle creeping down my spine. I aim the muted yellow beam of my light upward then follow its dim cone back toward the surface. I peer once more down into the depths at the gray lady that has lost her fleet. I see the silt cloud closing over it like an open grave caving into itself.

On the Boston Whaler, I cannot get my dive gear off fast enough. We load our boat on a trailer and take it back to Lualualei Weapons Station.

Later, at Bill's house, I could not shake a feeling of deep dismay. I am troubled by the mental holocaust of immersion with a thousand drowned souls when I hear Bill say the words that would doom the end of my military career. "Want an instant attitude adjustment?" he asked holding up a marijuana joint.

"It just doesn't matter anymore," I thought regretfully watching Bill take a hit. Reaching for the joint, I do not grasp that this smoldering cylinder is a coffin spike that seals my fate, hurling me down a dark path toward corruption and bereavement.

Bill rolls the smoking joint between his fingers, "This stuff is Maui elephant buds, it's the best, man," he said leaning forward. "I know where I can get an ounce of it pretty cheap."

"Get it; I'll buy some from you."

"Can't," lamented Bill, "I don't have the dough, but if you put up the cash, I'll sell three-quarters of it then I will give you back your money, and we'll split the rest. It'll be like smoking for free," he leers.

I put up the money, and Bill sold the three-quarters bag that night, which led to our buying more dope. Bill began every day with a joint. Once he even referred to marijuana as his best friend.

Two months before my enlistment was up, Bill and I were busted by the NIS (Naval Investigative Service). I heard them coming through the front door and ran to flush the evidence – and that is how I was arrested, kneeling at a toilet with my arm buried elbow deep into the bowl.

While awaiting my court-martial, Bill asked me to buy back Revelstoke as he and his new wife desperately needed the money.

It was a moment that will haunt me forever, as I stood before the court of five naval officers in total disgrace. Ours was an elite command, and I had tumbled from its ranks. Once so proud to be a Navy bomb disposal frogman, I was now an acute embarrassment to the command I loved. In the back of the court are seven men from the teams, five officers, and two senior chief petty officers. They have volunteered to make statements regarding my character before my drug problem. Before they can be called to the stand, the judge asked to talk privately with the prosecuting officer and my defense counsel.

The military lawyer defending me returns to our table. "Bad news," he said, "Since you're pleading guilty, they can't call witnesses against you. However, if anyone make positive statements about your character, the prosecution will get to call his witness."

"There is a witness against me?"

"Your buddy, Bill," he said with a shrug. "They are giving him a deal. He is going to testify that you were the one in charge of the whole marijuana thing and that he worked for you. It won't go well. You outrank him, so the board will assume that it's all probably true. I have to ask the judge to excuse our witnesses."

When the judge dismisses the men, I resist turning around to watch them go. I put my head down in my hands and close my eyes. I hear the men stand up. There is a brief conversation and then the sound of men walking, but they are not leaving, they are striding in my direction. All seven in their dress white uniforms with rows of ribbons on their chests walk in a file to the bench behind me. One places a comforting hand on my shoulder and squeezes reassuringly. They stand there for a moment at rigid attention then they sit down on the bench as one.

I turn to stare at the grim-faced men. They risk much regarding their careers by lending their support to a military felon. They are with honor; mine hangs about me in tatters. They deserve the respect their presence commands; I am throwing myself at the mercy of a military court. My defense counsel leans close and whispers, "I've never seen anything like this before. It is huge. They could not have made a more powerful statement regarding clemency. Whatever the judge rules, whatever your sentence, know that these men still believe in you."

I sit up straighter, turn in my chair, look each man in the eye, and nod my thanks. Each touches me, a pat on the shoulder or a handshake.

Despite the support of these respectable men, the court gives me a reduction in grade from chief petty officer to seaman recruit, a sentence of one month in the brig, and a Bad Conduct Discharge.

The Naval Brig at Pearl Harbor is an imposing two-story building of a cement block design. Crossed sledgehammers hang over the entrance as I step reluctantly inside. A stern-faced marine sergeant waits at a desk. He marches me into the guardroom where he orders me to remove all insignias from my uniform. From my collar, I take the silver and brass fouled anchors that symbolize my rank as a chief petty officer and place them on a scarred wooden table followed by three bars of Vietnam-era ribbons, including the Naval Certificate of Merit for lifesaving, my gold jump-wings and the silver insignia that identifies me as a bomb disposal *frogman. Memories of McNair pinning that device to my chest try to echo through my mind, but I shut it all out. Then, removing my khaki uniform and clad only in my boxer shorts, I sit on a wooden stool while the marine guard roughly shaves my head.*

I stand humiliated, then the marine guard leads me down a corridor still clad only in my boxer shorts and locks me into an isolation cell. The days pass slowly while I sit alone in that cell rummaging through my thoughts of personal failure.

Nothing in the world is more dangerous than sincere ignorance and conscientious stupidity. — Dr. Martin Luther King

* * *

Excerpt from Lieutenant Commander Thomas Marshall USN:

In 1978, I was the executive officer of EOD Mobile Unit One, where Steve served under me. He was two years out of EOD School and eagerly pursuing his career. Steve was highly regarded and encouraged to pursue a commission as a Limited Duty Officer. He was professionally qualified and considered our leading candidate. I departed the Mobile Unit before any selections were made and was not involved in any of the process.

Later, it was very surprising that Chief Arrington was not selected. It played a role in his fall, however, what utterly destroyed a fine naval career was his abuse of marijuana. In Hawaii, there was a very casual attitude towards marijuana, which continues to grow across the United States and around the world. It directly led to his involvement in the DeLorean Case and to a lengthy period of incarceration. Steve fell a long way, and it was a long journey for him to claw his way back. I am pleased that Steve now works so hard to keep youth off drugs and encourages them to make positive life choices. —Commander Thomas Marshall, USN, retired, November 25, 2017

Good decisions come from experience and experience comes from bad decisions. –Mark Twain

Chapter 17 - Boron Prison Camp, August 1984

We are on the hill in the education building. When the fire siren wails and the guard's radio squawks, "Fire crew, respond Code 3, a military aircraft has crashed north east of the camp."

Running to the fire engine, I see a cloud of smoke billowing into the sky. An Air Force fighter circles the site. I hope it is not a downed B-52 bomber. The giant Stratofortress is loaded with explosive hazards and components that when burning can emit highly toxic gases.

I key the ignition, switch on the radios, and hit the red light and siren. The high-low wail of the siren precedes the fire truck down the hill. Double clutching, I jam the shift lever into third even as a tracer of doubt flashes through my mind. If we are not careful, an inmate firefighter could die today. I think about the new man we added realizing I need to keep a tight rein on the men — ignorance combined with over-enthusiasm could put the crew in jeapordy.

We are responding with the 1965 Ford fire engine, a pickup truck with a small water pumper in its back bed, and the camp ambulance. In the rear-view mirror, I see a four-wheel drive carryall fall in behind us as I reach for the microphone.

"San Bernardino Command, Engine 52 responding Code 3 to a downed military aircraft. Be advised we are heading for a thick column of black smoke rising into the sky six miles northeast of Boron Prison Camp in open desert terrain. Engine 52 urgently requests multiple engine backup."

"Roger 52, advise size and type of aircraft."

I key the mic, "The smoke column is rising thousands of feet into the air and climbing. It's a large military aircraft, it could be a B-52 Stratofortress bomber with explosives and weapons."

"Company 52, did you say B-52 Stratofortress bomber?"

"Roger," I confirmed, "we don't know what we're responding to, but it is big. I can see an Air Force fighter circling the crash site. Call Edward's Air Base and ask if they are missing anything large and if there is ordnance and how many souls are on board."

"Roger, 52. Keep us posted on your progress."

The squelch on the radio hisses as the call goes out, "Three Alarm fire, Engine Companies 14, 18 and 24, respond Code 3, aircraft down: possibly a B-52 Stratofortress with ordnance, in rugged desert terrain. Assist Engine 52 enroute in the vicinity of Boron Prison Camp with best off-road capable engines."

I mentally see images of the other firehouses, fire engines rolling out of bays with sirens wailing. I glance at Henry in the passenger seat. It is the first time for me to drive the fire truck without a guard in that seat. The Safety Officer is well ahead of us in the pickup truck with an inmate fireman.

Down the highway, I see a cloud of dust where the pickup truck turned onto a firebreak. The ambulance takes the turn too fast. It slides across the dirt into a shallow ditch. The ambulance driver gets out and waves me on as I accelerate into the turn. The back of the fire truck fishtails throwing a broad swath of dirt and gravel. I hear the men on the back hollering happily. There are cuts and potholes in the firebreak. The carryall rides too closely in the thick dust cloud trailing my fire engine. The driver does not see a hole in the firebreak. The carryall hits the hole solidly. In my side mirror, I see it weaving sharply from side to side before it slows to a stop.

Later, I would learn that the battery broke free and slammed into the engine breaking the radiator fan. I follow the dust cloud of the pickup truck ahead. The guard I have left behind has never rolled with us, so I do not need him. In the side mirror, I see a compartment spring open spilling its contents. A fire extinguisher bounces off leaving clouds of dust with each impact.

Ahead, the pickup swings into open desert terrain, following a direct line toward the smoke column. I follow, employing skills learned in the Navy operating four-wheel-drive vehicles over rugged jungle roads and on sand beaches. I see the pickup mow down sagebrush that hid a two-foot drop. The truck launches off the edge; the right-side tires partially leave the ground. It crashes down hard with its heavy load of water in the back bed. It rolls 50 feet plowing down plants and knocking over cactus before rolling to a stop in a cloud of dust. The firefighter and the Safety Officer jump out and climb onto the big Ford as I slow alongside. The Safety Officer opens the side door and crowds in next to Henry. The firefighter rides on the doorstep holding onto the mirror.

I hope that we do not get stuck in the soft sand or in one of the shallow ravines. When the rough terrain gets worse, I send the inmate on the step running ahead to help pick a clear path. I use our heavy bumper to knock down shrubs and bushes. Soon the running man lags in his firefighter trousers and rubber boots. I honk my horn and beckon him back to the truck. Another inmate strips off his heavy jacket and leaps off the back of the truck to take his place, running against time, running to save lives.

We come to a flat area, and I hit the horn to call the running inmate back aboard. I pick up speed then abruptly see a gully. It is a wide drop-off, and there is no way around it. I can see that the other side has a soft two-foot tall slope. I glance left and then quickly right. The gully is too long. I commit to a split-second decision. I downshift as I let the RPM drop off and drive over the edge. The front tires collapse the gully's rim as the front of the truck noses down two feet. I feel the fire engine's undercarriage scooping dirt from the rim. The twin rear tires drop down and momentarily spin before our forward momentum carries us forward. I keep the front tires straight, yet the rear slides a bit in the soft sand. The gully is about 30 yards wide. I am gentle with the gas to keep the rear tires from spinning. I shift to neutral and then quickly downshift into first. The technique is known as double-clutching because the first gear is not synchronized. We are down to three mph, but I now have the added torque of the lowest gear. I increase the throttle as we slowly climb over the rim.

Abruptly, the accident site is before us. We are 200 yards from a raging fire, which is off to our left. It is the remains of the aircraft. Flames are shooting over a hundred feet into the air, fed by the burning wreck's exotic metals, tires, and remaining jet fuel. The leading edge of the fire races to the east driven by a gusting wind. Peering through gaps in a thick cloud of rolling smoke I see a glint of reflected light splashing off something shiny — stunned, I realize it is the cockpit of B-1A supersonic strategic bomber! The B1-A is still in prototype stage. It is America's newest top-secret deep-penetration warplane. My EOD training and skills will be extremely useful today. I know the hazards my men are facing. I speed up angling toward cockpit.

"It's the B-1A Supersonic Strategic Bomber," I yelled.

"Looks like it broke in half. The crew couldn't have survived," the Safety Officer said woefully.

"No, hopefully they just banged up," I said hopefully. "See the parachutes? The B-1A is the only plane where the whole crew goes out together. The cockpit is an ejection pod. The hatch is closed, that means the men inside are in trouble."

The spreading brush fire is threatening to engulf the escape pod. One of three drogue chutes draped over the back of the capsule is smoldering. We have to stop that fire, or the men inside will die."

Abruptly, there is a loud thumping noise, as two Air Force helicopters fly directly over us. The choppers are only 30 feet off the desert floor as they pass us on each side of the fire engine's cab. The wind from their passage washes over the fire engine as they pull up and half-circle the site at a steep angle.

"When I stop, you run for the pod, take two firefighters, and get those crewmen out. Henry, you and the new guy, will help me take care of the fire."

I keep my speed up then break hard while spinning the wheel as I try to throw a swath of sand and dirt from the rear wheels into the flames but am only modestly successful. The fire truck slides to a stop between the fire and the capsule. The Safety Officer and two inmates sprint for the ejection pod's hatch.

Jumping out of the cab, I use a fire extinguisher to knock down the closest flames that threaten the engineer's station. Henry and the new guy pull out the attack hoses. I charge the hoses to half the normal pressure to conserve water. This is an up close, in your face, fire attack. The helicopters settle to the ground amidst clouds of swirling dust. The flames about the engineer's station close in again. Heat licks at my faceplate and jacket. I am about to grab the fire extinguisher when Henry and the new man come running around each side of the fire engine with their hoses. They battle the flames with their nozzles on wide spray. Henry hits me with a cooling shower that washes over me.

"Just protect the fire truck, the capsule and the choppers," I yelled, "we don't have enough water for the bomber." I glance at the pod. The hatch is open. Air Force crewmen from the choppers run to assist. They pull three bodies out of the ejection pod. Two men are alive but unconscious. Someone yells that the pilot is dead.

With the hoses, we establish a firebreak between the crash site and us. The remains of the B-1A and its load of fuel are burning furiously. The blackened metal wings of the B-1A are a crumpled mass of broken and semi-molten metal, awash in flames erupting 60 feet into the air. The aircraft's tires are spewing heavy clouds of billowing black smoke. We increase the width of our fire line with shovels to protect the helicopters as they prepare to evacuate the injured crew members and the dead pilot.

We are fortunate that the sparse desert shrubbery makes the fire more manageable. I send my two firefighters returning from the pod to the north side of the crash site with shovels to contain the fire. Henry is attacking hot spots on the south side. To conserve water, I have the new guys use a fire extinguisher as needed.

With the main fire under control, I lean into the cab and grab the microphone, "San Bernardino Command, Engine 52," I said reporting in, "the aircraft fire is contained, but the wreckage is still burning. I have one dead aircrewman on the scene and two traumas being evacuated by military helicopters."

"Engine 52," the radio blared, "advise aircraft type."

I grab the microphone as two medi-vac helicopters lift off and climb right over the fire truck. I yell over the roar of the rotor wash, "Aircraft type B-1A Bomber."

There is a pregnant pause, and then I hear the radio dispatcher ask in awe, "Did you say B-1A Bomber?"

"Roger, some of it is still burning, but the fire is contained."

From the west, I see a wave of ground-hugging helicopters rushing at us. There is a dozen in three squadrons of four choppers each in diamond formation. It reminds me of a Vietnam airhead as the choppers settle quickly to the ground about us spilling security personnel with rifles at the ready. I wonder about the rifles; shovels would be far more helpful.

The soldiers run outward to set up a protective perimeter on the outskirts of the fire line. A gunnery sergeant runs up to me. "Chief," he asked urgently, "how can we help?"

"There are shovels on the truck's sides and fire extinguishers," I replied, "have your men hit hot spots on our fire line."

I enjoyed hearing him call me chief. Abruptly, I realize that I actually am in-charge of this accident response. I automatically took charge and coordinated the protection of the pod. The Air Force is looking after their injured men aided by the Safety Officer. I am the chief-in-charge. It is a magnificent realization.

The Gunny smiles at the insignia on the fire truck door. "Want to tell me how an inmate fire crew happened to be way out here in an isolated part of the desert?" he asked in wonder.

"Our camp is just six miles to the southwest," I said proudly.

He shakes my hand, "Well you saved our guys. The first two chopper crews would have been helpless if that fire engulfed the pod. It would have been horrible knowing our men inside were roasting alive and not being able to help," he said in admiration.

"Thank my men," I said, "we're inmates. They would sincerely appreciate it."

The radio blares, "Engine 52, be advised that Engine Companies 14, 18 and 24 with five engines are 30 minutes ETA from your location. Confirm if you still require backup."

Standing beside the fire truck, I see multiple dust clouds from military emergency vehicles rushing toward the scene. A big yellow crash truck pulls right up to the burning wreckage and sprays a stream of white foam onto the burning and smoldering wreckage with its top-mounted water cannon.

"That is a negative, command," relief floods through me. Getting the fire truck to this desert site is the biggest triumph of my life. I am amazed to have had this opportunity as an inmate.

I key the mic, "Command, be advised that multiple Air Force emergency vehicles including crash trucks are arriving in large numbers. Cancel 52's request for backup," I said with great satisfaction.

The inmate firefighters, carrying shovels over their shoulders, return to the sparse shade of the fire truck, their blackened faces are creased with smiles of satisfaction. I look at the tank's water gauge; it is a tick above empty. I shut down the pump. Through drifting smoke, I see the Gunnery Sargent walking up to the firefighters to shake their hands and say a few words.

A command chopper settles. The blast from its rotors blows stinging sand into my face. I drop my face shield. I see a man step down from the skids. He is an Air Force senior officer wearing a 45 automatic on his hip. He walks purposefully up to our fire engine and stops to read the door's insignia. "Boron Prison Camp." Stunned, he stares at me, "You guys are inmates!"

"Inmate Engine Company 52 at your service," I said proudly.

His hand rests on his pistol. "This site is classified top secret," he commanded, "inmates don't belong here."

"If we inmates weren't here," I said, "you'd still have a nasty fire to deal with, sir, and a dead crew from your B-1A."

He glares, "What makes you think it is the B-1A?"

"It's the only plane that has an ejection pod. I'm a pilot. I read about these things."

"Well, pretend you don't know it's the B-1A. This is to be kept totally under wraps. As of 15 minutes ago, this is designated as a top-secret site, that's directly from the Joint Chiefs-of-Staff."

I hold up the microphone, "Sorry, San Bernardino Command requested aircraft type," I said returning his glare, "I reported as ordered that it was the B-1A Bomber. It's standard procedure for coordinating a proper incident response."

The officer snarls, "It is a good thing you're inmates, or your careers would be over."

"Careers? What careers?" Henry exploded. "We're inmates."

"What do you want us to do?" I asked cutting to the chase.

"I want you out of here," he growled," like now."

"Okay 52, load up." I shouted. The guy is a complete jerk.

I have a sudden thought, 'Should I?'

"Very well, sir," I said with all the authority of a chief engineer standing up for his crew. I raise my hand in a snappy salute. "I surrender the site and stand relieved," I said officiously.

He almost saluted me back but caught himself just in time. Instead, he spies the Safety Officer, obviously our supervisory guard, and goes over to chew him out.

Following our tracks back out I am surprised at the number of Air Force vehicles that had accidents or gotten stuck littering the desert with broken down vehicles.

The Safety Officer has me stop alongside our pickup truck. "Arrington, you and I can nurse the pickup home after we dump the water tank. He has Henry drive the fire truck back to the camp.

The problem with the pickup is a broken leaf spring, and I suspect the shock is broke too. We drain the water tank, which reduces our load by almost 500 pounds. When we hit Highway 395, it is lined with television news vans and many other vehicles.

"This is your fault, Arrington," said the Safety Officer wearily.

"My fault?"

"That Air Force jerk chewed my butt good."

"Hey, I was just doing my job," I said defensively.

"It's why you're riding with me instead of driving the fire truck. This vehicle doesn't have a radio for you to cause more mischief. That guy is a Colonel, that's way above my pay grade. As we were leaving, he was on the radio to his ranking officer, a Major General. He was so mad, he was spitting his words into the radio. He knows your name. It's on the back of your helmet. He doesn't like you."

'How does this stuff happen to me?' I wondered. I knew the answer. My classmates were right at EOD School; I am a hog for attention. When I called in aircraft type to San Bernardino Command, I had a moment of mental hesitation, should I do this? The rascal in me said, 'Heck yeah.' Now, I feared that I was about to get far more attention than I wanted.

The Safety Officer suddenly chuckles. "My, my Arrington, you sure know how to piss off people in authority."

I grin, "It's because I have this thing about bullies."

"Well, I hope it was worth it because I don't think I am going to be able to protect you on this one," he said sadly.

I later learned that one of the news stations was monitoring the San Bernardino Fire Department Command Net. From there the news spread like wildfire. Within 20 minutes of which San Bernardino Command was receiving inquiries from as far away as New York City, about the crash of the B-1A Supersonic Bomber. This was a huge news story, and I was in big trouble.

Back at the camp, the word had quickly spread that not only were we inmates the first ones on the scene but that we also broke the story. The fire crew was suddenly extremely popular with the inmates, but the supervisory staff was secluded in the warden's office having a serious meeting.

I knew I needed help. I called an attorney friend who had been supplying me with inside information on the DeLorean Case, for some quick advice. Instead, he wanted a favor. The lawyer knew some high-level investigative reporters. He got one hooked up on a conference call. The reporter wanted inside information on the crash site, which I, fortunately, wasn't so dumb to share. Instead, I tried to feed him a story about the inmate fire crew, how felons were saving lives from a desert camp. He hung up on me.

Ten minutes after leaving the telephone bank, a guard snags me and marches me over to the unit manager's office.

"Why were you talking to the press, idiot?" he roared.

I remember that control monitors all inmate telephone calls from the bank of pay phones. Instantly, I realize the magnitude of my problem, which has placed me squarely back under the control of the Unit Manager. There is nothing I can say to make a difference with this man, not that he gives me a chance.

"I was calling an attorney; I didn't…"

"Shut up, inmate. You're off the fire crew," he yelled leaping up from behind his desk. He stomped up to me, then poking a very irritating finger into my chest, he yelled with spittle spraying into my face, "Get your butt up the hill, report to the plumbing shop!"

The plumbing shop is just below the top of the hill. The Unit Manager has me assigned to the tool bin. The inmate's place I am taking is ecstatic. "You're going to hate this job. It really sucks."

Because tools can be weapons, the shop guard locks the tool issuer into the wire cage during checkout and return. The tool issuer logs the tool's purpose and location. The returned tool goes on a pegboard with an outline of its shape or into a box, so it is easy to see if any tools go missing.

On the wall of the tool bin, there is a sign listing the rules for issuing tools. Someone has crudely lettered a set of inmate rules on the bottom: Rule #1. *Inmates have nothing coming. Rule #2. For all other situations, refer to rule one.*

Four days later, I am in my room, when the door slams open. Henry rushes in waving a newspaper. "The jury just acquitted DeLorean on all counts!" he yelled.

I had heard the news, but I looked forward to reading about it. I smiled at Henry, "Want to know why the Feds lost?"

"Do tell," said Henry sitting down on my bunk.

Having been careful for so long not to discuss secret aspects of the DeLorean Case, I decided to tell Henry all of it regarding John Z. DeLorean. "It begins with the British Prime Minister Margret Thatcher…"

A time later, an amazed Henry asked, "How did you learn all of this stuff?"

I chuckle, "I didn't know any of it before I was arrested."

"You learned all this while you were in prison?" queried Henry.

"Yes, some from an undercover agent who was trying to get me to snitch. I learned most of it from Morgan when they put him in my jail unit. The rest is from my file." I showed him a thick file of letters, reports, and newspaper clippings.

"Anyway, DeLorean was desperate. His company was going broke, he needed a big infusion of cash to save it, and that was when Hoffman called. DeLorean thought that Hoffman had serious money connections, so he agreed to meet with him.

"Hoffman lured DeLorean to a bar with the promise of $60,000,000 to save his company. DeLorean brought company records and financials, but Hoffman hardly seemed interested and wanted to meet in the back of the bar where it was dark."

"That in itself is a rather big hint," said Henry sagely.

"Meanwhile Hoffman was doing what he did best, looking out for himself. He wove a web of lies telling DeLorean it's strictly a money deal, a simple investment. But he needed 1.8 million up front to make it happen."

"Back at FBI headquarters, he told his handlers that DeLorean had two million dollars he wanted to invest in a drug deal to save DMC."

"The FBI had that on tape?"

"Nope, supposedly, the FBI didn't tape this conversation."

"Why the hell not?" barked Henry. "This is the initial setup, of course, they had to tape it."

"The Feds claimed it was just a social meeting, that DeLorean wasn't yet a target of the DEA. They even put it in writing and submitted it as Exhibit B, items 15 and 16."

"Why? Falsifying evidence is a case sinker," said Henry. As an ex-politician and CIA agent, he knew a lot about the law.

"Exactly," I grinned, "which means he may have said things that shouldn't have been recorded. Rather than risk losing the case before it even got started, better to just loose that first tape."

"However, I don't think that is what happened," I said throwing in twist. "Hoffman is sinking the hook into DeLorean. I think he didn't want the FBI knowing what he was up to, so he turned off his wire."

"Hmm," muses Henry, "that's a gutsy move. Puts Hoffman in charge right from the beginning."

"Yep," I agreed. "As the case developed, Hoffman kept weaving his web around DeLorean and not all of that is on tape either. Such as when Hoffman revealed that his backers were Colombians. DeLorean balked; he didn't want to be a part of what he now believed was a drug deal. Hoffman threatened him, saying that he knew too much."

"What kind of threat?" prodded Henry.

"That the Colombians would kill his children. The threat was graphic, child's head in a grocery sack type of a threat."

"That's assault!" yelled Henry, "It's a felony offense. Hoffman should have been arrested. They had that on tape?"

"Not quite, in that tape there was a missing 47-minute gap."

"Which is where Hoffman made the threat?" asked Henry.

"So, it seems. Just a simple flip of the switch on the wire."

"That is suppressing evidence in a federal case," Henry said.

"It's worse than that," I agreed, "if those agents were hiding a criminal act — it would make them co-conspirators."

"Wait," interrupted Henry, "it doesn't take 47 minutes to threaten someone."

"I think that Hoffman put that 47 minutes to good use. He's manipulating DeLorean and keeping the FBI out of the loop. Later, the agents would discover that Hoffman had around 50 telephone conversations with DeLorean that the FBI didn't know about."

"DeLorean is still trying to bail on the deal. So, one of the undercover agents posing as a drug dealer leveled a death threat at DeLorean for trying to back out."

"DeLorean wanted out, and they're using threats to keep him in," queried Henry. "They are forcing DeLorean into a criminal conspiracy. That's felony coercion by a federal agent. He should have gone to prison for that!"

"Exactly, DeLorean was scared for his children. He wrote it all down in a letter including names and places, which he mailed to his attorney. One of the names was a supposed crooked banker, James Benedict, AKA FBI Agent Benedict Tisa, from the Eureka Savings and Loan. "What disturbs me," I added, "is that they figured DeLorean deserved to be set up. So, it was okay for them to take him down even though he was innocent."

"They seem to have forgotten the FBI code of ethics."

I continued, "The agents needed an actual cocaine smuggler. So, they allow Hoffman to bring DeLorean and Morgan Hetrick together. Morgan drops his defenses because he knows DeLorean and has fond memories of Cristina."

"What?" said Henry stunned, "Morgan knew DeLorean and his wife Cristina before all of this went down."

I smile pleased to have delivered such a major bombshell. I grin, "Here's the best part. It concerns a mega millionaire named Fletcher Jones. He owned a 3,600-acre ranch called the Westerly Stud Farm. Fletcher liked to fly in young Hollywood starlets from Los Angles to his ranch in San Ynez for wild weekends."

"That's why he called it a stud farm, huh?" chuckled Henry.

I wait for the moment, "One of his buddies was DeLorean."

"I never read any of this in the newspapers," said Henry.

"Swingers try to fly under the press. Anyway, Fletcher had his pilot, Morgan Hetrick, flying in the starlets. Morgan was rubbing up against all that money and it made him hungry. Morgan was a conman. He wanted wealth and beautiful women too."

"That must have been enticing for a lecher like Morgan," said Henry. "Is that how DeLorean got into drugs?"

"I'll tell you my source on this, Henry," I paused as he leans forward eagerly. "It was Hetrick. He said it was wild times, but he never saw DeLorean doing drugs or mess with the starlets."

"There's got to be more," inquired Henry.

"Wait for it," I teased, "Fletcher met a real Hollywood actress, who co-starred in a couple of movies. She was a supermodel and a regular on the cover of fashion magazines. Fletcher Jones fell in love, which ended his messing around. He had Morgan fly her in regularly to the Westerly Stud Farm. She and Morgan became good friends during all those flights. When Fletcher proposed marriage, she told him she wanted to think about it. Then she confided to Morgan that she was going to say yes. But suddenly, in a matter of days, Fletcher died in a plane accident, which was a real surprise as he was a careful pilot."

"Who was this movie star?" pleaded Henry.

"Cristina Ferrare!"

"DeLorean's Cristina?"

"They got married the following year. But remember, Christina was friends with Hetrick. After Fletcher died, she wrote Morgan a note saying, "She didn't know that men like him existed.""

Henry leers, "That must have gotten his lustful fires burning."

"Ten years later, the flames hadn't died out," I said. "Morgan met DeLorean for dinner during the case, and Hetrick insisted that John bring Christina."

"A few days later," I said, "Hetrick ordered me to drive the coke out to Los Angeles, where Scotti and a dozen agents arrested me in a parking lot at the Van Nuys Airport. That slob Hoffman was there breathing down my neck. I can see why the jury could not stand him. Soon as they had me in custody, they arrested Hetrick at a transvestite restaurant and bar."

"Transvestite bar?" asked Henry intrigued.

"There were a few transvestite dives in this conspiracy — I haven't figured that one out yet. Nothing surprised me anymore about this case. However, the agents and the Department of Justice people had a big meeting that night about how to set DeLorean up for his arrest. The important part was that Gerald Scotti was at that meeting."

"The meet with DeLorean went down in a Los Angeles hotel room, where a federal agent was pretending to be a major cartel hitter. He handed a kilo of cocaine to DeLorean, while they videotaped him saying it was better than gold."

"Yeah, they aired that scene a lot," said Henry.

"It made DeLorean look bad, but the facts were that he did not put up any money for that cocaine, or real collateral and he was never intended to take possession of the cocaine. The only criminals in that hotel room were the FBI agents setting up a man who just wanted to save his dream of building a totally cool car."

"So how does DeLorean get off?" asked Henry.

"Hoffman, their star witness, was caught lying, and the jury saw that he was a real dirtbag."

"How does the jury know that?"

"The tapes of he and DeLorean in a bar. They hear Hoffman saying lewd things about women and drinking profusely. Hoffman loses all credibility. The jury doesn't like him, and neither does the Judge."

"Wasn't the Judge supposed to be unbiased?" asked Henry.

"Not after it comes out that the prosecution failed to reveal that Hoffman demanded a share of any money seized. It came out behind closed doors. The jury never heard it, but Judge Takasugi was offended, he called Hoffman, a hired gun."

"Next, DeLorean's lawyer, Howard Weitzman went after special agent Benedict Tisa who admitted in court that he knew John did not want to participate in the drug deal. Then Weitzman showed that there were inconsistencies in Tisa's case notes. After three days of cross-questioning, Tisa finally admitted, 'I may have rewrote the pages.' He also confessed to destroying the original notes."

"That equates to the destruction of the chain of evidence."

I grin, "After Tisa's damaging testimony, they broke for lunch and, a DOJ supervisor severely rebuked the agent for telling the truth—unknowingly in front of an open microphone. Every word was heard in an adjoining pressroom that was full of reporters."

"After lunch, Agent Tisa was back on the stand. The man was now a nervous wreck. Howard Wiseman set him up with a loaded question." He said, 'This whole case is built around Hetrick delivering 55 pounds of cocaine that costs $1.8 million, that Hoffman is supposed to sell for no less than $50 to $60 million in just a couple of weeks.'"

"Wait, that's impossible. A kilo of pure cocaine in bulk goes for about $40,000 to $50,000. It has to be cut dozens of times before it can turn that kind of money," said Henry.

"The DEA would know that," I agreed. "Once Hoffman had the money, Tisa was to launder it then give it to DeLorean."

"And what does DeLorean part with for $50 to $60 million?"

"Half of the stock of DeLorean Motor Car Company."

"Well, that's worth something, isn't it?" asked Henry.

"No, it's worth nothing. DeLorean Motor Company makes the DeLorean car, DeLorean Motor Car Company is an empty shell corporation that DeLorean put together just for this deal. They all knew it was a hollow company — worthless," I pointed out.

"Well that's the stupidest plan ever," interjected Henry. "Who would ever believe that?"

"Certainly not the jury," I concurred. "However, Agent Tisa's answer was, 'Yes that was essentially the basis of our plan.'"

"Wow," laughed Henry, "you would think the Department of Justice would have done a better job of briefing their witnesses, particularly in such a big trial."

"Yeah, the case was falling apart, but then it came out that the Feds were hoping that the trial would put them on the cover of Time Magazine."

"Who said that?"

"James Walsh, the federal prosecutor, he said it in front of Gerald Scotti at a meeting the night before DeLorean was arrested."

"How did the defense find that out?" asked Henry.

"Scotti was appalled with how his bosses were mishandling the case, and he was disgusted with how they let Hoffman stuff his pockets with reward money."

"Scotti is the guy who was burglarizing cars and houses."

"Yeah, Scotti was willing to break into people's homes and cars for evidence. When he got caught in Buzz Hetrick's house, Scotti was seen as an over-enthusiastic cop. It was not a career burner. However, the other agents were manipulating evidence and that's a serious felony."

"Therefore, the Feds go after Scotti?" speculated Henry

"They accused him of leaking information for money in another big case known as the Grandma Mafia case. But a corrupt agent may have duped Scotti into it. That's why the DOJ never prosecuted him."

Henry points at the newspaper he brought in, "Says here that Scotti was the defense's star witness."

"Yeah, he destroyed what was left of the prosecution's case. He was the one who alleged that it went all the way to the White House. He testified that the agents paid Hoffman huge rewards for his efforts. The government had already claimed under oath that they only reimbursed Hoffman for his actual expenses."

"What kind of rewards."

"Over $160,000 and that was just for 1983," I said.

"So, DeLorean got off for entrapment," said Henry smugly.

"Entrapment implies that DeLorean committed a crime," I said. "He didn't. He was found not guilty on all charges."

A bend in the road is not the end of the road… Unless you fail to make the turn —Helen Keller

Author's note: As a motivational speaker for youth in many back drops, from public schools to youth lockups, from churches to Conservation Corps, from Boy Scouts to Indian Reservations, from Kindergarten classes to college prep schools and Universities to 49 states and seven countries as a speaker, I get around. Surprisingly, the advice I offer for all these groups is basically the same — simply because it works. I will share these as An Arrington Minute.

An Arrington Minute: Mentoring 101. Being a mentor changes lives big time, including your own. I often hear people dodge mentoring because they don't feel qualified or maybe not even worthy. So, begin at the beginning. Start with a child. Children live in an exceedingly small world. They have a limited number of friends, some which have paws, others are only imagined, but they are all very real to the child. When something happens in their small world — it is always a world class event! It is a great way to learn about dealing with crises.

Mentoring youths and teens is challenging and hugely rewarding. The family unit is not what it used to be, not with rampant divorce, massive drug abuse and constant child endangerment.

Therefore I refer to our modern society as "Battlefield America." You are needed on the frontlines.

The Rockwell B-1A prototype #4 supersonic bomber.
We responded to B-1A #2. Photo courtesy USAF

Note: The ejection capsule is the whole cockpit less
the front section including the nose cone forward
of the cockpit windows, and the support section
beneath the cockpit. They were so low when
they ejected it didn't give the chutes enough time
to slow the ejection pod so it struck hard. An inflatable
bag was supposed to deploy cushioning the front
base of the pod. Its failure may be why the pilot died.

Chapter 18 - Boron Prison Camp, Sept - Dec 1984

In the Boron plumbing shop, the days seem longer, while I whittle away the hours in my dusty cage. The tool bin is a wire mesh pen inside a steel building that gets roasting hot under the desert sun. The wire-mesh enclosure is a bit smaller than a prison cell and not as tall. The low wire ceiling is hugely depressing – a mini version of J-1. The ceiling is a mere foot above my head. Motivation is hard to find as I stare at the old tools about me.

The tool cage is more bearable because I have my Bible. The guard, who likes to keep me busy cleaning tools, seldom disturbs me when he sees me reading my Bible. In prison, there is respect for Jesus Christ. Inmates value hope and the guards have hopes of their own. After all, Jesus is the Prince of Hope and of Peace.

At T.I., gang bangers stepped out of my way when I was on a Christian undertaking to help someone in one of the dormitories. Some say that the only way to leave a prison gang is in a body bag. However, I knew of several ex-gang members who accepted Jesus Christ into their lives and the gangs left them alone. However, the conversion had to be real. Guards and gangs see through a cloak of Christian deception when someone wears their faith falsely. Guards scornfully call it a jail house conversion.

After a week, the Plumbing Shop Officer lets me out of the cage when I am not issuing tools or signing them back in, but I remain restricted to the shop during working hours. The worst part about being in the plumbing shop is hearing the fire siren wail. My first reaction is an urge to run for the firehouse. Instead, I stand immobile at the open door of the plumbing shop staring after the fire truck as it drives down the camp access road.

It is frustrating watching the Unit Manager replace most of the crew. The reason for removing me is that I am a too-high profile inmate, the celebrity thing working against me again.

The crew did not pick their new chief engineer. The Unit Manager assigned his inmate clerk to the position. Someone wrote *I Spy* on his helmet. Morale was low among the men and training non-existent. The chief engineer was not mechanically inclined and had problems priming the pump. In an emergency, he panics. On their second fire response, the crew lost a motorhome because the new engineer was too slow getting water to the attack hoses.

The next few months pass slowly. Fortunately, I was still in the honor dorm because I had broken no rules. Battling depression was a constant vigil. I kept my Bible close.

* * *

It is dark-thirty as I rise off my bunk. My frogman training conditions me to wake and immediately get up. I hope one day to get over it, but not until prison is in my past.

I slip quietly out of the room. The other inmates think I am nuts to rise so early, yet in prison to be considered mentally off balanced only works in my favor as it keeps the riffraff away.

I am carrying an old blanket and a mug with a tea bag. I stop at an old banged-up drinking fountain. I place the mug under the hot water spigot and push down on the rusty bent handle. It coughs, gurgles, and then slowly sputters, before spitting up a weak trickle of hot or tepid water depending on its mood. I enjoy listening to the old fountain going through its liquid warming labors as it leaks wisps of steam.

A wire-covered night light is about 15 feet away, by its dim glow, I admire the cup in my hand. I made it in the camp pottery shop. I have a whole collection. Each is carefully hand-painted. This one has an underwater scene. A sunken sailing ship that lies on a submerged reef, its tattered sails flutter in the current, while long-leafed seaweed drifts about the hull. There are sharks and fish with a deep-sea diver stomping across the seabed with a treasure box in his arms. His air hose weaves up among the ship's broken rigging. I put hours into each of my cups, something to remember my quieter times in prison.

I find a clear area to lay my blanket and then between sips of tea go through my stretching routine. I adopt a variety of yoga postures. Mentally I follow the paths of muscles and structure of bones, consciously aligning my skeleton, while taking the joints through their full range of motion.

My transition to Gung Fu is purposeful as it begins with a solemn bow of respect to my old Chinese master in honor of what he has taught me. Each karate move must conform to what precedes and to what follows, harmony and physics equally applied seeking perfect balance. Yet, I am far from perfect, but contentedly so. I enjoy moving nearly silent about the large room, gliding around chairs and tables as I weave the obstacles into my improvised kata. Imagined attackers dance with me as I go through my various routines.

At 6:00 AM, I am at the door wearing a pair of old jeans, a T-shirt, and two sweatshirts. It is cold outside, a high-desert winter cold that chills to the bone. I hold old leather work gloves in one hand and a second half-empty mug of warm tea in the other. The new year is coming, I am being indulgent. Frost covers the corners of the door's glass pane. I sip my tepid tea waiting for the guard to open the door so I can go lift weights. The weight pile is tucked against a barren hillside behind a dormitory protecting it from the relentless wind blowing outside.

I see a gleam on the glass, which brightens. A corrections officer approaches. The guard's flashlight swings in pace with his rapid step. The brightness on the frosted glass comes and goes like the sweeping beacon of brilliance from a lighthouse. Even in the desert, thoughts of the sea accompany me. As the guard nears the door, the light steadies. The ice crystals gather the cone of light and scatters it into mini specks of radiant color like tiny jewels. I hear the key go into the lock and the deadbolt sliding back then the light sweeps away receding into blackness.

I step out into the crisp desert darkness filling my lungs with the bracing cold air. Except for the retreating guard, I am alone, and I revel in it. I walk with confidence in the dark, knowing the location of the obstacles, bushes, and large rocks until I am blindsided by a tumbleweed hurling out of the dark.

The weight pile is mostly in darkness except for a dim glow from a security light under the roofline of a nearby dormitory. A thin coat of frost covers the weight bench, which I sweep away with my gloved hand. The falling ice crystals tumble downward in a gently glowing cascade of frost diamonds.

I load up the barbell with two 45-pound wheel weights, then lie down on the bench and lift off the heavy bar. The metal is cold through the worn leather of my gloves, even colder at the palms where the gloves have two large holes. I have owned the gloves since my last Christmas package at T.I. I try to ignore the cold as part of my mental discipline. Quietly, I go through my morning routine, wondering if I am slightly crazy to be doing this in the bone-chilling cold. I stare up at the vast, dark heavens glistening with starlight. I listen to birds rustling and chirping in the bushes.

Being on the weight pile in the cold darkness is me expressing my will. This is my moment. As the camp awakens, I will lose a portion of this freedom. I will sacrifice it to the demands of the prison staff and the often-bizarre acts of other inmates. Living with criminals puts a sharp perception of how inmates think, adapt, and attempt to enforce their will upon others through various malicious manipulations. There seems to be a greater inmate satisfaction in taking something by force or deception than by simply asking. A primordial thought process, *'I take; therefore, I am a stronger and more of a man than you.'*

One of my favorite actives is swimming down to the bottom of the small pool with a large rock. I sit on the bottom with the smooth stone in my lap holding my breath. It took some time for the guards to get used to seeing a body on the bottom of the pool. On occasion, I take a candy bar down with me. I take a bite and slowly chew. It is something unique to do. On their path to self-discovery, many inquiring men have gone to the ends of the earth—I have come to a desert prison camp.

The following week I am inside the tool ben when Henry comes rushing into the plumbing shop waving a newspaper. "They sentenced your buddy, Hetrick. Despite his cooperation, Judge Takasugi nailed him with two ten-year sentences, to be served concurrently, plus an additional five years of special parole."

"Let me see," I asked.

He sits down on a chair outside my cage. "I'll read it to you," he said with an evil grin, "it will add drama to the moment."

"No wonder you were a politician," I groaned.

"Don't forget the corrupt part," laughed Henry, "that's what will make me interesting to the ladies when I get out." He crosses his legs, snaps the paper twice, grins at me, then begins to read, "Mr. Hetrick sat silently before the judge in the crowded courtroom and heard himself described by his attorney as, 'A man who is broken.'"

I considered the words, "Nope, he may be broke financially, but he is not broken. Morgan has an exceedingly high opinion of his intellect and abilities, and he has a vast network of connections. When he gets out, he will land on his feet."

"The prosecutor, James Walsh, told the Judge that Hetrick had cooperated handsomely with the government. Amazingly, the prosecutor argued for a reduced sentence for him."

"Would you just read the stupid story," I asked good naturedly.

Henry continues, "James Walsh, who led the unsuccessful prosecution of Mr. DeLorean, urged the judge to consider Mr.

Hetrick's past as an aviation engineer and his outstanding accomplishments before he turned to drug smuggling."

"Truly? Both sides are arguing in his defense?" I asked in surprise. "But the judge didn't buy it?"

Henry nodded, "There's more, 'This is a man who may border on genius in aviation engineering,' Mr. Walsh said. 'He is not the typical sort of person we see in narcotics cases any more than John DeLorean was a typical person to see in such a case.'"

"Did I hear that correctly?" I asked. "The prosecutor is using DeLorean's acquittal to argue in defense of his favorite snitch?"

"Very odd stuff, so how do you feel about it?" asked Henry.

I shrug, "It just doesn't really matter. Morgan is out of my life. My sentence is almost over while he is still getting started because now, they will move him into the general population. He has sat in a jail unit cell this whole time. His punishment has been far worse than mine. Morgan's intellect hates being idle."

"Looks like he is going to be idle for a long time," Henry said with a smile. "The judge sentenced Morgan to a total of 39 years on six different charges, the longest being 10 years for conspiracy."

"Actually, I already know that the judge ordered the counts to be served concurrently," I said. "That means ten years less good time. He will probably just serve the five years that the prosecution offered him."

Henry gives me the newspaper. "Seems I'm moving on, the Unit Manager got the parole board to release me to an early halfway house," Henry said soberly. "He is looking for every way he can to rid himself of all the old inmates from our fire crew."

I smile encouragingly at my friend whom I will miss dearly, "So when are you leaving?"

"Tomorrow."

* * *

Two months pass, I am in my cage working out with some of the tools. I have a whole routine. I have a heavy pipe wrench tied to a toilet plunger with a piece of rope. I am repeatedly raising and lowering the pipe wrench by rolling the rope up and down with the toilet plunger. It is a mindless workout.

"Arrington, I keep telling ya to stop playing with the tools," ordered the plumbing shop guard as he unlocked the cage door. "You're wanted in the Unit Manager's office."

I step out, wondering what mischief the Unit Manager is planning for me now.

"Move it," growled the guard, "he said immediately."

The Unit Manager's door is open, so I walk cautiously into the office. Four staff members sit around a long table. The Unit Manager, my enemy, sits at one end of the table. He stares sternly at me and frowns. The Unit Counselor opens the conversation with a surprise statement, "The Warden wanted us to do an immediate evaluation of your file."

I am not due for evaluation for two more months. I am very wary of this meeting. My inmate alarms are firing.

The Unit Counselor has my file in front of him, "Arrington, because of your good conduct and service on the fire crew we are going to send you to an early halfway house."

"Early?" a sudden grin slopped over my face, "how early?"

He smiled, "How does five months early sound to you?"

I am astonished. It means I will leave Camp Boring Boron in less than four months. "Thank you," I stood eager to tell Ralph.

"Ah, there's something else," added the Unit Counselor. He looked at the Unit Manager then asked soberly, "How would you feel about going back on the fire crew?"

"What?"

"It seems you are needed on the fire crew," snarled the Unit Manager.

The Safety Officer comes to his rescue, "An embarrassing event happened. Two congressional representatives are visiting the camp, and they heard wonderful things about our inmate fire crew — it's the B-1A Bomber thing. One of them is an ex-Air Force pilot. They wanted to see the fire crew in action. I set a 44-gallon trashcan on fire in my driveway at staff housing. The truck arrived with the lights flashing and siren wailing, which attracted all the kids in the reservation. The fire burned itself out while the engineer was trying unsuccessfully to prime the pump."

"The Warden is a bit upset."

"Upset?" questioned the Unit Counselor. "He was standing with the congressmen while all those kids were laughing. The stupid firefighter just stood there with his slump hose hanging until one of the other men thought to grab a fire extinguisher. But by then it was too late, the fire had already burned itself out."

"Yeah, the only thing burning then was the Warden. He was smoking," laughed the Unit Counselor.

at 300 feet and accelerates toward the rising moon and then disappears into the vast night sky.

From the heightened perspective on the hose bed, I look at the patches of bright light that pool upon the accident site that now seems vacant, like a movie set after the cameras have stopped rolling and the main actors have left the stage.

I leave the twin spots on while the men store the equipment. The ambulance takes the woman with her baby to the hospital. The highway patrol officer waits patiently for a tow truck, having studiously ignored Box of Rocks, who now sulks in the passenger seat of the fire truck.

I shut down the spotlights. Standing on top of the fire truck, I stare up into the heavens. The full moon rides the skyline above a distant mountain range. A feeling wells up from deep down inside as I realize I am happy and so right with the world.

Driving the fire truck back toward camp, I explore a wondrous feeling of pleasure I am experiencing. I am reliving an emotion I had thought lost forever. It is that feeling of camaraderie, of being part of a team, after completing a dangerous mission.

I have spent so much of my adult life as a Navy diver and bomb disposal frogman. The extensive training was incredibly exciting, the missions wonderously challenging and adventurous. I am still only 34-years old. A new life beckons, yet I cannot suppress the staggering realization that I must begin again from scratch and with a convicted-felon handicap.

I glance at the two other men in the dark cab. What an odd trio we make. Ralph is here for his need for drugs, which stole the last days of his youth. Box of Rocks is a slave to an insatiable appetite. The vast amount of fat he carries is an enormous burden that continuously weighs on him. He works at a job he hates with charges he despises — yet does nothing to change any of it. Last, there is me, the imbecile with the idiotic desire to smoke marijuana, thus forfeiting a life full of challenge, achievement, adventure, and patriotic purpose. I love America and served my country with pride. So, which of us is the greater fool?

'It is me; it is me,' screamed my mind. All that I am and all that I will ever be is dependent upon my mental abilities — and I put it all on the line just to get foolishly stoned.

The obese guard may have never known the joys of being healthy and athletic, so his may be a fault of profound ignorance and lack of discipline. Eating is probably his only pleasure in life, but it is seasoned with guilt. Ralph is also a victim of drug use, but I suspect there are family factors he is hiding.

Therefore, it is I who am without excuse. I had it all, the best teachers, and an adventurous career. Mine was a free lifestyle enhanced with an active, inquisitive intellect. I was perpetually challenged by a stimulus-rich military environment tempered with spasms of severe danger—and I tossed it all. What a dope!

My self-recrimination does not spoil my buoyant mood. It is just a startling realization of how far I have progressed in looking at myself in an open, honest way.

I glance at the fuel gauge, then look at Box of Rocks and am surprised to realize I do not know his real name. I tap the fuel gauge to draw his attention, "Need to stop to top off the tank."

"Good idea," he grunted.

We have an account at the gas station at Four Corners. I pull the truck up to the pumps. I get out to fill the tank while the men on back step off to stretch and talk excitedly about the accident. I notice Box of Rocks waddling into the station minimart no doubt in pursuit of sugarcoated nourishment.

A minivan pulls up to the opposing pump. The kids inside are excited to be so close to a fire truck with the men standing about in their turnouts. The driver steps out and smiles at me, as he is about to head inside to pay for the gasoline. I see him stutter-step as he reads the seal on the door, *Boron Prison Camp, Inmate Engine Company 52.* He suddenly looks at us from a different perspective as we go from trusted firefighters to a gang of leering murderous inmates. He spins about, hurries back into the minivan and drives rapidly away with his wife yelling at him.

I offer a friendly wave to his rearview mirror, which he does not return—but his children do enthusiastically. If I had been quicker, I might have touched off the siren for them, which would probably have given Box of Rocks a fatal heart attack.

The man in question is stepping through the minimart's double doors, a real convenience for the hugely fat man. "Who are you waving at?" he asked bluntly.

"Kids, they liked the fire truck."

Box of Rocks frowns, does he think he should not have left us alone? Then I realize that he is facing a dilemma. He carries a box of a dozen chocolate-covered doughnuts. Box of Rocks is wider around the waist than he is tall. He is short with fat; stubby legs and he is looking unhappily at that first tall step into the truck's cab. He cannot manage that much height with but one supporting hand. I can see his reluctance to ask for help because then he would have to share part of his doughnut horde and there are five of us. Instead, he goes through a laborious process of setting the doughnut box down on the floor mat, and then he uses both hands to lever himself up onto the running board. Next, he lifts the box of doughnuts to the seat and raises a ponderous leg onto the cab's floor, and then he places one large ham onto the seat. Next, he uses his broad butt to push the box of doughnuts over, and then quickly grabs it before it can invitingly touch Ralph. Finally, he lays the doughnut box onto his lap.

Ralph and I have been watching intently.

Box of Rocks smiles at us; it is a smile of accomplishment in solving a problem with the bonus of doughnut denial for the inmates. Fat man made it into the truck without having to ask for any help and, therefore, need not share his doughnuts with anyone beneath his station. It is his first smile of the evening. I guess we all measure accomplishment in our own way.

During the final six-mile drive to the camp, he gobbles all dozen doughnuts. Rather than watch Box of Rocks' heavy jowls working the chocolate pastries, I think about how we helped that young family tonight.

I turn onto the government road that leads up to the prison camp and radio control to raise the gate. We pull through the barrier then stop to let Box of Rocks out of the truck. He said nothing, not a good job or that it was a pleasure, just grunts with a lot of heavy breathing as he lowers his ponderous bulk to the tarmac, spilling doughnut crumbs, he waddles into the control building. I watch his massive frame silhouetted by the dim light from the doorway. He hitches up his pants and turns sideways to pass through the opening then steps out of view. I wonder at the hollowness of his life, but then decide I am being too judgmental.

Sliding over to the window, Ralph stares unhappily down into the empty donut box. "Nothing," he lamented, "he left us nothing but the lingering smell of real donuts."

"At least he didn't leave us a lingering fart," I said cheerfully.

The next morning an incredibly surprised inmate Arrington stands before the Unit Manager's desk. "Who said you could leave the camp without my authorization?" he yelled.

"What authorization are you talking about?"

"I put you back on the crew to train them," he raged, "I did not say anything about your leaving the prison camp."

"What is the point of being the chief engineer if I don't lead the crew on fire responses?" I asked, thinking it a fair question. The best training is responding to real emergencies.

"Listen, inmate," he snarled, "I don't care about fighting fires outside this camp. You go through that gate again, and you will have me to contend with—you got that?"

* * *

In mid-February, in the middle of the day, the fire siren wails, and despite the threats of the Unit Manager, I prepare to take my team out the gate. Each attack I lead is an opportunity to teach the new men from experience. This is my 17th, and undoubtedly last, response. I have only two more months to serve. I climb into the cab, knowing it is for the last time. It is a strange, hollow feeling, yet I am making a choice, knowing the ramifications. I am not breaking a rule as I have already cleared it with the Safety Officer. He said I am the chief engineer, and with that assignment, I must answer to my own obligations.

Not far from the camp, a Toyota pickup truck collided head-on with an 18-wheeler at a combined speed of over 130 mph. The driver of the big commercial rig has a broken arm, but the driver of the pickup is dead and mutilated.

The red Toyota is a flattened, crunched-up mess. The engine, driven inward and upward with tremendous force, is half in the cab, impaling the driver on the broken steering shaft. We spend over an hour just cutting the ravaged body out of the mass of ripped and torn metal. The force of the impact disemboweled him, and his legs are half-torn from the mangled corpse. A stream of blood mixed in a hideous collage with oil, radiator fluid, and gasoline runs in a wide slick across the hot black tarmac. It is a depressing sight. I flush the gross wet mess from the road with a fire hose. The high-pressure jet chases the horrific collage of body and engine fluids into a swirling pool glistening with dark-hued rainbows of gruesome red and black colors.

Seeing the highway patrol trooper walking toward me, I shut off the hose. "Hey, inmate," he said smiling, "remember me? I saw you standing on top of the fire truck when that helicopter flew right over it."

"Yeah, that was me." I offered my hand, "Stephen Arrington."

"Hugh Benson, you're the chief engineer of these guys?"

"Yep, the best darn inmate fire crew in the United States."

"I believe it; you guys have a professional way of handling things. I liked how you lit up the power lines for the chopper pilot—he's a friend of mine."

"Seemed the right thing to do," I am enjoying being an inmate visiting with an officer of the law.

"What are you in for?"

"Smuggling cocaine, shouldn't have done it—wish I didn't."

"You're a Christian, aren't you?" he said confidently.

"Discovered Him in a prison cell, how could you tell?"

"The way you told me what you did, that you knew it was wrong and took responsibility for it all in a short sentence."

"Well I'm in trouble again," I said, suddenly wondering why I am volunteering that information.

He glanced out into the desert then his eyes slice back to me, an officer of the law about to hear about trouble.

"One of the staff doesn't want me leading the crew off base anymore," I said, "it's a personal thing between him and me."

"So why did you do it?"

I spill my guts to a stranger in uniform. Well, he is not a stranger; he is a Christian, which makes us brothers in Christ. We just happen to be on opposite sides of the law, but I am trying to get back over to his side as best I can.

"You know he's going to pull you off the fire crew?"

"No doubt about it," I said looking down at the ground.

"But you went anyway," he said confirming my intent.

"Had to," I kick at a clump of dirt, frustration expressing itself.

"I understand," he said knowledgeably.

"You do?" I asked hopefully.

"Yeah, I wear a uniform and with it comes responsibility. You are wearing a uniform too, and these men are your team. You owe that uniform, those men, and the family of the boy in that body bag the best you got. A man or woman in a uniform cannot resist doing what their training requires. When you go back and see that man you've got a problem with, stand straight and tall—make that firefighter's uniform look good," he commanded.

Thoughts of McNair reverberate through my mind.

I take a better look at this trooper, "Thank you," I said softly.

"Got a job for when you get out?" He inquired.

"Na," I laughed, in my mind, I see that question repeated by law enforcement officers checking that I am not a vagrant in their town. "Sending resumes from Boron Prison Camp might not be the best of ideas," I quipped.

"What would you like to do?" he asked encouragingly.

"In Los Angeles Harbor, there is a commercial diving school, the College of Oceaneering. It's owned by a man I met named Jim Joiner. It's the most prestigious commercial diving school in the USA." I stared into the desert. "I would like to teach there."

"Do you have the qualifications?" he asked seriously.

I laughed, "Actually, I do. I have been a scuba instructor for over a dozen years, was a Navy hardhat and combat frog diver, am a CPR and First Aid Instructor, was a Machinist Mate Chief in the Navy, love rigging and knots, and I have a California Community Services Teaching Credential."

"How do they feel about ex-felons?" he asked cutting to the chase, which law enforcement officers are particularly good at doing.

"I have no idea," I shook my head. "It's a college, co-ed no less, so I don't think my chances are that good."

"It's worth a try," he encouraged.

"Most everything is," I agreed.

We shake hands, and I turn to go.

"Hey, Arrington."

I stop and turn around. The patrolman has a ticket book out and pen in hand. "What's the name of that Unit Manager?"

Climbing into the cab, Ralph shows me a crumpled piece of blood-stained paper. "Suicide note," he said, "the kid was only 19. I'm locked up dreaming about freedom and this kid just throws his life away."

"Excuse us, officer," I say to the guard. I take Ralph over to the Highway Patrol Officer.

"Hugh, this is Ralph, he has something," I said solemnly.

Ralph hands the note to Hugh, who reads it.

"Thank you, Ralph," he said shaking my friend's hand. "This is a real tragedy, but the note will be a comfort for the grieving family. Least, they will know why he did it. I'll take it to them."

"But he threw away his life, his freedom," Ralph's emotions strained his voice. "I was 19 when I went to prison. There's no coming back for him."

Hugh nods, "Yeah, but there are many kinds of prisons. One day your time will be behind you, he just did not see an escape from his situation. Therefore, every person you meet, look them in the eye. Recognize that person as a human being. It's more important than you might think."

Ralph stares at the wet dirt and sand beside the road.

"As an officer of the law, most people are not happy to see me. I never know how they are going to react. The first thing I do is take their measure. Instead of just writing them a ticket my priority is to protect and to serve." Hugh nodded towards the wreck of the pickup truck, "If I pulled him over for speeding before the accident. I might have been able to save his life, just by noticing him as a real human being, and listening to what he had to say."

He puts the note in his pocket, "If I can get someone to talk, I can find out what's going on in their head. I have faced more than a few angry men driving around to burn off their rage. Got them to calm down, to accept their responsibilities, and to go back to their wives and children—had my share of angry wives too."

Ralph wipes his eyes.

"One day, you'll be taking that uniform off, but don't ever shed the fact that you are a real lifesaver. Take that with you when you get out and look people in the eye. Wonderful things will come of it, not just for them but for you too," he said sagely.

As I drove back to the camp, I realized that Hugh's advice to Ralph would forever be a part of my life. That talk gave added meaning to my driving the fire truck out of the prison camp. I sighed as I prepared to confront the Unit Manager. I imagined Hugh having to comfort that family. My situation will be easier.

I radioed control to raise the barrier. Driving the truck through the gate, we passed the Unit Manager's office, and I saw him at his window glaring at me with a radio in his hand.

While the men stored the gear in the firehouse, I took off my turnouts, hung the chief engineer's helmet from its peg, stared at it, and then walked over to the Unit Manager's office. I knocked firmly on his door.

"Enter," said the gruff voice.

I step inside. "Figured you wanted to see me," I said politely remembering to stand tall and make eye contact. My hands are in front of me holding my ball cap. My posture resembles an old saying, "Hat in hand." It is a visible token of respect, which he notices as he glares at me.

"You disobeyed me, Arrington," he snarled.

"I am terribly sorry, sir. I just had a personal obligation to lead my men," I said respectfully. "It is what a chief engineer does," I paused, "it's nothing more than that."

"You know I could severely punish you," he threatened.

I simply followed my job profile, but it is a losing argument, so I keep it bottled inside of me. There is no benefit in our fighting, not for him and certainly not for me.

"Sir," he looks at me, surprised by my willingness to use that word so respectfully, "I take this assignment seriously. When I walked through this door a year ago, I told you I wanted to be a firefighter more than anything. That is still true. I did not lead the team out of the camp to be defiant or to make you angry. I did it because I felt it was my sacred responsibility," I said standing tall.

"Well, I have a duty to do too, inmate. You've had a couple of months to train the crew, and let's hope they are ready because you're off the fire crew effective immediately."

"Yes, sir, I expected that," I acknowledged respectfully.

"I have already cleared it with the Warden so don't get your hopes up in that direction," he said watching me intently.

"I won't," I awaited the punishment we both know is coming — then the hint of a smile crosses his face just before he sent it away.

"Plumber or dishwasher?" he asked.

"Well, actually sir, I would like to be a teacher," I said hopefully.

"What?" The pencil he was holding dropped to the desk.

"Can I maybe go to work in the Education Department?"

"Why?" he questioned with a frown.

"Because I can teach. I have a California Teaching Credential in Marine and Related Technologies."

"You want to teach Marine Biology to inmates in the desert?"

"No Sir, math or English, I am also writing a book about my time in prison."

"What does that have to do with anything?" he asked.

"They have a typewriter up there."

He leaned back in his chair studying me.

"I can write about what I've learned from you," I offered.

"What did you teach again?"

"Scuba diving, Ventura City College gave me a limited services teaching credential to run a scuba program for them. They needed to give it an official-sounding name, so I suggested Marine and Related Technologies."

The smile was there again, it was neither huge nor radiant, yet it lingered, and he is amused. "Okay, get your butt up the hill to the Education Department." He made a note in my file.

"Thank you, sir." I turned to leave.

"Hey, Arrington," he said not unkindly.

I stop at the door and turn to face him.

"When you came in, I was going to throw you back in that cage in the plumbing shop. What just happened?"

"We got off to a bad start, and we never corrected it. It was a mistake, after all this is the Department of Corrections."

"Make me a promise."

"What's that, Sir?"

"When you get out, I do not ever want to see you again."

* * *

I awaken slowly in the darkness—then my mind rushes to full consciousness. I grab my plastic digital watch on the nightstand. It is 2:00 AM—my last day in prison!

I slip out of the room carrying one of my hand-painted cups and a tea bag. I have been sharing the tea and am now down to my last one. I fill the cup with warm water at *old gurgle and spit* then pad barefoot into the television room. I quietly clear a small circle and then sit down on the old wooden floor. I sip my tea smelling the fragrance of jasmine, which reminds me of my time in Asia during the Vietnam Conflict. This will be my last tranquil moment for some time. Life is about to descend upon me with its time schedules, responsibilities, chores, and bills, as I prepare to start my life over from scratch. The government has released Revelstoke, which is in Sam's care. I have a surfboard and a wetsuit, also in Sam's care. That's it; I have nothing else, except for a $3,000 student loan—making the $200 in my prison account seem insignificant. I also have a modest $6,501,215 tax lien, courtesy of the IRS.

I look at a picture Sam sent of himself. He promised he would keep Revelstoke safely parked in front of his mother's house. In the picture, Sam is standing beside Revelstoke at the beach. He has taken my only possession on a road trip. I know its registration is expired and that it has no insurance. All that I have he has foolishly placed at risk. Anger does me no good; it is simply his irresponsible view of the world according to Sam.

I quietly go through my Gung Fu routines. I do sit-ups and push-ups on the wooden floor and pull-ups from a doorsill.

A few minutes before six, I lace up my running shoes then wait at the door. When the guard unlocks it, I step outside into the predawn darkness. The guard is walking heavily away, but he stops and turns, the beam from his flashlight washes over me, "Good luck, Arrington."

"Thank you, Sir," I responded. *'Amazing, I still do not know Box of Rocks' real name.'*

The desert wilderness just before sunrise has a lonely beauty that washes away the thoughtless chatter of my mind while encouraging a certain purity of inspirational contemplation. I set a fast pace up the hill and hear the rustle of small paws in the darkness. I barely see the young rabbits that flee my approach. The Jackrabbits are of an age to have left their mother and are now learning their survival skills as they scurry off the road for the dubious safety of the desert shrubs. I often see rattlesnakes, rarely coyotes, and sometimes owls; living in the wild is not easy on young rabbits.

Running the loop, I watch the rising sun, its brilliant red light spreading over the vast desert floor. I listen to the rhythm of my feet pounding on the road; the cadence is like the ticking of a clock counting off time, each step carrying me closer to 8:00 AM, my scheduled release time.

Returning to Dorm 7, Ralph is leaning against the door to my room. I remove my running shoes and hand them to him with my sweat socks, which are still warm from my feet. He would not ask for the socks, but I know he wants them. It is just one of those inmate things. The entire time I have known Ralph, no one has sent him a Christmas care box. Like I said, family problems.

Opening a drawer, I take out my treasured radio and place it in his hands. For a moment, I see the little radio from a civilian perspective. It is a cheap mono box radio with a 50-cent speaker. I look at the little radio with heartfelt fondness, knowing that no entertainment system will ever have more value than this little-scarred plastic box radio resting on a pair of old running shoes and sweaty socks.

After a cool shower, I put on worn-out jeans, a holed T-shirt, and a pair of frayed tennis shoes. From the dresser top, I pick up a small cardboard box. It is the same size that I carried from J-3. Inside is my Bible, both of my journals, my pictures, a half-dozen hand-painted coffee cups, and my toothbrush. I take a last look at my room, then close the door and wander casually down toward control to pick up my release papers.

Walking past the firehouse, I look at the fire trucks in their shaded bays. Who would have ever thought I would have such exciting memories from prison? I walk up to the big Ford and run a hand over its fender. I see my reflection in the brightly polished paint. I press my thumb firmly onto the shiny surface leaving a print; Stephen Arrington was here. I walk to the 48 Mack and run a hand over the siren. It's okay that the fire crew is at breakfast. I want my leaving prison to be a private affair.

Walking down to control, I stop at the barrier and look at the camp one last time. I have learned many things about myself, here and at T.I., yet I will not miss prison in any way.

After collecting my papers, I walk to the freedom side of the barrier and stare down the long, straight highway. Time passes, finally, I see my brother's car approaching. Jim stops beside me. I am about to get into the car when I hear the distinctive wail of the Mack's siren. The fire crew is driving the 48 Mack across the dirt baseball field trailing a cloud of dust with its red lights flashing. The truck comes to a halt as the dust cloud settles about it. The fire crew is hanging off the back and sides. They wave, and then at the back rail of the truck, I see Ralph waving. I realize that the crew has been waiting for my ride to arrive before driving out onto the field.

My brother Jim smiles as I climb into the car with tears clouding my eyes. As Jim begins to drive down that long, straight road, I turn in the seat to stare at the fire truck and the waving inmates until distance fades them from sight.

When we reach the main highway, I stick my head out the open window and feel the wonder of freedom rushing past all around me. It blows through the open window, playing with my hair, causing me to blink in its intensity. That wind carries within it fresh scents remembered and the sounds of life, civilian life unhindered. Looking back, I see the prison camp hill with its radar dome on top slowly fading with distance. Suddenly I am a civilian again — well almost.

As we climb the long grade going south, I look back and to the east where the B-1 Bomber crashed. Soon we pass the spot where the Volkswagen burned, my first fire response, then where the young man died, and I washed his blood into the dirt and sand. Ten minutes later, I see the spot where I stood on top of the fire truck when the helicopter flew right over my head. I glance at Jim,

"Ventura City College needed a scuba instructor. If you have seven years' experience in a profession, you can teach that subject at a junior college level."

"As an ex-machinist mate chief," I continued my pitch, "I can repair almost any kind of diving or boating equipment. I have studied expository writing so I can help draft teaching lessons."

"What's in the paper bag?" he asked peering at the bag I had tucked under my chair.

"My lunch," I said defensively.

"Really? Hope it's not peanut butter and jelly."

"I am on a bit of a budget," I admitted.

Tom continued asking questions. His interview was complex, and I realize just how deeply I have prepared for a diving career. Two cups of coffee and a full bladder later, I finally must ask, "So, any ideas on a diving job for an ex-felon?" I asked hopefully.

"Sure," he said off-handedly, "you're going to work as a core instructor. Come on, we'll get you a set of keys, take your instructor picture, and I'll give you a tour of the school."

"I got the job?" I asked astonished.

"Sure, you did—hope you don't think I have that much time to waste just sitting around jawing with a stranger," laughed Tom.

"But I thought you said you weren't looking for anybody."

Tom grins, "I was just funning you. I have needed a new core block instructor for months." Tom happily punches me in the shoulder, "Yesterday, Jim Joiner, the president of the college told me you'd be dropping in and that I was to hire you right off." Tom smiled at my look of surprise. "I've known since yesterday that I would be hiring you, which meant I wasn't looking for anyone. Get it?" He put an arm around my shoulder and smiled.

"I guess, but why me?" I wondered out loud.

"Jim got a call from a highway patrol officer up in the Mojave Desert last month. He even sent down a couple of reference letters. Want to see them?" he said digging in a drawer. Tom hands over three letters, one from the Hugh, the Highway Patrol Officer, one from the Safety Officer, and one from the Unit Manager, who said I was a model inmate with an excellent record and a cooperative disposition.

"That's not all," Jim Joiner called NAUI Headquarters, and they pulled your file. It seems you were a real active instructor up in Oxnard and that you completed a master scuba instructor certificate for teaching other instructors. He's very excited to be hiring you," said Tom, "thinks you add character to the staff."

Instructor Arrington three days out of prison

Tom leads me into the instructor lounge and knuckles a locker, "This is yours, and here's your keys." He said. "The receptionist has your employment papers and your medical insurance card. I'll see you in the morning at 7:30."

Half an hour later, I walk out the front door of the College of Oceaneering. I turn around and stare at the administration build's pillars. There is a diving bell next to the flagpole. I look up at the Stars and Stripes waving in the wind. '*Very classy*,' I thought listening to the squawk of seagulls and the signal horn of a tugboat in the harbor. For a year, I have worried about finding work as an ex-felon. All along, the LORD was laying out a plan for me. "Trust in Me," says the LORD, suddenly takes on greater personal meaning.

Boarding a bus, I grab a schedule. Occasionally looking out the window to orient myself to the town of my employment. I reach into my pocket and finger the ring of keys. How surprising, to start the morning with low hopes, and now in the afternoon to be a responsible person with a ring of keys. I settle into the bus seat, totally enjoying a true sense of belonging. On the ride out, I was an ex-felon, just out of prison, casting about, but not belonging. Now I am an instructor at a commercial diving college, just call me Professor Arrington.

Back at the halfway house, I unpack a bag of groceries. I am in a celebratory mood though it is sobering to have spent $9.85. That is another 5% of my money gone, which means I have already spent one-quarter of my funds. Thankfully, I now know that my first paycheck is just eleven days away. That is eight workdays, meaning I must allocate $8.60 per day for the bus. That equals 34% of my total funds, counting the 24% I have already spent—over half of my money gone. Not springing for that box of tea was a good choice.

That night I am early to bed, wanting to be fresh and bright for my first day at work. At 9:00 PM, I happily watch the fireworks streaking into the sky over Disneyland. The brilliant colors rocketing across the dark sky are like a seal of approval on a promise fulfilled. I settle deeper into my blankets, smiling at the world, and fall asleep.

The first few days at the college are very hectic as I learn my schedule and get to know the students.

On Saturday, the clerk at the halfway house rings the room. I have a visitor. Our telephone only receives incoming calls. I rush to the gate to see Sam at the curb with Revelstoke looming over his shoulder. The truck is looking older, yet so many wonderful memories reside in its wood interior and metal chassis. Sam and I visit about old times and all too soon, it is time for him to head back to San Diego.

After Sam leaves, I step inside Revelstoke's backdoor. It feels like coming home from a long trip or a near-fatal sickness. I sit on the bed and glance about Revelstoke's wooden interior, and I am so incredibly happy. There are pictures of Susan and Puu on the walls and places we visited together. This old truck means so much to me. I open the oven and see a steel pot with a dented lid, which gives me an idea.

Back from the supermarket, I have spent a mere five bucks. I have a bag of brown rice, a sack of beans, and a cylinder of old-fashioned oatmeal, which was on sale. Though I am staying in the halfway house, I will prepare and eat my meals in Revelstoke. For the next six days, for lunch and dinner I eat rice and beans, and for breakfast, oatmeal — no honey, no milk. These simple meals are spiced with the acute pleasure that I am eating them in my true home. I pause to think about Sam and am thankful that he brought Revelstoke to me as a surprise. I say a prayer of thanks and forgive him for all that has bothered me. That simple act restores our friendship in a good way.

Friday payday arrives. I have three dollars left. Opening the envelope, I see a check for $853.35, a vast sum. I purchase auto insurance, register Revelstoke, fill its gas tank, top off the propane cylinder, and fill the refrigerator and cupboards. I get a haircut then buy work boots, a pair of swim trunks, and another set of jeans — life is good, I be having things.

The next two months pass quickly. On the diving barge, which is moored in Los Angeles Harbor, I am teaching the night diving class. It gives the students a feel for diving in a working harbor in the dark, which can be disorienting and dangerous. We start at sunset and wrap up the class by 10:00 PM. I had to get special permission with a letter of explanation from the college to arrive late back at the halfway house.

Standing on the wet rusty deck of the diving barge, I stare out over the dark water at the lights of the harbor. The College of Oceaneering is but a mile from Terminal Island Prison. We are a bit up the channel on the same side of the harbor; the sights are so like what I saw through the prison fence. I am deeply disturbed by the prison's foreboding presence, which lurks too close to where I am standing. Sometimes school business takes me near the institution's gray walls, which always causes me to tremble deep down inside.

Beyond the floodlights on the dive barge, I see the dark hills of San Pedro. The view recalls prison memories. I see the same city lights on the hills and all but hear the prison's siren call and feel it is seeking to pull me back into its walls. Shadowy inmate memories linger about me and haunt my sleep. I do not rest well at night as phantom DEA agents, correctional officers, and inmates stalk my dreams. Often, I wake up in a cold sweat. I live with the secret terror of a simple parole violation, such as missing daily count at the halfway house.

On the dive barge, we run long securing the equipment. It is lightly raining causing me to hit heavy traffic. I am later than I should be as I walk through the office door to sign in — then stop dead in my tracks when I see a horrifying sight. Sitting on the clerk's desk is a cardboard box stuffed with my few possessions.

The thought that they are sending me back to Terminal Island Prison is overwhelming, 'Are they sending me back, just for being a little late?'

I stand there at a total loss and in complete dismay. My heart collapses into itself as I vividly remember the cold and dank T.I. holding cell, which is where they would take me for a parole violation. It is the closest federal prison.

"About time you got here, Arrington," grumbled the night clerk shuffling papers. "Sign these discharge papers."

"Discharge papers?"

"The judge commuted your sentence to three years."

I scan the document, Judge Takasugi has ruled on an appeal my attorney Rick submitted over two years ago.

Who would have ever thought he would rule on my appeal after my release from prison?

"You know you can't spend the night here," he said sternly.

"What?"

"Served your sentence," quipped the clerk, "The halfway house cannot be responsible for your safety around the inmates."

'He said the inmates,' I think gleefully, not other inmates. I am no longer an inmate; I am now a parolee!'

I signed the papers, grabbed the box and dashed out the door.

I drove Revelstoke to Huntington Beach and slipped into a parking space after paying a five-dollar overnight fee.

I walk along the water's edge, staring out to sea. The rain has washed the night sky. Stepping across the threshold of freedom is so unexpected. I still have three years of special parole. This means any violation will launch me like a lightning bolt back inside prison walls. However, I am no longer Inmate Arrington — just call me, Steve.

Early the next morning, I drive Revelstoke to the college arriving before sunrise. I park by a little green lawn. It is a tiny park in the middle of the college. It is smaller than a small house lot, but there are trees, flowering bushes, the little green lawn and two wooden benches.

I stare at the college's wooden administration building with the upstairs classrooms. Beside it is the hyperbaric chamber room and two diver-training tanks with portholes for viewing underwater training. A raised platform provides a deck for tending the divers. To the right are the rigging locker, knot-tying classroom, and the rigging yard. Behind me are three diving barges with various underwater projects.

In the middle of it all is Revelstoke. I perk a small pot of coffee and take a cup outside to sit on a wooden bench. I arrived early to revel in this moment. My life after prison has come together in a surprising way. I also know that I serve a purpose. What better place than a college to teach young men and women not just the commercial aspects of diving, but also about life.

I love camping at Huntington Beach at night and beside the little park in the day. However, there is a sign in the beach parking lot that restricts camping to only ten days. I begin the search for a place to live where I can park Revelstoke on a long-term basis. It needs to be affordable and close to the college. I rent half of a Mexican family's driveway on the poorer side of Los Angeles Harbor in the town of Wilmington for 40 bucks a month. It is only a mile from the College of Oceaneering so Terminal Island Prison still lurkers in the too near distance.

Across from my driveway, an oil well dips and pulls with an endless, reciprocating squeal 24-hours a day. It is like the mechanical heartbeat of this tough Mexican neighborhood, where police cars only patrol with backup within sight.

Revelstoke becomes a refuge of good memories, and I use it as a place to hide at night. I am fleeing the social life I fear for a self-induced cage. I want to be with people but know no one outside of the college. My mother lives just 50 miles away, but she has a problem. She told me not to expect to rely on her for anything and that, "Once a felon, always a felon. It's only a matter of time before you go back to prison." There is nothing there for me.

My brother lives further away yet we have little in common. With the death of our father, we had drawn even further apart.

On some Sundays, I attend church. It is a large warehouse affair with thousands of people in attendance at each service. But I am lost in the crowd. At the beginning of each service, they ask us to say hello to someone and to shake hands, but nothing comes of it. I feel awkward standing alone in the lobby. I arrive alone and leave alone. Finally, I just stop going. Instead, I should have found a friendlier church.

My life outside the college is hollow and uneventful. I would like to talk with teens at public schools about choices. But my drug felony makes it difficult to approach a school principal. Inmate conditioning prevents me from looking someone that respectable in the eyes. I am too fragile to face moral scrutiny.

Author checking a commercial diving student.

On September 8, 1986, I was teaching a core subject, when a student explodes through a door yelling, "Mr. Arrington, Mark is drowning!"

I grab my first aid kit and run.

On the diving barge, semi-controlled panic rules as a team of divers quickly don their gear. Five minutes ago, the student diver screamed over the radiotelephone that he was trapped. The project he was working on had fallen on him. Then from the speaker came the dreadful gurgling sound of water filling his helmet—just before the line went dead. The standby diver jumped into the water.

From the deck speaker, I hear the standby diver, who is 45 feet down on the muddy bottom of the harbor, "A heavy metal cylinder is lying across his back. I can't get it off him."

"What about his helmet?" The instructor yelled into the mic.

"His helmet's off—he looks dead!" static punctuated the reply.

Coming up on seven minutes," said the timekeeper. His voice broke as he stuttered, "Mr. Arrington—is Mark going to die?"

I turn away, not wanting to echo what he has guessed. Seven minutes and counting was just too long. I feel helpless while a young life ebbs away in the cold, dark mud at the bottom of the harbor. I peer anxiously at a mass of bursting bubbles surfacing in a large boil from the divers working desperately below.

"Got him," erupts from the speaker, "we're coming up."

The size of the bursting bubbles decreases as the divers ascend. Mark's head surfaces, he is surrounded by the rescue divers wearing Kirby-Morgan helmets with dark reflective faceplates. Each of the hard-shelled helmets is a different color: red, yellow, and blue with pieces of shiny brass and chrome. The men look huge in their black wetsuits, coveralls, and working harnesses. There is a lather of splashing water as they work to lift Mark up high enough for me to grab him. His head flops lifelessly, his open eyes stare sightlessly from a froth of whitewater. Kneeling at the edge of the barge, I reach down and grab Mark's harness. My face is just inches from those lifeless orbs as I remember the same look in the eyes of the teenage driver we lost in the desert.

Getting a grip on the harness straps, I haul the limp body upward. Other hands grab my belt from behind to help, and then onto Mark as we drag the flaccid student onto the unyielding metal deck. We are losing a desperate race. His skin is a ghastly shade of deep purple from excess carbon dioxide. The black pupils of his eyes are widely dilated, fixed, and staring—as if he has already passed from this world.

Ignoring what those terrible eyes foretell, I place one hand under Mark's neck and the other firmly on his forehead, then tilt his head back to establish an open airway. Mark's skin is cold and clammy—like touching a refrigerated cadaver. I seal my mouth around his icy, blackened lips and forcefully blow air into his lungs. I see his chest rise under the black wetsuit while in my mind I ask the LORD for His help, *'Father, let us not be too late. Let it be Your breath, not mine.'*

With the first breath, seawater gushes out of Mark's mouth from his distended stomach. I roll him toward me to keep the water from flowing back into his lungs. I give him three more rapid breaths then unzip his wetsuit to relieve pressure on the chest before locking my hands over his sternum and thrust downward, as I begin cardiopulmonary resuscitation (CPR). It is surprising how easy it is to do CPR on a real person. I have actively taught CPR for over 15 years. After all those late-night classes working with mannequins, I am doing CPR for real. I see his chest convulse inward a full two inches under the driving force of my clenched hands. Though his purplish skin slowly waxes to a deathly pale shade, I know his chances are poor or nonexistent. He has been down too long. I continue my efforts to revive him despite being convinced that he is already gone.

In my mind, I see Mark, the young student, who just hours earlier wished me an enthusiastic, "Good morning," as he hurried to the diving locker. I continue the compressions on his chest while another instructor takes over the breathing.

It is a full 20 minutes before the fire department arrives. They connect Mark to a portable EKG machine to measure his vital functions. They order us to pause CPR while they check the meter, which reflects a flat line indicating clinical death. I begin the CPR again as one of the medics readies an Ambu bag with an oxygen reserve. The lead medic kneels opposite me, "Okay, we got him now," he said as his hands take the place of mine. I am reluctant to surrender my position and awkwardly stand then step back. I am uncomfortable to be merely a concerned observer.

"Where's his wallet," yelled a firefighter. They interrupt CPR to lift Mark onto a gurney. From the barge's locker room, a student runs holding up Mark's wallet.

A medic flips the wallet open checking the driver's license. "Got an organ donor," he yelled.

The firefighters rushed the gurney up the barge ramp to the pier. They shove the body through the back of an ambulance. Then the doors slam shut, and the vehicle speeds away.

As the yelp of the siren slowly fades, I stare at a dark pool of rusty water where Mark's body had lain on the barge deck. I recall the sheen of black oil, and bloodstained desert sand in the Mojave after the coroner took away that poor teenager's body and a deep sadness settles over me. I step to the railing and stare down into the dark water lapping at the side of the barge.

On the pier, the firefighters are stowing equipment, when one of them with a radio yells, "They got a heartbeat!"

Everyone stops what they are doing, and we all stare.

"Spontaneous breathing," he yelled excitedly.

We crowd around him full of hope as he listens to his radio earpiece. "They're diverting to a chopper for air evacuation to Northridge Hospital's hyperbaric facility."

At the end of the workday in the instructor's lounge, we are all very sober; no one's hopes are high. The odds are that brain damage has already occurred. The word from the hospital is that Mark is in a deep coma—as expected.

The next day they move Mark to intensive care, his condition is extremely critical. His mother sits weeping at the side of his bed throughout the long night. It looks hopeless. The doctors warn her to expect the worst. If his heart stops again, they should be ready to harvest his organs.

At mid-morning, Tom Mix barges into my classroom. "Mark is going to live," he yelled. "He woke up, and he's talking. No sign of brain damage," the words are spewing forth. "The doctor thinks it's a miracle. He doesn't know of anyone who's recovered after over eight minutes without oxygen. Mark woke up with his mom there. He asked her what was going on."

"I thought you couldn't live that long without oxygen?" blurted one of the students.

"They think the cold sea water slowed his metabolism and the high partial pressure of oxygen in his body from being at almost 50 feet of water depth helped." Tom Mix smiled, "Good job, Arrington."

The next day Tom calls me to his office. "Come in, Steve," he said standing up. "Do me a favor and sit in my chair."

"What?"

"I just want to see something," he pulled me around the desk. "Come on, sit down."

I drop into the chair as Tom goes around to the other side of the desk and looks at me. He raises his hands forming them into a rectangle and peers through the opening like a camera operator framing a shot. "Perfect. It works."

"What works?"

"My desk fits you."

"It does?"

"Yep, you are the new Air Diving Supervisor."

"Huh?"

"Yep, I'm leaving, got a job with a treasure-diving outfit."

"Treasure?" I asked intrigued.

"Can't tell you a thing," he picked up a duffle bag and begins randomly stuffing items into it, "just that I'm leaving, and Jim Joiner has authorized your promotion."

Tom drops the duffle and leans his hands on the desk, "Everyone thinks you did an incredible job taking charge of Mark's CPR. Don't worry, you've got what it takes, and the students like you."

"Wait a minute," I stood up, "when are you leaving?"

Tom glanced at his wristwatch, "Now."

"You're leaving now?"

"Yeah, your promotion is immediate. You're getting a 50% pay raise, effective today."

Tom looks around the office, shoves a couple more items carelessly into the duffle, then shrugs his shoulders, and glances at his watch, "What do you know? My time is up."

With those parting words, he steps through the door.

I glance around at — my new office. *'I have an office?'*

Mark returns to the college with no apparent brain damage and joins a class just beginning practical harbor diving. It is startling to see him walking the hallways — I too vividly remember him looking dead.

The day he is to dive the mud monster, the project he almost died on, I arrange the schedule so I will run the dive operations.

I am like a mother hen, checking everything. I walk over to double check Mark's harness while the tenders suit him up.

"You okay?" I asked.

"Yes," he said, his smile strained. It is understandable; the mud monster almost killed him last time. "You know," Mark has a momentary faraway look in his eyes, "I remember drowning."

"All of it?" I placed a comforting hand on his shoulder.

Mark's deep brown eyes look directly at me. It is disquieting seeing those eyes full of life. "I was cheating on the project."

"Really…" I smiled encouraging him to tell me all about it.

The mud monster is an advanced underwater project. It is a thick iron cylinder five-feet tall and over two-feet wide. It is bolted at its base to a cement footing. The diver's task is to attach a webbed bridle with a lifting bladder to the top of the cylinder. Next, he unbolts the mud monster's feet and fills the bladder with air from his nemo (depth indicating air hose). The bladder makes the cylinder lighter, but not light enough to float it. This is a planned safety feature because teaching commercial diving is a dangerous occupation. The diver's job is to lever the cylinder up from the suction of the mud, move it to another footing, bolt it back down, and remove the lifting bladder. It is a timed grade.

"What I did," Mark is looking down at the deck, "is remove the footing bolts, but instead of attaching the lifting bridle, I removed the cylinder's inspection port and inserted my nemo."

"You were going to save time by using the air from the nemo to displace the water inside the cylinder to lighten it."

"Yeah, but it got away from me," said Mark. "The darn thing started to lift up off the bottom. I was afraid it would shoot to the surface and that I would be kicked out of the school for cheating. I grabbed it with both arms and hugged the stupid thing so I could roll the inspection port up to dump out the air."

"At which point it became negatively buoyant," I ventured.

"About 300 pounds negative—a great big iron casket. It knocked me facedown into the harbor mud and then it rolled onto my back. As more air dumped out, it got heavier, driving me deeper and deeper facedown into that thick mud. I knew I was going to die and panicked—so I removed my helmet."

Mark is staring at me with those now innocent eyes, "I remember how stupid I felt as the water and mud closed around my face. It was so dark and so very cold. I tried to scream, but couldn't underwater. It's the last thing I remember."

"Mark," I said carefully, "you don't have to make this dive."

Mark straightens up on the diving stool, "Yes, I do."

For the next 50 minutes, I pace the barge's deck. Then I hear Mark's triumphant voice over the radio-microphone, "Project complete, stop the clock, diver coming up."

When he surfaces, I help Mark remove his mud-smeared helmet. He smiles, "It's smaller than how I remembered it.'

Because so much time had elapsed while he was trapped underwater, the Los Angeles Fire Department and the Red Cross credits me with saving the young student's life. The Red Cross arranged an award ceremony to present me with their highest award for lifesaving, the Red Cross *Certificate of Merit*.

In the audience is James Walsh, the prosecutor in my case. I invited Mr. Walsh wanting him to see that an ex-felon could turn his life around. He now seems almost like an old friend. When they hand me the award, I look down at the signature upon it in wonder. The Director of the Red Cross had already told me that President Ronald Reagan signed these awards personally. Looking at that signature, I remember hearing President Reagan announce the war on drugs while I drove that drug-laden car in Florida.

The Red Cross Director takes out a small gold award and pins it to my jacket. I finger the shiny metal and remember the terrible sadness I felt when I removed my naval uniform for the last time. I think about my tragic state six years ago when I placed my military medals and chief's insignia into that little wooden box and sadly closed the lid. Receiving this honor for lifesaving washes away much of that old sadness, yet it makes me realize that I really can step into a new future and put prison and its awful memories behind me.

That night, in Revelstoke, I look at the awards. Ronald Reagan's signature on the Certificate of Merit feels like a Presidential Pardon. Ronald Reagan, Disney's Daniel Boone, and Jacques-Yves Cousteau were my heroes. Each was the father I wish I had. My father always worked late, returned home under the influence, and regularly whipped my brother and me. So, I fled into my imagination with daydreams that took me anywhere, but home.

I wonder when Reagan signed this award — did he know it was me — the smuggler in the drug car? I think not, but it does not take away from the wonder of it all.

I stare at the award from the Los Angeles City Fire Department. It is very ornate and colorful. There is another tie-in happening here. The LORD allowed me to become an inmate firefighter in prison, which gave my life inside meaning and purpose. Now, He comes back at me with a lifesaving award from the fire department no less.

Saving Mark's life became the turning point to get my life back in focus. I truly feel good about being me again and can deal with people knowing my criminal past. It also gives me the courage to approach school principals with my desire to speak with students about drugs, crime, and prison — one so often follows the other.

There is one more thing I must do before I can truly put my past behind me. It is time to part with Revelstoke. After ten years, the Stoker is getting old, and I am ready for a more secure home. The FOR-SALE sign is not on the old truck for long before I get a buyer. It is an old man living alone. He wants to retire to Mexico and live alongside a river.

I watch a stranger driving Revelstoke away. It slows at an intersection, turns, and disappears down the corridors of my mind where memories of Susan and Puu reside.

Fire Department

Steve Arrington

The Los Angeles City Fire Department considers your actions on September 8, 1986, to a reported drowning at the College of Oceaneering, a commercial diving school, located at 272 South Fries Avenue in Wilmington, to be worthy of special recognition.

Official reports state that on this day you became aware of a life-threatening drowning accident which required immediate action. Without hesitation, you immediately started cardiopulmonary resuscitation on a student diver who had been in respiratory and cardiac arrest as a result of being trapped under water for 10 minutes. Due to your timely intervention and proper use of cardiopulmonary resuscitation, prior to the arrival of Fire Department personnel, you were successful in saving the young man's life.

Your actions demonstrate a high level of responsibility and initiative and provide an excellent example for others to follow.

It is indeed a pleasure to commend you and to extend to you my personal thanks.

DONALD O. MANNING
Chief Engineer and General Manager

Los Angeles Fire Department
award letter for saving Mark's life

American Red Cross

CERTIFICATE OF MERIT

awarded to

STEPHEN LEE ARRINGTON

for selfless and humane action

in saving a human life.

Issued at Washington, D.C.

Honorary Chairman

Chairman

The Red Cross highest award for life saving
signed by President Ronald Reagan

"To save a life is a real and beautiful thing. To make a home for the homeless, yes, it is a thing that must be good; whatever the world may say, it cannot be wrong." –Vincent Van Gogh

Chapter 20 - Wilmington, California, May 1987

I have been working at the College of Oceaneering for two years. I enjoy my job but yearn for the adventure I had known in the Navy. I lust for travel to exotic places and chafe to get back into an active diving career. However, my special parole will not run out for another year, so until then I am stuck in Los Angeles County — or so I thought.

Global travel and underwater adventures only dreamed about are sprinting toward me — it is all linked to a potted houseplant growing behind my desk. I purchased the broad-leafed plant at a Mexican market along with a frozen pizza. Someone knocked the little plant off a shelf then ran it over with a cart. I felt sorry for it lying on the vinyl floor with other debris, its split pot spilling out dirt — its future did not look good. The clerk would only accept a quarter for the abused plant.

I put it in a pot and placed it under the skylight in Revelstoke, but it quickly grew too big for those cramped quarters. I took it to my office and put it in a dented steel bucket with a rusted bottom that I found under a pier. The other instructors wondered why I would use a rusty bucket as a decorative pot, but I kept my J-3 Yard memories to myself.

When pouring water over the dirt, I would run my hands over the old pail's sides. *The wonder, I carry water.*

The plant thrived as more vines climbed out of the bucket and went off in various directions in search of anchors and a sunbeam or two. The vines draped over picture frames, hung from shelves, swirled around electrical cords, and became a serious presence on the wall. If I left the window, open questing appendages tended to slip outside.

Two months ago, an instructor asked, "What are you going to do when that thing reaches the ceiling?"

I carelessly replied, "Move on to another job."

Now as I sit at my desk admiring the morning light coming through the office window with the gargantuan plant looming behind me, Doug, my lead instructor, quips innocently, "So tell me about your new job."

Confused, I asked, "What are you talking about?"

"Your plant," Doug pointed to the giant vegetative growth lurking behind me, "it just reached the ceiling."

Spinning about in my chair, I see that the plant has sprouted yet another leaf, which is on the verge of opening. The green tip is brushing against a ceiling tile with the movement of a gentle breeze blowing through the open window.

"Maybe I spoke too carelessly," I answered despondently.

I pour the rest of my coffee into monster plant's pot. I think it likes the caffeine; maybe that is why it is growing so rapidly.

Collecting the diving log for my class, I head for the door. I am teaching on the barge today. Outside it is a beautifully clear spring day in early May. The bright morning sunshine is dancing in a sparkling tapestry upon the seawater that laps ever so gently against the barnacle-encrusted wooden pilings of the inner harbor.

Down at the barge, I wipe black oil from my hands with a red cloth. I am teaching the students how to hand-crank start the diesel air compressor without hitting themselves in the head with the detachable crank. Over the heavy pant of the diesel engine, I faintly hear the pier phone ringing. I catch it on the sixth ring. While trying to blot out the heavy pant of the diesel engine that rumbles in the background, I hear the voice of Don Santee, chief diver, and expedition leader for the Cousteau Society. Don enjoys going for shock value, so he begins with 11 mind-jarring words, "Steve, how would you like to come work for us?"

Earlier in the year, Don had sat in on my diving medicine class just to brush up on any new changes that had occurred in treating divers' maladies. Like almost every other diver Don met, I offered him my services should he ever need a diver. I sincerely meant it when I made the offer, but I never expected him to call. I was just voicing a childhood dream I thought was too impossible to come true — particularly since I was an ex-felon, on special parole, and did not even speak French.

Listening to Don on the phone, I cannot believe that my childhood dream is setting down roots. "Don, it would be my absolute pleasure to come to work for you," I said eagerly.

"Great! You should give the college notice right away. I need you as soon as possible. "Oh, one more thing," Don added casually, as if it is just an afterthought, "your title is going to be chief diver and expedition leader."

'I'm going to be a chief diver and expedition leader for the Cousteau Society?' My mind boggles at the thought, 'Really?'

My happiness is uncontainable as I hoot and holler while dancing about the barge's rusty old deck. The students stare wondering if their instructor has just gone crazy. I leap from the barge and bolt up the pier, scattering them.

I find Doug in the recompression chamber room where he is conducting oxygen tolerance tests on a junior class. I dance about him waving my arms, "Guess what? Guess what?"

"Whoa — slow down," implored Doug, "you look like a hovering helicopter trying to take off with a heavy load."

"I got a job offer," I gasped. "Shake hands with the newest chief diver and expedition leader for the Cousteau Society."

"Nah," laughed Doug, "you're kidding me."

The next day, I went to see my Parole Officer regarding my three-year special parole, which would hamper my leaving the country. Considering that I am going to work for the Cousteau Society, my parole officer calls James Walsh my prosecutor. He agreed to end my special parole and to remove my $6,501,215 tax lien. I am suddenly a free citizen a year early.

* * *

A few months pass as I learn about the Cousteau expedition office in West Hollywood, and then Jean-Michel Cousteau sends me to Costa Rica on my first expedition. I board an 85' long Swedish wooden schooner named *Victoria*. Our destination is the solitary island of Cocos in the warm Pacific waters 300 miles due west. This beautiful volcanic island, lush with tropical foliage and sheathed in spectacular waterfalls, according to legend, is the renowned Treasure Island.

We make numerous dives in the virgin splendor of Cocos. We swim with thousands of jacks and barracuda in huge schools that part before us like a glittering curtain, flashing metallic in the submarine light we venture into their midst. There are schools of hammerhead sharks, numbering in the hundreds. From the relative safety of the seabed, 110-feet down, we watch the hammerhead sharks swimming overhead like a ghostly squadron of death raiders.

Back aboard *Victoria*, in the warmth of the tropical night, we dine topside on the bounty of the sea at a large communal table under the broad rope-wrapped sails. Laughter leads us into the night. We toast the glorious sunsets and listen to the music of the trade wind as it rustles through the furled sails and sings lightly in the rope rigging. The old wooden hull creaks and groans in its dance with the rolling swell of the ocean inside our protected bay.

At the end of the expedition, three of us descend in a tight formation with silver underwater scooters flying in synchronized loops and rolls for the underwater cameras and then dive to a depth of 130' to pass through an awesome underwater cavern. Trailing buoyant streams of iridescent bubbles, we fly through a spacious underwater grotto; its walls draped with vibrant corals. Suspended in the cavern are numerous schools of fish, each patterned differently in bright colors that part before our passage like successive shimmering veils as we traverse the length of the 200' long submarine cavern. *See image of us Cousteau divers with the scooters at* ***www.drugsbite.com***

* * *

A few weeks later, I am working late in the basement of the Cousteau office. I hear voices upstairs then two sets of legs descend the circular staircase into the basement. The second pair is long, feminine, and riveting.

Bruce Hamren, one of our diver researchers, eyes me suspiciously while introducing me to his younger sister. I look too enthusiastic about meeting Cindy. She has a captivating smile and an easy manner. We talk about diving and other harmless subjects while Bruce hovers worriedly at her side. Bruce only brought his sister by this late because he did not want her to meet any of the overly friendly Cousteau divers.

He is right to worry—I am in love at first sight. I soon become lost in Cindy's playful hazel eyes, which are on a level with my own. She is almost six feet tall.

Bruce looks unhappily from her smiling face to mine.

Reluctantly, he leaves us alone only long enough to pack a dive bag. However, judging by how he is rapidly stuffing his gear into it, I will only have a few seconds alone with Cindy.

"Would you like to go out with me next weekend?" I blurted.

Cindy's eyes crinkle, "I live in Northern California,"

I glance at Bruce, who is having problems jamming the wetsuit into his dive bag as he looks anxiously in our direction.

I make up my mind, "I'll buy you an airline ticket."

"Okay," giggled Cindy.

"Okay?" Bruce does not like the implication of that word as he arrives dragging the still open dive bag. "Okay, what?"

"Just okay, all right?" Cindy glared, "Can't I even talk with a guy without your overbearing protectiveness?"

"He's not a guy," Bruce argued, "he's a Cousteau diver. They have horrible reputations with women."

On Friday, I arrive at the airport carrying 101 long-stemmed red roses. I do not intend to tell Cindy I got the flowers on sale.

Cindy's height makes her easy to spot as she walks off the plane. I cannot decide if I should risk a hug, so instead, I present the flowers. "You shouldn't have," she said. "They must have cost you a fortune."

"Nah," I said with a sweeping gesture, "I got them on sale."

"You're not supposed to tell me that," she laughed.

While Cindy has her face buried to the nose in the roses, I have a closer look at this beautiful woman. She is wearing a short khaki jacket with a long matching skirt, which accents her blonde hair. She looks very outdoorsy. According to Bruce, Cindy is into skydiving, mountain climbing, mountain biking, whitewater kayaking, snow and water skiing, and scuba diving. Bruce also warned me she packs quite a wallop when upset. Cindy does not look violent as she smiles at me over the roses. It is a busy weekend of hiking, outdoor adventures, and mutual discovery. By the end of the weekend, she owned my heart.

An Arrington Minute: Learn the basics of life. The more you know about a diversity of subjects the more prepared you will be to react to situations. At the College of Oceaneering, I taught rigging. I told my students that every knot they learned to tie was a tool going into their 'Dealing-With-Life Box.' A knot can save or take a life. Knots are important. To pass my rigging class, they had to learn to tie all the knots behind their backs. Why? Because your hands need to know how to tie the knot in the dark, when its cold or freezing, when you are befuddled from an injury, when you are wearing gloves, etc. Only an improperly tied knot will fail. I also taught them CPR, Advanced First Aid, Water Rescue, global weather, ocean wave dynamics, river awareness, and more. Except at the College of Oceaneering, I was never paid for Teaching CPR, first aid or water safety for almost 18 years. My time investment in CPR saved Mark's life. With first aid add another half dozen lives saved and many dozens helped through injuries. As an ocean lifeguard, the best rescue is the one that is prevented by seeing someone heading for a bad situation and helping them before they get in trouble.

Going up the Gordon River in Tasmania, aboard
RV Alcyone. Photo Captain Jouet-Pastre

One can never consent to creep when one feels an impulse to soar. —
Helen Keller

I am on the island of Maui leading a Cousteau flying team. Our motel is next to a highway. Late night traffic noise makes sleeping difficult. I decide to find us a better motel, which may be difficult, we are under a budget of $75 a night per room. I open the yellow pages. A hotel catches my eye. The name sounds expensive, but why not. Talking to the hotel's manager, I explain that we are a Cousteau flying team filming humpback whales.

"And you're looking for a place to stay?" he asked eagerly.

"Yes, but it can't be too expensive," I said cautiously.

"Well, you're staying here," he replied.

"Ah, don't I have to see the rooms first?" I asked politely.

"No, no you don't," he said blowing off my question.

"But what if they're too expensive?"

"They're not...you're staying here," he said firmly.

We load up our gear and check out of the motel. Throughout the day, the divers asked me questions about the hotel. I am vague since I only have the hotel's name and directions to get there.

Just before 5:00 PM, we arrive at 2780 Kekaa Dr., in Lahaina. We pull up to the hotel's grand entrance, and the divers get out of the trucks and stare in awe. "The Royal Lahaina Resort?" asked Clay.

A man in a Hawaiian shirt and khaki pants strides out of the towering hotel. The man smiles, "Come with me, please."

He leads us through a classy lobby, out a back door and along a path lined with exotic flowers, broadleaf ferns, and dwarf coconut trees. He stops at a wide two-story bungalow, climbs a flight of hardwood stairs, and opens a door that leads into a luxurious suite. It is the size of a large beach house with a kitchen, dining area, front room, bedrooms, two bathrooms, and a balcony overlooking the ocean and a white sand beach.

"So, what's your budget?" asked the manager smiling.

"Seventy-five dollars a night," I replied regretfully.

"Perfect, you can have all of this for $37.50 a night. This suite will sleep two of you quite comfortably." He grins, "I am giving you the top two suites of our most expensive bungalows."

"What do they normally rent for," asked Michel DeLoire.

"About a thousand dollars a night," said the manager grinning happily. "How long will you be staying with us?"

"A month, maybe more," I answered warily.

"Perfect, here are your keys." He said heading for the door.

"Excuse me," I asked, "why are you so gracious to us?"

"I grew up watching the Underwater World of Jacques-Yves Cousteau, and you are helping the humpback whales. They often swim just off our beach, which keeps our resort full during the season. Having you here and knowing your team is helping the humpbacks will make our guests very happy."

He steps to the door, "Besides, the other resorts are going to be very jealous that you are here." He closed the door.

I go to a table, pick up the telephone.

"Who are you calling?" asked Michel DeLoire.

"Jean-Michel, to see if he will let me bring Cindy to Hawaii."

* * *

I greet Cindy at the airport holding a giant sunflower.

"In Hawaii, people meet guests with a flower lei," said Cindy, who is wearing a jogging shirt that says, "I will run you over."

"I'm not most people," I said with confidence.

"That's certainly true," agreed Cindy as we step outside. "When you called with an offer to fly to tropical Hawaii, there was a freezing storm blanketing most of Northern California. What girl wouldn't leap at an offer like that?"

"Remember that when you see where we're staying," I teased.

"That bad?" laughed Cindy.

"It rents for $37.50 a night. They should have named it the Cockroach Manor," I said brightly.

The next morning, walking down the pier at the Lahaina Yacht Harbor, Cindy says, "You got me with that Cockroach Manor jest. But be serious now. I want to be a working member of the team. I can cook, do dishes, help with gear, whatever is needed."

"I already have a job for you," I smiled mischievously as we arrive at our destination. We are standing before a 36' long cabin cruiser. She has graceful lines and a flying bridge. Her white paint and varnished woodwork glisten in the light. Her name is *Kai Kekoa*, (Ocean Warrior). She has twin engines and can do 30 knots. She has the most prestigious berth in the yacht harbor. We got a huge discount on her charter because the owner has high regard for Captain Jacques Cousteau. She flies the Cousteau flag."

"What a beauty," said Cindy running a hand along a polished wooden railing. "So, what's my job, chief deck scrubber?"

"I thought you might like to skipper the boat."

"What?" Cindy sputtered.

"Which would you rather be," I asked playfully, "the skipper or chief pot scrubber?"

Cindy grabs my T-shirt, "Are you teasing me again?"

"No," I said, being close I stole a kiss on her cheek.

"Then treat your skipper with more respect, or I'll have you scrubbing the bilges, sailor," she said punching me in the chest.

"Yes ma'am, Captain Bligh." I liked taking punches from Cindy.

Cindy's job is to keep the charter boat close to our operations as a support vessel. From it, we reload the cameras and launch the rubber Zodiacs. For safety reasons, this means Cindy is always a distance from the whale activity — until that one glorious day.

It is a blustery morning. The wind is whipping the ocean into a froth of whitecaps. Sea spray drenches my skin, but it feels good in the tropical heat. I am in a Zodiac with Jean-Michel Cousteau, Clay Wilcox, and Michel DeLoire. Jean-Michel sees a fast-moving pod of whales heading for the *Kai Kekoa*. He grabs a walkie-talkie, "Cindy, shut down your engines, a user baleine is heading for you."

"Going dead in the water," answered Cindy.

I wonder what the French words *user baleine* means. Baleine is French for whale, but a *user baleine* is a mystery.

Unbeknownst to me, Jean-Michel is referring to a *user whale*, which is the name for a cow in heat with bulls in pursuit. Unable to outrun her hefty admirers, she needs a place to rest, which is difficult for a whale that can be 45' long and weigh up to 90,000 lbs. Jean-Michel knows that the cow is heading for the *Kai Kekoa* as a hiding place, which is why Cindy must shut down the engines.

I see Cindy in the distance sliding down the ladder from the flying bridge. She rushes to the railing not knowing why the whale pod is heading for her craft. She is just ecstatic to be in their path, not realizing that her vessel is their destination.

Cindy sees the cow surface just an arm's throw away. The humpback shoots a column of water high into the air as she takes a rapid breath then dives. The humpback torpedoes straight for the *Kai Kekoa*. Cindy sees the submerged whale going underneath the cabin cruiser's keel. She rushes to the other side anticipating seeing the huge whale swimming away. Instead, she is about to get the whale-watching experience of a lifetime. The cow is trying to hide beneath the cabin cruiser. The 36' long boat only shelters the front half of the whale. Cindy can see the whale's pectoral fins protruding out from each side of the yacht and the tail extending out from beneath the stern. The deck shifts as the whale tries to get as close as she can to the *Kai Kekoa*.

Abruptly, a mass of plunging and breeching bull whales surrounds the *Kai Kekoa*. The cabin cruiser rocks wildly as the bulls brush against the hull or whip it about with blasts of water current from their huge tails. Two bulls propel their massive bodies high out of the water in dual flanking breeches then slam back into the ocean. Whitewater from whale belly whoppers explodes into the air sending a deluge of saltwater cascading across the boat's deck, soaking Cindy — much to her delight.

The Bulls are maneuvering to get close to the cow as they ram each other. Slabs of skin and fat float on the water from the violent impacts. An aggressive bull attempts to nudge the cow out from under the *Kai Kekoa*. Its huge body is so close Cindy reaches out to touch the descending bull as it plunges down right alongside the hull. A bull swings its towering tail high into the air. The fluke is taller than the flying bridge, and then it slams down. The impact echoes across the water like a cannon shot. The yacht rocks wildly in the thrashing tempest of whales.

We are 200 yards away when the cow makes a run for it. She surfaces next to the *Kai Kekoa* for a quick breath and then flees. The bulls charge in pursuit passing closely under the vessel as their wakes send the yacht spinning.

The whales are racing toward us in the Zodiacs. Jean-Michel cuts the engine and yells, "Everyone into the water!" Michel DeLoire and Clay, his safety diver, roll over the side. Clutching an underwater still camera, I quickly slip in after them. We descend beneath the frothy water. I will stay at a shallower depth to keep from hindering Michel's cinema camera. I am still clueless about the term *user baleine*.

The humpbacks appear abruptly, a pod of huge charging bodies that fills the underwater horizon of my faceplate. The whales are racing at the divers below. The gigantic marine mammals are each the size of an 18-wheeler truck. It is a subaquatic stampede with the whales charging ten times faster than human swimming speed. The humpbacks' pectoral fins extend outwards like the wings of giant birds in flight. Incredibly, each of the racing whales alters its course upward or to one side to keep from running over the two tiny creatures hovering in the path of their lustful rampage. The cow passes just above Michel, but then, perhaps feminine curiosity has her wondering what these little silver creatures are, she rolls onto her back and carves a sharp, descending vertical U-turn for a second look. As the cow comes level with Michel DeLoire's camera, she accelerates with strong beats of her tail. The trailing bulls are jostling to get closer to her. A bull nudges her underbelly, which prompts her into overdrive. The bulls charge in pursuit, each executing sharp-cornering U-turns just feet from the wide-angle lens of Michel's 35mm movie camera. For 30 long seconds, we are in the vast stampeding pod. The enormous bodies gliding by seems almost surrealistic because all this frantic mammoth activity is taking place in the silence of the submarine world.

Watching the nimble humpbacks, I think how amazing life is when one pursues adventure. I am fortunate to be here, yet it is not by accident. To seek adventure, to go on a life quest, one must develop a variety of skills, indulge in serious physical and mental training, broaden their knowledge, and develop true character because team trust must be absolute. One must pursue and create opportunities to put dreams within the realm of the possible.

I aim my camera at the last bull whale as it passes beneath my flippers. The rapidly swimming whale takes only seconds to pass before disappearing into the gloom of deep water. I feel a wisp of remaining current from its passage, and then we are abruptly alone in the wake of a mighty adventure.

Surfacing, out of breath, I see the whales again arriving at Cindy's boat. Their spouts of water and mist surround her small craft in an aquatic celebration of life. Cindy is running from rail to rail hollering happily at the whales.

That is one of the wonderful benefits of pursuing and achieving your dreams; it means you can take the ones you love with you. A dream shared is the best kind of living fantasy, and just like in a fairy tale, it leads to a purer, happier, and deeper love of one's companion. Before Cindy arrived, the expedition had been full of adventure and excitement, but her presence lends a sense of wonder and playfulness that convinces me I want to spend the rest of my life with this exciting woman.

The next morning I am drifting alone in a Zodiac looking for whales at sunrise. Warm light shimmers on the shifting surface of the deep blue ocean. A trade wind blowing from Maui gently ripples the water's surface. I place my ear to the Zodiac's rubber pontoon; it is a way to discover if a singing humpback is nearby. Faintly, I hear the soft echoing notes of a bull whale's song. The water density transmits subsurface sounds with more speed and intensity than those generated in air. Sticking my head over the side and dunking it into the water the sound of the whale's song increases dramatically. The bull is close. I don a dive mask and peer over the side. Below the Zodiac, is an enormous bull whale. It hovers in a head-down position singing. The whale is not moving as all its attention focuses on its song.

The trade wind has blown the Zodiac over the whale, which is unaware of my presence. Grabbing fins and a snorkel, I quietly slip over the side. Beneath the surface, the water resonates with untamed music. Taking three quick breaths through my snorkel to purge off excess carbon dioxide, I then take a final deep inhalation and swim silently down into the deep blue water. My heart thuds with eager anticipation. I descend toward the giant leviathan with the lust of the breeding season pounding in its arteries — sweet!

As I plunge downward with vigorous strokes of my fins, the humpback looms majestically within the narrow confines of my dive mask. The whale's song is a commanding, living presence. As I close, I feel the music washing over and through my body. It penetrates my bones. The effect is like holding a giant throbbing tuning fork in both hands in an atmosphere where gravity does not exist. Nothing distorts or hinders each perfect tone as I feel my skeleton almost vibrating in accord with the bull's serenade.

One of the wonders of whale harmonics is that their songs are a physical force. Submerged, I feel the leviathan's melodies as soft, tickling vibrations that play upon my body. The deep notes echo through my lungs and sinuses, while the softer gurgling tones bounce against my skin in a trembling cadence that feels like the gentlest body-hugging tickle. Swimming downward in an ocean alive with dynamic sounds and rhythmic vibrations is like descending inside the bass pipes of a cathedral organ.

I sink impatiently deeper. The whale's head-down position allows me to approach unseen. I wonder if the whale is bouncing its song off the ocean floor to increase its range. The majestic tail hovers at a depth of 45 feet. Rays of sunlight filtering down into the depths waver in harmony with the undulating surface. The sea-softened light washes across the giant humpback.

I yearn to reach out and touch the giant mammal. I am like a mouse in tall grass wondering at the massive passage of an elephant only a few feet away. One does not purposefully startle such a large creature. Swimming just yards from the giant bull; I wonder what it would be like to lay a hand on a singing whale. I can only imagine the power behind each note as it causes this part of the vast ocean to dance in harmony with its song.

Abruptly, the giant bull becomes aware of my presence. I am descending past its pectoral fin when the whale's eye rotates in my direction. The pupil is nearly the size of a softball. The whale's song abruptly ends on a deep, rumbling note — an ominous sound that seems to hover somewhere between majestic disappointment at my intrusion and royal anger that I, such a small creature, would dare to trespass in a world of giants.

The sudden silence and lingering glare cause me to shudder, and for a moment, fear freezes my flippers into immobility. I feel so tiny and vulnerable in the whale's massive presence. The whale's tail begins to move ponderously. It passes a few feet away, enormous, and majestic. With increasing beats of its fluke, the huge leviathan descends, trailing a rising stream of bubbles that glitter softly as they pass through a wandering ray of sunlight. A wake of depth-chilled water rushes upward from the whale's passage through a cold thermocline. The chilly water is like a winter wind sweeping away the last of the whale's presence. Involuntarily, I cough accidentally allowing water to rush down my snorkel. I try to spit it out and then cough again losing precious air. Water seeps into my mask; I look upwards and clear it losing more valuable air. I watch the lost air bubbling upwards. Then as if in passage with the departing humpback, a cloud passes in front of the sun. A lingering shadow casts the chilled depths into gloomy twilight. The darkening surface is far away, as I realize I am deeper than I thought!

Caught in the enchantment of the moment, I forgot to pay attention to my depth. The surface looks to be 70 feet away, my heart races as I begin to swim urgently upward.

Unexpectedly, from the corridors of my memory, stalks another remembered instant of absolute panic. I unexpectedly dredge up the moment when I woke for the first time inside a federal prison. I had gone from a deep sleep to an alarmed awakening in a heartbeat. In wild panic, I hoped that it was all just a bad dream — that the guns and the handcuffs were just imaginings of a bad night's tossing and turning. Then I hear a cell door slam shut and an inmate cursing. I knew without a doubt that the nightmare I so feared was now my living reality and that I was caught in its icy grasp. My usually buoyant spirit collapsed into a dark hole of dread knowing that my mistakes were real. The dungeon certainty of jail bars and inmate brutality was now my world to endure.

Swimming vigorously upward, terrifyingly caught between two worlds, one of cold shadows and the other of warm light, I consciously decide that the dark gloom of prison would not be my last thought. I stare at the softly rippling surface and focus my thoughts on the sunlight and air that awaits me. My pounding heart slows, my anxiety calms. Finally, just feet from the surface the cloud's shadow passes from the sun. Ascending into dazzling light, I rip my snorkel from my mouth and inhale deeply the sweetist breath of my life. For a full minute, I float on the surface, taking deep lung washing breaths.

Climbing into the Zodiac, I take off my fins and mask and then look toward *Kai Kekoa*. The cabin cruiser, flying a green Cousteau Society flag is underway and motoring toward a rainbow trailing a rain squall off Maui. I think about my life as a chief diver and expedition leader for the Cousteau Society. I am leading flying team and shipboard expeditions on a round-the-world odyssey of adventure. I am a free man, something only someone who has lost his or her freedom can fully appreciate. I am in an island paradise, and deeply in love with a woman I hope to marry. I regret that Cindy must fly back to California tomorrow.

Abruptly, I hear Cindy calling on the radio. "Where have you been?" she asked. "Jean-Michel is eager to find whales."

I place my ear against the Zodiac's rubber pontoon and hear the bull singing again. "Tell Jean-Michel he doesn't have to go far. A big guy is looking for love under my rubber boat."

* * *

Back in the Los Angeles office, Jean-Michel hangs up the telephone after talking with Captain Cousteau in French. I have no idea what they were discussing. I have been studying French for a year, but the romantic-sounding language remains a mystery.

"Stephen are you ready for a little adventure?" he asked. "I want you to take a flying team back to Hawaii to film lava flowing underwater from the Kilauea Volcano." Jean-Michel smiled, "I'm thinking close-up footage."

"Close-up footage," I echoed weakly, "of lava underwater?"

"Yes, try to get below the lava flow with it coming straight down at the camera," Jean-Michel grinned, "think dramatic."

"How do you film lava flowing underwater?" I blurted.

Jean-Michel swings his feet up off the desk, "Well, you go to Hawaii and look for where the ocean is smoking," he said placing a hand on my shoulder he walks me to the door. "Stephen, you'll figure it out, and if you're careful, it could even be fun."

* * *

Two days later, in my hotel room in Hilo, Hawaii, I glance at the clock. It is 11:00 PM, I must be up before dawn. I consider just some of the hazards lurking beyond the sunrise. All the diving activity will be in an exposed surf zone. It is where big breakers will be regularly pounding the shoreline. That means we will swim in strong underwater currents, in limited visibility water, while playing hide-and-seek with 2,000°F liquid rock in motion that also sometimes sprints. Underwater, flowing lava is very unpredictable, like a shifting tide, the molten lava can abruptly surge, creating flash floods of racing liquefied rock. There are daily earthquakes, occasionally punctuated by a real earthmover.

My first concern was finding the right boat and captain for going into harm's way. I chartered a local boat designed for Hawaii's heavy surf. The *Tsunami* (tidal wave in Japanese) is 30' long. She has an open back deck beneath which are dual V-8 engines. The boat is quick and agile. The owner, a barrel-chested Hawaiian named Russell, is a professional angler, who often fishes this coast; he knows the local wave and current patterns.

I also hire an underwater lava guide, the owner of a dive shop in the town of Hilo. Harry has logged a dozen dives on the lava flow. He was one of my students at the College of Oceaneering. Harry is disabled. He has three-fused neck vertebra. He cannot turn his head without rotating his upper body. It makes his more animated conversations with multiple people visually distracting.

I snuggle down into the covers confident that we are as ready as can be expected for tomorrow's challenges. Taking a relaxing breath, I prepare for sleep when an earthquake hits. It is a modest trembler as the bed shakes and the clock's red glow vibrates on the nightstand. The shaking fades, leaving me visualizing underwater earthquakes and landslides.

At first light, we trailer *Tsunami* behind a monster truck with huge knobby wheels to a little-used boat ramp. Most boaters avoid this south-facing ramp because getting out into open water is a boat-threatening experience. A small cement pier and tiny rock jetty provide little protection. This morning large breakers are pounding the south shore. I watch waves repeatedly wash over the jetty and smash into the small wharf.

"What do you think, Russell?" I asked the Hawaiian angler.

"Can do, brah." Many Hawaiians speak in Pidgin, a local blend of English and Hawaiian that uses as few adjectives and adverbs as possible. "More better, come back lunchtime," he mumbled cramming a doughnut into his mouth; a blob of red jelly squirts out sprinkling his T-shirt with red droplets.

"Why do we have to be back at lunchtime?" I repeated for Michel DeLoire's sake. He is listening closely, but the Frenchman is lost in this strange Hawaiian way of talking in pidgin.

"Tide be high, brah, surf bigger," replied Russell, wiping at the jelly globs effectively spreading them across his white T-shirt.

Russell's plan was simple. We get into the boat while it is still on the trailer. Standing at the helm, Russell watches the rhythm of the waves, and then abruptly yells at his cousin, who revs the truck's engine, slams it into reverse, and quickly shoves the boat trailer down the ramp, then stands on the brakes, which slides the boat off the trailer. It crashes into the water. Russell fires up both engines, spins the wheel, and slams the dual throttles one forward the other in reverse. The stern of the powerful boat digs in and turns 180 degrees then Russell pushes the throttles to the stops, launching us explosively forward. The whole process takes about 15 seconds before we are plowing into the first oncoming wave. Russell takes the waves at an angle slicing through the powerful surf, yet the hydraulic force drives our sturdy vessel towards the vertical with each wave face. The most interesting aspect of his crashing through the breakers is that there are surfers riding the waves. Russell sets a course and leaves it to the surfers to get out of his way.

As we begin our high-speed run toward the lava flow, I ask, "If the surf is going to be bigger when we return, won't it be trickier bringing the boat back in?"

Russell grins, "Yeah, harder than getting out."

"What's your plan?"

"Same plan," laughed Russell, "only go faster."

At 9:00 AM, we reach our destination and begin motoring just beyond the turbulent water at the lava flow. The boat engines' water inlet temperature is 90°F, and we are still 200 yards from shore. The water is varying shades of dirty brown with large blotches of black soot. The surface is a giant bubbling swamp with floating black shadows of submerged debris clouds.

Yesterday when I surveyed the lava flow from a helicopter, the lava spilling into the ocean looked scary, but it could be dove. This morning, from the up-close perspective of a small boat, the lava flow is downright terrifying — it looks like a war zone. I watch a wall of molten rock and fire spilling into the ocean. Sometimes the lava weeps slowly into the bubbling water, but mostly the fiery rock gushes forth in thick globs of fast-flowing streams. A billowing wall of sizzling steam laced with sulfur rolls off the turbulent water. At the heavy flow points, the liquid rock is so hot that on contact the ocean water flashes into rolling clouds of steam.

A wave breaks off a large chunk of steaming lava that falls, hissing loudly, into the water, and then it explodes, hurling long liquid tracers of lava through the air. One of the tracers falls back into the water 30 yards from our boat. I watch it spin spewing spits of steam like an errant firework.

"It's certainly out-of-control today," offered Harry staring at a large chunk of lava as it falls into the frothy water.

"Think it is safe enough to dive?" I asked seriously.

"Nah," he shrugged, awkwardly turning his whole body from the shoreline toward me, "it's never safe. It's why so few people dive the lava flow."

"Let's go," I said with forced enthusiasm.

I look at the black, frothy water beneath my flippers and consciously beating down my anxiety, step overboard. The water is hot and dirty, much like dumping burning charcoal into a bubbling Jacuzzi. The hot liquid rushes through the openings in my wetsuit, runs up my legs and arms and down my back. Hot yellowish water half floods my mask and sloshes up my nose. Inside the mask it reeks of sulfur and charcoal, my nose tickles outlandishly. We swim urgently down as the water is hottest nearest the surface. Submerging to a depth of 30 feet, we level off in the-sweltering water, which feels muggy like wading through a hot swamp.

Checking my compass and the direction of the sun, I orient us toward the shoreline as we descend deeper. It is very murky as we pass through black underwater clouds of soot and drifting ash. Closer to shore the sunlight dims to a dull red glow that fades to dark shadows with each passing soot cloud. The lava flow is creating a pounding cascade of underwater explosions. The liquid atmosphere pulsates with loud, crackling shockwaves. This is raw energy announcing its presence with the horrendous sounds of rock ripping, tearing, and blasting apart. As we get closer to shore, the crunching, tearing reverberations intensify.

I do continuous buddy-checks. Michel swims with his camera to my left. I see Michel's faceplate sweeping side-to-side as he looks for the first sign of liquid lava. I am used to seeing light reflected off a diver's faceplate, but Michel's is a dead black oval, a dark mirror reflecting an underwater hell.

On my right, Harry swims oddly because of his fused neck. He is doing exaggerated kicks with his fins. Each of the long strokes causes his body to roll off keel. He does this on purpose to create the rolling effect that permits him to look to each side with a passing downward glance. During one of his partial revolutions our eyes briefly lock, he smiles grimly around his mouthpiece and then rotates away from me. At this moment, swimming into the jaws of a crazy dangerous adventure, my mind pauses to admire Harry. He has a serious handicap but does not let it slow him down. He is my co-leader on this risky venture of a lifetime.

My compass needle swings wildly. The metal ores in the underwater lava flow are making the compass almost useless because of the shifting magnetic fields below us. It is the wondering of what hot vastness is moving beneath me that is the most alarming. Never, has a simple compass warned me of impending physical danger, it is a startling consideration.

I look for the sun to check my direction, but it is hidden by the shadowed twilight of the underwater soot clouds. I determine our heading by feeling the concussion of sound striking against my faceplate—that is when I realize the bulk of the terrible noise is now coming from directly beneath us. We are passing right over a main part of the lava flow. The water becomes hotter and more active. Abruptly, heated currents swirling up from the depths lick at us like a hot, wet dragon's tongue. Sudden liquid concussions bombard us as we swim on through dark clouds where bubbles and debris cascade upwards. I see my first ever dirty bubbles.

I'm sweating inside my wetsuit, an odd sensation underwater. Swimming more slowly, peering fearfully into the dark water below, my mind paints terrifying images of the inferno beneath us. Looking forward, I see a looming wall of darkness. The soot cloud is terrifying; it is a black wall without bottom, sides, or ceiling—it pulsates like a beast breathing. The water is surging from wave activity above us. We are close to the shore, which is where the lava pouring into the ocean is exploding. It means going up is not an option because of extreme heat and explosively flung lava splashing about the surface. I stare at the pulsating wall of darkness, and all my senses argue against swimming into it.

I look right and left, we have become slightly separated, the other two divers swim at the edge of the water's visibility, yet we are only six feet apart as we slowly enter the dark cloud. I watch Harry as his body rotates away, for a moment, he is lost in the gloom, almost disappearing. Then he rotates back toward me, but his form is waiflike in an emersion of drifting shadows. I have an unsettling feeling we could lose each other in this intensifying darkness. Holding up my fist while Harry and Michel can still see it, I signal them to stop. It is too dangerous to go on. Michel swims closer as I shake my head and jerk my thumb in the direction of the boat. He shrugs, an adventurous spirit pulled back from the edge of an alluring quest.

I made my decision based on justifiable fear and that it would be impossible to film in this dim to non-existent light.

As we swim back out, I hear a deep rumble followed by a far-off submarine sound of rolling thunder and grinding rock. Behind or below us, a serious avalanche is happening. I am thankful not to be near it as the water around us brightens.

We spent a month trying to film the lava flow underwater without success. Most of the lava flow is flowing deep within questing lava tubes that are beyond our diving limit. The high surf has beaten many of the lava tubes into rubble, which causes perilous underwater landslides. It is just too treacherous.

I call Jean-Michel to tell him I am aborting the expedition. Instead of returning to the mainland, Jean-Michel orders our team back to Maui to get more humpback whale footage. I wonder how I will explain to Cindy that I am off on another whale adventure without her.

* * *

It is a sunny day off the coast of Maui. Fifty yards from the stern of our Zodiac a gust of water shoots high into the air, followed immediately by a deep inhalation as a massive humpback tail slowly disappears beneath the rolling swells.

Floating on the surface, I hear the high-pitched squeals and rapid clicks of approaching dolphins. Michel DeLoire grins at me through the glass of his faceplate then nods. We take deep breaths together and then plunge down into the path of an approaching humpback pod. Holding our breath, we descend quickly to a depth of 40 feet. The water is especially clear. The surface water throws wandering sunbeams of shimmering light into the blue depths. About us, the ocean is full of sea mammal sounds. Nearby a bull humpback bellows out its love song.

Beneath the waves, there are no interfering noises to distract from the mighty leviathan's melody that reverberates through the water. Immersed in the deep tide of whale music, I hear on a softer scale the chirps, clicks, and twitters of excited dolphins. I am floating on a wave of living music. A melody of nature suspended in the rapture of the deep.

Peering anxiously into the broad vista of light and water, we wait eagerly, and then the marine mammal pod is upon us. Playful dolphins lead the way. There is a half-dozen of them riding the bow wave of the lead bull whales. It is an amazing sight. I know dolphins ride the bow wave of ships and boats, sort of like underwater surfing. I wonder if dolphins ride the bow wave of submerged submarines.

The dolphins are tiny compared to the brace of whales that swims behind them. Michel and I separate, he films the oncoming whales, but I find the playful dolphins captivating. Two of the bottlenose break away from the lead pack and rush toward me. Sunbeams play across their bodies as the dolphins gracefully wheel, they circle so tightly I could reach out and touch them. I aim my camera and release the shutter. I do not know it then, but I have just shot my first Cousteau poster.

The dolphins race back to join the lead whales. The massive marine mammals, like giant underwater zeppelins, pass only yards away. Behind the lead whales, a large humpback cow swims into view. Beside her is a newborn calf, and I abruptly realize the incredible magnitude of what I am witnessing.

An ancient Hawaiian hula tells a story about dolphins that protect humpback calves. A very elderly woman, whom I had sought out to interview, told the story to me just a week ago.

Jan came to Hawaii as a little girl in the early 1900's. Daughter of a missionary, she played and learned with the Hawaiian children of the royal court of the last great Queen Regent of Hawaii. Queen Lili'uokalani. She told me how the little dolphins are the protectors of the great whales. Then she stood with the aid of her cane before leaning it against a chair. For a moment, I saw the girl within the ancient woman as she danced the hula of the dolphin protectors of whale calves.

As I watched the rather spry elderly woman dance the hula, I thought what an amazing way to teach a child visually the legends and history of Old Hawaii.

Recent science lends credibility to her Hawaiian story. When a whale calf is born, berthing fluids drift down current in an odor corridor. Sharks that swim into the scent stream go crazy with hunger. This is whale blood, a prelude to a feast, a grand banquet for whoever arrives first. The sharks will charge up that odor corridor to attack and kill the calf — but for the dolphins. The bulls cannot defend against the sharks, which are too quick and agile — but the dolphins can. The dolphins sense when a whale calf is about to be born, nature's incredible ultrasound machines at work. The dolphins ring the cow and calf driving off or killing the marauding sharks by ramming them. Yet, the best action is for the whales and dolphins to flee the birthing site quickly.

That is what Michel, and I are witnessing, an underwater wagon train with dolphin scouts leading the way, followed by the bulls, which are the heavy cavalry. The cow and calf are at the center of the wagon train, and if the sharks arrive, they are the marauders that dart in to attack the calf.

The cow changes course toward me. Her name is Daisy, a diver-friendly humpback that we filmed yesterday, when she had no calf. This may be just moments after the berth. The whales are swimming away from the birthing site.

A cloud of giant bubbles rises out of the depths. Beneath me, a bull is releasing a long bubble steam. I shoot an image of the rising bubbles as they mask the calf, but it swims boldly through them, straight at me — which creates a problem. Somewhere, Michel is filming with his 35mm movie camera. I may be between him and the calf. I am not wearing Cousteau silver; my wetsuit is black. I must get out of his shot.

I swim backward, but the calf keeps coming, and seeing me swimming away, becomes bolder. My lungs labor for air as I continue to shoot pictures. The calf is a little longer than a dolphin, yet it has far more mass, nearly a ton of wide-eyed innocence. I see the calf's eye regarding me.

Beyond the calf, Daisy swims in close parental attendance. As the small humpback comes right alongside me, it fills the sports action finder on my underwater camera. I release the shutter then swim desperately for the surface. I have been down for almost two minutes and am lightheaded from lack of oxygen. Rocketing upward, I see the calf's tail beat strongly as the calf swim alongside me. The newborn calf's skin in the sun lit water is perfectly clean, pale in color, and without mar. It is perfectly gorgeous. It's right eye, larger than mine, is curious and innocent as it regards me.

A foot beneath the rippling surface the sunlight intensifies. I shoot a final picture, capturing the humpback calf in a halo of light, and then we both rise to the surface to breathe. Gasping through my snorkel, I lay on the surface, watching the little whale tail disappear beneath the shimmering water.

Author with humpback calf and dolphins.
Illustration by Andy Charles

Once I knew only darkness and stillness... my life was without past or future... but a little word from the fingers of another fell into my hand that clutched at emptiness, and my heart leaped to the rapture of living. — Helen Keller

Chapter 22 - Los Angeles, and Hawaii, HI Feb 1988

I sit at my desk in the basement of the Cousteau Society office in West Hollywood. I look forward to picking Cindy up at the airport. I am considering asking her to marry me when the telephone rings.

"Steve, a fresh lava flow is heading for the ocean," said a volcanologist from the Hawaiian Volcano Observatory, "It should begin dumping into the water at a new point in two days. The diving conditions look to be ideal."

Excited, yet with a sinking heart about Cindy's and my date, I carry the news upstairs to Jean-Michel Cousteau.

"Wonderful," he exclaimed. "Assemble the team."

"Uh, Jean-Michel," I said weakly, "Cindy's arriving tonight."

Jean-Michel chuckled, "Good, she can help you pack."

I nod, "That's what I thought you'd say."

Jean-Michel grins and says, "Must be good advice."

* * *

I wait with a bouquet of roses as Cindy walks out the airline gate wearing my favorite outfit, 501 jeans, tan shirt, and red converse high top sneakers. I buy jeans with a 32" inseam, Cindy's are 36" with a 26" waist. She gives me a quick hug then buries her face in the velvety red flowers inhaling deeply. "Is this because you love me?" she asked, hazel eyes sparkling happily.

"Well, yes and no." 'What a stupid answer,' I thought.

Cindy lowers the flowers, her eyes taking on a fiery quality. I wonder if she is freeing up her slugging hand. "You're leaving on another adventure, aren't you?"

"Hawaii to dive with the lava flow again," I answered meekly.

"And you didn't call me?" The flowers transfer to her left hand, she is freeing up that right slugger. I take a step backward, Cindy has a four-inch reach on me, which is one reason she is such a good climber. Cindy grew up with her brother and his adventurous friends. She had to hold her ground being the little sister hanging out with a group of macho teenagers. She learned to do it well. She is tough and lovely. In other words, the perfect woman for me.

"I just found out two hours ago," I said lamely.

"And you're flying out tonight?"

"Actually, I don't have to leave until tomorrow morning."

"It's okay," she said noticing my defensive posture, "I never hit a date who brings me roses."

"We have to change your return flight," I said getting out all the bad news up front. I know this date is not going well.

Cindy shrugs, "I'll just tell them that my fiancée got hurt, and I have to fly home unexpectedly.

"Got hurt? How did he get hurt?" I asked warily.

"Don't know, this date isn't over yet." Cindy turns and walks away. Those long legs carrying her rapidly along as it hits me. Cindy clearly said her fiancée. Was that an accidental Freudian slip or is she dropping a hint the size of an elephant?

I move quickly, well I run, to catch up.

Cindy smiles, but not with her eyes, "You know, Steve, if this were our first date, it would be our last date."

Driving from the airport, Cindy is in a dangerous mood, claws extended, like a cat daring someone to pet it. Her temper makes her incredibly attractive.

"Where are we going?" asked a very perturbed Cindy.

"Griffith Observatory. I Need to show you something."

Cindy's look is penetrating, "Fine."

We arrive at a promontory overlooking the vast Los Angeles basin. Before us, an ocean of twinkling lights sprawls as far as the eye can see. The broad freeways pulsate with swift moving ribbons of red and white light while vibrant neon signs define the borders of the darker suburban streets. At the center of the metropolis, as if rising above a shimmering sea of light, stands glass-walled skyscrapers. The towering buildings glisten with inner and reflected radiance, like windows into a futuristic world, which is what I am doing—reaching into the future.

"It's beautiful!" she said stepping over the protective railing to peer downward then glances back at me. I know she wants me to kiss her. Instead, I ask Cindy to marry me.

"Of course, I will marry you, Stephen," Cindy punctuated her statement with a kiss, "but this doesn't get you off the hook for leaving me for another way cool adventure."

"It's why I brought you here," I said looking toward the vibrant metropolis beneath us. "Life is a great big adventure full of wonder and mystery. I want to explore these wonders with you. All of my escapades are less fun when you aren't there."

Cindy whispers, "Write that into a prenuptial agreement."

* * *

I stand at the stern of the *Tsunami* with my team. The lava flow is pouring into the ocean at a single point. Leaping into the hot water, I hear a bombardment of concussions punctuated by louder explosions. We swim toward the loudest of the sounds. The water darkens as we descend. I peer into the dark smoky depths and suddenly see a faint red glow. It looks like a giant red glowing worm crawling down the side of a cliff. It slips in and out of view as black debris clouds drift over it.

Triggering his cinema camera, Bob Talbot swims in with me hovering at his side. The surging water clears revealing a thick lava tube weaving its way down the steep shelf. While Bob films, I watch other lava worms flowing toward us. Taking Bob's elbow, I squeeze a warning when one gets too close. Bob shifts the camera lens to capture the questing tube as it drops over a shelf. I realize that unlike a waterfall — water spilling over rock — I am looking at liquid rock spilling over water.

When the camera empties, we beat a hasty retreat to the *Tsunami*. Heading back to the boat launch, everyone is in high spirits. Our excitement lasts all the way back to the hotel, right until Bob's assistant opens the underwater cinema camera and instead of film on rollers discovers plastic confetti. The complex threading system slipped a cog, and the sharp-edged gears chewed all our footage to shreds.

The next morning, we prepare to jump into the frothy water. The lava flow has increased dramatically. What was a stream of flowing lava yesterday is now a river of cascading molten rock. It pours into the water in broad fiery sheets, a liquid avalanche of red-hot gushing stone. Jumping into the stifling water, we swim quickly downward. It is much hotter than yesterday. A barrage of underwater sound and shock waves intensifies. Beneath us, a steep slope leads down into the dark foreboding depths. I signal Bob's assistant and David to maintain a position well above us.

Descending toward a steep rocky shelf, we film unstable lava rubble upon which a lava worm is rapidly flowing. Below it lies a sharp incline upon which lava boulders are tumbling down each side of another pillowing lava worm. A large area of lava debris abruptly slides, quickly becoming a minor avalanche that plunges rumbling loudly into the dark depths below.

We descend capturing on film a huge smoking boulder that narrowly misses us. It tumbles down from above fully two yards across. Weeping jets of steam and laced with fiery red cracks, it looks like a falling meteorite burning its way through a fluid atmosphere. Bob and I separate as it bounces between us then somersaults over a shelf and disappears into the deep blackness below. Wisps of debris floating in the water slowly dissipate in the wake of its furious passage.

The water visibility keeps changing as the surging water sweeps us back and forth. Then we see a faint glimmer of red glowing at a depth of 60 feet. Swimming down, we find a lava tube over a yard in diameter. It pauses on a ledge. A black crust forms, and then the leading edge of the lava tube bulges outward. The crust splits open like an alien egg hatching as a cascade of molten rock spews in a fountain of thick liquid fire. We follow the weaving tube as it plunges downward. The water contacting the super-hot lava worm causes implosions and explosions that shoot out bone-rattling shock waves. The concussions visibly move the dive mask against my face. The increased water pressure at depth magnifies the shock waves to a painful level.

I am just below the leading edge of the lava worm when I see something moving desperately. It is a lobster with a singed tail fleeing the hot lava. Determined to save it, I exhale, letting the reduced buoyancy carry me down. I am reaching out for the injured lobster when—something alive brushes up against me!

My heart surges as the image of a tiger shark, common in Hawaiian waters, cuts through my mind. Fearfully I turn my head to see a large predatory eye just inches from my faceplate. The animal attacks! I feel its body sliding against my shoulder and arm as I swiftly pull back my hand from the lobster. A huge mouth opens and snatches the lobster. Powerful jaws crush down as the lobster's tail beats frantically. Then the huge predatory fish swallows half of the four-pound lobster after biting it in half. It snatches the other half and glares at me.

It is a large Mahi, four to five feet long. I have never seen one underwater before. Unalarmed, it stares at me, neither of us is a threat to the other. Its metallic-green streamlined body glistens in the dull light as it moves away patrolling ahead of the lava worms looking for more injured prey.

I glance over at Bob, who is still filming the lava tube. When the camera empties its film load, we beat a fast retreat.

At the hotel, we are ecstatic to discover the film intact inside the camera. Our celebration is dampened by sinus headaches caused by the violent shock waves beating against our skulls at depth.

We have many spectacular days diving with the molten lava. However, our final dive proves to be almost fatal; it is one of my closest brushes with death with the Cousteau Society.

Bob and I are filming two large lava tubes at a depth of 80' when a massive shockwave slams upward out of the darkness below hitting us like a giant hydraulic sledgehammer. A deep rumble echoes about us from the dark depths. Something large is moving. The hardened lava rubble upon which the tubes are crawling shakes violently and then large chunks of lava rock begin to tumble downward. A massive landslide rips the tubes apart spilling rivers of lava. The whole face of the shelf slides downward in a jumbled cascade of rock and red molten lava.

Beneath us comes heavy rolling thunder of an enormous avalanche. A black thunderhead of debris rushes upward from the depths as sweltering heat washes over us. The spilling rocks and debris accelerates downward as the black rising cloud engulfs us. Bob and I wrap our arms around each other with the 35mm movie camera between us. We are lost in absolute blackness — then a massive undertow pulls us irresistibly downwards into the mayhem below. The plunging current pulls us down tumbling and spinning in complete darkness. I hear and feel terrifying sounds beating against us. Boulders are colliding with head-crushing force, and rocks grind against each other. As Bob and I tumble down with the landside, we pass over wave after wave of billowing heat. I imagine rivers of lava passing just beneath us.

Finally, the turbulence slowly subsides. Bob's arms shift, so I know he is okay, yet we are lost in darkness, not knowing up from down. I place a hand on my faceplate and exhale; the escaping bubbles leak out the side of my mask. I use the bubbles to orient us towards the surface as we begin to swim upwards.

It takes three long minutes to struggle back to clearer water. I check my depth gauge. Bob and I had been pulled down to an astounding depth of 135 feet.

We join the other divers and retreat to Russell's boat. At a depth of 40 feet, I motion for the other divers to go up, but shake my head at Bob and hold him at depth. We need decompression.

They say that a diver should never memorize the dive tables. I consider that absolute foolishness. In a dangerous situation, I want every edge. I do not know the decompression schedule we must follow, but I can easily determine a serious safety factor. During the long decompression, I think how much I love this job. So yeah, I'm an adventure hog.

Ascending from lava dive.
Illustration by Margery Spielman

Death is no more than passing from one room into another. But there is a difference for me, and you. Because in that other room I shall be able to see. — Helen Keller, born deaf and blind.

I fly to Sacramento, where Cindy picks me up at the airport in her Toyota MR2, which she refers to as her Pocket Rocket. We drive to the quaint town of Paradise on a ridge in the Sierra Nevada Mountain Range. She grew up there living an amazing Norman Rockwell type of childhood. We spend little time in the house before Cindy leads me outside and innocently asks, "Want to go for a hike in the canyon?"

The house stands at the top of a high ridge, which drops 900' feet into a deep gorge. Trees line both sides of the gorge for as far as the eye can see. The west branch of the Feather River snakes its way along the bottom. I gladly accept her offer, not understanding that I am about to undergo a test that is a family tradition, much to the amusement of everyone involved. That is except for the victim.

As a girl, Cindy determined that she would not be stuck with any klutz of a fellow who could not keep up with her in the canyon. While lacing up my hiking shoes, I wonder why the rest of Cindy's family has come outside to see us off. I do not know her family sees me as the sacrificial lamb. No one has ever passed Cindy's canyon test. I would learn there had been some serious contenders, including expert mountain climbers, extreme athletics, and serious mountain bikers. They all failed.

Cindy takes off, her long legs flying down the steep rocky path. Having expected a hike, I am surprised to see her running over the sharp-edge lava cap that plunges down at a steeper angle than I would ever consider rational for rapid walking let alone running. My greatest fear is falling from any steep place that involves rocks. Cindy is rapidly pulling away. I am just trying to keep the fleeing figure in sight as she yells playfully, "Keep up, slowpoke."

After descending 300 feet, the steep trail levels off at a flume carrying water from up canyon. Cindy runs lightly along a pathway beside the flume but then she jumps up onto the top edge of the flume's wall. It is a narrow edge, maybe an inch and a half wide and she is balancing along it walking toward the other end rather rapidly. What makes the feat impressive is that she is doing it backwards with her hands in her front pockets, whistling. It has slowed her down, allowing me to catch up. I jump onto the narrow edge as she drops off at the other end and begins running again. I glance down at the water flowing beneath my boots and do not get six feet before losing my balance. I drop back down to the pathway and charge after Cindy, who is just disappearing down a narrow trail that leads into a Manzanita Forest. The trail is more like an animal path with low branches and exposed boot snatching roots.

The path abruptly breaks out of the Manzanita forest, and I find myself on slippery rock and loose shale, which reminds me of my serious fear of falling. Cindy is running down a steep stretch, she jumps over a rocky ledge, lands on one leg and lowers her body into a one-legged squat as she slides rapidly downward. She is on a steep hillside covered with leaves, which reduces the friction of her passage. Her smooth soled Converse shoes are sliding over roots and half-buried rocks. She has her other long leg stretched straight out in front of her while she holds her arms out for balance.

Cindy has been doing this almost daily since she was five-years-old and has been continuously trying to improve her performance. I did not stand a chance as I watch a rooster tail of leaves flying in her wake. I do not exactly leap over the rock ledge, but I am soon sliding down on one leg catching up with Cindy. The difference is that she is graceful while I am out of control and picking up speed. My knobby hiking boot keeps catching on exposed rocks and roots threatening to hurtle me end over end down the canyon.

Cindy glances over her shoulder and comes to a stop just before some dense brush. I slide by leaving a wake of tumbling rocks and swirling leaves. As I pass Cindy heading for a thick patch of brush, she shouts, "You do know that's poison oak, don't you?"

Cindy easily beats me to the river. Yet, I am suspicious that she is holding back. She is standing on a big rock looking at her watch as I arrive at her side huffing and puffing, scratched, bruised, beat up, and soon to have poison oak issues.

"Rats," she exclaimed, "we're a bit slow."

"Slow?" I asked, "what do you mean slow? We just ran down the side of a thousand-foot tall mountain."

"That is not a mountain silly it is just my backyard. We'll just have to make up the time on the way back up."

I think she is kidding—she is not. As I chase her back up the steep slope of the gorge, I realize this is one challenge I dare not lose too badly. I am a little lightheaded when we break out of the brush at the base of her parents' house. We are almost side-by-side, well maybe I was ten yards behind her gasping and wheezing, when her stepfather yells from the back porch, "How did he do?"

She looks at me critically, "I think I am going to keep this one."

Author's note: for years, I assumed that I had passed the canyon test, but after I wrote about it, Cindy gently revealed that I had failed.
"I failed?" I asked, surprised, and disappointed.
"Miserably," confirmed Cindy, "but your spirit did just fine."
Two years later, I had an incredible opportunity to buy the 40 acres behind out house for only $12,000. I may not have passed her canyon test, but I did her one better – I bought Cindy the trail.

* * *

I spent the next few days helping Michel DeLoire load gear for his trip to Papua New Guinea. He was to join the crew of *Alcyone*, the Cousteau's research vessel, nicknamed the Wind Ship

Jean-Michel calls me into his office. "It seems that Michel DeLoire forgot something. Want to know what he forgot?"

"What did he forget?" *Am I responsible for the forgotten item?*

Jean-Michel consults his notebook. I anxiously await my fate. His finger pounces on the missing item. "Ah ha, it's you!"

"Me? What?" I asked imploringly.

"You," he pointed a finger at me. "You are what he forgot."

"He forgot me?"

Jean-Michel slid an airline ticket across the desk. "You're leaving for Papua New Guinea tomorrow at 8:00 PM."

"But, but," I sputtered hopelessly, "Cindy's arriving tonight."

"Great, you're going to need her help." Jean-Michel handed me a lengthy telex. It is a date-busting three-page shopping list.

* * *

Days later, I am again looking out a window at a nighttime rain. A bright stab of lightning emphasizes that this is not a modest California rain shower. I am aboard the *Alcyone* sailing toward a giant thunderhead. Looking at the revolving light bar on the radar, I see towering clouds painted in angry shades of luminous red, orange, and yellow light. I see we should hit clear water in another hour. It is my first watch aboard the Wind Ship, and other than being a bit seasick life is terrific. At the helm of a world-famous research vessel, with a course set for adventure; how cool is that?

A thick bolt of lightning strikes the ocean off the starboard bow. I go to the chart table to check our position. Our destination is the Bismarck Archipelago, a long chain of tropical islands in the waters of Papua New Guinea. I use the chart to plot our course then realize that our lives are like a charted course. The chart shows the marine hazards, shallows, reefs, etc. With this map, I can navigate *Alcyone* past the obstacles if I know my starting point.

Being a Christian gives me my daily starting point. The chart I use to plot my life is from Mark 12:30-31. Here Jesus is asked, "Of all the Commandments, which is the most important?" He replied, "Love the LORD your God with all your heart and with all your soul and with all your mind and with all your strength. The second is this, love your neighbor as yourself. There is no commandment greater than these."

The weeks slip by under a hot tropical sun. We visit various islands and dive beautiful reefs. Late in the expedition, we anchor at Wuvulu Island, the last and one of the most isolated islands of the Bismarck Archipelago.

The next morning, we encounter three orcas hunting amongst the reefs. Encountering orcas in the tropics is extremely rare. To find them in clear tropical waters is incredible.

For eight hours, the Cousteau crew splits into two teams taking two-hour shifts to dive with the killer whales. My team exits the water as Jean-Michel's team takes over. The sun will set soon. My team decides to stay in our rubber boat and drift with their Zodiac. Jean-Michel, surfaces, and yells, "The orcas are eating sharks!"

We lunge for dive masks to peer over the side. Beneath us, a 28' long orca swims toward the other team with an eight-foot-long reef shark in its jaws. The divers closest to the orca hear cartilage crunching as the killer whale consumes most of the shark in three gigantic bites. Afterward, all that remains is the shark's tail and head. I watch them slowly drift down into the depths.

As the surrounding water grows darker with the sunset, the orcas become more active. We do not see them catching the sharks. The killer whales hang vertically suspended just under the surface. Facing downward, while they wait patiently, almost without movement. It is the classic posture of a hunter waiting in ambush. They descend without warning, torpedoing downwards. Soon they ascend with a shark draped lifelessly in their jaws.

Surprisingly, the whales purposefully return to us to eat their prey. Watching small clouds of shark blood and guts drifting in the wake of the feeding killer whales, *'I wonder why these super predators do not eat people.'*

Earlier in the day, I found myself alone in the water with a large Orca cow. She was resting just beneath the surface slowly drifting. I shoot my last frame of film then hang suspended a dozen feet below the surface staring at this magnificent creature. She is at an angle to me when I notice she is turning in my direction. Her eyes look at me with raw, primal intelligence — suddenly, I feel distinctly like prey under that predatory stare!

My heartbeat surges. It is beating out a cadence of fear. For a marine predator, this must be like ringing the chow bell.

From a head-on perspective, I see her tail go up and then down. The killer whale comes slowly toward me, and I am not sure what to do. I glance about, but there is no Zodiac or diver in sight from my limited underwater perspective. There is nowhere to flee. The surface beckons. I desperate for air but cannot tear my eyes from the approaching predator. I watch the head growing rapidly in size as she closes on me. I am aware of her predatory attributes, the huge mouth filled with sturdy teeth, her broad girth, and the muscled hump of her massive back. My heart jackhammers as she looms only eight-feet away — then she slowly turns sideways.

For long seconds, I stare at this magnificent hunter, and then I look back to her head, and our eyes lock. It is an instant of intensity that seems to last an eternity. I do not know what she is thinking or what the moment might mean to her. I stare into her wild intelligence lurking behind her eye. Intrinsically, I feel she turned sideways to appear less threatening. I don't want to look away, but my urge to breath is overwhelming. I shoot to the surface in a wash of fluttering fins. When I look back under water, she is gone.

I am alarmed! Where is she? I spin in a rapid circle looking all about and for a heart-stopping moment stare beneath me, but the water below is suspiciously empty. Unnerved, I quickly swim over to the Zodiac, which is floating empty 50' away, and climb aboard. I peer back over the side, but the water below is still empty. Floating alone beneath the hot tropical sun, I ponder the whale's actions. Was she curious or did her lingering look imply more?

It is an amazing thing that orcas in the wild do not eat people. They occasionally have harmed and killed their trainers in ocean parks. However, those orcas are inmates, confined in small tanks where every sound they voice echoes back at them. Confine any intelligent creature for too long, and they drift towards insanity. I think it is truly fortunate that killer whales to not hunt people. If they did humans would have hunted them to near extension.

Now, back in the water floating next to the Zodiac, I see the whales descending after consuming their prey. As the sun slowly drops behind the cloudless horizon, the light fades, casting the depths into shadowed darkness. Thirty feet down, I see Jean-Michel signal the team to return to the surface. They cannot film in the submarine twilight, and maybe there is a hint of fear of what lurks below that helps propel the divers back to the Zodiac.

With dusk turning to night, we drift under the evening sky as it fills with stars. We hold the twin Zodiacs together; everyone bubbles with excitement as we share the wonder of seeing the killer whales hunting sharks. Twenty yards away there is a froth of bubbles as a bull orca fin rises almost five feet out of the dark water. Faint starlight glistens on the wet black fin as it cuts through the glassy surface, then the whale disappears downward with a powerful flick of its tail.

Cousteau chief diver and expedition leader.
Stephen Arrington 1987 - 1993

The most beautiful thing we can experience is the mysterious. It is the source of all true art and science. — Albert Einstein

I stand nervously next to an altar covered with wildflowers. At my side, Jean-Michel Cousteau wears a black tuxedo. The piano begins to play as the wedding party comes down the aisle. Sam walks with Cindy's best friend, Dagmar. She will give birth to a son, but then cancer will take her two years later.

Next is Margery Spielman, one of my best friends. With her walking proudly is my big brother, Jim. I would lose him in five years to a tragic suicide. Jim is one of so many Vietnam Vets who ended their lives early.

Next, I see Cindy and can hardly believe this beautiful woman, my best friend, is about to become my wife. At the altar, we link hands and, just before the ceremony begins, we look at all our guests gathered in the small church. I see our families, a wealth of friends, and expedition companions from the Cousteau Society. Then, I turn to face Cindy. In her smiling eyes, I see a future yet to be, made of dreams, hopes, and aspirations. Whatever the future brings, we will face it together.

Cynthia Elizabeth Arrington with Jacques-Yves and Jean-Michel Cousteau. Photo Arrington

Upon our return from our honeymoon, Jean-Michel asked both of us to come to his office. "I have a dilemma," he said, looking at Cindy as if I was not even there. "I'm sending Steve to Australia to dive with great white sharks (*this is news to me*). We have never had women Cousteau divers, and I have a filming sequence I would like to do in the Bahamas. I need three very fit women, who can hold their breath for long periods of time, to dive with dolphins."

"I'll go," grinned Cindy.

"How long can you hold your breath?"

"Don't know, never timed myself."

"Two minutes, at least," Jean-Michel said sternly.

Cindy smiles, it is her accepting-a-challenge look, "I can hold my breath for over two minutes." She looked Jean-Michel in the eye, "Or I will be able to by the time we leave."

Jean-Michel laughs, "Good, you leave in two weeks."

"What about me?" I asked foolishly.

Jean-Michel turns as if noticing my presence for the first time. "Why you're leaving immediately, of course."

"I am?"

"See my secretary on your way out; she has your tickets."

"I'm leaving tonight?" I asked unhappily.

"Steve," He spread his hands, "I am not cruel. You have just got back from your honeymoon. You don't leave until tomorrow. Go look at your tickets; I even got you a red-eye."

* * *

Sunrise in the Great Australian Bight, I stare at the golden light glistening on the ocean's rippling surface. Standing at the stern of *Alcyone*, I place my hand against a plastic cylinder. It is 10' tall, 5' in diameter and rather flimsy. Not reassuring, considering that this is the world's first all-plastic great white shark cage, and it is my design. Its biggest flaw is that I ordered a sheet of *Lexan* 20' by 10' by 3/8" thick. Unfortunately, the French engineer mistakenly ordered a sheet only half that thick, just 3/16 of an inch.

In the plastic's distortion, I see Jean-Michel Cousteau walk out of the bridge door carrying a white porcelain cup of steaming tea. His reflection joins mine on the plastic cylinder.

"How do you like our plastic shark cage?" asked Jean-Michel.

"I wish it were thicker," I said wistfully. I knuckle it and watch my reflection quiver on the thin wobbling plastic.

Jean-Michel gives the cylinder a solid wallop. The thin plastic wobbles more, causing our reflections to shimmer and dance. "This is not just plastic; it is super-tough *Lexan*, 3/8" of an inch-thick, "said Jean-Michel, "*Lexan* has been known to stop a bullet."

"But this *Lexan* cage is only half that thick, and a bullet weighs less than an ounce," I answered. "But will the thin plastic stop a determined 3,000-pound super-predator after a bit of lunch?"

Jean-Michel shrugs, "I am going to give it the tuna test."

A bit later, Michel DeLoire and I jump from the Wind Ship into the open hatch of a steel shark cage floating on the surface.

An 18' long great white shark, we named Peaches, swims over to investigate. She peers through the viewing slots in the upper sides of the cage, then chomps down on one corner and gives the steel bars a vigorous shaking. It's startling to see the massive great white's body flex as she shakes our cage about like a pit bull with a stuffed toy. Keeping one's balance inside a shark cage bobbing with each passing ocean swell is challenging, particularly when wearing slick rubber booties on a web grate. Having a 3,000-pound shark knocking the cage about looking for a snack makes standing in one place tricky. Michel DeLoire and I are both trying to stay in the center of the cage away from those large, clashing teeth. Michel is doing a better job, and he is catching some exciting, but unstable, footage. I stumble bouncing off two of the cage's wire-mesh walls, half-flooding my dive mask. I want to clear the mask, but that requires my hands, which are holding a camera. Peering myopically through the distortion of the salt water, I see teeth the size of my thumb industriously shredding paint chips from the cage inches from my face.

The shark worries a few more feet of the steel bars before turning away and heading downward. Her tail slams against the cage as the super-predator charges after another great white shark below the cage. Two staggering steps later, I regain my balance, quickly clear my mask, and then realize that besides a rational level of fear, I am seasick.

The water visibility is poor as I feel my stomach rumble in protest at the constant bouncing and jerking of the floating cage with each passing swell. I can only see 30' into the gloomy water as I watch the two great white sharks swim in and out of view with Peaches predominately in pursuit of the other shark. Michel looks at me and grins. As always in dangerous situations, he is having an extraordinarily good time. I attempt to steady myself inside the bobbing cage and try to suppress my seasickness. Instead, I burp and taste an unpleasant acid tang inside my regulator — then I abruptly heave my guts out.

Blowing chow underwater requires that the regulator stay clenched firmly between the teeth, otherwise during the spontaneous gasping inhalation one could drown. The key to vomiting into your mouthpiece is to blow out to clear the bigger chunks just before that big gasping inhalation that follows. I go through the heave, blow, and gasp routine three times. Through my faceplate, I see an expanding multicolored cloud with floating chunks drifting just beyond my facemask. A gang of fish charges into the cloud going after a bit of breakfast. The leatherback fish, each about eight inches long, are always in close attendance with the cage, which provides protection from the sharks while they gobble fish chunks from the bait stream pouring from our stern.

I watch the disgusting cloud drift slowly in a slight current away from me. Then I notice Michel DeLoire staring at the approaching cloud — he cannot get out of the way. The yellow vomit cloud with its attendant horde of swarming fish descends upon Michel. He is ineffectively waving his 35mm movie camera at it. The vomit cloud engulfs his head as he paws frantically at it with his hands to clear away the half-digested debris.

Afterwards, a thoroughly angry Michel shoves me into the down-current side of the cage and glares at me. He is yelling. Fortunately, the water distorts his words, and anyway, I do not understand French, particularly not that kind of French.

I feel better after heaving and offer Michel a tentative smile, but he just glares at me with sincere hostility.

Looking up through the shimmering surface, I see the crew lower the plastic cylinder into the water, which instantly commands Peaches' attention. She swims around it eyeing the nearly transparent cylinder suspiciously. The huge shark nudges it once sharply with her snout, but the lifeless plastic cage does not seem to hold much interest for her. That is until Jean-Michel drops a 40-lb. frozen tuna into it. Peaches behavior changes dramatically as she gets the aroma of that decomposing tuna. She repeatedly swims through the odor corridor of the tuna as it defrosts, sending shark-tantalizing fish smells into the water. The shark circles the cylinder trying to get at that enticing fish.

The tuna's arrival brings in two more great white sharks. Seeing all the shark activity, Michel DeLoire decides to film with the front door of the cage wide-open, which means he can get unrestricted shark footage. Since Michel needs both hands to operate the movie camera, it falls on me to hold the door open, and that means I must lean out through the narrow opening. This allows Michel to position his camera on my shoulder — a hinderance to my getting out of the way of aggressive shark teeth. Another shark swims up from beneath our cage. Michel cannot see the oncoming shark because he is filming a great white torpedoing in out of the gloom.

My concern revolves around the teeth in the upper jaw of a great white, which can dislocate and extend outward from the shark's formidable mouth. The cage bottom's grid is wide enough that a biting shark can extend its teeth several toes' worth into the cage. Two loud grunts into my regulator does not get Michel's attention, so I resort to head nodding in a downward direction. My antics gain Michel's attention as I am causing his camera to wobble, ruining his shot of the shark swimming beside the cage, so he whacks me alongside the head with the big movie camera to get me to settle down.

For no apparent reason, the shark beneath us reverses direction and plunges back down into the depths. I breathe a sigh of relief, which elicits another crack alongside my head from Michel's camera. Trying to breathe softly without moving is causing my faceplate to fog up. Through the mask's reduced visibility, I see Peaches patrolling in a tight circle around the plastic cylinder. I would like to take a couple of pictures with the camera hanging from my hand — instead, I get to be Michel's camera rest.

Peaches is getting angry at the tormenting tuna; she whacks the plastic cage with her snout. The impact rocks the plastic cylinder causing the tuna inside to bounce about enticingly. The swaying fish is too much of a temptation for a 14' great white cruising below our cage. It makes a sudden rush for the dancing tuna. Peaches charges to head-off the smaller intruder, who turns away and flees toward the bottom.

A 15' male shark rockets out of the gloomy water straight at the cylinder. Peaches charges the shark — which turns away in panic and bolts straight toward our open door.

When leaning out into open water with a large movie camera resting on your shoulder and a still camera hanging from your hand, it is startling to see a great white shark torpedoing at you. I desperately reach for the door, which opens outward.

From a diver's perspective, things always look a bit bigger and closer underwater. Michel is backing up as fast as he can, yet the resistance of the water and the bulky camera slows him down. I pull the door closed and drop my camera as my faceplate fills with a jaws-wide-open, charging, super-predator. I see the shark's eyes roll back as he extends his jaws, and then it crashes into the door and chomps down onto it. My faceplate is only inches from the shark's snout. The lightweight steel mesh shudders and bends inward under the massive collision. The gigantic tail swishes from side to side as the shark repeatedly bites down on the wire mesh barrier and then shakes it ferociously. I have not latched the door. I cannot let go of the steel wire mesh. Otherwise, the shark might jerk the door open and rip it off its hinges. Barely two inches from my fingers are some startlingly large, serrated teeth going about the business of industrious chewing. I watch the teeth grinding off paint and steel slivers as the shark rattles the cage like a hobo with a tin cup looking for a handout.

Abruptly, the enraged shark releases its toothy grip, but only to go for a better bite. I let go of the door while he resets his dental work more aggressively in my direction. I see the upper jaw dislocate in anticipation of the bite. The serrated teeth flash in the gloomy light as he chomps down into the wire mesh again. His jaws are now a little further from the latch. I grab the door with one hand and am reaching for the latch—just as Peaches crashes into the opposite side of the cage. The jar helps as I feel the latch's bolt slide into its slot. Retreating backward toward the center of the cage on my knees, I feel Michel's camera sliding back over my shoulder and then he grips my arm with his now-free hand as a signal to remain still. Kneeling, with my heart pounding wildly, I watch the shark finally abandon its attack and depart. The sharks depart as I turn to look at Michel and see he is laughing.

Picking up my camera, I find his good mood irksome and motion with my thumb that we should open the top hatch of the floating cage so we can talk about it. We emerge from the battered cage. Michel is in high spirits, "You were very busy holding that door closed with the shark chewing on it."

"Why didn't you help me? I asked. I couldn't close the latch."

"I was catching it all on film," grinned Michel, "that's my job."

"What if he had gotten the door open?" I asked seriously.

"Would have gotten that on film too," he laughed."

I look at the mirth in his eyes and cannot help laughing with him. "Did you see the size of those chompers?" I asked.

Michel has us pulled to the stern of Alcyone so he can climb out and service his camera. I stay in the cage over lunch to get some more great white still images. I am a distance from Alcyone to prevent the cage from banging against her hull.

Later, someone tugs on the rope that secures the cage to the stern of Alcyone. I open the hatch and climb out onto the top of the cage. Capkin, our youngest diver, and Bruno, our chef, are on the stern. Bruno holds a pink balloon with a ribbon tied to it. Hanging beneath it is a paper party plate inside an inflated plastic bag.

"You missed lunch," shouted Capkin," you got to try this dessert. It's peanut butter and chocolate cheesecake with raspberry swirls, and topped with chunks of rich Dutch chocolate, and heavy whipping cream. This is the last piece. Michel said we should float it out to you — even though you blew chow all over him."

Bruno places the balloon and plastic bag in the water. I watch the little colorful convoy drifting slowly down current towards me. Abruptly a two-foot-wide mouth erupts from the water — massive teeth chomp down on the cheesecake party bag. A giant tail thrashes wildly throwing water and shredded pink balloon high into the air. Then, the shark and my dessert plunge beneath the swirling surface.

On the ship's stern, Capkin and Bruno have been soaked head to toe by the shark's trashing about. I am highly amused, yet disappointed that I didn't get to try that cheesecake.

* * *

In building the world's first plastic great white shark cage, it is logical there might be a few flaws in the design. The cylinder's height, ten feet, prevents me from climbing in through the top hatch while the cage is onboard *Alcyone*. The thin plastic cage also cannot withstand a sharp blow against the side of our metal hull. That means we must lower it into the water, well beneath the threat of the metal stern. That leaves only one way for me to get into the cylinder. I must jump into the water and swim down to it after making sure there are no sharks lurking near the *Alcyone's* stern.

I take a deep breath and leap. Splashing into the cold water, I find myself surrounded by a cloud of bubbles from my entry — and many imagined sharks. Desperately, with my mask half-full of water from the rushed entry, I see the top of my nearly transparent cage. Kicking frantically downward, I lunge for the hatch cover, throw it open and pull myself urgently down into the dubious protection of the thin plastic cylinder. Inside the cage, I feel better though I am upside-down; it takes a couple of clumsy moments to right myself. All I see is empty water, except for the ever-present leatherbacks, one of which is chewing on the tip of my flipper.

I notice Capkin and Michel in their steel cage. Capkin is pantomiming my panicked entry while Michel pretends to be a great white shark hiding behind him. I put my hands on my hips and give them *the look*, which probably loses some of its impact through a dive mask, but then I notice the ballistic arrival of Peaches. The shark arrows straight up from the depths. She is just two feet away when she notices I am not the 40-pound tuna she was expecting. The disappointment brings her to an abrupt halt beside the cylinder. Hovering, she peers intently, but there is no doubt about it. I am not a succulent decomposing fish. She makes one pass behind the cylinder to make sure I am not hiding the tuna behind my back. Then with a complete lack of interest, she swims away and so ends our human-bait experiment for the day.

An Arrington Minute: As much as you can take every opportunity to do something good for someone else. Practice this regularly. It is surprising the ripple effect that a simple act of kindness creates. A tiny undulation in a small pond will always reflect on its source. That being you. Acts of goodness announces you as a caring person, it makes you likeable. People will want to include you in their circle of friends and that creates unforeseen opportunities. Such as, it wasn't an accident that the inmates of Engine Company 52 chose me to lead them. Note the incredible impact it had on my life. It helped lead to my becoming the Air Diving Supervisor at the College of Oceaneering. My position at the college led to my becoming Chief Diver and Expedition Leader for the Cousteau Society despite my being an ex-inmate who did not speak French. As such, good acts build one upon the other. Be consistently good but know that one negative response can destroy many acts of goodness.

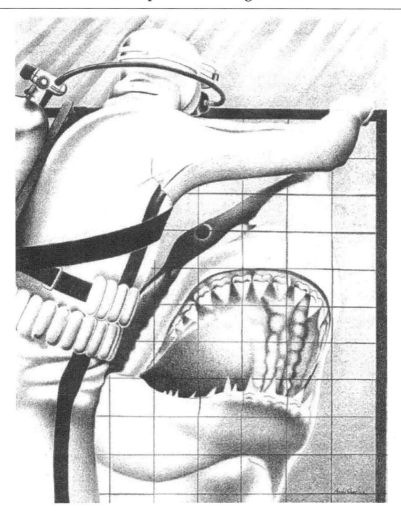

Author holding shark cage door closed. Note all the extra lead weights to help me stay standing while in a cage that is bouncing and rocking. Illustration by Andy Charles

Humor is the great thing, the saving thing. The minute it crops up, all our irritations and resentments slip away, and a sunny spirit takes their place. — Mark Twain

* * *

It is now late fall on the underside of the planet. Looking to the east, the dark sky lightens slowly as nautical twilight fades before the rising sun on a stormy day. I am just finishing the early morning watch at the stern of *Alcyone*. The wind is howling across Dangerous Reef, causing *Alcyone* to swing at her anchorage. I am trying not to breathe through my nose. Riding the wind from Dangerous Reef is a horrible cargo of pungent odors. The tiny spit of rock is a seabird rookery and seal whelping sanctuary. The reef smells worse than an over-stuffed diaper pail.

There is no chance of launching the shark cages today, yet part of my watch requires that I continue the chum corridor drifting behind the Wind Ship. Scooping up a bucket of fish offal, tuna oil, and pig blood, I lean over the stern and pour it into the dark water. I am trying to keep the awful stuff from getting onto my jeans as I pour it slowly. It gives the great white shark in the depths of the dark water all the time she needs to zero in on the source. Amy erupts at my feet, biting viciously at the chum stream. Leaping out of the way, I inadvertently spill fish offal onto the crotch and legs of my jeans. I wipe off the grosser chunks then rush to the bridge to grab my camera and dash back outside. I am busily tying a rotting mackerel to a piece of rope with a yellow balloon on it when Capkin arrives.

"Wow! That's some smell out here," Capkin stated the obvious as he stepped through the bridge door. "Why are you tying that decaying fish to a balloon? Making a party favor?"

"It's an experiment," I said in a friendly way, mostly because I am looking for a second set of hands, "want to help?"

"Sure, if I don't have to touch your stinky fish."

Capkin is the most enthusiastic person I know other than Cindy. He is a tall, slim, yet muscular Australian. He is 21-years old. The girls love him because he is so kind-hearted and very good looking.

I tell him that I want to re-create the poster from the movie *Jaws*. It depicts a great white shark leaping right at you with its massive jaws wide open. Only I want to do it with a real shark. Amy's morning leap has given me the idea of dangling a fish from the Wind Ship's crane, which is why I need Capkin's help.

I thread the rope through the pully on the tip of the crane then lower the fish into the water. The floating yellow balloon will keep the fish near the surface. Also, its bobbing action on the surface is making the rotting fish dance enticingly. When the shark lunges, Capkin will pull the fish up. Amy will have to leap for it.

"Where are you going to stand to take the picture?" he asked.

"The swim step," I answered. Taking off my shoes and socks, I jump down onto the small platform, which is eight inches above the water and two plus feet from the dangling fish depending upon the angle of the swell. The movement of the *Alcyone* on the rough water has the dangling fish swinging toward and away from me — something I had not reckoned into my plan. I am barefoot because salt water is sluicing over the swim step with each passing swell.

"This should be fascinating," Capkin deadpans. "What happens if the shark lands jaws first onto the swim step?"

"I imagine I'll be getting off it rather rapidly," I responded while peering down at the still dark water from which had recently leaped a 17'-long great white shark.

"Okay, lower the fish," I said wondering if standing on the plunging swim step is a good idea. The dangling fish dips into the water and sinks a few inches below the floating balloon. I am prepared to be patient; this could take a while.

The shark is not so patient. I see a startling flash of white ascending out of the depths.

"Here she comes," I yelled as Amy lunges for the dead fish, which surprises her by flying up and out of the water. The astonished shark tries to pursue with her rapidly beating tail, but lacking momentum, she instead falls back into the water.

Amy makes repeated lunges for the fish before her bad disposition sends the now thoroughly angry shark into a biting frenzy. Shark scientists refer to this activity as display behavior. Amy is swimming in circles biting the empty water. I nervously watch her working out her frustrations from the swim step.

"Looks like Amy is getting a mite stirred up," said Capkin tugging on the line making the dead fish wiggle invitingly.

The enraged shark circles the floating balloon with its fish baggage then reverses direction and swims straight down.

"Uh oh," I cautioned Capkin, "I think this might be it."

The shark is torpedoing upward like a ballistic missile. As Capkin jerks the fish upward, the 3,000-pound shark explodes mouth wide-open from the water. Her tail drives furiously, propelling her a full five feet out of the shark thrashed water. Quickly, leaning out with my camera, I shoot a full-frame picture of the enraged predator from less than three feet away. Then the balloon and fish land with a solid plop onto the swim step as Capkin accidentally lets go of the rope. The shark, still in aerial pursuit, glares in my direction. She slams back into the water next to the platform. The shark's belly flop flushes me head-to-toe with cold salt water, which sends Capkin into a fit of laughter.

Author pondering sharks.
Illustration Margery Spielman

Creative man lives many lives, some men are so dull they do not live even once. — Dagobert D. Runes.

Chapter 25 - Dangerous Reef, Oct 1991

It is a sunny spring day; *RV Alcyone* is back at Dangerous Reef. I am standing at the stern in my dive gear watching a 17-foot-long great white shark glide by just beneath the shimmering water. A small tag beneath her dorsal fin identifies this shark as Amy; whom I know is extremely aggressive.

The cage is eight feet down and nearly invisible from the surface, which is not reassuring. The more primal part of my brain is having difficulty with jumping into shark-infested waters to swim down to a barely visible cage. Usually swimming down eight feet to the shark cage is not that big of a deal, but this morning Amy seems to be showing abnormally high interest in my short journey. Is she devising a plan to catch me at the halfway point? Watching the great white shark circling beneath my flippers, I have a distinct feeling I am about to find out.

Seeing a shark's dorsal fin knifing through the smooth water 30' from the stern, I make a quick jump for the cage. Just as my flippers clear the stern, I hear our chef shout, "Shark!"

Looking down, I see a large dark torpedo shape slipping out from under *Alcyone*. Instantly, I realize that the shark in the distance is not Amy. The crafty predator has been hiding under the Wind Ship's stern, and we are now on a collision course. My point of impact is exactly where Capkin and I dangled the fish.

An instinctive fluttering of my flippers does not prevent me from splashing into the chilly water. My mask half floods with water. A froth of bubbles from my entry further obscures my vision. I barely see the shark at first because of all the bubbles drifting about from my entry, but as they clear away, I have an unmistakable close-up view of a 17' great white shark swimming toward me. I do not have time to look again as I turn my back on the huge predator and bolt for the *Lexan* cage. It is disconcerting having my back exposed to the giant shark, but I know my only hope is to get into the plastic cylinder quickly. A few heart-fluttering seconds later, I reach for the double top hatches of the plastic cylinder, open them, and pull myself vigorously down into the cage. Granted I am upside down in the plastic cage with a half-flooded dive mask, but at least I am inside. Glancing upward and clearing my dive mask, I see the great white shark passing overhead, its black orb regarding me with mischief on its mind just before it descends back down into the gloom beneath me.

The great white is not long in swimming back up. I watch her ascend out of the depths. The massive head swings side-to-side as she approaches then nudges the bottom of my plastic cage with her snout. The black eye regards me coldly from inches away. Confused by the invisible barrier, the shark keeps returning, though not actually attacking. That is until she is joined by a second shark, and then by a third. It seems I have rung the sharks' dinner bell with my frantic entry.

The sharks grow bolder and confident with numbers. They circle my plastic cage aggressively. I wonder if they sense my fear, when abruptly a 15-footer attacks. Its snout thumps the side of the Lexan cylinder solidly. I am so intent on watching the 15'-long shark that I do not notice the 17-footer has returned — until I see a shadow passing over me.

Turning, I see the huge shark hovering vertically alongside my cage. Its pectoral fins hug the five-foot diameter plastic cylinder as it seeks to get as close to me as possible. Just the thin Lexan separates us. Her belly rubs against the plastic as she seeks a way inside. Twisting her head, just inches from my own, I feel the alarm of real fear as I stare into that cold, dark orb. She gashes her teeth against the thin plastic scoring it. Turning her head to one side for a better bite, I find myself leaning forward into that giant maul. Because of the warp of the cylinder, my face is mere inches from her teeth. I peer deep into her throat and stare in awe at sunlight radiating in through the gill slits. The marine softened light paints shadows deep down in her gullet. I wonder if anyone else has seen this far into the throat of a massive great white shark underwater and lived to tell about it. She hovers alongside the cage seven long seconds before swimming off.

I breathed a premature sigh of relief, but then the huge shark reverses direction, now swimming rapidly up.

Arrington in shark cage with 17 ½ -foot long
Amy in close attendance. Illustration Courtesy of
long-time Cousteau artist Dominique Serafini.

'Uh oh!' The thought came suddenly, *'This is the shark that spent the most time investigating the plastic cage.'* She comes up like a speeding torpedo, straight toward the bottom of my cage, its weakest point. Just a single layer of hollow two-inch tubes, with sides less than a quarter-inch thick, lines the bottom of the plastic cylinder. I instinctively raise my feet off the bottom of the cage an

instant before she rams into the plastic tubes. The collision drives the cage over a foot upwards. I watched wide-eyed as the tubes bend apart, admitting her thick snout. Then with brute force, she thrusts her massive head forward, biting furiously at the thin *Lexan* tubes. Fortunately, her mouth is not far enough into the cage to bite down on the far-too-frail tubes. After some diligent chewing, she vigorously swings her head side to side, shaking the cage violently.

Earlier, I had placed two 25-pound lead weights in the bottom of the cage to hold it vertical in a current. As Amy's head bangs about, one of the lead clumps slides across the hollow tubes and smacks her in the snout. Amy pulls back, glares indignantly at the lead weight then swims off into gloomy water without a backward glance. As the aggressive shark swims away, I look affectionately at the lead clump.

At the lunch table, everyone is excited about the filming, which has gone very well from Michel's perspective. He said, "Stephen, it is very exciting jumping into the open water with a great white shark so close, yes?"

"Yes, Michel, it was terrifying."

Good," exclaimed Michel. He reaches across the table to pour me a half-glass of red wine, which he knows is my limit on diving days, "Because, I want to film it."

I look at Michel, who is smiling. The Frenchmen are such good practical jokers. "Right, Michel," I chuckled.

"You will do this for me?" he asked pleasantly.

I realize he is not kidding.

After lunch, I am standing on the swim step peering over the side. There are four great white sharks in attendance. Sometimes they swim leisurely pass the Wind Ship, at other times they rocket by in pursuit of bait or each other.

Michel is in his steel cage floating just beneath the surface. Capkin is inside the cage holding his hand up through the bars. The hand signals one. Three is my signal to jump. I nervously watch a shark swimming in and know that Michel is filming it. The hand flashes two as the great white passes beneath me. The hand suddenly shows three fingers. Taking a deep breath, and questioning my stupidity, I jump.

The splash startles the shark, which arrows for the bottom while I rocket for my cage. Seconds later, safely behind the plastic barrier, I see the 14' long shark returning. She swims in to investigate nudging the side of the cage, and then she swims up to examine the top of the cage. She glides over the rim as I fearfully watch her sliding against the lifting bridle that raises and lowers the plastic cage. If she gets snagged in those lines causing her to bite through them — it means she could swim off with a to go snack. With her at the top of the cage, I would be along for the ride. With great relief I watch her swim down. She pauses for an upside-down stare off — then thankfully swims away.

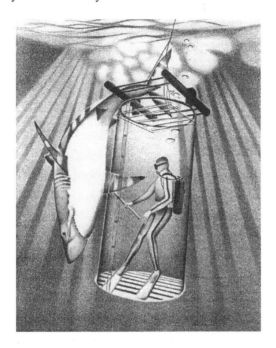

The 14′ long shark upside-down stare off.
Image Andy Charlies

At dinner, Michel smiles at me, "That was very exciting your jumping in with the shark, Stephen."
"I guess," I said sarcastically.
"I only wish the shark hadn't been quite so far down," said Michel wistfully.
"What do you mean?" I asked suspiciously.
"How do you say it in English?" he asked. "Oh, take two."
The next morning, I am again on the swim step — peering over the side at sharks. There are seven today. The water at the back of the *Alcyone* is beginning to look like the carpool express lane for large hungry predators.

Abruptly, a silver-gloved hand shoots up out of the water with the index finger pointed skyward — one!

My heart leaps as I look just beyond my flippers. This shark is much shallower. The top of its dorsal fin cuts through the water while another shark disappears under *Alcyone*. The hand abruptly flashes two and the shark is right beneath me.

Paul, our engineer, peers over the side and says with a shrug, "Is okay, Stephen. She's only a small one."

The shark is 15'-long and weighs at least ten times more than I do. The hand suddenly has three fingers in the air. I take a deep breath and like an idiot leap into the cold water.

With the splash of my entry, I have lost visual on the shark. I swim frantically to the cage, quickly open the top hatches, and vigorously pull myself down — halfway in my tank valve hits the top edge of the plastic cage and jams. My lower torso and legs are outside of the cage. I panic and swim harder but go nowhere. I imagine my frantically fluttering fins are attracting great white sharks. I have no choice but to push myself backward, freeing my tank valve and then drop frantically down into the cage. Looking rapidly about, I am surprised to see there are no sharks in close attendance. Later, Capkin would share that my entry was so close to the great white shark that it raced away in panic.

That evening, I go to the bow and sit down on the fairing that turns *Alcyone's* forward metal sail. I lean my back against the curved sail to watch the sunset fade to twilight and then ever so slowly to full darkness. I am deep in thought. Looking at the glittering light of the vast heavens, I hear the rest of the crew in the dining salon. There is the subtle tinkle of glasses and the sound of muffled laughter. The forward salon windows glow warmly from the flickering candlelight within, luring me toward the camaraderie below, yet I am not willing to leave the solitude of the Wind Ship's bow. Soon, all of this will be but fond memories.

Staring at the twinkling heavens, I think about my promise to Judge Takasugi to help motivate youth towards a better life. I also remember telling Ralph that the LORD was preparing me for important work. These are commitments I need to honor, as a promise not kept is a lie fulfilled.

I realize that this is a tough time to be a youth living in America. Teen and adult suicide rates grows statistically every year.

Author's note: In 2018, according to the CDC (Center for Disease Control) suicide is the #2 killer of children 10 to young adults 35-years old. The #1 killer of children 10 to adults 25-years old is Unintentional Death — however the primary cause of unintentional death for those children, youths and adults is drug overdose, which has been brought on by synthetic drugs, pain pills, heroin, meth, PCP, ecstasy, cocaine, etc. People who think marijuana is a harmless drug are ignorant of the facts. It is classified as a Class 1 Drug by the CDC. In its natural state marijuana has a THC content of just 2% to 3%. Tetrahydrocannabinol (THC) is the active ingredient that gets people high. Growers are pushing out new strains of marijuana and hybrids with a THC content of 27% and more. Vaping marijuana oils are nearing 100% THC. Marijuana toxicity is overwhelming our hospitals with children, youths and adults who are smoking and vaping high levels of THC and eating marijuana ingestibles that are often made to look like candy (as are synthetic drugs like pink heroin), all of which explains why many children 5 to 10-years old are now dying of drug overdose. The prison population in the United States is by far the largest in the world. So yeah, I and my message about, "Hope that never surrenders," is needed.

Sitting on the bow of Alcyone 29 years ago, even I didn't imagine how bad it was going to get. Yet I knew the answer to these staggering problems is hope. Without hope, children will fall through the cracks in the American dream. Hope is something I understand. I have seen my wildest hopes fulfilled in prison.

Hope offers a way back from a life-destroying mistake. Hope is the kiln in which broken dreams are re-forged. As an ex-inmate, I see the world from a different perspective and with a greater sense of appreciation. Hope a person can believe in is worth sharing. With that thought, my decision was made. It is time for me to serve a greater purpose with my life.

The next morning, I am in my dive gear at the stern of the Wind Ship starring at a double rainbow that stands out against nimbus clouds from a recent rain. Stepping to the edge of the deck, I glance at a six-foot-tall mirror leaning against a shark cage. We are using the mirror to see how a great white shark will react to its reflected image. I stare at myself in the mirror. The metallic silver of the wetsuit is dazzling in the morning light. The French tricolor ripples proudly over my shoulder and beyond it gleaming are the radiant twin rainbows in the mirror's upper corner.

I am reminded of the LORD's promise that when we see a rainbow, we are to remember His covenant with us. Taking a deep breath, I smile and step from the stern of the Wind Ship.

For an instant, my splash disturbs the smooth, calm water. Then an iridescent stream of bubbles rises to the surface where they gurgle and burst before they dissipate and are gone.

Alcyone at anchor at Dangerous Reef.
Image by Margery Spielman

Life is a mirror and will reflect back to the thinker what he thinks into it. – Ernest Holmes

The photo of Amy, the 17' long great white shark, leaping out of the water can be viewed at **www.drugsbite.com**. Because of copyright law, I can print these images in my book.

Chapter 26 - West Hollywood, Jan 1993

I am alone in the basement of the Cousteau Society office. It is the end of the workday, and everyone is gone. A squeak from the floor reminds me that I am not alone. I look fondly at the portable playpen beside my desk. Stetcyn, my four-month-old daughter, is awake from her nap. She gurgles at me as I reach down and lift her up. I realize I must leave or be late picking up Cindy from the physical therapy office where she works.

With the sadness of a put-off-decision made, I place Stetcyn into her car seat on my desk and tuck a fuzzy blanket about her. Then carry the crib out to my Ford Explorer. I have packed my personal items, mostly remembrances from various expeditions. I return to the basement office to get my now-cooing daughter. I place my keys to the office on the desk, then carry Stetcyn out the door. I turn to watch the door automatically close and audibly lock. I stare blankly at it for several seconds then carry my baby girl out to the car and get inside. I glance once more at the closed office door then slowly drive away.

After five-and-a-half years, I am leaving the Cousteau Society. I choose to walk a new path. I will be a full-time husband to Cindy and a father to our daughter. I also have a promise to Judge Takasugi to honor regarding talking with youths about life choices. Most of all I have a private commitment to God to do His work.

* * *

Many persons have a wrong idea of what constitutes true happiness. It is not attained through self-gratification but through fidelity to a worthy purpose. — Helen Keller

An Arrington Minute: We are happiest and most in control of our lives when we are centered. Jesus Christ is at the center of my life. During times of stress or anger we are more likely to be pulled from our center. Outside our center we tend to make poor choices and must live with things we may regret for a long time. This is exactly what happened with me regarding Roxanne and Morgan. As such, our center needs to have a lot of influence over choices. The center is our feel-good place. Go there often.

Crew of the Alcyone for the Great White Shark Expedition
from top down and left to right: Capkin Van Alphen, Author,
Captain Christophe Jouet-Pastre, Paul Martin, Michel DeLoire,
Antoine Russet, Dominique Sarifini (the artist), Cluck Davis,
Patrick Allioux, Marc Blessington, and Bruno our chef.
Illustration by Dominique Sarifini

Yesterday, I left the Cousteau Society office, and this frosty
winter evening, I am standing on the College of Oceaneering
diving barge overseeing nighttime diving operations while
wrestling with some serious emotions. I feel like I have stepped
backward in time.

The students are wondering about me. They are impressed that
their instructor was a chief diver and expedition leader for the
Cousteau's, but they are also pondering what I am doing back here.
Actually, so am I. I am the in-between man waiting to see where
life is taking me.

Seeing a puddle of rusty water, I go stand in it. I am near the
edge of the barge at dive station three. This is where I kneeled to do
CPR on Chris. It is where the LORD used my breath to save a
young life, and in the process, to give purpose and meaning to my

life. I stare at the dark water where a boil of bubbles bursts above a student diver working on the harbor bottom. He is probably wondering where his diving career will take him. For all of us on the diving barge, it is a point of transition, a temporary way station on life's weaving journey.

Looking up, I stare at the glistening lights of San Pedro with echoes of Terminal Island Prison fluttering through my mind and absolutely know that I have made the right decision. As I told Ralph in the high Mojave Desert, the LORD has been preparing me for this exact moment, a door is opening, and I am running towards it as fast as I can.

When one door of happiness closes, another opens, but often we look so long at the closed door that we do not see the one, which has been opened for us. — Helen Keller

* * *

With the wisdom of hindsight, 28 years have passed since I left the Cousteau Society, I know beyond doubt that the LORD had a plan for me, to share a message of hope. I am a motivational and drug education speaker at public schools, for universities, at churches, and for organizations. I have done over 3,700 school assemblies in 49 states and spoken in seven countries. I also have done many dozens of teen suicide interventions. If I cooperated 35 years ago, none of this would have been possible. I probably would have served a longer prison sentence then disappeared into the witness protection program.

Yes, I made the best decision by not cooperating against my codefendants and as such against their families who had suffered enough already, mostly through no fault of their own. It allowed me to pay my debt to society.

It was my faith in God that gave me the courage to confess to what I had done wrong and to tell why I did it. That faith has allowed me to help almost a million children and youths at live presentations. Through worldwide media, add untold millions more. As I write these words I was recently in Hong Kong and then Taiwan speaking at a Christian colleges, academies, and elementary schools. Obviously, I love my work with children, youth, young adults, and families.

Speaker for Week of Prayer at Hong Kong Adventist College and Academy. I stand accused of eating the last cookie! March 2019

In this work, I have tried to share my relationship with Jesus Christ in a gentle, thoughtful manner. You see, this book is not actually about me — it is about Him.

He gave me hope in prison, protected me from the worst kind of abuse and dangers, and washed away my sins. It was not that I was worthy of this blessing, rather it was a gift of perfect love.

He brought me out of the darkness and clothed me in the uniform of a hero, of a firefighter and a lifesaver, giving my life meaning and purpose though I was a felon and an inmate.

He surrounded me with people who helped me to get the perfect job just days out of prison.

I wanted to help youth, so He taught me that my breath could physically save a life thought by all to be lost. That miraculous moment was the key that opened thousands of doors for me to speak to youth and young adults about true hope.

What are the odds that a felon on parole would be hired as a chief diver expedition leader aboard a famous French ship when he did not even speak nor understand French? It gave me an avenue to speak with youth capturing their attention with whales, dolphins, and great white sharks, while my prison and cartel experiences give me a path for teaching about the tougher choices in life.

I stand in amazement at the depth of His love for a broken man in a prison cell and that even then He had a plan for me.

My job as a Christian is to introduce people to Jesus Christ and then to let the Holy Spirit work in their hearts.

Therefore, if you do not yet know Him, this is your personal invitation. Are you ready for the most incredible adventure of a lifetime? Would you like to be accepted and loved just as you are? He is waiting—this is that moment when it truly is all about you. After all, you are why I wrote this book.

THE BEGINNING

With dreams begins responsibility, it is the bridge that connects the realm of fantasy with the world of reality. –Stephen Lee Arrington

AFTERWARD

In 2016, I received four security boxes of DeLorean trial files from my attorney. They contained official copies of the FBI secret transcripts, reports and FBI court filings as ordered by the judge. Also, there were John DeLorean's investigative files looking into the FBI and DEA agents, James Hoffman, and Morgan Hetrick.

The boxes also contained the records of my Court-Martial and of the Appelate Court ruling. These were documents I had never seen. In March 1980, prior to my leaving Hawaii, the Navy convened the Appellate Court to reconsider my court-martial. Their findings were given to a review board. Dozens of people had written letters on my behalf, including numerous naval officers and chiefs, several public service organizations, and two doctors whose lives I had saved. The doctors had surfaced from a deep dive with serious symptoms of the bends. One was unconscious, the other couldn't walk. I was their inside medical tender for a dangerous 36-hour hyperbaric treatment. There were numerous Naval Citations for my service including the C-5 Galaxy Minuteman Operation, Secret Service support for foreign Heads of State, and other dangerous assignments.

The review board ruled in my favor stripping away my sentence and awarding me an Honorable Discharge with the separation rank of chief (E-7). The Executive Officer at EODMUONE never advised me that my Court Martial had been thrown out. I can only imagine that he hated me and wanted to see me suffer, which I certainly did for almost four decades.

I did not correct this in the book because I have lived 38 years with the misconception that I had dodged a Bad Conduct Discharge by error. It is an essential aspect of my story and key to my slipping into Morgan's clutches. In the box was the letter of recommendation that Hetrick wrote to the board, where he said, "If the Navy is not proud to have Stephen Arrington then please send him back to me." In Author Jones' book, "The Gods Laughed," he wrote that Morgan targeted hiring military men who had been released from service for drug problems. Again, my bad choices had put me in the crosshairs of Morgan Hetrick's speculation and manipulations. The fault for all my problems laid solely upon me.

* * *

In the DeLorean Files, I made many significant discoveries. There is one however that only someone on the inside could have appreciated for its significance. It points to a 48-year-old suspicious death. A mysterious airplane crash that killed a mega-multi-millionaire who could have rivaled Bill Gate's impact in the world of computer software and technology.

The largest part of the DeLorean Files is what I refer to as the Hoffman Papers. I have an affidavit from DeLorean's Investigative Law Film from a man and his wife, who were present with James T. Hoffman when he flew to Santa Barbara on Dec 2, 1972. They drove out to the Westerly Stud Farm to meet with Morgan Hetrick who was a broker for the Fletcher Jones Estate. Hoffman claimed to be representing a wealthy person from Texas to purchase the estate's Morgan Paris Jet. The man noted that Hoffman and Hetrick acted like old friends. *No big surprise there.*

Morgan was an engineering genus. Fletcher Jones was known to be a careful, experienced pilot. Why did his aircraft, a single-engine Beechcraft Bonanza Debonair, crash on a ridge eight miles from the Santa Ynez Airport on a clear day?

It should be noted that this was a complex airplane, and it would not take much skill to sabotage it. However, an aviation engineering genus could do it with little chance of getting caught.

The twin-engine Aztec Stretch and I flew to Colombia almost crashed because of a disconnected heater fuel line that caused 20 gallons of 100 octane fuel to spill onto the heater's spark inducer. It was an easy way to set a plane on fire and send it burning from the sky. There would be no traceable evidence that someone had tampered with the plane.

Using this same basic premise, I asked a dentist who owned a Beechcraft Bonanza how easy would it be to crash the Debonair by tampering with the heater.

Here is his response, "There is a sheet metal shroud around the exhaust headers on one side of the engine. The heater pulls air around the hot metal shroud and into the cabin. A common failure is an exhaust leak that brings carbon monoxide into the cabin. It is odorless and colorless, and it out competes hemoglobin in our blood for oxygen. People go to sleep and crash. Creating a small exhaust leak would be easy. "

As a Navy bomb disposal technician, I can think of several ways to accomplish this in flight with either a time delay or altimeter trigger. When the plane reaches a certain altitude, it arms the trigger with an inexpensive time delay. On the return trip from Santa Monica the trigger gets the second altitude signal triggering the release of carbon monoxide into the cockpit. The crash occurs on the return trip thus reducing suspicion that the plane had been sabotaged in its hanger in San Yenz.

Hetrick told the FBI that he was the last one to work on the Bonanza Debonair and that he felt a certain responsibility for the accident as per a recorded interview of Morgan Hetrick by the FBI in 1983. Fletcher had to fly himself down to Santa Monica because Morgan claimed to be doing critical work on a Lear Jet.

It should also be noted that Morgan confessed that he thought Fletcher was getting ready to fire him because he had not delivered on his promise to get the Morgan Paris Jet certified for Fletcher Jones to fly it. The certification application had already taken over two years.

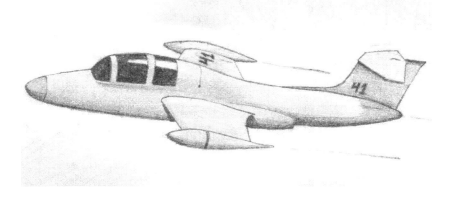

Morgan Paris II by Stetcyn Leigh Arrington

Fletcher Jones died on November 7, 1972. I met Morgan Hetrick just over a year later in the spring of 74, while I was attached to the EOD team at Point Mugu.

- In that short amount of time Morgan had gone from earning the wage of a pilot and airplane mechanic to becoming a multimillionaire.
- Morgan was in possession of Fletcher Jones' custom Morgan Paris Jet, which was supposedly sold through Hoffman to a Texas buyer. In an FBI file Hoffman noted that Morgan had taken possession of Fletcher's jet, which Morgan recertified as the Morgan Paris Jet II.
- Morgan had acquired expensive specialized tools for aircraft maintenance. Could those tools be traced back to the estate?
- I wonder about other assets he sold from the estate, such as a 36' Hatteras Yacht, a 40' Fleetwood motorhome, and a Moony 231 aircraft (valued at $250,000).
- Morgan was a thief. As a younger man, he and his wife cleaned out his father-in-law's house and shop of everything of value. A crime for which his father-in-law, Author Jones was prepared to kill him for in revenge as written in his book, "The Gods Laughed."
- Morgan's obsession with Christina Ferrare may have been a factor. They flew together often, where Morgan described their conversations as close and very personal. He told me several times that she written him a note that said, "I didn't know that men like you existed."
- Though Morgan wasn't much to look at, he could certainly be a charmer. He could have misinterpreted her friendship as actual feelings for him. It may be more than a coincidence that Fletcher's airplane crashed before Christina could accept his proposal of marriage.
- For a meeting at a restaurant with John DeLorean, Morgan insisted that he bring Christina. She was extremely reluctant to go and asked if this mystery person who wanted to surprise her with his presence was a pilot who wore glasses (as per an FBI file). She had less than fond memories of Morgan Hetrick and never wanted to see him again. He had asked her out on a date shortly after Fletcher Jones died.

Author Jones, Morgan's father-in-law, wrote that Hetrick once purposefully crashed a B-25 bomber for the insurance payout. Of interest, Morgan's sidekick, James T. Hoffman, had one of his own twin engine planes go down into the ocean off Mexico with three individuals aboard. It is believed that the plane was sabotaged, yet Lloyds of London Insurance Company had to pay Hoffman's claim. Reportedly none of the funds went to the three men's surviving families.

Since Morgan died in 2004 there is little incentive for an investigation. I contacted the Fletcher Jones Foundation, but they saw no advantage in pursuing an investigation.

Here are a few interesting bullets regarding the near crash of the plane Stretch and I flew:

- Hetrick knew Stretch to be a blabber mouth, particularly when drunk. Morgan hated drunks and thought them untrustworthy.
- Stretch was trying to cut his own deal with Max to increase his profits. Morgan had strong feelings regarding loyalty from people he employed.
- Stretch's father was a judge and thus he was potentially more of a threat as a witness against Morgan in a plea agreement. *Note: Stretch did enter into a plea agreement with the FBI and DOJ and thus avoided incarceration.*
- I had refused to make the flight and was a liability as Morgan knew me to be a patriot, (despite my court martial). I knew far too much about Morgan's illegal operations.
- Morgan was suddenly under scrutiny by the Ventura Police Department, the FBI, the DOJ, and the DEA. Hetrick's future was looking bleak.
- If his plane crashed it could solve most of his problems.
- The loss of the plane and two of his pilots would give him the excuse to stop flying for the Medellin Drug Cartel without life-threatening repercussions. The mysterious crash of Hoffman's plane a few years earlier suspiciously eliminated three potential witnesses against him. One of their wives said that Hoffman owed her husband money before he died. She never got any of it. I have her written interview by DeLorean's investigative law firm. Morgan was a quick

study, what worked for one conman could easily work for his partner.

- Morgan was a very greedy man, he could claim an insurance payout for the $185,000 Aztec, which had been significantly upgraded at great additional cost. This would be legitimate money, which he desperately needed. Yes, I believe he would kill two troublesome men particularly for a tax-free, quarter of a million-dollar insurance payout.
- If there was any residual evidence associated with the aircraft, it would be destroyed in the crash. This is why auto thieves burn stolen cars after stripping them.
- Morgan's criminal past from the 1960's as an importer of illegal wild animals and drugs pulled him deeply into a criminal underworld that thrived in lawless jungle towns where murder was always a quick and viable solution.

"I am guilty of betraying your trust more than you will ever know," William Morgan Hetrick. As he said to me in J-3.

EPILOGUE

1. Susan is happily married, has four boys, and lives in New Zealand. I am forever grateful that she helped me during my greatest emotional trials. I wish Susan and her family all the happiness in the world.

2. Morgan Hetrick, after serving five years in prison, retired to Arkansas, where he later died in an airplane accident. He was teaching three youths how to fly when their aircraft clipped a power wire severing a wing. Morgan took control from the student pilot and crash-landed the plane, saving the lives of the students. He perished from the resulting fire. Amazingly, Morgan died a hero — over 500 grateful people attended his funeral. It is interesting that Morgan Hetrick burning to death in a plane crash was the fate that I believe he planned for Stretch and for me.

3. James Timothy Hoffman simply disappeared. I have no idea what happened to him. However, the movie "Driven," was written about Hoffman, DeLorean and Hetrick. Supposedly, it was inspired by true events. It did well as a dark comedy. But Hoffman as the hero of the film — go figure.

4. Gerald Scotti resigned from the DEA after coming under investigation for possibly revealing information about the Grandma Mafia Case. He became a criminal defense attorney. In 2003, he murdered his best friend and business partner by putting three bullets into his chest at point-blank range. He did this in the law office of Carl Capozzola, attorney to the stars. Capozzola was terrified that he would be next. Instead, Scotti put the gun to his own head and pulled the trigger. He left a suicide note.

   In March 1986, the UPI reported that Steve Gibbs, a DEA special agent was indicted on charges that he gave law enforcement secrets to the "Grandma Mafia" money-laundering ring's attorney. Scotti was innocent of the charge that ruined his career and led to him becoming a key witness in John DeLorean's defense.

5. Buzz Hetrick attempted to disappear into the witness protection program. While flying back from a nine-school speaking tour on the East Coast, my commuter landed at a small airport in Chico, California. Chico is a university town just 12 miles from Paradise. Walking down the plane's steps, I abruptly saw Morgan's Mooney 231 parked on the flight line. I discovered that Buzz owned it. I got his telephone number and called to let him know that the Witness Protection Program was not working out so well and that he had nothing to fear from me. He disappeared. A month later he popped up in Texas on a friend's Facebook page. I still wonder how he wound up with a quarter of a million-dollar airplane after the Hetrick's surrendered all their wealth?

6. James Walsh, the District Attorney, became a friend and wrote the introduction to this book. That both he and Judge Takasugi became supporters of my work with youth is a powerful testimony to the wonders of walking with Jesus Christ in one's life. Note: visit **www.drugsbite.com** to see a NBC primetime news story. In it I am speaking to a boy scout troop with James Walsh standing next to my wife Cindy. He is wearing shorts and a scout leader shirt. Also, in the NBC story John DeLorean is seen in a chain gang being led out to a marshal's van. Chained next to DeLorean is Clayton from J-3. That was not accidental — think snitch placement seeking opportunity. The Rat Wrangler at work.

7. Judge Robert Takasugi helped to sponsor my application for a Presidential Pardon. He died in 2009 from medical complications. He and I had several telephone conversations over the years — I am pleased that he considered me one of his success stories and that he enjoyed our conversations. I shared how drugs were impacting families and youths nationwide. Regularly crisscrossing the country speaking in schools, small towns and large cities has given me a unique understanding of what works best for helping youth find a successful path in life.

8. Max Mermelstein was arrested in 1985 because of evidence delivered by Morgan Hetrick. Max cooperated extensively and only served 25 months at Terminal Island Federal Prison. He then disappeared, with 16 family members, into the witness protection program. The Medellin Cartel put a $3,000,000 bounty on his head.

   Max gave the government evidence against Manuel Noriega, the ex-President of Panama, who is serving a life sentence in a federal prison. He gave details regarding the inner workings of the Medellin and Cali Drug Cartels, including their secret codes, command structure, drug routes, and money laundering techniques. He exposed cartel murders. He connected the murder weapon that he provided for the killing of Barry Seal with the Colombian hit team that shot him. He gave evidence that the murder of Barry Seal was personally ordered by Fabio Ochoa and Pablo Escobar and directed by Rafael Cardona. Max also gave up his own operation, which resulted in the arrest of ten men including Jan Roberts, who he claimed was involved with the Barry Seal murder contract. Tom Cruz played Barry Seal in the movie, "American Made." The film only loosely portrays the life of Barry Seal.

   Because of Max's cooperation, many dozens of boats, cars, airplanes, houses, and structures were confiscated along with millions of dollars in cash and over a thousand pounds of cocaine. He was the key witness against Luis Javier Castano-Ochoa, who got 16 years for money laundering, his codefendants got maximum sentences, and the government confiscated $22,000,000. Max provided evidence that instigated another half-dozen cases that the government pursued and won. For Max's sentencing, the

Judge received 26 letters from law enforcement officers asking for clemency. Max served only 36 months at T.I. before being released. Such are the fruits of the justice department's, "Let's make a deal program." Max died in September 2008 from bone and lung cancer. A movie, "The Man Who Made It Snow," is currently listed as in development.

9. Pablo Escobar died on December 2, 1993, in a shootout with Colombian authorities. As the King of Cocaine, he was the wealthiest criminal in the world, richer than many small countries. Several movies and a Netflix series titled, "Narcos," ran for two years and was hugely successful.

10. I have no idea what happened to, Rodrigo Restrepo, AKA Scar Face.

11. Fabio Ochoa (Vazquez) was sentenced to 30 years in a federal prison in 2003.

12. Twelve-year-old Pedro disappeared into the criminal underworld. I can only hope that someone rescued him from the path that was being forced upon him.

13. Rafa was killed in Colombia at his car dealership. He was machine-gunned by several assassins.

14. Ralph was released after spending six years in prison. I have no idea what happened to him.

15. To learn more about the Grandma Mafia Case, read *Dirty Money*, by Robert J. Perry, the federal prosecutor of the Grandma Mafia Case. It is well worth the read. On a side note, my wife Cindy was working for Flight Suits, which made the skydiving suit the IRS agent was wearing when he died base jumping off Half Dome in Yosemite. His fatal fall was witnessed by mountain climbers. During that period, Cindy was an active climber at El Capitan. She remembers all the fireside talk about the mysterious motorhome full of bundles of cash and secrets.

16. Sam told me that I made him look goofy with the things I wrote about him. However, his girlfriend said, "Those are exactly the type of things you do." He still lives in San Diego where he continues to surf.

17. John Z. DeLorean served a total of eight days in prison. I believe John suffered the most of us, three defendants. He was on the verge of securing a loan to save his company, which could still be thriving. According to the Los Angeles

Herald Examiner, "A few hours before John DeLorean's arrest, the money he was desperately trying to raise to save his automobile company was made available to him from Midwestern investors. A Mr. Larry Watts, President of Midwest Funding and Development Co., said he called DeLorean's office twice on Oct 19, 1982, to inform him of $200 million loan arrangement. The agent had 100% authority to commit and release the funds." The message that would have saved John did not reach him in time.

Federal agents targeted a man who was innocent of any drug crime, yet it caused DeLorean to lose his company. Though the jury found him not guilty, his reputation was ruined, the cost of defending himself was devastating. His wife divorced him and took the children. He died in March 2005. He was buried wearing jeans, a black leather jacket, and motorcycle boots — a rebel to the end.

18. The DeLorean is being manufactured again in Texas by the DeLorean Motor Company under a government license. They have enough parts to make 300 vehicles. It will get a new 300 to 400 horsepower engine making it the high-powered sports car DeLorean's fans always wanted. A feature docudrama for the big screen, "Framing DeLorean," won several major awards. It is the most accurate work on DeLorean to my knowledge.

In loving memory of Captain Jacques Yves Cousteau.
Born June 11, 1910 and died June 25, 1997.

In 1996, *Calypso* sank after an accidental collision with a barge in Singapore. All that remains is her wooden skeleton in a Brittany shipyard. Her machinery and hardware are in storage. There is a coordinated effort by the Cousteau Society to save Calypso. To learn more please visit: www.cousteau.org

Calypso on the harbor bottom in Singapore.
Painting by Domonique Serafini

MY APPLICATION FOR A PRESIDENTIAL PARDON

At 7:00 AM, on January 17, 2017, I received the most amazing telephone call of my life. It was the Presidential Pardon Attorney calling to advise me that of many thousands of applicants, President Obama had selected only 64 felons for full pardons and that he was at that moment signing mine. They were the last of just a total of only 202 pardons of his presidency. I am very honored and will use my pardon as evidence of "Hope that never surrenders," as I share my story with youth to give them hope for their future.

BARACK OBAMA

President of the United States of America

To All To Whom These Presents Shall Come, Greeting:

Be It Known, That This Day The President Has Granted Unto

Stephen Lee Arrington

A Full and Unconditional Pardon

FOR HIS CONVICTION in the United States District Court for the Central District of California on an indictment (Docket No. CR 82-910(A)-RMT) charging violation of Sections 841 and 846, Title 21, United States Code, for which he was sentenced on September 2, 1983, as amended on July 24, 1985, to three years' imprisonment and three years' special parole.

THE PRESIDENT HAS DESIGNATED, directed and empowered the Pardon Attorney as his representative to sign this grant of executive clemency.

In accordance with these instructions and authority I have signed my name and caused the seal of the Department of Justice to be affixed hereto and affirm that this action is the act of the President being performed at his direction.

Done at the City of Washington, District of Columbia, on January 17, 2017.

By Direction of the President

PARDON ATTORNEY

Full and Unconditional Presidential Pardon
January 17, 2017

THE WHITE HOUSE

WASHINGTON

January 19, 2017

Mr. Stephen Lee Arrington
5234 Country Club Drive
Paradise, California 95969

Dear Stephen,

I wanted to personally inform you that I am granting your application for a pardon.

The power to grant pardons and clemency is one of the most profound powers granted to the President of the United States. It embodies the basic belief in our democracy that people deserve a second chance. Thousands of individuals have applied for a pardon, and only a fraction of these applications are approved.

I am granting your application because you have demonstrated your commitment to turning your life around. Your work to accept responsibility for and overcome the mistakes you have made is admirable. I trust that you will continue to make good choices. By doing so, you will affect not only your own life, but also the lives of those close to you. You will also influence, through your example, others in similar circumstances who are looking for the strength to get their own second chance in the future.

I applaud your ability to prove the doubters wrong, and to change your life for the better. So good luck, and Godspeed.

Sincerely,

Letter to me was written by President Barack Obama on his last day in office.

Stephen Arrington in Paradise, CA, May 2016.
Steve is available to speak at schools, churches,
universities, corporate events, and for conventions.
Contact him at **www.drugsbite.com**.

THE DREAM MACHINE FOUNDATION

Finding new ways to do good work is always rewarding. In 1998, Cindy and I founded the Dream Machine Foundation (DMF). We offer free mobile medical and dental clinics in Fiji in the South Pacific. In 31 years, we have treated tens of thousands of rural Fijians, saved 100s of lives, and brought seven Fijians to America and other countries for limb- and lifesaving surgeries.

In Buca Bay, Fiji, the DMF owns a beautiful 100-acre ocean-front site in a rain forest with a volcano. We would like to build a tropical youth camp with bamboo and thatch tree houses in old growth hardwood trees. There would be rope walkways and wooden bridges between the tree houses that will be handicapped accessible. Imagine the impact that would have on physically challenged youths who have never been able to climb a tree.

For physically challenged youth gravity is their worst nemesis, so we will teach them to scuba dive. Underwater they can learn to hover and to fly in slow motion. Outside our bay is Rainbow Reef, one of the top ten dive sites on the planet.

However, my dreams of a youth camp must take a backseat to our far more serious work of providing mobile clinics to rural Fiji.

Below, my youngest daughter, Cheyenne, Dr. Larry Cohen and I led a medical and dental team and 16 youths to Fiji. At four rural public schools, we did health evaluations for 600 Fijian students and mobile clinics for over 400 villagers.

Our mobile clinics go into the villages. That means we see many patients who are too old, too sick, or too poor to take the hours long bus trip to the government hospital, which has only one overworked doctor. Few will make the journey until they are extremely sick. So many will die, mostly babies and the elderly. There is a rural Fijian belief that you go to the hospital to die.

We have taken thousands of volunteers to Fiji. In Buca Bay, we have improved the communities' health by installing dozens of slow-sand water filtration systems to provide clean water and put in dozens of septic tanks. In 2012, a category 4 cyclone slammed into Buca Bay. We provided medical support, fresh water, and emergency food along with building and gardening supplies.

One of five, Dream Machine Foundation
emergency food drops from the 2012 cyclone.

On February 22, 2016, the Fiji Islands took a devastating direct hit by Cyclone Winston. It was the most powerful category 5 cyclone to make landfall in recorded history in the Southern Hemisphere with 188 mph winds gusting to 220 mph. Tens of thousands were left homeless, and 42 people died.

Because of contaminated water, cholera walks in the wake of cyclones. Yet, in Buca Bay, our Fiji Clean Water Program and years of teaching sanitation and health is still saving lives. We didn't lose one soul. This is also why the septic tanks we have installed are so critical.

THE CAMP FIRE

On November 8, 2018, the town of Paradise, California was almost destroyed by the Camp Fire. It was the most destructive event in 2018 — not just for California, nor the United States, but for the entire planet. When the towering flames hit Paradise, they were advancing at the rate of 80 football fields a minute. Over 18,000 structures (14,000+ homes) were destroyed, and 85 people lost their lives.

Feather River Hospital was Ground Zero for the Camp Fire. The morning of the fire, I arrived at the hospital at 5:00 am. I was

Patient zero, scheduled first for surgery at 7:00 am. At 6:45 am, I was on the gurney, IV in and ready to be rolled in for surgery.

Abruptly, the nurse who was paging through my medical file asked, "Where's your EKG?"

"What," I asked?

"Your electrocardiogram. It's not here. You're on hold. We can't do your surgery without one. She left to get an EKG machine.

That lost file caused my surgery to be delayed by an hour.

At 7:45 am, I was again about to be rolled into the operating room, when an emergency announcement was made to evacuate the hospital. A fire was roaring out of the Feather River Canyon.

Had my EKG not gone missing, I would have been one hour into a three-hour surgical procedure to reattach my right external bicep and to repair a massive full-thickness tear of my right shoulder rotator cuff. Both were caused by my old military adventures, mostly involving jumping out of things at high speed: helicopters, planes, and fast boats.

The lost file may have saved my life and the lives of my family.

The nurse pulled out my IV and I ran out of the hospital. Outside, the morning had morphed into dark twilight. Flaming embers were blowing across the parking lot. A gusting wind was hurling the glowing embers into dry trees and bushes. My son, Chase, 22-years old, soon pulled up next to me and I jumped into his car. We could not speed away, there was already congestion in the parking lot.

We finally got out onto Pentz Road, one of only three main escape routes off the Paradise Ridge. There were thousands of flaming cinders blowing across the tarmac. The brightly burning embers swept under cars in fiery waves like an ocean surge flowing over a beach. Burning pieces of wood and dead birds were falling onto the road. The sky, swirling with dense clouds of black smoke, got darker. There were thunderous explosions caused by exploding propane tanks and pine trees. I had never heard nor seen a tree explode before.

I saw billowing flames lick at a huge pine tree — it instantly burst into a towering torch like a flaming Roman Candle. Paradise was suffering from a seven-year long drought.

Our home was a mile away, south of the hospital on the edge of the Feather River Canyon. Chase dodged around a couple of slow-moving cars, we were racing against the fire in the canyon, which like us was headed for our home

Finally, we pulled into the driveway and a desperate situation. My wife, Cindy, and daughter Stetcyn were frantically carrying loads out to the cars. There was no time for packing, just grab and run. Our other daughter, Cheyenne was racing home from Chico State University. I ran to our back deck— but there was too much smoke to see anything, but I heard the roar coming out of the canyon. It reminded me of the roar the fire made as it raced across the desert towards the escape capsule of the B-1A bomber. This roar was of a magnitude more powerful. It proclaimed a monstrous fire sweeping across the canyon.

"No more loads," I yelled, "we go now!"

Cindy and the girls were reluctant to leave, we've been evacuated for canyon fires before. They assumed this fire was like the others—it wasn't! The fire was being driven by 80 mph winds, it was leaping from ridge line to ridge line and now it was inside the Town of Paradise.

My son, Chase, who had seen the hospital on fire, yelled, "Dad's right! We got to go now!

At Pentz Road, our main escape route, a police officer wouldn't let us out. There was a line of cars fleeing down Pentz from central and northern Paradise. I knew why we were delayed—further up Pentz Road people were dying.

A break in traffic allowed us to join the line of cars moving slowly towards safety. The sky was getting darker as burning embers shot through dark rolling clouds turning draught-dry pine trees into torches in seconds. Fire licked under the cars; I saw where two had pulled over burning. The people were gone.

It took us 2 ½ hours to reach safety. Two of our car's engines were so damaged by flames that they had to be salvaged.

As I laid in an unfamiliar bed that night at a friend's house, I wondered about the missing EKG and came to a conclusion. I did not believe that the report went missing by accident, but rather by divine confusion. It was a way for God to save my family but not at any expense to others. It is upon moments like this that faith builds its foundation. If it was but a singular incident, I might not have been willing to so trust that it was of His design. Yet, I believe God leads us to Him in steps as witnessed in this book. It is my living proof of His unrelenting love for us. It is also my proof that I have work yet to do for Him.

Two months later, that work announced itself with a telephone call from a Fijian chief from the House Matairoko (1st chiefly house of Fiji). Ratu (chief) Waisea Vuniwa and I became brothers in Christ when he was the Fiji Mission President of the Seventh-day Adventist Church. Together, we saved six Christian schools from closing because of debt. Later, he became the Transpacific Union President.

Waisea was visiting Sacramento, California and he wanted to see me about something important. It concerned Waisea's great grandfather, who had been high chief of the ancient Nasukamai war clan. In the early 1800's, he united most of Fiji's Northern Providence of Ra under his leadership. At the time, Fiji was known as the Cannibal Isles.

Nasukamai Village is high up on the side of Fiji's tallest and historically most sacred mountain, a towering volcano. Until recently, no one was allowed to drive up to Nasukamai village. One had to climb the mountain on foot as a sign of respect. In 1990, Waisea took me up to the village to meet his uncle, the High Chief of the Nasukamai. For reasons not apparent to me at the time, it was important to Waisea that I and my companions ride horses up to the village. It was a memorable trip not to be forgotten.

For our meeting, Waisea and I met in at a coffee shop as Cindy and I were living in an RV. He told me about the cyclone's massive devastation in Nasukamai Village and across the Northern Coast of Viti Levu Island. Wind and waves swept away whole villages.

So, I took Waisea to Paradise, to my Ground Zero. He had been a witness to the full destructive force of wind and water, now he was looking upon a barren landscape devastated by a fire storm.

Standing where our house once stood, Waisea stared at all the burned lots. Waisea looked at me and said, "You and I are brothers. But now we are brothers who have lived through fierce devastation on opposite ends of this planet. I need to tell you something that is hugely important to my people. It is the Nasukamai prophecy of, 'The American Eagle.'"

What follows is written by Ratu Waisea Vuniwa:

"How did the story of the American Eagle start? My great grandfather, who I am named after, was a high chief and a great warrior. He united the clans of the Nasukamai, and other clans, through the power of his war club. This was before Christianity arrived in Fiji in 1835. My great grandfather lived 100 years.

Then my grandfather, Ratu Peceli Taukei became high chief of the Nasukamai. He accepted Christianity and became a Seventh-day Adventist in the 1890s. He lived 106 years and died in 1963.

His eldest son, Ratu Poate Dakuni, my great uncle, became the high chief of the Nasukamai at the death of his father. He told me and my family when I was young that one day l would become the leader of the SDA Church in Fiji. This was realized many years later when I became President of Fiji Mission and then President of the Transpacific Union.

He told us about the American Eagle. That the American Eagle would one day come to roost in Nasukamai Village to bring good fortunes to the people of the clan. He said the blessings should be used to further the work of Jesus Christ. Not just in Fiji, but to all the South Pacific Islands and even out unto the whole world. This great uncle of mine died in 1995 when he was 100 years-old."

Waisea then explained that the American Eagle prophecy was greatly anticipated by the people of the Nasukamai. My visit to Nasukamai Village in 1990 had caused much discussion amongst the chiefs and elders of the clan. They had heard of the work of the Dream Machine Foundation, that we built three churches, and remodeled two more in desperate need of repair and saved six Christian schools from closing. We also invested over $200,000 in the Savusavu Government Hospital and remodeled the children's wing. We established a medical and dental clinic in Buca Bay. We provided cyclone relief. Our free mobile clinics treated tens of thousands of Fijians and saved hundreds of lives, mostly through preventive medicine. They felt it was a convincing argument that I was the American Eagle of his great uncle's prophesy.

I was stunned into silence.

"Steve," he said kindly, "it has been decided, we want to adopt you and your family into the Nasukamai Clan. I am adopting you as my brother into the House Matairoko, the first chiefly house."

In this book, I made extensive references to the embarrassment and humiliation I suffered for my self-inflicted fall from the ranks of heroes as the chief of Navy Bomb Disposal Team 11. I knew that I would never again be the chief of anything.

I fled into the surfer community in San Diego where I lived in a marijuana fog. I was at the crossroad of my life and I did nothing. So, the darkness found me, and I slid foolishly into the criminal underworld of organized crime. I wouldn't truly come out of that terrible world until I was arrested and found Jesus Christ in prison. I was amazed at how much He loved a sinner like me, which He proved with life-changing miracles. Then He returned to me my title, "Chief." Being chief engineer of an inmate engine company restored purpose, meaning and focus to my life. My firefighting turnouts were my garments of salvation.

Two years out of prison, He returned the title to me again, when I became chief diver and expedition leader for Captain Jacques Yves Cousteau and his son Jean-Michel. A wonderful odyssey of underwater adventure followed, of diving with humpback whales, dolphins, great white sharks and even swimming with lava. After 5 ½ years, I resigned the job of my childhood dreams to become a full-time lay youth minister and motivational speaker for public schools, churches, and youth organizations. I did not doubt that the title chief had slid quietly into my past.

This honor comes with serious responsibility for the Arrington Family to help the Nasukamai Clan. It also extends to 20 villages that lay alongside the long dirt road that leads from the coast to Fiji's vast northern interior. We are building a medical and dental clinic for the rural families. Currently, this vast area is only served by a single nursing station which is constantly short of even simple first aid supplies. Nasukamai is Viti Levu's most remote village.

July 2019, The Arrington's on being adopted into the Nasukamai Clan. Left to right, Stetcyn Leigh, me, Cynthia Elizabeth, Chase Greystoke and Cheyenne Summer Arrington.

I hope to turn this gift into broader service for Fiji by becoming that country's Ambassador for Goodwill to the United States. I believe this would be a powerful steppingstone for furthering the LORD's work in Fiji, across the South Pacific Islands and yes, out unto the whole world. I would be an advocate for bringing help to rural Fiji from corporations, organizations, churches, schools, and universities. I would like to create a Fiji youth and adult "Ocean Ranger Program," to help study and protect Fiji's magnificent reefs. Fiji is known as the Soft Coral Reef Capital of the World

So, who am I? I am an ex-criminal, a felon, and a sinner. I was facing 144 years of incarceration. On my knees in a jail cell — covered in blood, I feared I would die in prison. In hopeful desperation, I opened my shredded and battered soul to Jesus Christ — and He changed my life forever.

So, now, that royal invitation is being offered to you...

My brother, Ratu Waisea Vuniwa with his great grandfather's 300-year old war club. I am wearing an ancient whale's tooth signifying that I am Ratu Sitiveni Vuniwa. We bring hope in His Holy Name to rural Fiji.

The Dream Machine Foundation is an approved 503-C non-profit organization since 1989. Your donations are fully tax deductible. We are also a Fijian non-government organization since 2002, which means we pay no importation tax and work with the full approval of the Fiji Government. When we open the Nasukamai Clinic, the President of Fiji said he would be pleased to do the honors.

We also need volunteers: physicians, dentists, nurses, medical professionals, builders, teachers, and agricultural professionals. We want to help increase the yield of crude family farming plots which are made with digging sticks, machetes, and the occasional hoe or shovel.

But most of all we need you. Mission work changes lives, particularly for children and youths. That is why Cindy and I have taken over 3,300 people to Fiji, mostly families.

Fijians are the friendliest people in the world, and they particularly love Americans.

During World War II, the Japanese Imperial war machine was rolling over the Mid and South Pacific. They were unstoppable and threatening to cut off Australia and New Zealand. Fiji was their next main target. Viti Levu, Fiji's main island, had the best natural harbor in the South Pacific. It was over three miles wide and Japan was eager to take it. The Fijians had no real defenses.

America came to Fiji's defense. We deployed 10,000 marines to help defend Fiji. We turned Suva Bay into a major working harbor to supply the war effort. We built runways, roads, hospitals, and much more important inter-structure.

We stopped Japan's advance first at Guadalcanal in the Solomon Islands. Then we took the rest of the Solomon Islands with the aid of Fiji's 7,000-man battalion. The fierce Fijian fighters were feared by the Japanese and respected by the Americans. Fijians knew how to fight in jungles, which greatly reduced American casualties.

Fiji is enormously proud of the role they played in stopping the frontline of the Imperial Japanese Army.

Now you know why, Fijians love America more than any other country in the world. You can also appreciate how humbling, and what a great honor, it is for me to be recognized as the American Eagle. It places an incredible responsibility upon me and my family. God is opening a door. I stand at the entry eager to do His service. Will you come with me? The Fijians love Americans and Jesus Christ has a mission there for all of us. Mission work always yields dual blessings that go both ways, particularly in Fiji. America has one of the highest rates of murder and suicide amongst youths in the world. Fiji has one of the lowest teen murder and suicide rates in the world. Fijians happily minister to our families, to our children and youths with love, unhindered friendship, and non-judging acceptance.

American youths return home with a new sense of purpose and meaning in their lives. Many go on to become physicians, dentists, nurses, teachers, and builders who are eager to return to Fiji; to their favorite country in the world and to the people who have so touched their hearts and souls.

www.dreammachinefoundation.org
PO Box 3234, Paradise, CA 95967

TIMELINE

1967 – 1971	Served 4 tours to Vietnam, earned 7 campaign stars
1971	Naval School Deep Sea Diving, Washington DC
1972 – 1975	EODGRUONE Detachment Point Mugu, CA Earned Naval Commendation Medal for Life Saving. The Navy's highest non-combat award
1975 – 1976	Naval School Explosive Ordnance Disposal, Indianhead, MD
1976 – 1980	EODMUONE, Lualualei Weapons Station, Oahu, Hawaii. Served aboard USS Enterprise (CVN 65), USS RANGER (CVA 61) & USS CONSTELLATION (CVA 64). Led Flying Teams to Kwajalein Atoll, Truk Atoll, Philippines, Canton Atoll, and Guam
1980	My time with Susan and Puu in Hawaii and California
1980 – 1982	Lived in Revelstoke in La Jolla Shores, attended San Diego State University, worked at La Jolla Surf Systems.
1982	Went to work for Morgan Aviation in Mojave, CA. Copiloted plane to and from Colombia, drove the drug car from Florida to California and was arrested on October 18.
1982 -1984	Confined at Terminal Island Federal Prison, pled guilty and was sentenced to five years.
1984 – 1985	Transferred to Boron Prison Camp and served as chief engineer, Boron Inmate Engine Company #52
1985 – 1987	Air Diving Supervisor and Medic, College of Oceaneering. Awarded Red Cross highest award for lifesaving, the Certificate of Merit signed by President Ronald Reagan. Also received lifesaving award from Los Angeles Fire Department.
1987 – 1993	Chief Diver and Expedition Leader, the Cousteau Society, Hollywood, CA. Led flying teams to Costa Rica, Treasure Island, Papua New Guinea, Australia, Tasmania, Hawaii, Alaska, Turks and Caicos Islands, Baja California, Socorro Island, Kwajalein, Truk Atoll, and Nauru Island.
1989	Church of the Recessional, Glendale, CA., married Cynthia Elizabeth Hamren on April Fool's day.

1992 – 1996	Stetcyn Leigh born 09/02/92, Cheyenne Summer born 11/11/1994, Chase Greystoke born on 06/06/96
1993 -	Moved to Paradise, CA and became a national and international motivational and drug education speaker for over 3,500 public school assemblies, hundreds of churches and youth organizations, youth lockups and prisons.
1998 -	Cindy and I started the Dream Machine Foundation in Fiji.
2017	January 17 received a full and unconditional pardon from President Barack Obama. On January 19, received a personal letter of encouragement from President Barack Obama on his last day in office.
2019	My family and I were adopted into the Ancient Fijian War Clan, Nasukamai. I am now the brother of Ratu (chief) Waisea Vuniwa of the House Matairoko (first chiefly house.) Waisea will soon be the High Chief of the Nasukamai. I am recognized as a Fijian chief and as part of the adoption and am now known in Fiji as Ratu Sitiveni Vuniwa.
2020	Much to my surprise, the Governor of Kentucky, award me the title, "Kentucky Colonel," which is the highest title of honor bestowed by the Kentucky Commonwealth. Surprisingly, this award was initiated in recognition of my leading the emergency response to the crash of the B-1A Bomber as an inmate and for my work with youth, and in Fiji. Another surprise is that this ex-inmate is now entitled to be addressed as the Honorable Stephen Lee Arrington. Another proof that no matter how great your fall, you can come back, but you can never do it alone. With Jesus all is possible.

An Arrington Minute: I believe that our minds and bodies are our adventure machines. All our adventures will involve our minds and bodies. This is why I am into gravity and self-propelled sports. I studied martial arts and yoga to better understand how my body works and to test its limitations and then to go beyond them. A strong and finely tuned body and mind withstands and recovers faster from injuries. The best fuel is natural foods — learn to cook.

Made in the USA
Las Vegas, NV
24 January 2021